CHANGING PERSPECTIVES
IN CANADIAN HISTORY

Selected Problems

CHANGING PERSPECTIVES IN CANADIAN HISTORY

Selected Problems

K. A. MacKIRDY
University of Waterloo

J. S. MOIR
University of Toronto

Y. F. ZOLTVANY
McGill University

J. M. DENT & SONS (CANADA) LIMITED
DON MILLS, ONTARIO

ACKNOWLEDGMENTS

Grateful acknowledgment is made to the following for permission to include copyright material.

Miss Anne Bourassa: *Les Ecoles du Nord-Ouest*, by Henri Bourassa.

M. Brunet: "Les Canadiens et la France révolutionnaire".

A. L. Burt: "The Frontier in the History of New France".

Canadian Broadcasting Corporation: "Origin and Historical Record of the Separatist Idea in French Canada", by Maurice Séguin, from *Conference*, March-April, 1962; *The Image of Confederation*, by F. H. Underhill; reprinted by permission of the Canadian Broadcasting Corporation.

iv

Canadian Journal of Economics and Political Science, Toronto: James Eayrs, "The Origins of Canada's Department of External Affairs", by permission of the author; R. McQueen, "Economic Aspects of Federalism—A Prairie View"; M. P. O'Connell, "The Ideas of Henri Bourassa", by permission of the author; N. McL. Rogers, "The Compact Theory of Confederation"; D. V. Smiley, "The Rowell-Sirois Report, Provincial Autonomy, and Post-War Canadian Federalism", by permission of the author; Melville H. Watkins, "Economic Nationalism", by permission of the author; reprinted by permission of the Canadian Journal of Economics and Political Science.

The Canadian Journal of Theology: "The Church and the Workers", by D. J. M. Heap; and "The Lord's Day in a Secular Society", by A. M. C. Waterman; reprinted by permission of The Canadian Journal of Theology.

Carnegie Endowment for International Peace: *The United States, Great Britain and British North America, from the Revolution to the Establishment of Peace after the War of 1812*, by A. L. Burt.

The Champlain Society: *Loyalist Narratives from Upper Canada*, J. J. Talman, ed.

The Clarendon Press: *Lord Durham's Report on the Affairs of British North America*, C. P. Lucas, ed.; reprinted by permission of the Clarendon Press, Oxford.

Clarke, Irwin & Co. Ltd.: *Arthur Meighen:* Vol. II, *And Fortune Fled*, by Roger Graham; reprinted by permission of the author.

Le Devoir: Programme of the *Action libérale nationale.*

Mrs. Mary Doyle: The lyrics of "An Anti-Confederation Song", from a collection of folk-songs published by Gerald Stanley Doyle.

Les Editions de l'Homme: *La libération économique du Québec*, by Raymond Barbeau.

Les Editions Fides: *Histoire du Canada par les Textes*, M. Brunet, G. Frégault, M. Trudel, eds.; *Histoire du Canada français depuis la découverte*, by L. Groulx; the extract from A. Buies, *Chroniques canadiennes, humeurs et caprices*, quoted in their publication *Arthur Buies*, by L. Lamontagne.

Gérard Filteau: *Histoire des Patriotes.*

Guy Frégault: *Canadian Society in the French Régime*, and *La Civilisation de la Nouvelle France*; reprinted by permission of the author.

The Globe and Mail: "Mr. Pearson Abstains", and "Our Only Real Hope"; reprinted from *The Globe and Mail*, Toronto.

Victor Gollancz, Ltd.: *Left Turn, Canada*, by M. J. Coldwell.

Lionel Groulx: *Lendemains de conquête*, and "Ce Cinquantenaire".

Harvard University Press: excerpts reprinted by permission of the publishers from Hugh G. J. Aitken, *American Capital and Canadian Resources*, Cambridge, Mass.:

Harvard University Press, Copyright, 1961, by the President and Fellows of Harvard College.

Harvest House Limited Publishers: *The Impertinences of Brother Anonymous*, translated by Miriam Chapin.

D. C. Heath and Company: *The Evolution of the British Empire and Commonwealth from the American Revolution*, by A. L. Burt.

Hutchinson Publishing Group Ltd.: *My Political Life*, by L. S. Amery.

The Literary Executors of Mackenzie King: *The Mackenzie King Record*, by J. W. Pickersgill.

Alfred A. Knopf, Inc.: *The British Empire Before the American Revolution:* Vol. 5, *Zones of International Friction: The Great Lakes Frontier, Canada, the West Indies, India, 1748-1754*, by L. H. Gipson; *Canada: Tomorrow's Giant*, by Bruce Hutchison.

Les Presses de l'Université Laval: *Economie et Société en Nouvelle-France*, by Jean Hamelin; *Papineau: Textes choisis et présentés*, by F. Ouellet.

George E. Levy: *The Baptists of the Maritime Provinces, 1753-1946*.

Librairie Beauchemin Limitée: *Great Britain and Canada*, by H. Bourassa; *La présence anglaise et les Canadiens*, by M. Brunet.

A. D. Lockhart: "The Contribution of Macdonald Conservatism to National Unity, 1854-78".

Longmans Canada Limited: *Colony to Nation*, by A. R. M. Lower.

Estate of the late Helen J. Mackenzie: *Maria Chapdelaine*, by L. Hémon, translated by W. H. Blake.

Macmillan & Co. Ltd.: *The Problem of National Unity*, by G. R. Parkin, reprinted by permission of Macmillan & Co. Ltd.; *The Imperial Idea and Its Enemies*, by A. P. Thornton, reprinted by permission of Macmillan & Co. Ltd. and The Macmillan Company of Canada Ltd.

The Macmillan Company of Canada Limited: excerpts reprinted from *Dominion of the North* and *The Commercial Empire*, by D. G. Creighton; *Canadian Economic History*, by W. T. Easterbrook and H. G. J. Aitken; *Northern Approaches*, by James Eayrs; *The French Canadians 1760-1945*, by Mason Wade; *Quebec States Her Case*, by F. Scott and M. Oliver, eds.; by permission of the author or editors and The Macmillan Company of Canada Limited. *Manitoba Essays*, by R. O. MacFarlane, by permission of The Macmillan Company of Canada Limited.

McClelland and Stewart Limited: *Joseph Howe: Voice of Nova Scotia*, by M. Beck; *Upper Canada: The Formative Years*, by G. M. Craig; *Frontenac, The Courtier Governor*, by W. J. Eccles; *Troubled Canada, The Need for New Domestic Policies*, by Walter L. Gordon; *The Policy Question, A Critical Appraisal of Canada's Role in World Affairs*, by Peyton V. Lyon; *The Atlantic Provinces: The Emergence of Colonial Society*,

1712–1857, by W. S. MacNutt; *Peacemaker or Powder-Monkey*, by James M. Minifie; *The Rowell-Sirois Report: An Abridgement of Book I of the Royal Commission on Dominion-Provincial Relations*, D. V. Smiley, ed.; excerpt from *Lament for a Nation*, by George Grant; reprinted by permission of the Canadian Publishers, McClelland and Stewart Limited, Toronto.

Kenneth McNaught, *A Prophet in Politics: A Biography of J. S. Woodsworth.*

Mrs. A. R. Menzies: "General Economic History of the Dominion, 1867–1912", and *The Life and Times of Sir Alexander Tilloch Galt*, by O. D. Skelton.

Ministère des Affaires Culturelles du Québec: extract from *Rapport de l'Archiviste de la Province de Québec, 1947–1948.*

André Montpetit: "Vers la supériorité", by Edouard Montpetit.

W. L. Morton: "The Western Progressive Movement, 1919–1921", and *The Progressive Party in Canada.*

Mouvement laïque de langue française: *Le Mouvement du 8 avril*, by Jacques Godbout.

John Murray (Publishers) Ltd.: *A Narrative*, by Sir F. B. Head.

Ontario Department of Public Records and Archives: extracts from the Bureau of Archives *Report*, 1904, and the Bureau of Archives *Report*, 1916.

The Ontario Historical Society: *The Correspondence of Lieut.-Governor John Graves Simcoe*, E. A. Cruikshank, ed.; "What Was the Family Compact?", by Robert Saunders; *The John Strachan Letter Book: 1812–1834*, George W. Spragge, ed.; "The War of 1812 in Canadian History", by C. P. Stacey.

Oxford University Press: *Empire and Commonwealth*, by Chester Martin; and *The Quebec Act: A Study in Statesmanship*, by Reginald Coupland.

Maurice Pope: *Correspondence of Sir John Macdonald*, by Joseph Pope.

The Presbyterian Church in Canada: extracts from *Acts and Proceedings of the Forty-fifth General Assembly of the Presbyterian Church in Canada, 1918* and *Acts and Proceedings of the Fifty-seventh General Assembly of the Presbyterian Church in Canada, 1930.*

The Queen's Printer, Ottawa: *British North America at Confederation: A Study Prepared for the Royal Commission on Dominion-Provincial Relations*, by D. G. Creighton; *The Elgin-Grey Papers, 1846–1852*, Sir A. G. Doughty, ed.; extract from a speech by Maurice Duplessis in *Proceedings of the Federal Provincial Conference 1955: Ottawa, October 3, 1955*; *Decisions of the Judicial Committee of the Privy Council Relating to the British North America Act, 1867 and the Canadian Constitution, 1867–1954*, by Richard A. Olmsted; *Documents Relating to the Constitutional History of Canada, 1759–1791*, A. Shortt and A. G. Doughty, eds.; reprinted by permission of the Queen's Printer.

Antoine Roy: *Inventaire des ordonnances des intendants de la Nouvelle France*, by P. G. Roy.

The Ryerson Press: excerpts reprinted from *Why I Am a Separatist*, by Marcel Chaput, translated by Robert A. Taylor; *George Pidgeon*, by John Webster Grant; *Methodism in the Middle West*, by J. H. Riddell; *After Tippecanoe: Some Aspects of the War of 1812*, Philip P. Mason, ed.; by permission of The Ryerson Press, Toronto.

G. F. G. Stanley: "Act or Pact: Another Look at Confederation".

The Toronto Public Library: *The Arthur Papers*, C. R. Sanderson, ed.

P.-E. Trudeau: "Politique fonctionnel", and *La Grève de l'Amiante*.

F. H. Underhill: "Some Aspects of Upper Canadian Radical Opinion in the Decade before Confederation".

The United Church of Canada: excerpts from *Record of Proceedings of the Sixth General Council of the United Church of Canada, 1934*, and *The Christian Guardian*.

University of Maine: "An International Community on the St. Croix (1604–1930)", by Harold A. Davis.

University of Michigan Press: excerpt reprinted from *Canada: A Modern History*, by J. Bartlet Brebner, by permission of The University of Michigan Press.

University of Minnesota: *The Old Province of Quebec*, by Alfred Leroy Burt. Copyright 1933 by the University of Minnesota. Renewed 1961 by Alfred Leroy Burt. University of Minnesota Press, Minneapolis.

University of Toronto Press: "George Brown", by J. M. S. Careless, in R. L. McDougall, ed. *Our Living Tradition: Second and Third Series* (1959); "Henri Bourassa", by A. Laurendeau, in R. L. McDougall, ed. *Our Living Tradition: Fourth Series* (1962).

University of Toronto Press and *Canadian Historical Review:* G. M. Craig, "The American Impact on the Upper Canadian Reform Movement before 1837", by permission of the author; A. W. Currie, "Freight Rates on Grain in Western Canada", by permission of the author; Helen T. Manning, "The Colonial Policy of the Whig Ministers, 1830–37", by permission of the author; Chester Martin, "Lord Durham's Report and Its Consequences"; George Metcalf, "Draper Conservatism and Responsible Government in the Canadas, 1836–1847", by permission of the author; W. H. Parker, "A New Look at Unrest in Lower Canada in the 1830's"; Allana G. Reid, "Representative Assemblies in New France"; W. S. Wallace, "The Growth of Canadian National Feeling"; Alan Wilson, "The Clergy Reserves: 'Economical Mischiefs' or Sectarian Issue?"; by permission of the author.

Vancouver Sun: extract from an editorial, 14 May 1934.

Warwick Bros. & Rutter Ltd.: *Sir Oliver Mowat . . . a biographical sketch*, by C. R. W. Biggar.

Wherever possible, the source of quoted material has been traced and acknowledgment given. Apology is made for any inadvertent errors or omissions.

The use of the following material is acknowledged.

C. P. Lucas, ed. *Lord Durham's Report on the Affairs of British North America*, Vol. II; W. P. M. Kennedy, *Statutes, Treaties and Documents of the Canadian Constitution, 1713–1929*; O. D. Skelton, *Life and Letters of Sir Wilfrid Laurier*, Vol. I; Margaret Fairley, ed., *The Selected Writings of William Lyon Mackenzie*; W. A. Riddell, *Documents on Canadian Foreign Policy 1917–1939*; an abridged excerpt from James Eayrs, *The Commonwealth and Suez: A Documentary Survey*; published by Oxford University Press.

Egerton Ryerson, *The Loyalists of America and Their Times*; Edith Fowke, Alan Mills, and Helmut Blume, *Canada's Story in Song;* published by The Ryerson Press.

John Romeyn Brodhead, *Documents Relative to the Colonial History of the State of New York; procured in Holland, England and France*, Vol. IX, edited by E. B. O'Callaghan, was published in Albany, New York, in 1855.

PREFACE

Although the "problems approach" to the teaching of European and American history has long been used by Canadian university instructors, we believe that this book represents the first attempt to present a collection of such problems in Canadian history. The book is designed primarily for use in discussion groups of introductory survey courses in Canadian history. Just as the discussion group is designed to supplement and enrich the learning experience of the mass lecture, so we hope this book will supplement and deepen the student's understanding of historical processes which he derives from his basic textbook and other assigned reading.

In the opinion of the editors the ideal presentation of a study problem would include some relevant primary documents, accounts of the event by major historians of earlier days, and some accounts by more recent scholars drawing different interpretations from the same body of evidence. It is a commentary on the current state of Canadian historiography that it was rarely possible to follow this ideal pattern. No excerpts from later commentators have been included in the first and last problems, for instance. As the last problem deals with contemporary events the omission is to be expected, but the absence of such commentary for the first problem reflects a failure of historians to comment on an important facet of our early history. On other problems there has not been the diversity of comment and revisionist scholarship to provide the spectrum of interpretations which are represented in Problems 4, 5, and 6.

Readers should note that we are offering only selected problems and make no claim to cover all the important issues of Canadian history. Some have been chosen because of their obvious importance in Canadian history. Others because, being within our personal areas of interest and research, we were aware of documents that are both unfamiliar and interesting. Others recommended themselves because of their relevance to questions which Canadians are asking today about the nature of their country, the ownership of its economy, the orientation of its foreign policy, and the prospects of national survival.

Some of our readers might have preferred to examine other problems. No selection can hope to meet the variety of interests possible within such a large field. The number of Problems included here is intended to provide a unit of study for each effective teaching week in the average academic year of Canadian colleges and universities. This plan and the necessity of keeping each Problem within the physical limits of what a student may reasonably be expected to absorb and criticize week by week, in addition to lectures and outside reading in his various subjects, have necessitated restricting the contents of each problem to those documents and comments that the editors judge to be an irreducible minimum. At the end of each Problem the editors have added a brief bibliography for further reading, listing a few books containing general background information and any relevant books or articles for which no space could be found in the body of the Problem. Where older books have been reprinted, the references are to the most recent edition, but students are reminded that the volume may originally have appeared some years earlier. Titles in paperback have been indicated thus: *.

In selecting the readings which follow, and in deciding upon the method of presentation, we have profited from the direct and indirect assistance of a large number of colleagues, students, and those librarians and archivists upon whose co-operation all historians depend. We wish specifically to acknowledge the assistance of Professor John Wilson of the Department of Political Science, University of Waterloo, for his comments on a number of the modern problems from the vantage point of a related discipline; of Professor J. M. S. Careless, Chairman, Department of History, University of Toronto, for his help in connection with Problem 10; of Mr. Dale Miquelon, a doctoral candidate at the University of Toronto, for his assistance with Problem 4; of the Rev. Professor Jacques Monet, S.J., of Loyola College, for advice on certain translations; and of Professor William Ormsby, Brock University, St. Catharines, for his assistance with Problem 9. Y. F. Zoltvany also wishes to thank the Canada Council, whose short-term research grant helped him to prepare his share of the book.

The three editors accept responsibility for all the errors of omission and commission which might have slipped into type. Although we assume joint responsibility for the project, there has been a division of labour under which Y. F. Zoltvany undertook the initial preparation of Problems 1, 2, 3, 4, 14, and 20; J. S. Moir of Problems 5, 6, 7, 9, 10, and 18; Y. F. Zoltvany and J. S. Moir of Problem 8; and K. A. MacKirdy of Problems 11, 12, 13, 15, 16, 17, 19, and 21. Sources and documents originally in French have been translated by the editor of the particular Problem, unless indicated otherwise.

May 1967

K. A. M.
J. S. M.
Y. F. Z.

CONTENTS

ANALYTICAL CONTENTS

Problem 3

Problem 6

Problem 7

The War of 1812 — Seed-Bed of Canadian Nationalism?

Problem 8

From Reform to Rebellion — What Caused
the Conflicts of 1837?   **117**

Problem 9

Responsible Government — Political Principle
or Political Patronage?   **139**

Problem 10

Problem 13

Problem 14

The Struggle for *La Survivance* — Misguided Effort
or Source of Permanence?

Problem 15

Problem 16

Problem 17

Problem 18

Problem 19

Problem 20

Problem 21

Problem 1

France's View of Canada — Asset or Liability?

"A few acres of snow!" These celebrated words attributed to Voltaire are the ones that usually come to mind when the question of how France regarded Canada is raised. Many Frenchmen undoubtedly shared this opinion of the famous *philosophe*, but another important school of thought also existed which regarded France's North American colony as a very valuable possession. In this problem, the highlights of the debate between the pro-Canadian and anti-Canadian schools will be presented.

Any serious study of France's attitude toward Canada must begin with the Ministry of the Marine, the department of government to which the King had entrusted the administration of the colonies. From 1663 to 1760, the period studied in this problem, one soon notices a certain continuity in the activities of this body. In the first place, the purpose of its Canadian policy was always the same. For the duration of the French Régime the ministers of the marine were striving to improve the performance of the Canadian economy so that it might prove useful and profitable to France. Secondly, they were invariably followers of the doctrine known today as mercantilism, according to which colonies were useful only if they served as outlets for the manufactured goods of the mother country and as producers of raw materials for her industries. Trade with foreign powers was discouraged or altogether forbidden.

While the ministers subscribed to the same doctrine, changes in context, personalities, and emphasis did cause modifications in their policies. Jean-Baptiste Colbert (1669–1683) wanted Canada to develop both her manufactures and her trade with the French West Indies. Fearing, however, that too vigorous an emigration policy might depopulate France, he refused to go as far as his Intendant, Jean Talon, who wanted to establish a powerful French state in

North America. Jérome de Pontchartrain (1699–1715), on the other hand, whose mercantilism was far more doctrinaire than Colbert's, discouraged Canadian manufacturing and all forms of trade except that carried on directly with the mother country. With the advent of Frédéric de Maurepas (1723–1749), manufacturing and intercolonial trade were once again encouraged, and generous subsidies were offered to Canadian entrepreneurs to encourage their participation in these activities.

As the eighteenth century wore on, another colonial policy gained many supporters in both Canada and France. This school of thought can be referred to as the imperial, because it was concerned with France's position as a world power. This approach differed from that of the mercantile school, which viewed the colony as a purely economic venture whose usefulness could be measured by its imports and exports. The origins of the imperial interpretation can be traced back to the Treaty of Utrecht, concluded in 1713. By virtue of this treaty, Great Britain gained Hudson Bay, Newfoundland, and Acadia from France, and several important concessions in the Great Lakes and Mississippi Valley regions. The more astute French observers now began to realize that measures had to be taken to check the growth of Great Britain's overseas power. Otherwise, the English might ultimately drive the French from Louisiana and Canada and remain the sole masters of the North American continent. Such crushing superiority in the New World would soon enable Great Britain to become the most formidable power in the Old. Governor Vaudreuil first expressed this idea in embryonic form in 1714; but its most eloquent exponent was another Governor of New France, Michel Barrin de la Galissonière, whose memoir on the colonies of France in North America is one of the most statesmanlike papers of the entire French Régime.

For the imperialists, then, Canada's value to France was different from that of the West Indies. The islands were useful because their economy complemented that of France; Canada was useful because it was the most powerful obstacle that could be raised against the further progress of the English in the New World. For this reason it was an extremely valuable possession which had to be kept and fortified. The mercantilists, for their part, approached the problem quite differently. Canada, they stated, despite France's aid, produced little of utility apart from a few beaver pelts; it remained a burden to the kingdom's finances. Therefore it was dispensable. It was this second view which prevailed during the latter stages of the Seven Years' War, perhaps because the mercantilists controlled the Ministry of the Marine. But of the two schools of thought, which was the more lucid and far-sighted? From the selections that follow, the reader can decide this question for himself.

King or Company — Who Was Reponsible for New France?

Talon Presents Colbert with a Choice for Canada

The team of Jean-Baptiste Colbert, the brilliant minister of Louis XIV, and Jean Talon, the Great Intendant, gave New France the most dynamic leadership of its history. With Colbert providing capital and general directives, and Talon on-the-spot management, the colony developed rapidly between 1666 and 1672. However, the two men viewed the colony differently, as the following exchange of correspondence illustrates.

... Canada is of a very vast extent; ... I know not its limits on the North, they are so great a distance from us, and on the South there is nothing to prevent his Majesty's name and arms being carried as far as Florida, New Sweden, New Netherland and New England; and that through the first of these countries access is had even to Mexico.

That the whole of this country, diversely watered by the river St. Lawrence and by beautiful rivers . . . communicates by these same rivers with several Indian Nations, rich in furs, particularly those who inhabit the North; . . .

That the Climate, which causes a residence in the country to be feared on account of the excessive cold, is nevertheless so salubrious that people are seldom sick here, and live here very long; that the land, very unequal on account of its mountains and valleys, is covered with trees which form but one forest, stifling in my opinion, rich and beautiful products. Its fertility in grain is evident to us by the abundant harvests furnished every year by cleared and cultivated lands; . . . when it will once be supplied with all sorts of animals, agricultural and domestic, for the raising of which it is well adapted, it will have in 15 years a sufficient surplus as well in grain, vegetables, meat as in fish, to furnish the Antillas of America, even the places on the continent of this vast quarter of the globe. I do not advance this lightly, and do not state it until after having well examined the strength of the soil in a state of nature. . . .

I pass from the fertility of the soil to its fecundity, and from its fruits to its minerals, and say that . . . you ought to expect great advantages from this country for His Majesty. . . .

* * * * *

... I explain myself as to the motives that might have led him [the King] to make this surrender to the Company [the Company of the West Indies, which had been recently granted proprietary rights to Canada] and say,—that if it were to increase the profits by furnishing him large means to meet his first expenses; to augment the number of his vessels, and to carry on an extensive commerce, useful to his state, without having in view the extending settlements and the multiplying colonists in this country, it is, in my opinion, more advantageous to the King to leave this property to the Company without any reserve. But if he have [*sic*] regarded this country as a fine field on which to establish a great Kingdom, or to found a Monarchy, or at least a very considerable State, I cannot persuade myself he will succeed in his design, if he leaves in other hands than his own, the Seigniorage, the property of the soil, the nominations to parishes and dependencies ... and even the trade which constitutes the soul of the establishment.

Jean Talon to Jean-Baptiste Colbert, 4 October 1665
Documents Relative to the Colonial History of the State of New York [*N.Y.C.D.*]
(Albany, 1853–1887), Vol. IX, pp. 30–1.

Colbert Refuses to Make Canada a "Great and Powerful State"

The King cannot concur with you in the whole of your reasoning as to the means of rendering Canada a great and powerful State, perceiving many obstacles thereto which cannot be overcome except by a long lapse of time; because, even though he should have no other business and could direct both his application and his power to that object, it would not be prudent to depopulate his Kingdom, which he should do to people Canada. Besides this consideration, which will appear important to you, there remains yet another, namely, that if his Majesty removed thither a greater number of men than what the land, now cleared, could feed, 'tis certain that if they did not all perish at once they would at least suffer great privations, which, reducing them to continual langor, would weaken them little by little; and besides the inconveniences they would themselves endure, they would increase those of the old inhabitants, who, without this augmentation of Colonists, would live by their labor and the cultivation of the soil. You will understand sufficiently, by this observation, that the true means of strengthening that Colony is to cause justice to reign there, to establish a good police, to preserve the inhabitants in safety, to procure them peace, repose and plenty, and to discipline them against all sorts of enemies; because all these things, which constitute the basis and foundation of all settlements, being well attended to, the country will get filled up insensibly, and in the course of a reasonable time may become very considerable, especially as his Majesty will afford it all the assistance in his power according as he shall have more or less occupation within his Kingdom.

Colbert to Talon, 5 April 1666
N.Y.C.D., Vol. IX, p. 39.

Talon Expresses His Faith in the Future of the Colony

I am no Courtier, and assert, not through mere desire to please the King nor without just reason, that this portion of the French Monarchy will become something grand. What I discover around me causes me to foresee this; and those colonies of foreign nations, so long settled on the Sea-board, already tremble with affright, in view of what his Majesty has accomplished here in the interior within seven years. The measures adopted to confine them within narrow limits, by the taking possession which I have caused to be effected, do not allow them to spread without subjecting themselves at the same time to be treated as usurpers, and to have war waged against them; and this, in truth, is what they seem, by all their acts, greatly to fear. They already are aware that the King's name is spread so far abroad among the Savages throughout all those Countries that he alone is there regarded by them as the arbiter of Peace and War; all detach themselves insensibly from the other Europeans, and with the exception of the Iroquois, of whom I am not yet assured, we may safely promise ourselves to make the others take up arms whenever we please.

Talon to Colbert, 2 November 1671
N.Y.C.D., Vol. IX, p. 73.

Pontchartrain's Guidelines for Canada

In spite of their differences of opinion, both Talon and Colbert were agreed on the fundamental point that Canada should develop into a strong and self-sufficient extension of the French kingdom. Under Jérome de Pontchartrain this ideal gave way to one that was more in keeping with doctrinaire mercantilism. Both colonial self-sufficiency and intercolonial trade were to be discouraged as prejudicial to French manufacturing.

His Majesty has been very pleased to learn that the growing of hemp has met with the success that we had hoped for. But he must explain that he never intended to allow cloth to be manufactured in Canada so that the settlers might do without that of France. Thus, no weavers will be sent to the colony. The settlers must forward their hemp to France to be sold either to the state for the servicing of the royal navy, or else to private parties to dispense them from buying this product from foreigners. Generally, they [Vaudreuil and Beauharnois] must observe that whatever can compete with the factories of France must never be produced in the colonies. Colonies must act as suppliers of raw materials to enable the factories of the kingdom to do without imports from foreign states. They must consider this as one of the principal purposes of colonies which are established solely for the benefit of the mother countries and never to permit them to do without those countries.

Memoir from the King to Governor Vaudreuil and Intendant Beauharnois,
14 June 1704

Archives des colonies [AC], série B, Vol. 25, ff. 117–18 (translation).

It has been proposed to His Majesty as a good thing to send ships from Canada to the islands of America to carry out a reciprocal trade in the products of the two colonies. On this point His Majesty wishes to explain . . . that since colonies must be considered only in relation to the kingdom, they must be carefully prevented from supplying each other with the merchandise that they are accustomed to draw from France. It would not be fitting, for example, that Canada supply wheat to the islands in return for refined sugar since this would be prejudicial to the cities of La Rochelle, Bordeaux, Nantes and the others that send vessels to the colonies and support all the charges of the state.

It is equally important to prevent every type of trade between the inhabitants of Canada and the English, since the latter could only supply them with the merchandise that they would otherwise obtain from France. . . .

Instructions from the King to the Intendant Jacques Raudot, 17 June 1705
AC, B, Vol. 27, f. 56 (translation).

A Governor Explains Why New France Must Be Preserved and Fortified

Philippe de Rigaud de Vaudreuil was Governor of New France from 1703 to 1725. During his long administration, the Anglo-French rivalry for control of America began in earnest. The following memoir, written shortly after the conclusion of the Treaty of Utrecht, reflects the impact of this dawning struggle on Vaudreuil's colonial philosophy.

The Marquis de Vaudreuil, Governor General of Canada, persuaded that Your Royal Highness is convinced of the need to preserve this colony, will not present in this memoir the reasons that make this necessary. He will only try to acquaint him with the measures that must be taken to achieve this end.

One of the surest is to prevent the imminent danger to which this colony would be exposed in case of a new war with the English.

It can be easily understood if we consider that there are in Canada at present but 4484 inhabitants, between the ages of 14 and 60, capable of bearing arms, and that the 28 infantry companies only number 628 soldiers. Meanwhile, in the colonies that border Canada, the English could place 60,000 men under arms.

We cannot doubt for a moment that at the first breach between France and England the English will make every effort to seize Canada and consequently all of North America. From this might ensue the loss of Mexico from which the English would expel the Spaniards without meeting any resistance.

Their intentions were sufficiently revealed by the war preparations which they made in 1711 and even since the peace, and by article 22 of the instructions of the City of London to its representatives directing them to ask the ministers of the preceding government to explain why they let France keep Canada and Cape Breton Island, now called Ile Royale.

If this island of Cape Breton should pass to the English with what remains of Canada there would be no resources left for the cod fisheries and this would result in a great loss for the commerce of the kingdom.

One cannot express to what point the power of England would increase if she acquired what remains of North America and how fearsome this power would become in Europe.

All this shows the necessity of profiting from the peace to fortify Canada by sending people there to fill the ranks of the infantry companies and to augment the number of settlers. . . .

> Mémoire de M. de Vaudreuil au Duc d'Orléans,
> Régent du Royaume, February 1716
> *Rapport de l'Archiviste de la Province de Québec, 1947–1948*,
> pp. 291–2 (translation).

A New Blueprint for Canadian Growth

For the greater part of the reign of Louis XV, France enjoyed considerable prosperity and a soaring trade. Her overseas empire, which at that time embraced a large part of India, the West Indies, Louisiana, Canada, and Cape Breton Island, was largely responsible for her affluence. In the following document, Frédéric de Maurepas tells his Intendant, Gilles Hocquart, in what ways Canada can prove most useful to France.

Since the colony of Canada is only valuable insofar as it can be useful to the kingdom, the sr. Hocquart must discover ways of making it so.

The establishment of fisheries is one of the ways by which the Canadians can best contribute to the advantage of France. Those of porpoises and seals which have been begun in some places might provide the kingdom with the oils which are always in great demand but which are now supplied by the Dutch. This commerce is liable to become very extensive and can never be overly encouraged. Besides the oils, it also provides sealskins, which can be put to different uses. In every respect, then, this commerce can only be most advantageous.

There are also masts and timber which can be obtained from Canada, not only to supply the royal shipyards but private industry as well. . . .

[The sr. Hocquart] will also report on what can be done to preserve the forests which are being uselessly destroyed. . . .

Canada can also sustain various cultivations which will be of great utility to France. There is hemp and flax, for example, which we are presently obliged to purchase in northern Europe. . . . Tar is also manufactured there, from the great quantity of pine trees, and His Majesty recommends that the inhabitants be encouraged to continue in this habit, so that this product may be later available for the royal shipyards. . . .

The King has also been informed that the wool of the Canadian sheep is of good quality. Since this product is in great demand in France, His Majesty wishes the sr. Hocquart to encourage those who have proper pastures to raise sheep. This should eventually procure considerable wealth to the colony as well as an easier and less expensive sustenance for the inhabitants.

His Majesty recommends that he increase as much as possible other cultivations, such as the growing of vegetables. These will not only provide the inhabitants with abundance but will also give rise to a lucrative commerce with Ile Royale and the West Indies, consisting of shipments of flour, peas, and biscuits.

By his letters patent issued in October, 1727, His Majesty has forbidden all commerce between foreigners and the islands and colonies of France. Measures were also taken at the same time to ensure that the Windward Islands would be provisioned by French instead of by English merchants as was the case in the past through a tolerance most prejudicial to the commerce of the kingdom. These measures have met with the success that we expected. All foreign trade has now been banished from the islands, and the French merchants have provided them with an abundance of salt beef, flour, and other foodstuffs, while cod, salt fish, and oils have been sent from Ile Royale. However, French commerce has been unable to replace the cattle, horses, planks, staves, and shingles which were formerly carried there in great quantities from New England. His Majesty had given orders to the sr. marquis de Beauharnois and the sr. du Puy [the Governor and the former Intendant of Canada] to find ways of making Canada carry out this part of the trade . . . This could be done by using Ile Royale as a clearing house, particularly for the horses and cattle. . . .

Before ending this article on cultivations, His Majesty will observe that the Canadians have not until now made the progress that we could have expected. It is true that long wars have prevented the growth of the colony. The inhabitants became accustomed to wielding weapons and to roaming the woods and they have taken no interest in tilling the soil since the return of peace. Yet this is what can best contribute to providing the colony with the basis of strength necessary to resist the hostile enterprises of its neighbours. For these reasons the sr. Hocquart must favour and encourage cultivations and the increase of the population as matters that are among the most important for the safety of the colony. . . .

Mémoire du Roy pour servir d'instruction au sr. Hocquart, Commissaire général de la marine ordonnateur dans la Nouvelle France, 22 mars 1729
AC, B, Vol. 53, f. 476 (translation).

Canada, an Imperial Factor in an Imperial Struggle

The great war for imperial hegemony between France and England began in 1744 and, after a brief respite, continued until the collapse of the first French Empire in 1763. This conflict, with its attendant questions of expenditure and strategy, caused many high-placed Frenchmen to express opinions on Canada. The following extract is taken from La Galissonière's remarkable memoir on the colonies of France in North America.

One might argue that only colonies like St. Domingue and Martinique, which are a source of great wealth and revenues, should be preserved, while others like Canada and Louisiana, which are a burden to France, should be abandoned.

I shall not try to minimize this objection. . . .

* * * * *

In this memoir, I shall consider Canada strictly as an unproductive frontier, as the Alps are to Piémont and as Luxembourg would be to France. . . . I will ask if a land, although sterile and a cause of great expenditure, can be abandoned if by its strategic position it provides its inhabitants with a great advantage over its neighbours.

This is precisely the case of Canada. We cannot deny that this colony has always been a burden to France and that it will probably continue to be so for a very long time to come. But it is also the most powerful obstacle we can use to check English ambitions. The only proof of this I need give are the many attempts the English have made against this colony over more than a century. However, I will also add that Canada alone can enable us to wage war on the English possessions in continental America, which are as dear to them as they are valuable in fact. Since their strength grows daily, they will soon swallow up our island colonies as well as those we have on the mainland unless we find a way of limiting their progress.

We know from past experiences that most of the establishments on the tropical islands do not support themselves by their internal forces so much as by the difficulty of transporting troops from Europe to subjugate them. . . . But if we do not interrupt the rapid progress of the English colonies on the continent, or what is the same thing, if we do not build up a counterweight that is capable of containing them within their present limits and of forcing them to remain on the defensive, they will soon acquire such great facility for making formidable preparations for war in continental America, and they will require so little time to transport considerable forces to Saint Domingue, Cuba, or to our Windward islands that we will be unable to preserve the latter without immense expenses.

*   *   *   *   *

Those losses, great as they are, would not be the only ones we would suffer. As an aftermath, France would lose the hegemony that she must claim in Europe. For if anything can destroy this hegemony, it is the naval forces of the English. These alone sustained the house of Austria in the early stages of the War of the Spanish Succession, and these again forced us to give up the Austrian Low Countries, which we had entirely conquered in the last war.

We should not deceive ourselves into thinking that we can have a navy that can compare to theirs for many years. Our only recourse is to attack them in their overseas possessions. To attempt this with troops launched directly from Europe would cost us dearly, and the chances of success would be slight. But by fortifying ourselves in America we can maintain the advantages we presently enjoy and even increase them by means of expenditures that are small compared to those European armaments would cost.

*   *   *   *   *

Nothing must be spared to strengthen our colonies, because we must consider them as the boulevard of America against the enterprises of the English, because they alone can compensate for our weakness on the high seas . . . and because we cannot abandon our colonies to their own resources without letting them fall into the hands of the English, whose superiority in America and the great wealth they would derive therefrom would most certainly give them superiority in Europe.

> Mémoire sur les colonies de la France dans l'Amérique septentrionale [*circa* 1750]
> AC, C 11 A, Vol. 96, pp. 178–9, 182–6, 211–12 (pagination of the Transcripts
> of the Public Archives of Canada), (translation).

Support for La Galissonière's View

The marquis de Silhouette, author of the next reading, occupied the important position of comptroller general of finance. He was also a friend of La Galissonière and had assisted him in drafting the memoir on the colonies of France in North America.

The debate today is between France and England. The English spare neither effort nor expense in the pursuit of their goal, and this proves that these people, at least, do not doubt the influence of the American system over the European one. . . .

* * * * *

I cannot help but suspect that it is because of the difficulties we may experience in trying to preserve Canada that some people are claiming that it must be abandoned. If their views prevail, we could soon witness a rebirth of the gothic system based on the idea that France can dispense with colonies and needs only soldiers and labourers. Russia does not lack soldiers; it does not lack labourers. . . . Russia, however, is subsidized by foreign powers, so true is it that something more is necessary for the dignity, grandeur, and power of a state, especially one which is largely bordered by the sea and whose greatest enemy is a nation whose strength resides principally in her naval forces. . . .

If we are so unfortunate as to lose Canada, we must find a way to have it returned to us at the peace treaty along with the other colonies which the English will have found easy to conquer once the threat of Canada is removed. The English will rightly attach such a great value to their American conquests that it may only be after we have threatened them with an invasion of England itself that they will agree to give them up.

A letter from the marquis de Silhouette, 8 February 1759
AC, C 11 A, Vol. 104, pp. 591–8 (pagination of the Transcripts
of the Public Archives of Canada), (translation).

The Value of Canada Placed in Doubt

The arguments put forward by La Galissonière and Silhouette did not convince French colonial policy makers that Canada was worth preserving. The sr. de Capellis, a highly placed official in the Ministry of the Marine, continued to regard this colony as a useless piece of property.

(France is not able to populate a country as vast as Canada.

Until today, this colony has produced little for the state in time of peace, for reasons which I cannot go into in this memoir, and has cost enormous sums for more than ten years.)The money spent on that colony which the King is about to lose represents the greater part of the funds allotted to the navy. If the money had been used to build vessels and to establish solidly our maritime forces, we would have been respected and even feared by our enemies, who seem inclined to flout us. We can, then, cede this land to England, but here is what we should ask for in return, and I daresay that the King will not lose in the exchange. . . .

The colony of St. Domingue has produced for the state in peacetime over twenty million *livres** annually. This amount can be doubled and some day may

---

* The *livre* was a basic monetary unit during the Ancien Régime. It was worth approximately 1/20 of the English pound sterling.

even exceed fifty million *livres.* Can we ever hope that Canada will sell that much to France? . . .

The island of Newfoundland will provide us with abundant fisheries. . . . France would derive an immense profit from the sale of salted fish for which she could find markets in Spain, Italy, and in parts of Germany. The fisheries are also a nursery of seamen, and that is perhaps their greatest value. The more extensive our fisheries become, the more sailors we will have. This class of men can never become too numerous. . . . It has also been said that there are beavers in the interior of the island and I have no reason to doubt this. . . . It can also be assumed that the lands in the interior are covered by immense forests, which would provide wood for masts and planks. . . . We could also extract pitch, tar, and resin . . . We might eventually draw from Newfoundland what we presently import from northern Europe. . . .

The advantages that the King's subjects would derive from the establishment of Newfoundland and from the cession of the Spanish part of St. Domingue would be far greater than those which the English would obtain from the cession of a part of Canada. I even dare advance that the island of Newfoundland and half of St. Domingue are worth much more than all of Canada; and I do not believe that we should hesitate to give it up entirely to obtain the other two establishments.

Mémoire de M. de Capellis concernant les colonies et relatif à la paix [1758]
AC, C 11 A, Vol. 103, pp. 656–63 (pagination of the Transcripts
of the Public Archives of Canada), (translation).

Support for the Views of Capellis

Like Capellis, M. de Beaucat saw nothing in Canada except a barren land and a harsh climate. The money spent there was wasted, for such a colony could never become profitable to France.

There are about 60,000 inhabitants in Canada, 180,000 acres of farmland, and 20,000 of pasture. The annual crop, on the average, consists of 400,000 bushels of wheat, 5,000 of corn, 130,000 of oats, 3,000 of barley, 6,000 of peas, 100,000 quintals of tobacco, 120,000 of flax, and 5,000 of hemp.

The value of beaver and other types of pelts does not exceed 1,500,000 *livres.* The seal fisheries are of very little account.

Canada has very little timber that is suited for construction, and it is very greasy. A few frigates and vessels are built there at costs that are as great as those that prevail in France. Furthermore, those ships do not last half as long as those built in Europe.

In years of drought the crops fail and we are obliged to send flour to Canada. The trade of this colony is so slight that in 1755, when colonial commerce was in a most flourishing state, sixty vessels were dispatched from France and over half of these had to return by way of St. Domingue to find cargo for their return voyage. In passing, we might note that this island has only 18,000 settlers, but its trade is so great that it occupies 400 vessels of 500 tons.

(The cost of maintaining troops in the Canadian forts is also very great. . . .

All of Canada is covered by a thick blanket of snow during half the year, and the Gulf of St. Lawrence is impassable during that time. The settlers are confined to their houses and only venture outdoors to hunt or to exchange a few pelts with the Indians. On this colony have we spent men and money in such great quantities! The Canadians are brave, vigorous, and active, but they lack the means of enriching themselves by commerce or agriculture. They live from day to day, so to speak, and in time of war are exposed either to dying of hunger or at least to doing without the most basic necessities of life.)

M. de Beaucat, Mémoire sur le Canada [1759]
AC, C 11 A, Vol. 103, pp. 626–8 (pagination of the Transcripts
of the Public Archives of Canada), (translation).

An Attempt to Refute the Arguments of the Anti-Canadian School

The following anonymous memoir bears the title *Is It Important to Preserve Canada?* and was written in 1759. It is an attempt to refute, point by point, the principal arguments used by those who were opposed to the retention of Canada.

At all times there have been people who have thought that it was not important for France to keep Canada, and perhaps there are some who still think so today. Some say that it has been and will continue to be the cause of great expenditure, and that it yields almost nothing of value. . . . Others claim that we are depopulating France to place settlers in a very harsh country, full of lakes and forests, frequently exposed to famine, while good lands in France lie fallow; that the commerce with the Indians is of little consequence and will continue to decrease since the fur trade cannot last for another century; that the voyages to Canada are long, difficult, and dangerous.

Finally, a third group maintains that Canada will be conquered, at least in part, each time that we have a war with the English, and that this will oblige France to surrender its European conquests at the peace treaty. And when Canada is finally well-established, revolutions can be expected to break out there. For will it not be natural for kingdoms and republics to emerge in that land and claim their independence from France? . . .

The territory owned by France in North America is vaster than the whole European continent. Its wealth is not yet known to us. The choicest areas remain to be settled. The glory of the King seems to require that we preserve such a vast country. In spite of the enormous sums of money we spend there, it is always sad to see the enemy grow greater at our expense. Besides, those expenses could be reduced considerably and are not so conspicuous in peace-time. It would even be easy for someone who is knowledgeable in finance to prove that the amounts of money France derives from the Canadian trade and from its exports to that colony are greater than those the King spends there. The reasons why it is important for a state to have colonies are related to this point.

It is wrong to object that it depopulates the realm. More men die during one year of European war than would be necessary to settle New France . . . How many thousands of useless men are there not in this kingdom and in other states? Every year, the English recruit a large number of families in foreign kingdoms and help them to settle in New England. Once New France is popu-lated, there will be no country easier to preserve. Our regular navy would guard Acadia and Louisbourg. But we can be certain that if France loses Canada, she will need more maritime forces than ever before, because the English will become absolute masters of the sea.

It is true that in the future these vast regions might break up into kingdoms and republics. The same will be true of New England. But how many centuries will this take? To look into a future so remote and so uncertain is to attempt to foresee too much.

And let us suppose that Canada will never be very useful to France and that it might even cost a little money. Must we regard it as of no consequence to prevent a rival nation from expanding, from establishing a despotic empire on the high seas, and from seizing all the trade?

*   *   *   *   *

Our immense forests and vast prairies will give the English abundance and provide them forever with the means of building as many ships as they may want.

And even if it were only the cod fisheries that were at stake, they would constitute an extremely important object. Of all the types of commerce, these are the richest, the easiest, the least expensive, and the most widespread. As early as 1696, the commerce of Newfoundland alone was valued at 15,000,000 *livres* annually. Once Canada is conquered we will have to relinquish all our fishing bases.

Without knowing all the commerce that Canada produces and is capable of producing, it can be said that if the King loses this colony, the trade of England will soon be increased by 150,000,000 *livres*.

[Anonymous], *Est-il important de préserver le Canada?* [1759]
AC, C 11 A, Vol. 104, pp. 600–5 (pagination of the Transcripts
of the Public Archives of Canada), (translation).

Further Reading

W. L. Dorn, *Competition for Empire, 1740–1763* (reprinted, New York, Harper & Row, 1965)* particularly Chapter VI, presents a good analysis of the role played by colonies in the national economies of the eighteenth century. Canada's economic utility to France can be ascertained from the old but still valuable E. Salone, *La Colonisation de la Nouvelle France* (Paris, n.d.). L. H. Gipson, *The British Empire Before the American Revolution:* Vol. 5, *Zones of International Friction: The Great Lakes Frontier, Canada, the West Indies, India, 1748–1754* (New York, Knopf, 1942), reviews some of the arguments for and against the retention of Canada that were voiced in the 1740's. G. Frégault, *La Guerre de la Conquête* (Montreal, Fides, 1955) is an important work written from the perspective of the French imperial school. W. L. Grant, "Canada versus Guadeloupe. An Episode of the Seven Years War", *American Historical Review*, Vol. 17 (1912), pp. 735–43, analyses some of the pamphlets published in England in the early 1760's on the question whether, in the peace treaty, Canada or Guadeloupe should be retained.

Problem 2

Freedom in New France — What Was Its Nature?

The nature of society and government in New France and the relationship that existed between the two is a problem that has long interested historians. How did the government act toward its Canadian subjects? What liberties, if any, did the latter enjoy? To what extent did they participate in government? These questions have been asked many times during the past hundred years.

The answer which has found its way into most textbooks goes roughly as follows. Because the government of France was a despotic one, Louis XIV and his ministers made no allowance for popular liberties or for the participation of the people in government when they fashioned the institutions of New France. All powers were vested in a few officials, appointed and paid by the Crown. But such an attempt to enforce complete obedience was doomed to failure because of the presence in Canada of a wild and antagonistic influence: the frontier. Settlers who yearned for freedom, for the carefree and adventurous life of the *coureur de bois*, or those who were simply offended by some aspect of government policy, fled to the wilderness, and an element of freedom, not orderly and institutionalized but savage and anarchic, was thus introduced into the society of New France.

This interpretation still has many supporters today, but some historians have adopted a different approach to the problem of liberty in New France. Absolutism, they claim, far from being an arbitrary and despotic force crushing subjects under its oppressive weight, was deeply Christian and humanitarian in character. The essence of the royal office, according to a long tradition going back to the Middle Ages, consisted of the King's obligation to do good, to maintain the various classes of society in their rights and privileges, and to protect the poor and the weak against the rich and the strong. The monarchy was a source of order, stability, and justice, not an instrument of oppression. Society itself was based on the corporate ideal, not on the assumption that the people had no rights before the King. A few words will clarify the meaning of this expression. Modern societies, as is well known, are the sum total of their individuals, all enjoying identical rights and all equal before the law. Ancien Régime societies, on the other hand, were the sum total of their social groups, institutions, and geographical areas: churchmen, nobles, bourgeois and peasants, universities, craft guilds and monasteries, provinces, towns and villages. It was membership in one or more of these groups that entitled a person to his share of freedom, extensive in some cases, limited in others. Nobles, for example, might enjoy exemptions from several taxes and a privileged status before the courts of law. The chartered freedom of a peasant, on the other hand, might consist of nothing more than the right to pasture a cow on the village common or to gather firewood in the nearby forest. Both, however, were equally sacred, and even Louis XIV at the height of his power recognized that he could not override them.

The notion that the people did not participate in government has also been revised. Although there was no institution in New France as powerful as the elective provincial assemblies of the British colonies to the south, the population could influence policy-making in a number of ways. The Sovereign Council, staffed principally by the colony's ruling class, sometimes shared legislative powers with the Governor and the Intendant, and possessed also the important right of registration by virtue of which no royal edict became law in Canada until officially promulgated by the Council. The Governor and the Intendant frequently consulted assemblies of notables on important matters affecting the welfare of the colony. Although the powers of these assemblies were purely advisory, the opinions they expressed frequently influenced the decisions of the officials. Merchants also had their assemblies in which they considered the state of their business and drew up petitions for presentation to the authorities. Finally, at the level of the seigneuries, assemblies of *habitants* exercised considerable control over matters of local interest.

In conclusion it can be said that historians agree that freedom existed in New France, but sharp differences of opinion arise on its nature, causes, and degree. Middle class liberals, who believe that freedom means an individualistic society operating with a minimum of government restrictions, will disagree with the paternalism of the French monarchy and emphasize the role of the frontier. Others, who consider that rational freedom only exists when individual initiative and enterprise are obliged to yield whenever they clash with the common good, will regard the social philosophy of the Crown as New France's most important safeguard against exploitation and injustice.

The Humanitarianism of the Ministry of the Marine

Jérome de Pontchartrain was Minister of the Marine from 1699 to 1715. The two readings that follow are meant to illustrate the philosophy of social justice on which he based his colonial policy. The first is his reply to a dispatch in which the Governor and the Intendant had outlined the progress of manufacturing in Canada. In the second, Pontchartrain explains why he will not send out the additional troops that the colonial authorities had requested to enforce discipline in the colony.

Since the settlers have been compelled by necessity to manufacture cloth, let us hope that they will also find means to satisfy their other needs. As a rule, however, it is not fitting that manufactures be established in the colony, as they would be prejudicial to those of France. The products of Canada ought instead to be shipped to France to be manufactured there. Such must be the general rule. But we must not absolutely prohibit manufacturing in Canada, especially for the poor settlers.

The Minister to Philippe de Rigaud, marquis de Vaudreuil and Jacques Raudot, 9 June 1706

Archives des colonies [AC], série B, Vol. 27, f. 235 (translation).

Nor does His Majesty believe that an increase in the number of soldiers is necessary to restrain the *habitants*. Their loyalty has been known to him for a long time, and he is persuaded that they will never change their attitude. There are very good methods for cultivating that sentiment in them. One need only uphold the rule of justice, and cause the people no vexation nor permit that any be caused to them. The Governor and the Intendant must not hinder them in the trade of their products but let them enjoy all ordinary liberties and be partial to no one. These precautions are based on justice and are in accordance with the views of His Majesty. Once they are adopted, it will not be necessary to employ authority to maintain order in the colony and to hold the *habitants* in dependence and respect.

Memoir from the King to Claude de Ramezay and Michel Bégon, 10 July 1715
AC, B, Vol. 37, ff. 180–1 (translation).

A Project for a Trading Post at Detroit

The following memoir was written in 1692 to show the necessity for a trading post at Detroit. Its interest lies in the type of company suggested to exploit the post.

The establishment of a post at Detroit appears necessary to facilitate the trade of the Canadian settlers with the Indians and to prevent the English from gaining control of it. The facility of this trade would be of great advantage to Canada, if His Majesty authorized the inhabitants of the colony to form a company with an exclusive privilege to carry it on in the posts above Montreal. This company would be obliged to accept everyone interested in joining it, for whatever sum he may choose to invest, but would give preference to the poorer settlers over the richer ones. If it found itself with surplus funds, part of the larger investments would be refunded in order to accept the small ones which the poor *habitants* might wish to make. Thus, the profits would not fall into the hands of a few parties but would be spread among the public.

An anonymous and undated memoir, probably written in 1692
AC, C 11 A, Vol. 12, f. 152 (translation).

An *Ordonnance* of the Intendant Jacques Raudot

Throughout the Ancien Régime the French economy was closely regulated by the government, and the place and role of each group in society were also carefully defined. The following document illustrates an attempt to extend this system to Canada.

The size of the population of Montreal is increasing daily as a result of the number of persons taking up residence there, and the number of craftsmen of all trades is growing proportionately. Until His Majesty decides to establish trade guilds in this city, we deem it expedient to prescribe a few regulations, particularly for the tanners and cobblers to follow, which should benefit the public by causing these craftsmen to apply themselves to their work. The said regulation should also enable the tanners and cobblers to subsist by limiting each one to the functions of his trade.

We order that there will be but two tanners in Montreal, to wit, Launay and Barsalot. So that each may have an equal amount of work, the city's five butchers will divide between them equally, as to quantity and quality, the skins of all the animals they will slaughter. In processing these skins the tanners will make use of all the methods that are necessary and required to provide the public with good merchandise, and this under pain of a fine of three *livres* for each item which our inspectors will consider below the standards set down in our *ordonnance*.

We forbid the butchers to make French shoes, under pain of a fine of three *livres*, but we do authorize them to make moccasins . . . We also forbid the butchers to engage in the traffic of animal skins with the *habitants* and order the latter to bring all said skins to the market established in Montreal. There they will place them on display and sell them only to the tanners.

> *Ordonnance* of M. Raudot, Intendant in Canada, fixing the number of butchers, tanners, and cobblers in the city of Montreal, 20 June 1706
> AC, C 11 A, Vol. 24, ff. 73–4 (translation).

The People of New France

In the following two documents, the people of New France are described by government officials. These descriptions seem to indicate that the settlers were not sufficiently submissive to accept government discipline and regulations.

Permit me to inform you, My Lord, that firmness, which as you know is absolutely necessary to bring about the execution of the King's orders, is considered a crime in this country. The religious communities state that it is not the custom in France to oblige them to contribute to the *corvées*; the nobility and the officers of justice declare loudly that it violates their rights; the merchant says that it disrupts the order of his business; the farmer who is taken from his field and the craftsman from his shop only obey with difficulty. They are vexed when they are conscripted for public works and notice that others are exempted from them . . . There cannot be too much sternness in dealing with a people so unruly and so hostile to obedience.

> Louis de La Porte de Louvigny to the Minister [*circa* 1707]
> AC, C 11 A, Vol. 25, ff. 20–20v. (translation).

The settlers of this country have never had any education because their fathers and mothers, like the Indians, have an inordinate affection for them during their childhood. Thus their faults remain unpunished and their temper is unformed. As there are no schoolteachers here, the children always remain with their parents, and growing up as they do without discipline, acquire a character that is hard and ferocious. They lack respect for their fathers and mothers as well as for their superiors and their priests. It also makes it impossible for them to show each other any civility in the affairs they have together. I have done my best, My Lord, to draw them from that barbarism and to cure them of the violence in which they are plunged by their ferocious manners, by sentencing them to heavy fines. But this can only produce effects on those who have some wealth, and since few of them have any means, they remain insubordinate for the most part.

> Raudot to the Minister, 10 November 1707
> AC, C 11 A, Vol. 26, ff. 167–167v. (translation).

An Encounter Between the Intendant and the Sovereign Council

The following reading is a report of the Intendant Jacques de Meulles (1682–1686) to the Minister of the Marine. It illustrates the defiant attitude the Sovereign Council could adopt toward the Governor and the Intendant when the councillors felt that the interests of the group they represented were at stake.

Upon returning from Montreal I discovered that the Sovereign Council had passed an *ordonnance* fixing the price of the spirits that are annually imported from France. This had produced such a stir that seven or eight of the most important merchants of Quebec had decided to send the large quantities of wines and spirits still aboard the ships to the Islands of the West Indies . . . I therefore thought it necessary to assemble the Council to find out if the matter could not be settled amicably. During two sittings I left nothing unsaid to prove to this body that commerce must be free and to persuade it to postpone the execution of its *ordonnance* until the King could advise on the matter or until the Governor's return to Quebec. But the Council would not be swayed. Its members had secretly joined together in a sort of league, the better to hold their ground, and they maintained that they could promulgate *ordonnances* regulating the sale of merchandise imported from France. . . .

* * * * *

From this episode, My Lord, you can infer to what length the councillors of this country would go if they were not held back by superior powers. Far removed as they are from the royal court, it is certain that they would rule as sovereigns and live in independence. . . .

I also take the liberty to inform you, My Lord, that unless you repress the boldness of the Attorney General of the Council he will be capable of anything in either word or deed. His speech is so brazen and forward that it borders on insolence. He once addressed the Count de Frontenac as one might a servant and would no doubt use the same language with me were it not for the fact that I avoid arguing with him. . . .

* * * * *

Permit me to say that unless you give the Intendant greater powers over the Sovereign Council, this country will always be a place of intrigue and injustice. The Councillors are allied to each other and also related to all the Canadian families. They will be the masters of justice. . . .

Jacques de Meulles to the Minister, 12 November 1684
AC, C 11 A, Vol. 6 Pt. II, pp. 147–9, 153–4, 160–1 (pagination of the Transcripts
of the Public Archives of Canada), (translation).

Extracts from the Minutes of an Assembly of Canadian Notables

In 1682 a new governor, Le Febvre de La Barre, arrived in New France. Soon after disembarking, he summoned an assembly of the principal settlers to confer with them on the Iroquois problem. Many other examples could be given of matters of importance being referred to the Canadians for deliberation.

At the Meeting held the tenth October, 1682, composed of the Governor, the Intendant, the Bishop of Quebec, M. Dollier, Superior of the Seminary of Saint Sulpice, at Montreal, the Rev. Fathers Beschefer, Superior, D'Ablon and Fremin, Jesuits, The Major of the City, Messrs. de Varennes, Governor of Three Rivers, de Brussy, Dalibout, Duguet, Lemoine, Ladurantais, Bizard, Chailly, Vieuxpont, Dulhut, de Sorel, Derpentigny [*sic*], Berthier and Boucher.

It is proposed by the Governor that it is easy to infer, from the records Count de Frontenac was pleased to deposit in his hands of what had passed at Montreal on the 12 Sept. last between him and the Iroquois Deputy from Onontagué, that these people are inclined to follow the object of their enterprize, which is to destroy all the Nations in alliance with us, one after the other, whilst they keep us in uncertainty and with folded arms; so that, after having deprived us of the entire fur trade, which they wish to carry on alone with the English and Dutch established at Manate and Orange, they may attack us isolated, and ruin the Colony in obliging it to contract itself and abandon all the detached settlements . . .

As he is not informed in the short time since his arrival from France of the state of these tribes and of the Colony, he requests the gentlemen to acquaint him with all they know of these things, that he may inform his Majesty thereof, and represent the necessities of this Colony, for the purpose as well of averting this war as of terminating and finishing advantageously, should it be necessary to wage it. . . .

Extract from the minutes of an Assembly of the Canadian notables
on the state of affairs with the Iroquois, 10 October 1682
Documents Relative to the Colonial History of the State of New York
(Albany, 1853–1887), Vol. IX, p. 194.

Petitions of the Canadian Merchants

In 1717 the Canadian merchants asked the French government for permission to meet periodically in order to discuss business matters and to consider the adoption of measures to promote their affairs. Their request was granted.

Given below is this demand, written by their agent, Benoit Collet. It is followed by a petition to the Governor and the Intendant, prepared by the merchants during one of their early meetings.

In the name of the merchants of Montreal and Quebec, whose commission he [Collet] claims to hold, he states that commerce, the principal means of sustenance and prosperity for the colony, will not flourish so long as the merchants do not have the right to assemble in a convenient place to discuss their affairs.

Assemblies of merchants have appeared so necessary for the betterment of commerce that places have been set aside for them in all the cities of France which engage in trade, which are called the Place or Exchange in some cases, or the *Bourse* in others. If the Canadian merchants are similarly favoured, they hope that the measures they adopt will soon result in a flourishing trade. They beg to be allowed to meet daily in a convenient place in both Montreal and Quebec to discuss business matters and also to appoint one of their number to act as their agent. His duties will consist of submitting their memoirs when necessary and of obtaining the permission of the Governor and the Intendant to present requests and demands either to them or to the Council of the Marine for the betterment of their commerce.

> Mathieu-Benoit Collet to the Council of the Marine, 11 May 1717
> AC, C 11 A, Vol. 37, ff. 202–3 (translation).

The King has favoured the merchants of this colony by bestowing on them the right to assemble for the good of their trade. Having thus assembled and conferred together on the poor state of their affairs, which has reduced them to the extreme necessity in which they find themselves today, they believe they have discovered the cause of their distress in the trade carried on by transient merchants from France, who spend the winter here, retail their merchandise, and send their agents into the countryside to skim off the cream of this land's products. . . . They claim they are entitled to do so because they are subjects of the same king as we are, and because the colony's trade is free to both resident and transient merchants.

We agree that commerce is free but not in the manner the transients carry it on, for it is of great prejudice to the residents and might ruin a colony which

the King wants to preserve. Thus, the reasons they advance to justify their
conduct can easily be countered by the following ones.

Please observe, Our Lords, that the residents have in this colony three
generations of ancestors; that they have their families, which are frequently
large; that they were the first to contribute to the establishment of the colony
by bringing land under the plow, building churches, putting up crosses, maintaining the faith, erecting nice homes, fortifying the cities, and prosecuting
war even with success against the Indians as well as against other enemies of
the State. They have obeyed all the orders transmitted to them and supported
all the hardships of war . . . they have spared neither their wealth nor their lives
to assist the King in establishing this country, which is a jewel in his Crown.

How will the unfortunate residents even be able to manage a living if they
cannot count on your customary goodness and justice to maintain their claim
to the retail trade and to exclude the transients from it . . .

> The merchants of Canada to the Governor and the Intendant [*circa* 1720]
> AC, C 11 A, Vol. 40, ff. 264–6 (translation).

Assemblies of *Habitants*

Like the merchants, the *habitants* also had their meetings, which
took place in the villages and the seigneuries, usually in the presence
of the parish priest and the captain of militia. The captain was
chosen from among the *habitants* to act as the local representative
of the Intendant. The following selections give an idea of the broad
range of topics that were put to these assemblies for deliberation.

Ordonnance advising the *habitants* of the parish of Ste. Geneviève of Batiscan
to assemble as soon as possible in the rectory of the said village to select, in the
presence of Father Le Sueur, missionary serving the parish, and of Claude
Loranger, captain of the militia, a suitable place near the church to build a new
bridge. This is necessary because the one that crossed the stream of the sr.
Veillet was carried away by ice floes last spring.

> *Ordonnance* of 4 June 1730
> P. G. Roy, *Inventaire des ordonnances des intendants de la Nouvelle France*
> (Beauceville, 1919), Vol. II, p. 63 (translation).

Ordonnance ratifying the election by the *habitants* of Ile Jesus of the sr.
Labrèche, bursar of the Seminary of Quebec, as their syndic. Jointly with the
srs. Date and Nantel, captain of militia, he will supervise the digging of a
drainage ditch to clear certain of the island's marshlands.

> *Ordonnance* of 10 July 1730
> *Ibid.*, p. 70.

Ordonnance decreeing that an assembly of the habitants of the seigneury **of** Sorel will be held for the purpose of electing three representatives to draw **up,** jointly with Father Pierre, Récollet missionary in the said seigneury, and with the captain of the militia, an estimate of the quantity of staves that will be required to enclose the cemetery of Sorel, as well as of the labour days, *corvées,* and expenses that will be required to complete this work. On the basis of this estimate an assessment roll will be prepared indicating what each *habitant* must pay or contribute in lumber or by labour or *corvées* as his share of the undertaking.

Ordonnance of 24 March 1732
Ibid., p. 115.

Ordonnance directing the principal *habitants* of St. Augustin to hold a **new** assembly to determine if the annex planned for the rectory to provide **the** *habitants* with a meeting place should be built in wood or in stone.

Ordonnance of 21 March 1741
Ibid., Vol. III, p. 6.

THE VIEWS OF LATER COMMENTATORS

The Mischiefs of Absolutism

Francis Parkman (1823–93), a New Englander, remains perhaps the best known of all the historians of New France. Although some modern scholars are finally questioning his judgments and conclusions, his influence is still enormous. Given below are the views of Parkman on absolutism, followed by those of L. H. Gipson, an eminent contemporary American historian whose specialty is the period of the American revolution. Sixty-eight years intervened between the writing of the two volumes, but, as the reader will note, their points of view are basically the same.

Not institutions alone, but geographical position, climate, and many other conditions unite to form the educational influences that, acting through successive generations, shape the character of nations and communities.

It is easy to see the nature of the education, past and present, which wrought on the Canadians and made them what they were. An ignorant population, sprung from a brave and active race, but trained to subjection and dependence through centuries of feudal and monarchical despotism, was planted in the wilderness by the hand of authority, and told to grow and flourish. Artificial stimulants were applied, but freedom was withheld. Perpetual intervention of

government, regulations, restrictions, encouragements sometimes more mischievous than restrictions, a constant uncertainty what the authorities would
do next, the fate of each man resting less with himself than with another,
volition enfeebled, self reliance paralyzed,—the condition, in short, of a child
held always under the rule of a father, in the main well-meaning and kind,
sometimes generous, sometimes neglectful, often capricious, and rarely very
wise,—such were the influences under which Canada grew up. If she had
prospered, it would have been sheer miracle. A man, to be a man, must feel that
he holds his fate, in some good measure, in his own hands.

But this was not all. Against absolute authority there was a counter influence,
rudely and wildly antagonistic. Canada was at the very portal of the great
interior wilderness. The St. Lawrence and the Lakes were the highway to that
domain of savage freedom; and thither the disfranchised, half-starved seignior,
and the discouraged habitant who could find no market for his produce,
naturally enough betook themselves. Their lesson of savagery was well learned,
and for many a year a boundless license and a stiff-handed authority battled
for the control of Canada . . .

*   *   *   *   *

This English conquest was the grand crisis of Canadian history. It was the
beginning of a new life. With England came Protestantism, and the Canadian
Church grew purer and better in the presence of an adverse faith. Material
growth, an increased mental activity, an education real though fenced and
guarded, a warm and genuine patriotism, all date from the peace of 1763.
England imposed by the sword on reluctant Canada the boon of rational and
ordered liberty. . . . A happier calamity never befell a people than the conquest
of Canada by the British arms.

Francis Parkman, *The Old Régime in Canada* (Boston, 1887), pp. 394–5, 400–1.

. . . If it, therefore, may be fairly charged that the activities of British colonials, along certain lines at least, were under-regulated, it may be as fairly charged
that those of French colonials along as many lines were over-regulated, depriving them of individual incentive and initiative. In this connection, it is not
without significance that within the bounds of New France there was no
escaping, for long, at least, the presence of the King's soldiers; they were
quartered in every town of importance, they were to be found at every trading
post of any consequence. Not only were these troops designed to defend the
territorial rights of the Crown along the frontiers in times of war but they were
the chief agency for maintaining its authority over the inhabitants in times of
peace. . . .

. . . The world of New France was not a world of industry and commerce but
really a world of officials, of *décrets*, of *ordonnances*, of King's soldiers, a world
in which religious monopoly and trade monopoly were incompatibly linked

together, a world without newspapers, without a press, without open discussion of public issues, a world of suppression of thought in which governmental policy affecting the most vital interests of the people was carried out without their consent expressed either directly or indirectly. . . .

> L. H. Gipson, *The British Empire Before the American Revolution:* Vol. 5,
> *Zones of International Friction: The Great Lakes Frontier, Canada,*
> *the West Indies, India, 1748–1754* (New York, 1942), pp. 342–3.

Absolutism Revisited

Guy Frégault, a French Canadian, is a leading contemporary authority on the French Régime. In the following passage he argues that the government of New France was more paternalistic than absolute.

When he pointed his accusing finger at the mischiefs of absolutism, Parkman uttered the great word, the key expression, which often takes the place of any form of reflection. It is indeed under the sign of absolutism that one must place the history of Canada during the French Régime. It is then illuminated, but by a light which is bright rather than precise. . . .

*　*　*　*　*

The supreme authority of the King—to say nothing of the extensive powers of the Minister—could have become a formidable instrument of oppression. Was this the case? Let us see. Basic psychology requires that we note first of all that the King could not have the same outlook as those petty tyrants who, having started from nothing, feel the need to assert themselves by crushing others beneath their astonishing superiority. The guiding principle for the Sovereign to follow was to behave like the Father of his people. . . . The character of the French monarchy was more paternalistic than absolute and the political history of Canada will be marked by this.

This particularity immediately limits in a singular way the exercise of power. Let us see how Louis XV defines authority in his memoir to Governor Vaudreuil and Intendant Robert. "True authority consists of doing what must be done, and when this limit is transgressed it is no longer legitimate authority that acts." The Minister Maurepas was later to write to the Bishop of Quebec: "There are undoubtedly occasions when rigour is absolutely necessary; but an enlightened gentleness is well suited to induce respect as well as love of authority." The King advises his colonial administrators to be kind and gentle toward the Canadians . . . by looking after their needs, facilitating their establishments, and by protecting the small settlers from the vexations of the powerful. One day, the Minister gave Vaudreuil a lesson in the art of governing. First, he must find ways to earn the love of the people, "and the surest way to attain this end is always to be just, to maintain peace and good order among the families, to intervene in private quarrels only to end them and not to meddle if you think yourself unable to conciliate the parties, never to listen to the talk of women, never to suffer the use of slander in your presence and not to speak ill of anyone yourself" ... The Intendant Raudot was familiar with this concept of authority. He once declared that Canada should be administered "as a good father conducts his estate".

The government could persevere in this attitude because it was based on personal contacts and because it was something more and something else than a bloodless administrative hierarchy, ignorant of human realities. Supreme authority maintained itself by using confidence rather than force as its bond with the people.

G. Frégault, *La Civilisation de la Nouvelle France* (Montreal, 1944),
pp. 126, 134–6 (translation).

A Look at Representative Institutions in New France

Allana G. Reid holds a Ph.D. degree from McGill University. Her dissertation was submitted in 1950 and bore the title *The Development and Importance of the Town of Quebec, 1608–1760.* She has also written several articles dealing with trade and commerce during the French Régime, and the institutions of New France.

In a country the size of New France, where there were abundant opportunities for law-breaking, it was obvious that a certain amount of co-operation had to be ensured from the leading men of the colony if there were to be peace, order, and prosperity. And while the principle that "What concerns all must be debated upon by all" could scarcely be described as a foundation stone of French-Canadian government, yet the practical truth behind it was easily recognized. Hence the practice of the governors of New France of convoking, at the Château St. Louis, assemblies of Canadian *habitants* to discuss current problems, to make suggestions, and to hear the plans of the home government ...

None of these assemblies, or meetings, was in any way democratic or representative. Their members were chosen by the governor, not by the people. Each gathering was held for a specific purpose and had no connexion whatever with any that went before or after. If the same persons appeared at a large number of the gatherings it was not from any right, but simply because they were the leaders in the economic life of the colony and hence best fitted to give the governor advice and support. When they voiced an opinion, they spoke for themselves alone except in so far as their influence would be likely to sway those of lesser wealth and prestige.

A. G. Reid, "Representative Assemblies in New France", *Canadian
Historical Review*, XXVII (March 1946), pp. 19–20.

The Influence of the Frontier

The frontier thesis was first developed in the late nineteenth century by an American historian, Frederick Jackson Turner, who was attempting to explain the origins and nature of the democracy of the United States. His conclusions were that this democracy stemmed largely from the presence of the frontier on the western rim of settlement—a zone where civilization gradually gave way to wilderness. There, class differences were minimized and equality of opportunity prevailed. At the Canadian Historical Association meeting of 1940, A. L. Burt, a noted Canadian historian, presented a paper in which he argued that the frontier thesis also applied to the history of New France.

American conditions of life emancipated the French peasants who crossed the Atlantic. With liberty forever beckoning through the trees and up the waters which flowed past their doors, how could they be ridden by feudal lords? If anyone found life in the colony too cramping, no power on earth could hold him from running away into the woods to live a wilder life of freedom with the Indians. . . . The earliest years of French settlement on this continent saw the emergence of the *coureur de bois* type. Long ago Turner described the same type on the fringe of English settlement. The condition of this escape was the adoption of savage ways of life, dictated by the environment. This was true of French and English alike, and both accommodated themselves in varying degrees.

*   *   *   *   *

Privilege sickened and died in the vigorous atmosphere of the New World. New France was no place for the *noblesse* of old France, who were preserved in the glass case of their hereditary caste. . . . The difference between society in the mother country and in the colony was as wide as the ocean between them. In New France, habitants frequently became seigniors, which they could never do in old France; and this made little or no change in their manner of living, for many other Canadian seigniors, including some titled ones, had to work and live like habitants. It was not uncommon for the lord of a manor, his lady, and his daughters to toil together in the fields. Such was the levelling influence of frontier life.

*   *   *   *   *

[The habitant] was a typical farmer of the North American frontier, where nature made men free and equal by enabling all to become economically independent. His economic independence was pretty complete, for he and his family produced practically everything they consumed. Their tastes were simple and their wants were few, but they lived well. They had so much more land than they needed that they cultivated only a corner of it. . . . It was the way of the frontier, which had no market for surplus agricultural produce, and it gave them an abundance. Though horned cattle were cheaper than horses as beasts of burden, these people invariably kept horses—mostly for pleasure. Many hands made light work in this self-sufficient household, the members of which had therefore plenty of leisure for the enjoyment of life. In short, the habitant of New France was one of the most independent men alive. By setting foot on this continent he had escaped from feudal bondage.

A man who thus stood erect on his own feet and could look the whole world in the face was not likely to be a hewer of wood and a drawer of water for his church, no matter how much he might be devoted to it. Nor was he a slave of the clergy, as a glance at the history of the tithe shows. When this ancient institution was introduced into the new country by the royal decree of April, 1663, which ordered the payment of one-thirteenth of all the fruits of human labour as well as of the soil, how was it received? With meek submission? Decidedly not! With one accord the people refused to pay. . . .

*   *   *   *   *

The freedom which permeated Canadian society also baffled the royal autocracy. Witness the many futile decrees to keep the people from wandering in the woods. The weight of the government fell heavily upon the masses at home but the population of the colony would not bear it. . . .

*   *   *   *   *

Here was real democracy, and it faithfully conformed to the familiar North American type. In contrast to that of the Old World, which developed out of a mass struggle to gain freedom which existing conditions of life denied, the democracy of this continent has existed because the individual would not surrender the freedom which the very conditions of life conferred upon him. It was the freedom of the frontier. This fresh and invigorating breeze from the West blew through New France as well as through the English colonies.

> A. L. Burt, "The Frontier in the History of New France", Canadian Historical Association, *Report, 1940*, pp. 93–9.

Further Reading

H. Méthivier, *L'Ancien Régime* (*Collection Que Sais-je?*, Vol. 925, Paris, Presses Universitaires de France, 1961)* and M. Beloff, *The Age of Absolutism, 1660–1815* (New York, Harper & Row, 1962)* provide short but informative introductions to the Ancien Régime in France. M. Giraud, "Tendances humanitaires à la fin du régime de Louis XIV", *Revue historique*, Vol. 209, (1953), pp. 217–37, is a scholarly analysis of France's humanitarian approach to problems of colonization. W. J. Eccles, *The Government of New France* (Canadian Historical Association Booklet No. 18) concludes that the administrative system of New France was efficient and that the people were satisfied with it. G. Frégault, *Canadian Society in the French Régime* (Canadian Historical Association Booklet No. 3) argues the revisionist thesis that control of affairs in New France rested with "the great commercial middle class". G. Lanctot, *A History of Canada*, Vol. II (Toronto, Clarke, Irwin, 1964) has chapters on society and political organization.

Problem 3

Westward Expansion — Choice or Necessity?

New France began in the early seventeenth century as a small colony in the St. Lawrence Valley. One hundred years later it embraced the larger part of the North American continent. Its settlements, forts, and trading posts ran uninterruptedly in a sweeping arc from Cape Breton Island in the North Atlantic to New Orleans on the Gulf of Mexico, hemming in the British east of the Appalachians. This expansionism is one of the more contentious issues of the history of New France. One school of thought contends that the clash with the English and perhaps even the Conquest itself could have been avoided had New France refrained from this headlong expansion; another maintains that contraction could only have resulted in the loss of the colony's fur trade and of its Indian allies and led to economic stagnation and political disaster. This division of opinion among historians reflects the one that existed among policy makers during the French Régime itself.

France's original colonization plan for Canada was formulated by Jean-Baptiste Colbert, the great minister of Louis XIV, and is known as the compact colony policy. It called for the population to remain concentrated in the St. Lawrence Valley, in order to provide a solid basis for the development of agriculture, industry, and the fisheries. The administrators sent to Canada were instructed to prevent the settlers from travelling to the distant West to trade with the Indians, and to encourage the latter to bring their furs to the colony. Thus, by a careful management of manpower resources, it was hoped that New France would gradually develop a strong and diversified economy.

Could such a plan have succeeded or was it necessarily doomed to failure? In 1678 the Intendant Jacques Duchesneau declared that the Minister's design could be implemented if Governor Frontenac enforced his orders instead of systematically eluding them. While some historians agree with this statement, most argue that Colbert's policy defied both geography and economics. By its magnificent system of waterways the St. Lawrence Valley was linked to the heart of the North American continent, and the French could not overcome the urge to expand and to claim for their country an imperial domain larger than Europe. The forces of expansion were further strengthened by the fur trade, the colony's chief economic activity. The settlers could follow the Minister's instructions and wait for the Indians to come to the colony, but going into the West after the trade held out the promise of far greater profits. Thus, for the sake of fur, New France gradually committed itself to an expansionist policy during the last thirty years of the seventeenth century. In growing numbers men travelled hundreds of miles from the main settlements, and garrisoned posts were established at several points in the hinterland. The Ministers of the Marine, however, disapproved of these developments, for their master plan for New France was still that of Colbert. Finally, in 1696, the collapse of the beaver trade brought about by years of reckless overtrading with the Indians presented the home authorities with a final opportunity to enforce their policy. An edict was issued abolishing the twenty-five trading permits (called the *congés*) and ordering the garrisons to evacuate the principal western posts. As the beaver boom had been the cause of the first period of French expansion, so the beaver crash had brought it to an end.

With the recovery of the beaver trade in 1715, French soldiers and traders once more began to occupy strategic points in the West. But this second period of expansion, unlike the first, was not mainly the result of economic motivation. In 1713 the War of the Spanish Succession had come to an end with the ratification of the Treaty of Utrecht. Shortly afterwards, for the first time in the history of North America, New France was faced with the phenomenon of English westward expansion as the fur traders and land speculators of New York, Pennsylvania, Virginia, and the Carolinas began to press steadily toward the Great Lake and Mississippi Valley regions. The Canadians soon decided that they had to resist this movement. They feared that the English, once they were allowed to advance into the West, would not only gain control of much of the fur trade but also of the system of Indian alliances, which was vital for the security of New France. For different reasons, the officials of the Ministry of the Marine also thought that English westward expansion had to be opposed. They considered that the overflow of the population of the Thirteen Colonies into the interior of the continent would be but the first step on a road that would lead to the conquest of the French and Spanish colonies, and eventually to the establishment of a formidable empire that would make Britain the greatest power in the world. It was therefore imperative to close the West to the English by establishing a chain of fortified posts in the rear of their settlements.

Such was French strategy in North America in the middle of the eighteenth century. In assessing it the historian must ask two major questions. Was such a policy sound? Was there any alternative to it?

New France's First Western Post

The foundation of Fort Frontenac in 1673 was the first significant departure from Colbert's compact colony rule. Built on the site of the present city of Kingston, the fort was separated from the main settlements by approximately two hundred miles of wilderness. In the following reading Governor Frontenac states his reasons for having established this post.

The intelligence received by the Count de Frontenac, on arriving in Canada, of the Treaty the Iroquois were negotiating with the Outaouaes, was of too great importance to the trade of the country not to oblige him to prevent its ratification. By this Treaty, in which the Iroquois were urged forward principally by their neighbors, they offered to supply the Outaouaes with all the goods they required, and the latter were to carry to them generally all their peltries, and the exchange was to take place on Lake Ontario.

The only means to traverse and upset this negotiation was, as had been frequently before proposed, to establish a Post on the same Lake, which would prevent the communication of the Nations of the South with those of the North, and force the latter to continue to bring us not only all the peltries that usually come by the River of the Long Saut, but even those our neighbors profited by, through the facility of being able to cross the Lake without any impediment. . . .

[Frontenac] was of the opinion, however, that the loss of the trade would infallibly entail in a short time the rupture of the peace, since the Iroquois and the Outaouaes, being in a position to dispense with us, and finding greater facility in their hunting and trade, would more easily resume that inclination they naturally feel for war, inasmuch as they had an idea that they could undertake it with less risk on the arrival of a new Governor, who they knew had no troops.

Journal of Count Frontenac's Voyage to Lake Ontario in 1673
Documents Relative to the Colonial History of the State of New York [*N.Y.C.D.*]
(Albany, 1853–1887), Vol. IX, pp. 95–6.

Colbert's Views on Expansion

Colbert was not pleased by the news of the construction of Fort Frontenac, for he realized that it was a step that might lead to the dispersion of the population over a very wide area and thus jeopardize all his plans for New France. In two cases, however, he recognized that the founding of distant posts might prove necessary.

. . . His Majesty's intention is not that you undertake great voyages by ascending the river St. Lawrence, nor that the inhabitants spread themselves, for the future, further than they have already done. On the contrary, he desires that you labor incessantly and during the whole time you are in that country to consolidate, collect and form them into Towns and Villages, that they may be placed in a position the more easily to defend themselves successfully, so that should even the state of European affairs be altered by a happy and advantageous peace, to his Majesty's glory and satisfaction, he deems it much more agreeable to the good of this service that you apply yourself to the clearing of those tracts which are most fertile and nearest the sea coasts and the communication with France, than to think of distant discoveries in the interior of the Country, so far off that they can never be settled nor possessed by Frenchmen.

This general rule may have its exceptions in two cases:—The one, should the countries of which you take possession be necessary to the trade and traffic of the French, and be open to discovery and occupation by any other Nation that may disturb French commerce and trade. But when such a category does not exist, his Majesty is always of opinion that you may and ought to leave the Savages at liberty to bring you their peltries, without giving yourself the trouble of going so far in search of them.

The other is, that the countries you might discover may approximate you to France by communicating with some sea, more Southerly than the mouth of the River St. Lawrence, such as would be the case with Acadia.

The reason for this is, as you are perfectly aware, that the greatest drawback to Canada is the mouth of that River, which being very much to the North, is open to vessels only for four to six months in the year.

Jean-Baptiste Colbert to Louis de Buade, comte de Frontenac, 17 May 1674
N.Y.C.D., Vol. IX, p. 115.

The Failure of Colbert's Compact Colony Policy

In 1678, in keeping with his policy, Colbert authorized Cavelier de La Salle to explore the southwest in order to discover the mouth of the Mississippi River. Once in the Mississippi Valley, however, La Salle engaged in the fur trade on an extensive scale. This was the signal for a number of other people to leave the colony in order to trade with the Indians in the remote interior. In the following document, Intendant Jacques Duchesneau describes this exodus and its consequences.

It is therefore an established fact, My Lord, acknowledged by everyone, that disobedience is general in this country. The number of persons who have taken to the woods is estimated at 500 or 600, not including those who are leaving every day. These are the people most qualified to enhance the value of the colony and to defend it against its enemies. They are led by Dulhut, a likely person to engage in dubious dealings, to encourage others to take their pelts to the English, and even to induce the Indians to do likewise. And all these evils have happened because the Governor, who could use force to impose his authority, has done nothing to prevent them and even lent his secret encouragement. This is so true that when he acted in good faith almost everyone obeyed.

Jacques Duchesneau to the Minister, 10 November 1679
Archives des colonies [AC], série C 11 A, Vol. 5, p. 52 (pagination of
the Transcripts of the Public Archives of Canada), (translation).

The Revival of the Compact Colony Policy

By 1696 the baneful consequences of western expansion had become evident to almost everyone. The beaver market was completely saturated by the reckless overtrading of the past years, and the Indian allies were being increasingly angered by the competition of the *coureurs de bois*. The Ministry of the Marine therefore decided to abolish the twenty-five trading permits known as the *congés* and to order the evacuation of the principal western posts. It was hoped that these measures would oblige the Canadians living in the interior to return to the colony.

It appears to his Majesty that the war with the Iroquois has arisen especially of late times from no other cause than their jealousy of the trade with the Upper Nations, in order to monopolize that between New York and these nations to themselves, through the advantageous position possessed by the Iroquois establishments which bar the communication of the English with those nations and of the latter with New York. Further, it results from the Narratives of Sieurs de Frontenac and de Champigny that the estrangement of the Outawas and others proceeds from the fact that the French, by ranging the interior of the country, have usurped the trade these nations carried on with the Upper Tribes, and that some of the latter are, on the same account, waging war against the Allies, or obliged to rally themselves to the Iroquois; and that, finally, the ranging of the woods, more unrestricted last year than it ever was before—notwithstanding his Majesty's orders and the reduction of licenses to the number of 25—is the source of all the disorders of the Colony, and has given rise to establishments which by dividing, weaken its strength in such distant regions, and upset the views his Majesty has entertained and which alone ought to prevail—to concentrate it and employ the settlers in the cultivation of the soil, in the fisheries and other pursuits he has always recommended and which they can derive from the nature of the country and their own application and industry.

* * * * *

They must, pursuant to his Majesty's invariable orders, observe as their main rule in all departments of the government of that Colony, to concentrate it, and to make it derive its support from the employment of the settlers within its confines and from their trade with the kingdom and with the Indians who will necessarily bring peltries into the Colony in order to procure there those goods of the Kingdom which they require. Such was their wont before the Canadians were permitted to go into the depths of the forest, where they contract every debauched and vicious habit which renders them useless and a burthen to civil society; leaving out of consideration the extortions they are guilty of towards the Indians in the excessive prices of the merchandise they carry thither, and the irregularity on account of the bad beaver they accept indifferently from them, because they are sure of being equally paid for it. . . .

> Louis XIV to Louis de Buade, comte de Frontenac and Intendant Jean
> Bochart de Champigny, 26 May 1696
> *N.Y.C.D.*, Vol. IX, pp. 637–8.

The Case for the *Congés*

In the years that followed the abolition of the *congés*, the Governor and the Intendant of New France frequently pointed out to the Minister of the Marine that these trading permits, in spite of the many evils they had caused in the past, were still vital for the security of New France. Philippe de Rigaud de Vaudreuil, in particular, regarded the *congés* as the foundation stones of Indian diplomacy.

We agree that the *congés* have been the cause of evils and that Frenchmen have led disorderly lives among the Indians. But we must also recognize that it was not the *congés* proper but their abuse that caused this. We must now ask if matters can long remain on the present basis and if the *congés* correctly used do not favour the conversion of the Indians and the well-being of the colony by preserving peace among the savages. Your Lordship has decided to re-establish a commanding-officer at Michilimackinac. We believe that all canoes going up-country must proceed there to carry on their trade. The Ottawas and other nations of the Great Lakes country will also make their way to Michili-mackinac to obtain merchandise both for their own use and for the trade which they carry on with nations located deeper inland. The profits they will make will strengthen their alliance with us. . . .

*   *   *   *   *

Once the post of Michilimackinac and the *congés* are reestablished, all the Indians will be more firmly committed to our side and we will be able to use them as we see fit. Their value as allies was demonstrated during the late war with the Iroquois when their war parties attacked our enemies. In those days *congé* holders travelled up-country and the Indians obtained the goods they required from them. Could they have waged war otherwise? They would have lacked everything and been useless to us. Thus, it does not appear that *congés* weaken the colony. On the contrary, they procure the help of which it often stands in need. . . .

Had there been a commanding-officer at Michilimackinac last year and had the *congés* been revived, the Chippewas would not have attacked the Pottowa-tomies, and the latter would not have cut off the ears of their Iroquois prisoners. The commanding-officer and the *congé* holders would have uncovered these plots and prevented their execution. The commanding-officer is also in a posi-tion to assemble all the Indians from the Great Lakes and turn them against the Iroquois if the latter ever decided to make war on us. This is what the Iroquois fear most, and it is one of the factors that keeps them from attacking us.

> Memoir on the *congés* by Philippe de Rigaud, marquis de Vaudreuil and
> Jacques Raudot [1710]
> AC, C 11 G, Vol. 6, ff. 80–1, ff. 86–8 (translation).

The Foundation of Louisiana

The foundation of Louisiana in 1700 added a revolutionary new dimension to New France's western policy. Until that time the purpose of the French establishments in the West had been to con-trol the fur trade. Louisiana, however, was meant to prevent English westward expansion. These imperial origins of the southern colony are aptly summarized by Pierre Le Moyne d'Iberville.

If France does not seize this part of America [the Gulf of Mexico region], which is the most beautiful, in order to have there a colony strong enough to resist that of England in the east, from Pescadoué to Carolina, the English colony, which is becoming very considerable, will increase in such a manner that in less than one hundred years it will be strong enough to seize all of America and expel all other nations. For if we reflect on this subject we will see that in the West Indies our numbers are not increasing in the same proportion as those of the English, who are a people with a genius for colonization. Although they enrich themselves, they do not return to England but remain in the colonies and make them prosper by their fortune and their spending. The French, on the other hand, abandon the colonies and retire to France as soon as they have amassed a little wealth because these are inhospitable countries which do not compare with France. I do not believe that this would happen on the coast of Florida if France colonized it. This is a perfectly good land where a population would grow rapidly, for the men we sent there would not die as they do in the islands. Thus they would become powerful and in less than fifty years, with the help of the Indians, would be able to hold all of New England in check.

> Pierre Le Moyne d'Iberville, Memoir concerning the coast of Florida and a part of Mexico [n.d.]
> P. Margry, ed., *Découvertes et Etablissements des Français dans l'ouest et dans le sud de l'Amérique Septentrionale* (Paris, 1879–88), Vol. IV, pp. 322–3 (translation).

If we pay a little attention to the country occupied by the English on this continent, to that which they plan to occupy, to the forces which they have in their colonies where there are neither priests nor nuns and where everyone helps to increase the population, and to what they will be in 30 or 40 years, we cannot doubt that they will not occupy the country between them and the Mississippi River, which is one of the world's most beautiful. Joined to the Indians they will then be in a position to raise considerable forces on land and sea in order to become the masters of all America.

*   *   *   *   *

It appears to me absolutely necessary to plant a colony in the Mississippi Valley at the Mobile River and to join with the Indians who are quite numerous there, in separate villages and nations. We must arm and support them against those who are in the English interest and force the latter back beyond the mountains [the Appalachians], which is easy enough at the present because they are not yet powerful to the west of them. But it will not be as easy if we wait until later. The English will fortify themselves and will reduce the number of Indians who are in our interest by obliging them to come to their side.

A memoir of Pierre Le Moyne d'Iberville [1701]
Ibid., pp. 545–8 (translation).

The Beginnings of Anglo-French Rivalry in the West

It was only after the Peace of Utrecht in 1713 that Anglo-French rivalry for control of the West began in earnest. By clause 15 of the treaty, the Iroquois were declared British subjects and the western nations were given the liberty to trade with the English as well as with the French. Legally, at least, the whole interior of the continent was now open to the English.

[Article 15] The Subjects of France inhabiting Canada . . . shall hereafter give no Hindrance or Molestation to the Five Nations or Cantons of Indians, subject to the Dominion of Great Britain, nor to the other Natives of America, who are Friends to the same. In like manner the Subjects of Great Britain, shall behave themselves Peaceably towards the Americans, who are Subjects or Friends to France; and on both sides they shall enjoy full Liberty of going and coming on account of Trade. As also the Natives of those Countries shall, with the same Liberty, resort, as they please, to the British and French Colonies, for Promoting Trade on one side, and the other, without any Molestation or Hindrance, either on the Part of the British Subjects, or of the French. . . .

Treaty of Peace and Friendship . . . concluded at Utrecht the 31/11 *
day of March/April 1713 (London, 1713), pp. 74–5.

The Clash on Lake Ontario

In 1727, capitalizing on clause 15 of the Peace Treaty, New York merchants crossed Iroquois territory and built a trading post at Oswego on the shore of Lake Ontario. This establishment, the first owned by the English in the Great Lakes country, was a direct challenge to New France's western trading empire. So great was the alarm it caused in the French colony that Governor Vaudreuil even considered declaring war on the English to force them to retreat.

The news of this establishment on territory which has been considered, from all time, to belong to France, appeared to him as much the more important as

---

* Until Britain adopted the Gregorian Calendar in 1752, diplomatic documents were commonly given both "Old Style" and "New Style" (O.S./N.S.) dates.

he was sensible to the difficulty of preserving Niagara, where there is no fort, should the English be once fortified at Chouaguen [Oswego], and that the loss of Niagara would entail at the same time that of the entire Indian trade of the Upper country; for these nations go the more readily to the English, as they obtain goods much cheaper, and as much Rum as they please from them . . .

The projects set on foot by the English, since the Treaty of Utrecht, indicate that Canada is the object of their constant jealousy, and the Colony has not a more dangerous enemy. By means of underground belts they have managed the Outawas of the Upper country, who are as much in their interest as they appear to be in ours. They have given these Indians to understand that all the Lakes belong to them, and that they have a right to trade there, as well as in the whole of the Upper country. . . .

* * * * *

Should the Iroquois refuse to listen to M. de Longueuil's proposals and de-clare openly for the English; should they desire to favor and support the estab-lishments of the latter, and oppose the construction of our barks and of the house at Niagara, the Upper country trade must be absolutely abandoned, and we must anticipate the seizure of all the posts we have in that quarter, one after the other. In this extremity it would be impossible to preserve the Upper coun-try otherwise than by force of arms, in which case there would be no need of Manifestos to show that the English have been the first to violate the Treaty of Peace. But as their force is at present numerically superior to that which we could oppose to them, and as the Indian Nations, whom they have almost wholly seduced by force of presents, might also declare for them, there is reason to apprehend that a war with them will be unavoidable.

[Vaudreuil] asks that extraordinary and considerable aid be sent him, both in money and munitions of war, and a large number of guns and pistols.

He also requires troops.

Abstract of Vaudreuil's dispatches regarding Oswego, 25 May 1725
N.Y.C.D., Vol. IX, pp. 949–51.

The Clash in the Ohio Valley

The crisis on Lake Ontario gradually receded, and twenty-five years passed before another major Anglo-French confrontation took place. The scene this time was the Ohio Valley, a region which France decided to occupy largely on the strength of the memoir of Governor Michel Barrin de La Galissonière on the colonies of France in North America. This was a fateful decision, for it caused the clash with the English colonies that led to the fall of New France.

What has already been said in the course of this memoir while speaking of Canada's utility for the preservation of Mexico should impress upon us the importance of maintaining a free and certain route between Canada and the Mississippi River. A break in this chain would leave a void which the English would no doubt exploit to draw closer to the sources of silver. They devote much space to such a project in their writings, but it will never be anything but a vain dream if France maintains herself in her Canadian possessions.

The River Ohio, otherwise called the Beautiful River, is very important to the English for the realization of their plans. It originates near the country occupied today by the Iroquois, flows to the south, merges with the Wabash, and then joins the Mississippi.

The Ohio River was discovered by the sr. de La Salle, who took possession of it in the name of the King. It would probably be occupied today by a large number of French habitations had not the fear of an illicit trade developing between these settlements and those of the English prevented the Governors of Canada from proceeding with a solid occupation of the area.

The English have no habitations there either. They had only carried on a clandestine trade there until the last war, when the revolt of a few Indian nations against the French encouraged them to come forward more boldly.

Since the conclusion of peace they have been told to withdraw, and we must be assured that the Governor of Canada will evict them by force if they do not comply. Otherwise, the same thing would happen as at Oswego, only far worse, for an establishment on the Beautiful River would give them far more opportunity to do us harm than Oswego alone.

1. There would be more occasions than at Oswego to debauch the Indian nations.

2. They would find it easier to interrupt communications between Canada and Louisiana. The Ohio River is almost the only route by which Canada can send to the Mississippi the contingents required to strengthen Louisiana, which is still a weak colony, against the enterprises of the Carolina Indians which the English are continuously stirring up against us.

3. If the English ever become strong enough in America to dare attempt the conquest of Mexico, they will have to descend by the Ohio.

4. It is also by way of the Ohio alone that the English can attack with forces at all considerable and with any hope of success the posts we have in the Illinois country and in the Mississippi Valley.

5. It is again by that route that they can attack the post of the Miamis, whose loss would deprive us of one of our most important links with the Mississippi and would entail the loss of Detroit, an important post to be discussed hereafter.

Therefore we think that one of our most urgent priorities must be the establishment of a few posts on the Ohio River. . . .

Memoir of Michel Barrin, marquis de La Galissonière, on the colonies of France in North America, December 1750

AC, C 11 A, Vol. 96, pp. 202–5 (pagination of the Transcripts of the Public Archives of Canada), (translation).

THE VIEWS OF LATER COMMENTATORS

New France Had No Choice

According to Lionel Groulx, it would no doubt have been preferable for the French to build a compact colony in North America, but the external threat of Anglo-American expansionism forced them to develop a continental empire. If New France had refused to intervene in the Great Lakes and Mississippi Valley regions, its downfall might have been hastened by as much as twenty years.

Who was right in this debate between the advocates of the Laurentian Valley colony and those of the Empire, the court or the colonial administrators? To answer this question we must examine the motives of French expansionism. Toward the Atlantic, at Ile Royale, in the Gulf, on the north shore, these motives were largely economic, namely the fisheries and the industries of oils and skins in which the colonials were encouraged to engage in order to complement the economy of the mother country. In the west and northwest, furs remained as important as ever. There were years like 1735, when la Vérendrye's furs saved the trade, threatened by a long period of troubles in the area of the Great Lakes. To those commercial preoccupations were joined as in the past the thirst for adventure and the curiosity of the explorer obsessed by the American enigma. The Laurentian Valley could not conceal from those of her sons who felt no inclination for agriculture the marvels of the Upper Country where impatient youths could freely roam. Yet it must be recognized that [after the treaty of Utrecht] the expansionist urge no longer came from the colony's inner self, from the irrepressible vital impulses of the missionary and the explorer. It came from an external pressure which is called Anglo-American expansionism. Let us look at each of the French advances in turn. In every case—Ile Royale, Crown Point, Niagara, Detroit, the Ohio, the West, the Prairies—a threatening shadow had appeared. To contain the English, bar his way, preserve the trade of the Upper Country, safeguard the alliance with the Indians, maintain communications between Canada and Louisiana, those were the imperatives that determined everything. . . .

Who then was right, the colonial or the French authorities? No doubt, it would have been preferable to settle a limited area, to build a compact colony instead of one so widely dispersed. But it remains to be known if the empire did not constitute a vital annex, an indispensable rampart for the inner colony and if the two did not somehow have to be reconciled. Suppose, after 1696, that the French had abided by Louis XIV's policy of withdrawal from the West; suppose, after the building of the fort at Oswego, that they had allowed the English and the Iroquois to hatch their intrigues in the Upper Country; who would dare deny that such a policy would not have hastened the colony's fall by twenty years?

> L. Groulx, *Histoire du Canada français depuis la découverte* (Montreal, 1962), Vol. I, pp. 209–10 (translation).

New France Should Have Stayed Out of the Southwest

Lionel Groulx's opinion is not shared by W. J. Eccles. In the following passage the latter argues that New France's attempt to control the southwest was economically unsound and politically unrealistic.

. . . In a memoir dated May 31, 1701, Louis [XIV] informed Callières and Champigny at Quebec: "His Majesty has resolved to found a settlement at the mouth of the Mississippi . . . this has become an indispensable necessity to halt the advance which the English from the colony of New York have begun to make in the lands which lie between them and this river."

It was not expected that this new colony, when established, would be of great benefit to France in the foreseeable future. It was to serve mainly as a base, an anchor, for a series of posts to be built on the rivers flowing westward into the Mississippi from the Great Lakes to the Gulf of Mexico. Just as Governor Nicholson had foreseen six years earlier, these posts were to be used to weld all the Indian tribes between the Alleghanies and the Mississippi into an alliance with the French to bar the English from the west. If this were not done, it was feared that the English would soon begin to press south and west until they came into conflict with the Spanish in Mexico; in order to secure his grandson's hold on the throne of Spain, Louis XIV had to demonstrate to the Spanish people that France was able and willing to protect their colonial possessions from a common enemy. The French now found themselves committed to occupying the entire western section of North America from Hudson Bay to the Gulf of Mexico and to holding the English colonials on the eastern side of the Alleghanies—this at a time when the population of the English colonies was doubling every twenty-five years.

Essentially, it was a dog-in-the-manger policy. In 1696 Denis Riverin, one of the leading *bourgeois* in the colony and a staunch believer in Colbert's policy, had advocated what amounted to the abandonment of the Illinois country to the English, on the grounds that this whole area produced only poor-grade furs which were a glut on the market. He observed that the English had relatively easy access to this region but that the country to the north of the Great Lakes, which produced the best furs, was inaccessible to them. Even though it was quite possible to exclude the English from the Mississippi valley, would it be wise, he queried, to strive, arms in hand and at excessive cost, to retain the very things that were proving to be a liability both to the economy and to the state? Champigny had recognized the logic of this, and he too had suggested the abandonment of the south-west, but his recommendation had gone unheeded and the authority of the king of France still extended, at least nominally, throughout the mid-west. It was this tenuous sovereignty that Louis XIV had now decided to strengthen.

The consequences of Louis XIV's decision were certainly to be of great moment, not only for France and New France, but for England and her empire as well. Nothing is inevitable in history but what is made so by the decisions and acts of men. It may well be that had Louis not made this decision and had the French not attempted to hold western North America south of the Great Lakes, there would have been no conflict in the Ohio Valley, some fifty years later, between the French and the English colonials as the latter pressed on beyond the Alleghanies. Perhaps then the English would not have thrown their full weight against Canada in the Seven Years War and it would have remained under the French flag . . .

W. J. Eccles, *Frontenac, The Courtier Governor* (Toronto, 1959), pp. 335–7.

Further Reading

L. P. Kellogg, *The French Régime in Wisconsin and the Northwest* (Madison, State Historical Society of Wisconsin, 1925) and the first part of C. W. Alvord, *The Illinois Country, 1673–1818* (Springfield, Illinois Centennial Commission, 1920) are basic accounts of French activities in the West. Both, however, stand in need of revision. H. A. Innis, *The Fur Trade in Canada* (Toronto, University of Toronto Press, 1956)* is a classic study of the economic force that played such an important role in westward expansion. W. J. Eccles, *Canada Under Louis XIV* (Toronto, McClelland & Stewart, 1964) contains critical reassessments of the role of Frontenac and La Salle in the western expansion of New France. L. H. Gipson, *The British Empire Before the American Revolution:* Vol. 4, *Zones of International Friction: North America South of the Great Lakes Region, 1748–1754* (New York, Knopf, 1939); Vol. 5, *Zones of International Friction: The Great Lakes Frontier, Canada, the West Indies, India, 1748–1754* (New York, Knopf, 1942) have a wealth of ideas and information about conditions in the West in the mid-eighteenth century.

Problem 4

The Conquest — Incident or Catastrophe?

In 1760, after six years of bitter warfare, Pierre de Rigaud de Vaudreuil, Governor of New France, surrendered the colony to the British general Jeffery Amherst, and approximately 65,000 French Canadians passed under English rule. That much is clear. But what were the effects of this event on the history of French Canada? This is one of the most controversial questions in Canadian history.

One group of historians view the event as a catastrophe which shattered French-Canadian society. They argue that in the seventeenth century and in the first part of the eighteenth, a *Canadien* society supported by France, the indispensable source of manpower, capital, and technical skills, had been developing in the St. Lawrence Valley. In every respect, it was a typical community of the western world. It had twin foundations in agriculture and commerce and was equipped with the classes and occupational groups to carry out the political, economic, and social operations necessary for its harmonious functioning. Membership in the French empire presented the inhabitants with splendid opportunities for self-advancement.

Then came the Conquest. The links with France, through which flowed the colony's life blood, were severed. This entailed the collapse of the *Canadien* business class, the school system, and several major institutions of the French Régime. Canada now had a new metropolis, England, and formed part of a new empire, the British. Political and economic power, social prestige, and opportunities for brilliant careers had been transferred to the English settlers.

Another group of historians view the event simply as an incident which did not cause any profound changes in the fabric of French-Canadian society. They reject the image of New France as a small but vital community advancing toward nationhood under the protective wing of the mother country and view it instead as a weak and deficient colony. According to them, what happened after 1760 was not caused by the Conquest but by a faulty socio-economic development during the French Régime itself. No French-Canadian business class existed after 1760 because none had really existed before. The economy of New France was controlled by French merchants or by the metropolitan government. The primitive institutional organization consisting of the parish and the seigneury, which appeared in the post-Conquest era, was also a consequence of the French Régime — a régime that had failed to generate strong native institutions. Even the low level of French-Canadian intellectual life under British rule could be blamed on New France, which had not possessed a soundly based school system and had even lacked a printing press to diffuse ideas and information.

These two theories are the product of modern historical scholarship. Before they appeared, the Conquest was viewed in simpler and somewhat different terms. Older historians who studied this event dwelt on its cultural rather than on its socio-economic aspect. The Conquest was particularly significant in their eyes because it might have caused the ethnic and religious disintegration of French Canada. The community, however, had closed its ranks and survived, and for this reason they concluded that it had successfully overcome this greatest of all challenges to its national existence.

These three interpretations give a preliminary idea of the complex nature of the Conquest. It is this complexity which makes it an outstanding example of how historians research and analyze a given problem, and how such factors as personality, time, and milieu influence their approach to it.

The Articles of Capitulation

The following articles have been extracted from the capitulation of Montreal, 8 September 1760. On the right-hand side appear the conditions requested by Governor Vaudreuil; on the left, the comments of the British commander Jeffery Amherst. The original document was written in French, the international language of the eighteenth century.

ARTICLE XXVII

Granted, as to the free exercise of their religion,

The free exercise of the Catholic, Apostolic and Roman Religion, shall subsist entire, in such manner the obligation of paying the tithes to the Priests will depend on the King's pleasure.

that all the states and the people of the Towns and countries, places and distant posts, shall continue to assemble in the churches, and to frequent the sacraments as heretofore, without being molested in any manner, directly or indirectly. These people shall be obliged, by the English Government, to pay their Priests the tithes, and all the taxes they were used to pay under the Government of his most Christian Majesty.

ARTICLE XXXVI

Granted

If by the treaty of Peace, Canada remains to His Britannic Majesty, all the French, Canadians, Acadians, Merchants and other persons who chuse to retire to France, shall have leave to do so from the British General. . . .

ARTICLE XXXVII

Granted . . .

The Lords of Manors, the Military and Civil officers, the Canadians as well in the Towns as in the country, the French settled, or trading, in the whole extent of the colony of Canada, and all other persons whatsoever, shall preserve the entire peaceable property and possession of the goods . . . They shall have liberty to keep, let or sell them, as well to the French as to the British; to take away the produce of them in Bills of exchange, furs, specie, or other returns. . . .

ARTICLE XLII

[They become Subjects of the King.]

The French and Canadians shall continue to be governed according to the custom of Paris, and the Laws and usages established for this country, and they shall not be subject to any other imposts than those which were established under the French Dominions.

A. Shortt and A. G. Doughty, eds., *Documents Relating to the Constitutional History of Canada, 1759–1791* (Ottawa, 1918), Pt. I, pp. 30, 32–4.

First Reactions to the Conquest

Initially, the Conquest meant the disappearance of the signs and symbols of French supremacy, the break-up of families, the departure of friends and relatives. The heartbreak of these moments is expressed in the letters of Mother Marie d'Youville, the founder of the Order of Grey Nuns.

Thus it came to pass that those who stayed behind had to mourn both for the devastated fatherland and for the loss of their friends and relatives. The letters written by our venerable mother [d'Youville] at that time are full of such regrets. We shall cite a few passages.

. . . 'We had flattered ourselves that France would not abandon us, but we were wrong in our expectation. God permitted it so. May his holy name be praised.' 'What is even more distressing for us is that this poor country is more and more forsaken. All the good citizens are leaving it.' We have the sorrow of seeing depart 'our parents, our friends, our benefactors, never to see them again. Nothing can be sadder. Each day brings new sacrifices.'

The forthcoming departure of one of her friends for France caused her to write these lines, touched with emotion: 'We are losing her forever. I have not visited her or her family for several days. Nor will I go until after she has left, since I lack the strength to bid her farewell. I will do my best to comfort her father and mother, her brothers and sisters, when she is no longer there. I very much fear that her departure will greatly upset the father and the mother. I must end; my tears are blinding me.' To an old benefactor: 'Please let us hear from you and your dear daughters. Forsaken by France, our only consolation is the news we receive from our friends. . . . I will not tell you anything of X and X, since they are writing to you. I know not how many times they kissed and bathed in tears the letter of your little ones.'

[Anonymous], *L'Hôpital général des Soeurs Grises de la Charité* (Montreal, n.d.), Vol. I, pp. 238–40 (translation).

The Beginnings of British "Leniency"

It is often argued that the lenient policy followed by the British after 1760 repaired the damages inflicted by the Conquest and won the loyalty of the *Canadiens*. Documents such as the following dispatch of Secretary of State Egremont to Jeffery Amherst, the British commander-in-chief in North America, play a central part in this interpretation.

His Majesty observes, with Pleasure, the laudable Gentleness and Mildness, with which you offer his Royal Protection indiscriminately to all his Subjects, recommending it particularly to the Troops, to live in good harmony and brotherhood with the Canadians, and as Nothing can be more essential to His Majesty's Service, than to retain as many of the French subjects, as may be, and to prevent their leaving their homes to repair to such Colonies, as shall remain in the possession of the French, when those, which are now His Majesty's by Conquest, shall be confirmed to him at the Peace, it is the King's pleasure that you should earnestly enforce, to the several Governors above mentioned, the conciliating part of the Instructions, which you have given, and that you Recommend it strongly to them to employ the most vigilant attention, and take the most effectual care that the French Inhabitants (who, as you very properly observe, being equally His Majesty's subjects are consequently Equally entitled to his Protection) be humanely and kindly treated, and that they do enjoy the full Benefit of that Indulgent and Benign Government, which already characterizes His Majesty's auspicious Reign, and constitutes the peculiar happiness of all, who are Subjects to the British Empire; and you will direct the said Governors, to give the strictest orders to prevent all Soldiers, Mariners, and others His Majesty's Subjects, from insulting or reviling any of the French Inhabitants, now their fellow Subjects, either by ungenerous insinuation of that Inferiority, which the fate of War has decided, or by harsh and provoking observations on their language, dress, Manners, Customs, or Country, or by uncharitable Reflections on the Errors of that mistaken Religion, which they unhappily profess; and as there is yet no regular Civil Government Established in any of the said Conquered Countries, it is the King's Pleasure that the several Governors do properly exert that Authority, under which they at present act, to punish such persons, as shall disregard His Majesty's orders in a Matter so Essential to his Interests; and you will direct that His Majesty's Intentions in this behalf, be forthwith made known to all those, whom it may Concern, to the End that the King's British Subjects may not, thru Ignorance, disobey his orders, and that his French Subjects may feel and Relish the full Extent of His Majesty's Royal Protection.

Charles Wyndham, Earl of Egremont, to Jeffery Amherst, 12 December 1761
Public Archives of Canada [PAC], Série B, Vol. 37, pp. 10–12.

The Conquest and the Roman Catholic Church

The Conquest of New France left the Roman Catholic Church in a very delicate position, for it was now subjected to the rule of the Protestant kings of England. The Catholic hierarchy soon decided that the wisest policy in these difficult circumstances was one of loyal co-operation with the new masters of Canada. Any other course of action might expose it to being deprived of the powers and privileges necessary for its future functioning.

The peace signed in Paris on February 10 last, and ratified on the 10th of the following month, has finally ended a cruel war. . . . You yourselves have experienced its baneful consequences, so I shall not recall them to your memories on a day that must be one of thanksgiving to God for having granted us peace, this invaluable gift, which we had so earnestly wanted and continuously demanded by our public prayers and our wishes. These wishes were perhaps not blessed in their entirety, for Canada and her dependencies have been irrevocably ceded to the British Crown. But trust in Providence, dear brethren, whose ways are often the more merciful when they do not entirely conform to our wishes and do not flatter all our expectancies. Do we not have manifest proof of this in the manner in which our victors have acted toward us since the conquest of the colony?

The surrender of Quebec left you at the mercy of a victorious army. At first, you were undoubtedly alarmed, frightened, and dismayed. Your feelings were justified . . . but you were ignoring that a kind and watchful Providence had reserved for you a Governor who, by his moderation, his stern justice, his generous and humane sentiments, his tender compassion for the poor and the wretched, and his rigid discipline towards the troops, would remove all the horrors of war. Show me the vexations, the distortions, the plunders, that ordinarily follow in the wake of victory. Did not those noble victors, once they became our masters, appear to forget that they had been our enemies, in order to concern themselves solely with our needs and with ways of satisfying them? Surely, you have not forgotten the good actions of His Excellency, the illustrious and charitable General Murray, and the alms he gave to help the poor subsist! You have not forgotten his wise and generous measures to prevent famine in his government!

After such deeds, must we not be convinced that God has not stopped loving us and that it rests with us to enjoy under this new government the pleasure of a long and durable peace. Punctually perform the duties of subjects who are loyal and devoted to their prince. You will then find a King who is good-natured, charitable, diligent in promoting your happiness, and favourable to your religion to which, with a joy that is beyond words, we see that you are so strongly attached.

Besides, dear brethren, it is not only temporal interests that demand your entire and perfect loyalty. This is also a duty prescribed by faith.

The apostle Paul, in many places, speaks of it as an indispensable obligation. By betraying the trust of your legitimate sovereign you would not only incur his wrath, lose his protection, and forfeit all the privileges he has been good enough to grant you, but you would also be guilty in the eyes of God. Twice guilty, since you would expose yourselves to being deprived of the right granted at the peace treaty to practise our holy religion, the only true faith. Consider carefully, then, dear brethren, how important it is for you to be loyal and submissive and how nothing can dispense you from a perfect obedience, a scrupulous and punctual fidelity, an inviolable and sincere attachment to our new monarch and to the interests of the nation to which we have just been united.

Given at the General Hospital, June 4, 1763
[by Jean-Oliver Briand, Vicar General of the district of
Quebec 1760–6, Bishop of Quebec 1766–84]

Mandement pour faire chanter un Te Deum en action de grace pour le
bienfait de la paix
Mandements, lettres pastorales et circulaires des Evêques de Québec
(Quebec, 1888), Vol. II, pp. 168–70 (translation).

The Conquest and the Seigneurs

The strategy of the seigneurial class following the Conquest was basically the same as that of the Church. They promised to co-operate with the British authorities and to make their tenants into loyal and devoted subjects of George III. In return for these services, however, they asked to be admitted to all offices of state.

The Seigneurs of the lands and proprietors of the fiefs of the district of Montreal, in the province of Quebec, at the foot of Your Majesty's throne, filled with the deepest Gratitude for all the marks of Favour with which it has pleased Your Majesty to honour them, since they have been under Your Government, Dare to take the Liberty of here presenting to You their most humble supplications in their own Names and those of their tenants.

The truly paternal Care which your Majesty has never ceased to bestow on their temporal Interests, and the signal Favour of possessing a Bishop have roused in the hearts of all the New subjects the liveliest sentiments of gratitude, of love, and of fidelity toward Your Majesty.

*   *   *   *   *

The frequently repeated Marks of a King's Goodness, always give ground for the hope of fresh ones, and it is on this ground that they dare plead for two privileges. These would fill up the measure of your Majesty's favours, & of their gratitude & devotion.

The first is the suppression of the Register, the expenses of which exhaust the Colony, without its receiving from it the least advantage.

The second is that all the subjects in this province, without any Distinction of Religion may be admitted to any Office, the only basis of selection being that of capacity and personal merit. To be excluded by the State from participating in it, is not to be a member of the state. If they feel such a humiliation they would appreciate all the more the value of a favour equally marked, for which they can only offer their hearts full of love and gratitude. Their Zeal, their affection and their devotion shall be the signal proofs of it for all time to come.

Their precepts and their examples shall perpetually tend to maintain their tenants in the sentiments of fidelity and submission which they owe you. They will offer without ceasing their vows and their prayers for the Glory and Preservation of Your Majesty and your august family.

Petition to the King from the Principal People of Montreal, 3 February 1767
Shortt and Doughty, eds., *Documents* . . . , Pt. I, pp. 272–3.

The Conquest and the Middle Class

The three readings that follow illustrate some aspects of the economic dislocation caused by war and conquest. The first is a letter by Simon Jauge, the Bordeaux correspondent of François Baby, a Canadian merchant. It relates to the transfer of Baby's accounts to England, an operation made necessary by the disruption of communications with France. In the second, a petition to King George III, a group of Canadians explain the nature of their plight and ask for royal protection. The third is a letter from three Canadian merchants to two English merchants. It shows the changed economic climate that prevailed in Canada after 1760, one to which the Canadians obviously found it difficult to adjust.

I am writing you this letter by way of England and sending it to my friends, Mssrs. Thomas, Thomas and Sons of London. You can write to them if you cross over to France and are captured or if you sail by way of England, as others have done. They will provide you with the help you may need. If conditions do not change, you can send them your furs and advise your friends to do the same. You can be assured of the integrity and solvency of this house. It is powerful, leaves nothing to chance, and your funds will be as safe in their hands as they are in mine or in your own coffers. There will be no lack of agents travelling from London to Quebec to offer their services in the name of important houses. But I advise you to stay away from them and not to trade your furs for letters of exchange drawn on London. You could be the dupe of such an operation. Send them rather for your own account and have them insured. The premium will be cheap. If Quebec remains in English hands, you could present your memoir of the merchandise you will need to Mssrs. Thomas, Thomas and Sons. I will even transfer your account to them if you so order and if you do not give them a remittance. . . .

Simon Jauge to François Baby, 5 February 1760
PAC, Baby Collection, Vol. III, pp. 1733–8 (translation).

Most humble and respectful address of the citizens of the
town of Montreal to His Britannic Majesty.

Sire:

The citizens of the town of Montreal in Canada venture to take the liberty
of prostrating themselves at the foot of Your Throne, fully persuaded that there
dwells the sanctuary of justice and the temple of all the virtues.

*   *   *   *   *

The scourges of war and famine, long before the surrender of Canada,
afflicted its unfortunate inhabitants, expenditures of funds multiplied beyond
reason had, long before its downfall, spread about an extraordinary quantity
of paper; companies as avaricious as they were powerful, were formed. All
the trade was captured, and the merchants of Canada were helpless onlookers
at business which should have been theirs. Would to heaven that the ministry
of France had been earlier informed as to these injustices! It would have
imposed a check on abuses so antagonistic to the welfare of a colony!

These same merchants had made purchases of goods in France in the years
1757 and 1758. The fear of these running risks on the sea in time of war led
them to take the resolution to await more favourable circumstances. They
adopted the expedient of leaving their goods in warehouses, until peace was
restored. This peace, so dear to them and so much desired, aroused the hope
of commencing their labours anew; but vain hope, Canada passed under the
dominion of Your Majesty.

From this time, paper money, the only kind which circulated in the country,
became totally discredited and entirely useless. The suspension of the payment
of bills of exchange brought upon us the last blow; in a word, all classes and
conditions of the people found themselves and are finding themselves in
terrible distress, and in a situation most deplorable. The public markets are
filled to overflowing with goods and chattels absolutely necessary to maintain
the existence of our families.

*   *   *   *   *

. . . The future casts dread over the people of Canada. What will become
of them if the payment for their money is long deferred? What will become
of their families? The rural labourer will find at least in the fertility of the
soil, a reward for his labours; he will live, but, more unfortunate than he, the
inhabitants of the towns will have no resources; they will do everything in
their feebleness to assist one another, because they suffer in common.

The truly Royal heart of Your Majesty is touched at the sight of this feeble
portrayal of our misfortune; it pities the fate of so many unfortunates. Permit
us, then, Great King, to seize this happy moment to obtain your favourable
notice. Deign to interest yourself in the prompt payment of our paper; long

enough and too long have we suffered without complaining; we are not the authors of the disorders which have been perpetrated in the finances of Canada; and nothing can be more just than to discriminate between the innocent and the guilty.

Deign also, to grant us permission to bring from France our merchandise which was purchased long since, and which will become a total loss if it lies longer in warehouses. This object is not so considerable as to be able to prejudice, in the least, the trade of your old subjects. . . .

[Signed]
The Body of the Clergy . . .
The Body of the Noblesse . . .
The Body of the Merchants . . .

February 12, 1763

A. Shortt, *Documents Relating to Canadian Currency, Exchange and Finance During the French Period* (Ottawa, 1925–6), Vol. II, pp. 969–71.

Only recently conquered, we have gladly submitted ourselves, we say, to the new government. We were hoping to find in it kindnesses that we could never have enjoyed under French domination, and up to a certain point we were not mistaken. But in order for us fully to enjoy these kindnesses, a material basis should also be present and this is exactly what we lack.

France used to spend annually ten or eleven million *livres tournois* for the maintenance of the troops or for other political purposes. This money, distributed among the people, constituted real wealth . . . Our new masters adopt an opposite method. Far from spreading wealth among us, they force us to assume a burden. We do not know how to carry it. We see only one solution, and that is to compensate for our new mother country's lack of aid and for the regulations she imposes on us by a trade that is free and extensive.

The English are reputed the best traders in the world. Their leaders, as a consequence, should be the most enlightened. They cannot but see what is best for us and what is the most useful. However, the distance that separates us makes them see things quite differently from what they really are. Our trade is declining. We lack many of the necessary, we even dare say, indispensable goods. We have a surplus of things we cannot use, and our own goods cannot be used in payment for what we would require from you. A sad situation! Money is no longer sent to us and we cannot obtain any by means of our own goods. These few words explain everything.

The consequences are evident. Trade is falling off. It will decline and wither until the colony, burdened with debts which it cannot pay, will become a useless member of the state, an insupportable burden to herself, and a lost cause to all those who would have liked to help her.

The decline of numerous business houses established in the last four or five years easily shows what we have always wanted your government to understand, that this colony cannot yet be self-supporting. It is absolutely necessary that she receive, at least for a little more time, either assistance or an equivalent encouragement for her commerce.

> Lemoine, Porlier, and Lévêque to Guinaud and Hankey, 27 September 1765
> PAC, Dartmouth Papers, Vol. I, pp. 126–8 (translation).

The Conquest and the Lower Classes

Among the French-Canadian peasants, in the unchanging countryside, memories of France lingered on for many years after the Conquest. The selection from Philippe Aubert de Gaspé's *Mémoires* captures this mood. Born in 1786 of a noble French-Canadian family, Gaspé is best known as the author of *The Canadians of Old* (Les Anciens Canadiens). His *Mémoires* are based on his recollections of life in French Canada during his early years. The second selection consists of a petition sent to the consul of France at New York by a group of French Canadians during the French Revolution. It shows the pro-French feelings of the people being expressed in a more forceful way.

For a long time after the Conquest, the French Canadians remembered with fondness their former French princes. When my father received his newspaper in the country, the old *habitants* would ask him for news of the King and Queen of France and of their children. During the Revolution, this unfortunate family had been struck by the executioner's hand. My father, and particularly my mother, often told them the story of their ordeal, of the sufferings of the young Dauphin under the infamous Simon's iron rod. Each time the *habitants* shook their heads in disbelief and said that this was all a story made up by the English.

It is a most remarkable thing that I never heard anyone of the common people ever accuse Louis XV of the disasters suffered by the French Canadians after he had abandoned the colony to its own resources. If someone did blame the monarch: "Bah! Bah!" replied Jean-Baptiste. "It's la Pompadour who sold out the country to the English." And they would launch into long discourses full of reproaches against her.

> Philippe Aubert de Gaspé, *Mémoires* (Quebec, 1885), pp. 85–6 (translation).

Citizen:

Accept the best wishes of the greater part of the *Canadiens*. They all love France, detest the English, and passionately desire to be re-united to the motherland from which they have been separated for too long. They see with sorrow that the Convention seems to forget them. Day by day the British tyrants, under whose yoke they groan, want to make their chains heavier. The *Canadiens* wish to break them, and all they require to do so is a favourable word and a little help from the Republic. For each oppressor in Canada there are three hundred oppressed. The former do what they can to reduce our strength. So greatly do they fear us that they began by forming a militia company and then divided it in two, then in four, so as to make it weaker. But all their efforts are in vain. . . .

With one voice the *habitants* say that their fathers took the oath of fidelity to the English but that they did not; however, that they will defend the English against all their enemies except the French, because they will never take up arms against their fathers, their brothers, and their parents. Their most cherished desire is to see France fix her attention on them. As soon as this has been proved by the presence of even a small French force it will soon be augmented by that of all the inhabitants, and they will then concentrate their efforts against a handful of helpless Englishmen who only preserve this fertile land because France has so far neglected to reconquer it.

The citizens hereafter named have the support of all their fellow *habitants*. Good patriots and good warriors, they will join forces with the French who will come to free them from the British yoke. As soon as the signal is given, they will be followed by all those whom it is impossible to name here but who all have the same courage and the same love of France and the French.

I will add that all have asked me to offer their hearts and their arms to France and that all would have signed if they could have done so without risk.

A letter by some Canadians to the Consul of the French Republic in New York
[*circa* 1792]

M. Brunet, "Les Canadiens et la France révolutionnaire", *Revue d'Histoire de l'Amérique Française*, XIII (1960), pp. 474–5 (translation).

THE VIEWS OF LATER COMMENTATORS

An Early Nationalist Interpretation

F. X. Garneau (1809–1866) was French Canada's first major historian as well as its first important literary figure. He began to write his history in the dark days that followed the collapse of the uprising of 1837, the Durham Report, and the Act of Union. By describing his nationality's past trials and heroic deeds, he hoped to instil into his contemporaries the will to continue the struggle for survival.

After three years passed in a state of alternate hope and fear, the Canadians had perforce to renounce their latest illusion. Their destiny was bound irrevocably to that of the British people by the treaty of 1763. Consequent upon this event, a second emigration took place: numbers of commercialists, lawyers, ex-functionaries, with most of the leading men still remaining in the colony, left for France, after selling or abandoning estates . . . None now lingered in the towns, but here and there a few subaltern placemen, some artisans, scarcely one merchant. The members of the different religious confraternities, with the rural populations, of course remained.

*   *   *   *   *

. . . The Canadians, meanwhile, felt all the chagrin arising from subjection to alien sway. The evils they had previously endured seemed light to them, compared to the suffering and humiliations which were in preparation, they feared, for them and their posterity. First of all, the British wished to repudiate whatever was Canadian, and to deprive the *habitants* even of the natural advantages Canada offered to them by its extent. The colony was dismembered. . . .

From parcelling out territory, the British passed to relegislating. Their king, by his sole authority, without parliamentary sanction, abolished those laws of olden France, so precise, so clear, so wisely framed, to substitute for them the jurisprudence of England — a chaos of prescriptive and statutory acts and decisions, invested with complicated and barbaric forms . . . and the above substitution was effected, merely in order to ensure protection and the benefits of the laws of their mother country to those of the dominant race who should emigrate to Canada.

> F. X. Garneau, *History of Canada, from the Time of Its Discovery till the Union Year (1840–1)* translated by Andrew Bell (Montreal, 1860), Vol. II, pp. 84–6.

The Religio-National Interpretation

Canon Lionel Groulx, the author of the following selection, has had a long, active, and very influential career as a historian and theorist of French-Canadian nationalism. The interpretation of the Conquest which he presents below has now become archaic. But historical thinking of this type was extremely widespread half a century ago, when French-Canadian nationalism was based essentially on race, language, and religion (see Problem 14).

In short, on the morrow of the Conquest, in that year 1766, there is a question full of anguish that the historian must ask himself. What will become, in the new environment tainted with creeping Protestantism, of the young, idealistic, and chivalrous race, sprung of such a pure history, the synthesis of the thoughts and labours of the ancestors, the offspring of those gallant knights with the flashing swords who had performed so many marvellous exploits? What will become of the race of New France so amorously moulded in the divine hands of the Church?

If the threats are great, thank God the protections are still greater and more powerful. In those arduous times the young nationality would be guided by a great bishop, a bishop in the best episcopal tradition . . . behind this leader was a clear-sighted and hardworking clergy whose devotion and attachment to the Holy See was without equal, as the abbé de La Corne once dared to inform the pope himself. Such noble qualities would enable the clergy to safeguard more effectively the integrity, the faith, and the customs of their people.

There also existed between the two races now facing one another — the one of Saxon background, the other of Latin descent — a mental opposition, an incompatibility of feelings, a lack of affinities that would reduce the dangers of contact. A juxtaposition of races took place but not a penetration. And ours being a historic race, one of those whose oneness is the result of the blending of several racial strains through environmental and institutional forces, ours kept this strength of never having mixed but homogeneous elements in its crucible. Perhaps the purest race on the whole continent, it would also have the quality of being the most impenetrable.

Finally, this is the time and the place to recall the memorable words of Mother Marie de l'Incarnation: "Canada is a country specially guarded by Providence." Mightier than all human protections was that of Divine Providence, the august guardian of our history, who has never abandoned the world, nor even a continent, to the disastrous uniformity of a single race or a single civilization.

L. Groulx, *Lendemains de conquête* (Montreal, 1920), pp. 234–5 (translation).

The Neo-Nationalist Interpretation

Lionel Groulx viewed the Conquest as a catastrophe but managed to remain optimistic about the future because of the continuing presence of the Roman Catholic Church. Guy Frégault, a contemporary French-Canadian historian, considers that nothing can undo the economic and political damage which French Canada suffered in 1760. In accounting for these different points of view, one must emphasize the different perspectives of these two historians.

While Groulx belongs to the generation studied in Problem 14, Frégault belongs to the one which forms the subject of Problem 20.

In 1760 Canada was completely crushed. The colony which passed to Britain three years later was an economic ruin. It was also a political ruin. . . . Finally, in 1763 the country was ruined socially. It had lost the most influential and competent part of its ruling class, a part which could not survive outside of the political and economic framework of New France and the French empire. The latter now disappeared from America, and the former from the map.

During the years 1760–3 Canada was not merely conquered and ceded to England; it was defeated. Defeat means disintegration. When an army is defeated there are still soldiers, but there is no longer an army. In 1763 there were still Canadians, but Canada was no more. Eliminated from politics, from commerce, and from industry, Canadians turned back to the soil. If they came to boast that they were "children of the soil", it was because defeat had affected not only their material civilization but also their ideas. They had had higher pretensions when their community was more complete.

The social development described in the preceding pages does not conform with the account given by most historians of Canada. The reason is that most of them attempted to reconstruct the society of the French Régime on the lines of that broken society which they could examine in the period following 1760. They have read history backwards. It is only because of this dubious approach that they came to conclude that, under the French Régime, the chief factors which conditioned Canadian society were neither the existence of the French motherland nor the fur trade but only the peaceful work of the countryside. The behaviour of the mother country was shown as being inadequate and, at times, uninspired; but that does not mean that it was superfluous. A simple examination of the facts brings into sharp relief the importance of big business and of the economic activity which implied the existence of a middle class.

In truth, the old-time Canadian society was something more than a rustic community. It had all the elements which made up the society of a normal colony. Like other American settlements, Canada possessed political and social institutions borrowed from the motherland and adapted to the conditions of the New World. Like other colonies it had its rustics and its townsmen, its clergy and its faithful, its workers and its merchants, its soldiers, its officials and its politicians, its middle classes and its aristocracy. Between Canada and the British colonies the chief difference was not one of kind but of size. It had very few people; they were populous. Hence, after an inevitable conflict, it was defeated.

G. Frégault, Canadian Society in the French Régime, Canadian Historical Association, Booklet No. 3 (Ottawa, 1962), pp. 15–16

A Recent Revisionist Interpretation

Frégault's view of the Conquest has not been accepted by all historians. In the following selection Jean Hamelin of Laval University argues that the absence of a business class in French Canada after 1760 is an outcome of the French Régime rather than of the Conquest.

Much is being said about the French-Canadian bourgeoisie before 1760. Its origins would go back to the formation of the Company of the Habitants in 1645, and the Conquest would have marked its decline. Part of this bourgeoisie would then have emigrated to France, and the other, cut off from its economic basis of the fisheries and the trading posts by the modification of the frontiers of New France, would have died of economic suffocation. Thus the annihilation of the French-Canadian bourgeoisie becomes the major historical factor which conditioned the economic evolution of French Canada down to Confederation.

This thesis is attractive, but does it correspond to the exact reality? This is a legitimate question, for the hypothesis was presented without any exhaustive research to support it. The case is therefore not closed but remains open to discussion. . . .

* * * * *

Could it not be supposed that the emigration of a few businessmen in 1760, and the ruin of those who remained in the colony — if indeed there was ruin — is but an aspect of a much deeper problem? Let us suppose that in fact bourgeois were established in the colony as masters of trade and commerce and as owners of lucrative industries. What would have happened then? They would not have emigrated. Did the *habitant* who owned his land emigrate? The majority of those who emigrated were clerks or associates of French companies, itinerants and civil servants who engaged in commerce, French Canadians whose businesses were tributary to those of French merchants and dependent on military contracts.

The absence of a dynamic French-Canadian bourgeoisie in 1800 thus appears as the end product of the French Régime, not as a consequence of the Conquest. For the tragedy of French colonization in Canada was its inability to form a French-Canadian bourgeoisie based on the rational exploitation of the natural resources of the country. Trade with the motherland, the fisheries, and the monopoly of the sale of beaver pelts, were in the hands of metropolitan Frenchmen. The shipyards and the St. Maurice ironworks were in those of the King.

J. Hamelin, *Economie et Société en Nouvelle-France* (Quebec, 1960), pp. 127, 137 (translation).

The Conquest Viewed as an Incident

Mason Wade, a native of New England and formerly a member of the University of Rochester's History Department, is one of the leading English-speaking authorities on French Canada. The interpretation of the Conquest which he gives below differs considerably from the preceding ones. According to Wade, the harmful consequences to which this event might have given rise were obviated by the generous policy of the conquerors and by French Canada's own indomitable will to live.

It is still possible today to start bitter controversy in Quebec by pointing out that the first British rulers of Canada did not try to crush the French Canadians under the yoke of military government, but on the contrary actually befriended them against the pretensions of the swarm of campfollowers and commercial adventurers who descended upon the newly conquered land like a cloud of locusts. Such, however, is the picture which emerges from sober study of the contemporary documents. In this age of ruthless oppression of conquered peoples the peaceful transition of Quebec from French to British rule is remarkable and noteworthy. The English conquest might well have meant the end of French Canada as a cultural unit in North America, and of the French Canadians as an ethnic group; instead the survival of both was assured by legislation adopted a decade after the peace treaty had been signed. The French Canadians benefited from the confusion of British politics from 1760 to 1774, when colonial affairs were almost completely neglected in George III's bitter struggle with the Whig majority. But their survival was not dependent, however, upon either British magnanimity or the force of circumstances; for French Canada possessed an indomitable will to live, witnessed in the first decade after the conquest by the attainment of the highest birthrate ever recorded for any white people. The whole history of Quebec since 1760 reveals how completely the French Canadians concentrated their resources and devoted them to the struggle for survival. This effort still continues, long after survival has been assured.

Mason Wade, *The French Canadians 1760–1945* (Toronto, 1956), pp. 47–8.

Further Reading

The extracts from the works of Garneau, Groulx, Frégault, Hamelin, and Wade illustrate the opinions of the principal schools of thought on the Conquest. The volumes and articles listed in this section were written to support, amplify, or refute one or the other of these five points of view.

T. Chapais, *Cours d'histoire du Canada*, Vol. I, *1760–1791* (Montreal, Editions Bernard Valiquette, 1919) concentrates on the efforts of the French Canadians to preserve their legal and religious rights. The social and economic effects of the Conquest are studied by M. Brunet in "La Conquête anglaise et la déchéance de la bourgeoisie canadienne (1760–1793)". This important essay was published in *La Présence anglaise et les Canadiens* (Montreal, Beauchemin, 1958). Brunet's thesis that the Conquest caused the disintegration of the bourgeoisie and deprived French Canada of its most dynamic class has been sharply attacked by F. Ouellet in "M. Michel Brunet et le problème de la conquête", *Bulletin des Recherches Historiques*, Vol. 62 (1956), pp. 92–101. Like Hamelin, Ouellet denies that the Conquest caused a major upheaval in French-Canadian society. He develops this point of view in his recently published *Histoire économique et sociale du Québec, 1760–1850* (Montreal, Fides, 1966).

For a provocative introduction to the attitude of English-speaking historians toward the Conquest, see M. Brunet "The British Conquest: Canadian Social Scientists and the Fate of the *Canadiens*", *Canadian Historical Review*, XL (June 1959). Francis Parkman's very influential interpretation has already been given in Problem 2. A. L. Burt, *The Old Province of Quebec* (Toronto, Ryerson, 1933) is one of the classics of Canadian historiography. M. Wade's description of conditions in French Canada after 1760 is largely derived from this source. The period covered by Burt has recently been restudied by Hilda Neatby, one of his former students who is now the head of the Department of History at the University of Saskatchewan. Her volume, *Quebec, the Revolutionary Age, 1760–1791* (Toronto, McClelland & Stewart, 1966) does not commit itself to any single theory of the Conquest, but tends rather to present the event as a "challenge or opportunity" for French and English alike. Such a point of view would seem to be well worth further investigation.

Problem 5

The Quebec Act — Generosity or Self-Interest?

The Quebec Act constitutes a historical problem because it marked a crucial decision for Canada's future development. In 1838 Lord Durham wrote in his famous *Report* of finding "two nations warring in the bosom of a single state". That conflict is described today in terms of "one Canada, or two?", or as the problem of bilingualism and biculturalism. This study problem introduces the first of those two historic events—the Quebec Act and the American Revolution—which laid the foundations for Canadian dualism.

The British acquisition in 1763 of the colony of New France, inhabited by some 60,000 people differing in religious, political, legal, and social customs from the settled population of the other British colonies in North America, created problems that were both quantitative and qualitative. Other non-English-speaking and non-Protestant areas had previously been incorporated into the British Empire, but in every case the "new subjects" of His Britannic Majesty had been easily assimilated to established British patterns either because they were numerically insignificant or because they were technologically inferior. Neither condition held true for New France, where a unified homogeneous society had grown over the previous century-and-a-half until, by 1763, the people could with justice speak in truly national terms of "the Canadian church" and a "Canadian society", and of themselves as "Canadians".

Never before the conquest of Canada had British statesmen faced the problem of ruling a nation so culturally distinct as New France —except perhaps in the case of unhappy Ireland. Should the Canadians be assimilated in language, laws, religion, and political institutions to the British colonial system in North America, or should they be left distinct within the Empire to enjoy their own way of life? This uncertainty lasted for a decade, and is reflected in the policies recommended by the Board of Trade and Plantations and in the opposing policies advocated by governors Murray and Carleton who, from their vantage point of residence in Canada, believed much would be gained from retaining the institutions of New France. British statesmen were faced then with the fundamental question: what was to become of a French colony in an English empire? Varied motives influenced their decision to abandon the policy of assimilation (a policy that had in fact never been seriously or consistently implemented), but that decision was basic to the nature of Canada for all time to come.

Every historian of Canada must inevitably answer the question: would assimilation of the French have been the wiser policy in the long run? Most have answered in the negative. But this answer does not solve all the problems raised by the Quebec Act. Was that Act an example of "British statesmanship at its best", or of calculated self-interest, or even part of a sinister plot to destroy British liberties in North America? Americans of Washington's day saw the Quebec Act as the evil companion of the so-called "Intolerable Acts". Some historians have agreed with this verdict; others have viewed the Act as pragmatic politics, and still others as British justice for French Canadians.

Among the related problems raised by the Quebec Act we must consider whether that Act was a breach of faith with the "old subjects" who settled in Canada by invitation after the Conquest. Are French Canadians justified or merely historically naïve in calling the Quebec Act their own "Magna Carta"? Did the Quebec Act in fact keep French Canada British when revolution destroyed the great promise of an undivided empire? Was the Quebec Act a sudden reversal or a simple maturing of British colonial policy? If it is true that politics is the art of the possible, was any other policy really applicable to Canada in 1774?

Policy for a New Province

As far as New France was concerned, the Treaty of Paris which closed the Seven Years' War did little more than confirm the policies hinted at in the Montreal Articles of Capitulation. Precise details of future British policy were announced in the Royal Proclamation of 1763. This document promised that the new colony of Quebec would become British in every respect. It also barred settlement from the Indian lands of the interior, a factor that was to have repercussions on the expansionist ambitions of the older seaboard colonies who had previously been shut out of the "west" by the presence of French soldiers and forts.

> . . . so soon as the state and circumstances of the said Colonies will admit thereof, [the Governors] shall, with the Advice and Consent of the Members of our Council, summon and call General Assemblies within the said Governments respectively, in such Manner and Form as is used and directed in those Colonies and Provinces in America which are under our immediate Government; . . . and in the mean Time, and until such Assemblies can be called as aforesaid, all Persons Inhabiting in or resorting to our Said Colonies may confide in our Royal Protection for the Enjoyment of the Benefit of the Laws of our Realm of England; for which Purpose We have given Power under our Great Seal to the Governors of our said Colonies respectively to erect and constitute, with the Advice of our said Councils respectively, Courts of Judicature and public Justice within our Said Colonies for hearing and determining all Causes, as well Criminal as Civil, according to Law and Equity, and as near as may be agreeable to the Laws of England. . . .

> Royal Proclamation for the Government of Quebec, 1763
> A. Shortt and A. G. Doughty, eds., *Documents Relating to the Constitutional History of Canada, 1759–1791* (Ottawa, 1918), Pt. I, p. 165.

"New Subjects" and "Old Subjects"

Despite his Instructions to encourage Anglicization, General James Murray, first governor of the colony of Quebec, adopted a liberal and sympathetic attitude toward the French-speaking Roman Catholics of the colony and urged a policy of "leniency" in the matter of privileges for these "New Subjects", a suggestion that antagonized the handful of English merchants who had taken control of the colony's economy after the Conquest.

> Little, very little, will content the New Subjects but nothing will satisfy the Licentious Fanaticks Trading here, but the expulsion of the Canadians who are perhaps the bravest and the best race upon the Globe, a Race, who cou'd they be indulged with a few priveledges wch the Laws of England deny to Roman Catholicks at home, wou'd soon get the better of every National Antipathy to their Conquerors and become the most faithful and most useful set of Men in this American Empire.

I flatter myself there will be some Remedy found out even in the Laws for the Relief of this People, if so, I am positive the populer clamours in England will not prevent the Humane Heart of the King from following its own Dictates. I am confident too my Royal Master will not blame the unanimous opinion of his Council here for the Ordonnance establishing the Courts of Justice, as nothing less cou'd be done to prevent great numbers from emigrating directly, and certain I am, unless the Canadians are admitted on Jurys, and are allowed Judges and Lawyers who understand their Language his Majesty will lose the greatest part of this Valuable people.

> Governor Murray to the Lords of Trade, 29 October 1764
> *Ibid.*, p. 231·

Governor Carleton's Proposals

Governor Murray's disputes with the "English party" of merchants led to his recall in 1765, but his successor, Guy Carleton, another career soldier, fully shared Murray's admiration for the French Canadians. Moreover, Carleton saw in the "New Subjects" a potential source of manpower should there be future hostilities in North America. In his despatches to Lord Shelburne, the Secretary of State in charge of the American colonies, Carleton recommended measures that he considered simple justice to the French Canadians —measures which he believed would win their gratitude and loyalty to the British throne.

The King's Forces in this Province . . . would amount to sixteen hundred and twenty seven Men, The King's old subjects in this Province, supposing them all willing, might furnish about five hundred Men, able to carry Arms. . . .

The new Subjects could send into the Field about eighteen thousand Men, well able to carry Arms; of which Number, above one half have already served, with as much Valor, with more Zeal, and more military Knowledge for America, than the regular Troops of France, that were joined with them.

* * * * *

Having arrayed the Strength of His Majesty's old and new Subjects, and shewn the great Superiority of the Latter, it may not be amiss to observe, that there is not the least Probability, this present Superiority should ever diminish, on the Contrary, 'tis more than probable it will increase and strengthen daily: The Europeans, who migrate never will prefer the long unhospitable Winters of Canada, to the more chearful Climates, and more fruitful Soil of His Majesty's Southern Provinces; The few old Subjects at present in this Province, have been mostly left here by Accident, and are either disbanded Officers, Soldiers, or Followers of the Army, who, not knowing how to dispose of themselves elsewhere, settled where they were left at the Reduction; or else they are Adventurers in Trade, or such as could not remain at Home, who set out to mend their Fortunes, at the opening of this new Channel for Commerce. . . . But while this severe Climate, and the Poverty of the Country discourages all but the Natives, it's Healthfulness is such, that these multiply daily, so that, barring Catastrophe shocking to think of, this Country must, to the end of Time, be peopled by the Canadian Race, who already have taken such firm Root, and got to so great a Height, that any new Stock transplanted will be totally hid, and imperceptible amongst them, except in the Towns of Quebec and Montreal.

> Governor Carleton to Lord Shelburne, 25 November 1767
> *Ibid.*, pp. 282, 284.

To conceive the true State of the People of this Province, so far as the Laws and Administration of Justice are concerned, and the Sensations, they must feel, in their present Situation, 'tis necessary to recollect, they are not a Migration of Britons, who brought with them the Laws of England, but a Populous and long established Colony, reduced by the King's Arms, to submit to His Dominion, on *certain Conditions*: That their Laws and Customs were widely Different from those of England, but founded on natural Justice and Equity, as well as these; That their Honors, Property, and Profits, as well as the King's Dues, in a great Measure Depended upon them, That, on the Mutation of Lands by sale, some special Cases excepted, they established Fines to the King, in Lieu of Quit Rents, and to the Seigneur, Fines and Dues, as his Chief Profits, Obliging him to grant his Lands at very low Rents—

This System of Laws established Subordination, from the first to the lowest, which preserved the internal Harmony, they enjoyed untill our Arrival, and secured Obedience to the Supreme Seat of Government from a very distant Province. All this Arrangement, in one Hour, We overturned, by the Ordinance of the Seventeenth of September One Thousand seven hundred and sixty four, and Laws, ill adapted to the Genius of the Canadians, to the Situation of the Province, and to the Interests of Great Britain, unknown, and unpublished were introduced in their Stead; A Sort of Severity, if I remember right, never before practiced by any Conqueror, even where the People, without Capitulation, submitted to His Will and Discretion.

*   *   *   *   *

The most advisable Method, in my Opinion, for removing the present, as well as for preventing future Evils, is to repeal that Ordinance, as null and void in it's own nature, and for the present leave the Canadian Laws almost entire. . . .

> Carleton to Shelburne, 24 December 1767
> *Ibid.*, pp. 288–9, 290.

The Board of Trade's Advice, 1769

The Lords Commissioner of the Board of Trade and Plantations advised the British cabinet to implement the Anglicizing policies promised in the Proclamation of 1763, thus ignoring or rejecting the on-the-spot reports of Murray and Carleton. The Board's report of 1769 on the state of the province left no doubt as to the Board's belief in uniformity for the administration of the Empire.

It is true indeed, that His Majesty has been graciously pleased to disapprove of such unwarrantable claims and proceedings, and to direct, that the Canadians shall be admitted to serve on Juries, and to plead as Advocates, in the Courts; but the same erroneous opinion, with regard to the extension of the Laws of England, still prevails; the Laws and customs of Canada, in respect to property, have not gained admittance into the Courts; And His Majesty's new subjects, though they have a full Confidence and reliance on His Majesty's Equity, and His paternal Regard for their interest, do yet express great uneasiness, and wait with impatience His Majesty's Determination on those points, which so materially affect their Properties, Quiet, and Happiness.

*   *   *   *   *

From these Letters, and from what has been said, it is evident, That the Colony of Quebec is in the greatest disorder and confusion, and that the authority of the Governor and Council, as limited by the Commission and Instructions, is in no respect competent to those regulations, which either the present state of it does, or the future progress of it may require; and as it appears to us, that there is no Method of curing these disorders, and giving effect and Stability to Government, but by establishing a competent legislative Authority, conformable to the Royal Assurances contained in the Commission and Proclamation; we are therefore of opinion, that it is necessary in the present State of Quebec, that a complete Legislature should be established; and that it would be advisable for the present to adopt not only the measure recommended by the Merchants of admitting, under proper regulations and restrictions, a number of His Majesty's new Subjects into the Council and House of Representatives, but also into the Courts of Judicature, and other Offices of Government, by exempting them from the obligation of Subscribing the Declaration against Transubstantiation declared in the Statute of twenty-fifth of Charles the second, conformable to what has been done in the like case in the ceded Islands, and has been found, both upon Antient precedent and late opinions of Law, to be a Matter entirely in His Majesty's Discretion.

*   *   *   *   *

Upon this occasion we have the satisfaction to find it declared in the Report of His Majesty's Law servants, annexed to your Lordships order of reference, that, as the several Acts of Parliament which impose disabilities and penalties upon the public exercise of the Roman Catholic Religion, do not extend to Canada, His Majesty is bound by no ties or constitutional necessity to prohibit the profession of this Worship there; and that as His Majesty is not bound to prohibit, He is at liberty to tolerate such Worship, so far, and in such form as not to impeach or violate His Royal Supremacy.

Report of the Lords Commissioners for Trade and Plantations relative to the
State of the Province of Quebec, 10 July 1769
Ibid., pp. 382, 383, 389.

The Solicitor-General's Report

In support of the aims of the Proclamation of 1763, His Majesty's "most dutiful and Loyal Subjects, the British Freeholders, Merchants and Traders in the Province of Quebec" petitioned for an Assembly in 1770, claiming that representative government would be good for the French Canadians. That this petition did not reflect French-Canadian wishes was immediately demonstrated by a counter petition from leading Canadians asking that French law be restored in the colony.

That same year Governor Carleton went to London to expound his views on the Quebec question. He obtained permission to grant lands under the French seigneurial tenure system in future. This was a departure from the policy of freehold tenure consistently advocated by the Board of Trade and the English merchants in the colony. It was also a precedent for the Quebec Act, which was passed just three years later.

Faced, however, with conflicting advice and opposing petitions, the cabinet ordered the Attorney-General and the Solicitor-General to study the relevant documents on the laws and government of Quebec and to recommend changes in the laws. Solicitor-General Alexander Wedderburn's report, made in 1773 but kept secret for years like all documents related to the Quebec Act, supports Carleton's preferences for an authoritative regime in Quebec, in the spirit and partial shape of the pre-Conquest French system. Prophetically, Wedderburn stated his conviction that English and French would be unable to co-operate politically in the colony.

The first consideration, in forming the political constitution of a country is in what manner the power of making laws shall be exercised. If it were possible to provide every necessary regulation for a distant province, by orders from England, it might, perhaps, be the most eligible measure to reserve that authority entirely to the British legislature. But there must be many local interests of police, of commerce, and of political economy, which require the interposition of a legislative power, acquainted with the affairs, and immediately interested in the prosperity of a colony. In all the British colonies, that legislative power has been entrusted to an Assembly, in analogy to the constitution of the mother country. The most obvious method would then be, to pursue the same idea in Canada; but the situation of that country is peculiar. The Assembly must either be composed of british subjects, or of british and Canadians.

In the first case, the native Canadian would feel the inequality of his situation, and think (perhaps truly) that he should be exposed to the oppression of his fellow-subjects.

To admit the Canadian to a place in that Assembly (a right, which, from the nature of a conquest he has no absolute title to expect,) would be a dangerous experiment with new subjects, who should be taught to obey as well as to love this country, and, if possible, to cherish their dependence upon it. Besides, it would be an inexhaustible source of dissension and opposition between them, and the British subjects. It would be no less difficult to define the persons who should have a right to elect the Assembly.—To exclude the Canadian subject would be impossible, for an Assembly chosen only by the British inhabitants, could no more be called a representative body of that colony, than a council of state is. To admit every Canadian proprietor of land would be disgusting and injurious to all the men of condition in the Province, who are accustomed to feel a very considerable difference between the seignior and the censier, though both are alike proprietors of land. Nor would it be beneficial to men of inferior rank; for every mode of raising them to the level of their superiors, except by the efforts of their own industry, is pernicious. It seems, therefore, totally inexpedient at present to form an Assembly in Canada. . . .

*   *   *   *   *

The point then, to which all regulations on the head of religion ought to be directed is, to secure the people the exercise of their worship, and to the crown a due controul over the clergy.

The first requires that there should be a declaration that all the subjects in Canada may freely profess their religion without being disturbed in the exercise of the same, or subject to any penalties on account thereof, and also that there should be a proper establishment of parochial clergymen to perform the offices of religion.

*   *   *   *   *

It would be proper, therefore, to give the parochial clergy a legal right to their benefices. . . . The governor's license should in every case be the title to the benefice, and the judgment of the temporal courts the only mode of taking it away. This regulation would, in the present moment, attach the parochial clergy to the interests of government, exclude those of foreign priests, who are now preferred to the Canadians, and retain the clergy in a proper dependence on the crown. It is necessary, in order to keep up a succession of priests, that there should be some person appointed whose religious character enables him to confer orders, and also to give dispensations for marriages; but this function should not extend to the exercise of a jurisdiction over the people or the clergy; and it might be no difficult matter to make up to him for the loss of his authority, by emoluments held at the pleasure of the government.

*   *   *   *   *

The political and religious constitution of the province of Quebec being established, the next matter of inquiry is, what plan of civil and criminal law is best adapted to the circumstances of the province? and this is not altogether an open question; for, Canada is not in the condition of a new settled country, where the invention of a legislator may exercise itself in forming systems. It has been long inhabited by men attached to their own customs, which are become a part of their nature. It has, of late, acquired some inhabitants superior in power, but much inferior in number, to its ancient inhabitants, equally attached to different usages. The prejudices of neither of these classes of men can be entirely disregarded; in policy, however, more attention is due to the native Canadian than the British emigrant, not only because that class is the most numerous; but because it is not the interest of Britain that many of her natives should settle there. The Canadian also has a claim in justice to the enjoyment of as much of his ancient laws regarding private rights, as is not inconsistent with the principles of the new government; for, as his property is secured to him, the laws which define, create, and modify it, must also be retained, otherwise his property is reduced to the mere possession of what he can personally enjoy.

> Report of Solicitor-General Alexander Wedderburn, 6 December 1772
> *Ibid.*, pp. 425–6, 428, 430.

The Debate on the Quebec Act

The answer of Lord North's government to all these problems was the Quebec Act, passed in the closing days of the parliamentary session of 1774 in an atmosphere of intrigue and government secrecy. No reporting of the debates was allowed, but Sir Henry Cavendish scribbled extensive shorthand notes inside his tall hat.

These notes, eventually published in 1839, are virtually our only first-hand account of the government's explanation of its policies.

LORD NORTH—. . . excuse me if I do not answer the questions which he has put with so much warmth, and so pointedly,—"Whose bill is this? Is it the bill of the governor of Canada? Is it the bill of the law officers? Is it the bill of the lord chancellor? Is it the bill of the lord president?" Sir, I apprehend that is a matter of no manner of consequence to this inquiry. It comes down to us a bill from the House of Lords: if the House of Commons shall approve of it as it is, or if they shall think proper to return it with alterations, when it goes from hence to receive the concurrence of the Lords and the concurrence of the Crown, it will be a bill of Parliament. His Majesty's ministers have been led to the proposal of this measure, in compliance with the repeated calls of several members of this House, as well as from the necessity of the case, and after having maturely considered the various opinions of those individuals who were able to give the best light and information upon the subject. Sir, this question has not been delayed from any other desire than that of being fully informed. Information has been sought from all quarters; from the officers of the Crown in Canada, and from the officers of the Crown at home; every person who could give information has been consulted. . . .

The first thing objected to by the honourable gentleman is, the very great extent of territory given to the province. Why, he asks, is it so extensive? There are added, undoubtedly, to it two countries which were not in the original limits of Canada, as settled in the proclamation of 1763; one, the Labrador coast, the other, the country westward of the Ohio and the Mississippi, and a few scattered posts to the west. . . . The House of Lords have thought proper to annex them to Canada; but when we consider that there must be some government, and that it is the desire of all those who trade from Canada to those countries, that there should be some government, my opinion is, that if gentlemen will weigh the inconveniences of separate governments, they will think the least inconvenient method is to annex those spots, though few in population great in extent of territory, rather than to leave them without government at all, or make them separate ones. Sir, the annexation likewise is the result of the desire of the Canadians, and of those who trade to those settlements, who think they cannot trade with safety as long as they remain separate.

The honourable gentleman next demands of us, will you extend into those countries the free exercise of the Romish religion? Upon my word, Sir, I do not see that this bill extends it further than the ancient limits of Canada; but if it should do so, the country to which it is extended is the habitation of bears and beavers. . . . The general purpose is undoubtedly to give a legislature to that country. It was very much, I believe, the desire of every person, if it were possible, to give it the best kind of legislature; but can a better legislature be given than that of a governor and council? The honourable gentleman dislikes the omitting the assembly; but the assembly cannot be granted, seeing that it must be composed of Canadian Roman Catholic subjects, otherwise it would be oppressive. The bulk of the inhabitants are Roman Catholics, and to subject them to an assembly composed of a few British subjects would be a great hardship. . . .

Now, Sir, with regard to giving French law—if gentlemen will remember, the most material part of the criminal law is to be according to English law. The civil law of Canada certainly is to be the French law. . . . It has been thought better calculated to secure the happiness of the Canadians, and more beneficial for all who live in the country, that they should have the civil law of Canada, and not that of England. If the Canadian civil law is incompatible with the present condition and wishes of the colony, the governor and council will have power to alter it. But there must be a general basis; there must be a law established, ready to be amended and altered as occasions shall arise, and as the circumstances of the colony shall require. It has been the opinion of very many able lawyers, that the best way to establish the happiness of the inhabitants is to give them their own laws, as far as relates to their own possessions. . . .

As to the free exercise of their religion, it likewise is no more than what is confirmed to them by the treaty, as far as the laws of Great Britain can confirm it. Now, there is no doubt that the laws of Great Britain do permit the very full and free exercise of any religion, different from that of the church of England, in any of the colonies. Our penal laws do not extend to the colonies; therefore, I apprehend, that we ought not to extend them to Canada.

> Sir Henry Cavendish, ed., *Debates of the House of Commons in the Year 1774,*
> *on the Bill for making more effectual Provision for the Government of the*
> *Province of Quebec* (London, 1839), pp. 7–12.

Terms of the Quebec Act

The hasty passage of the Quebec Act aroused the suspicions of the Whig opposition and of the restive colonists in America. The fact that the four "Intolerable Acts"—Parliament's reaction to the Boston "Tea Party"—had been passed in the same session added weight to their dark doubts about the motives behind the Quebec Act and brought protests from the future American revolutionaries. The Act extended Quebec's boundaries—and its constitution—deep into the Ohio Valley; it gave the Roman Catholic Church powers in law, while providing for the endowment of the Church of England;

it re-established French civil law; it imposed government by an appointed council only; it did *not* guarantee French language rights. In the context of Canadian history, the Quebec Act's reversal of the avowed policy of the Proclamation of 1763 and the Board of Trade's recommendations of 1769 marked out a new course for Canadian development. The Quebec Act also raised for historians a host of questions regarding its real purposes, its authorship, and its results.

... the said Proclamation, so far as the same relates to the said Province of *Quebec*, and the Commission under the Authority whereof the Government of the said Province is at present administered, ... are hereby revoked, annulled, and made void, from and after the First Day of *May*, One thousand seven hundred and seventy-five.

And, for the more perfect Security and Ease of the Minds of the Inhabitants of the said Province, it is hereby declared, That His Majesty's Subjects, professing the Religion of the Church of *Rome* of and in the said Province of *Quebec*, may have, hold, and enjoy, the free Exercise of the Religion of the Church of *Rome*, subject to the King's Supremacy, ... and that the Clergy of the said Church may hold, receive, and enjoy, their accustomed Dues and Rights, with respect to such Persons only as shall profess the said Religion.

Provided nevertheless, That it shall be lawful for His Majesty, His Heirs or Successors, to make such Provision out of the rest of the said accustomed Dues and Rights, for the Encouragement of the Protestant Religion, and for the Maintenance and Support of a Protestant Clergy within the said Province, as he or they shall, from Time to Time, think necessary and expedient.

* * * * *

And be it further enacted by the Authority aforesaid, That all His Majesty's *Canadian* Subjects, ... the religious Orders and Communities only excepted, may also hold and enjoy their Property and Possessions, ... and all other Civil Rights, ... as if the said Proclamation, Commissions, Ordinances, and other Acts and Instruments, had not been made, ... and that in all matters of Controversy, relative to Property and Civil Rights, Resort shall be had to the Laws of *Canada*, as the Rule for the Decision of the same; and all Causes that shall hereafter be instituted in any of the Courts of Justice, to be appointed within and for the said Province, by His Majesty, His Heirs and Successors, shall, with respect to such Property and Rights, be determined agreeably to the said Laws and Customs of Canada. ...

* * * * *

And whereas the Certainty and Lenity of the Criminal Law of *England*, and the Benefits and Advantages resulting from the Use of it, have been sensibly felt by the Inhabitants, from an Experience of more than Nine Years, during which it has been uniformly administered; be it therefore further enacted by the Authority aforesaid, That the same shall continue to be administered, and shall be observed as Law in the Province of *Quebec*. . . .

And whereas it may be necessary to ordain many Regulations for the future Welfare and good Government of the Province of *Quebec*, . . . And whereas it is at present inexpedient to call an Assembly; be it therefore enacted . . . That it shall and may be lawful for His Majesty, His Heirs and Successors, . . . to constitute and appoint a Council for the Affairs of the Province of *Quebec*, to consist of such Persons resident there, not exceeding Twenty-three, nor less than Seventeen . . . which Council, so appointed and nominated, or the major Part thereof, shall have Power and Authority to make Ordinances for the Peace, Welfare, and good Government, of the said Province, with the Consent of His Majesty's Governor, or, in his Absence, of the Lieutenant-governor, or Commander in Chief for the Time being.

The Quebec Act, 1774
Shortt and Doughty, eds., *Documents* . . . , Pt. I, pp. 572–5.

THE VIEWS OF LATER COMMENTATORS

Evidence of a Dark Plot?

In *Empire and Commonwealth* the Canadian historian Chester Martin accepted the traditional American interpretation of the Quebec Act, and twenty years after its publication stated that he would now print it "in blacker ink". For him the *bête noire* of the Quebec Act is Sir Guy Carleton.

In the face of this evidence the most mysterious features of the Bill—the boundaries, the insistence upon "the Laws of Canada, as the Rule" for Quebec, the systematic indulgence of the seigneurs in conjunction with the coercive measures of the same session against the American colonies—began to wear a sinister and menacing aspect. By North's own admission the Bill was included among the measures which were designed "to put an immediate stop to the present disorders in North America" and to make "permanent colonies". To that note the chief opposition to the Bill was pitched, and in the end perhaps no single measure of that whole cycle of coercion aroused more vehement defiance on both sides of the Atlantic than the Quebec Act. . . .

Thus the Quebec Act, which is now chiefly remarkable for its subsequent influence upon Canadian history and politics, belonged in its origin and in its context essentially to the age before the deluge. It was devised to preclude a "Catastrophe shocking to think of". Beyond all question, for weal or for woe, it was not without influence both upon the beginnings and upon the subsequent course of the American Revolution: though scarcely perhaps in the way its advocates intended.

*   *   *   *   *

In its effect upon the American situation, therefore, the Quebec Act proved to be a miscalculation. It had been associated by North and the King himself with other Acts "to put an immediate stop to the present disorders in North America" and to secure "the just dependance of the colonies". It proved to be not a deterrent but a violent irritant which did much to precipitate resistance by force in the thirteen provinces to the south and nearly lost a fourteenth, as we shall see, to the cause of the Revolution.

For Quebec itself the miscalculation was scarcely less disastrous. The [Roman Catholic] Church responded loyally to the privileges accorded to them by the Quebec Act, and to the fear of vastly different treatment at the hands of the dour New Englanders. . . . But the Church could not fight; and Carleton looked to the seigneurs to meet the obligations implied in the Quebec Act. . . .

*   *   *   *   *

Never were interested calculations more egregiously at fault than Carleton's reliance upon the old-world feudalism of Quebec. The governor, who had rested the weight of British policy in the Quebec Act upon the seigneurs and had believed only what he wanted to believe from their self-interested response, now discovered that a very important element had been left out of calculation. The "due subordination" of the habitants was not forthcoming. The disillusionment came swiftly and convincingly, and it is unnecessary to go beyond the letters of the Chief Justice and of Carleton himself for the ironical retribution visited upon those who had put their trust in the traditions of French colonial government for Quebec.

*   *   *   *   *

Had the opponents of the Quebec Act been in power in 1774 would their policy for Quebec have been radically different? "If it had fallen to Whig ministers to deal with it," writes Professor Coupland in his study on the Quebec Act, "they would inevitably, after studying the facts, have drafted a similar measure." With respect to many details that are sometimes regarded as though they were essential features of the Act this surely is the simple truth. . . . But there is a difference in spirit; and when one compares the comprehensive project of the Board of Trade in 1769 with that which supplanted it in 1774, the difference in time, in spirit, and in principle, becomes in truth unmistakable. Had French Canadians, who have shown themselves perhaps the most politically minded people in Canada, been introduced into full British citizenship in 1769 in the spirit of magnanimous toleration, might not such a union at such a time have enriched Canadian history and Canadian politics for all generations to come?

Chester Martin, *Empire and Commonwealth* (Oxford, 1929), pp. 129–30, 138–9, 146–7.

Proof of Practical Politics?

Sir Reginald Coupland, an imperial historian who emphasized the humanitarianism of British colonialism, disagrees with Martin and sees the Quebec Act as the necessary and justifiable conclusion to a pragmatic colonial policy—nothing, in his opinion, could have destroyed the solidly rooted tree of French-Canadian nationalism.

Apart from principles and treaty obligations, the one obvious motive of the Bill was to reconcile the Canadians to their conquerors. And the one obvious reason for trying to attain this end without delay was the possibility, or rather the probability, of a renewal of war with France. . . . Under these circumstances, to wean the Canadians as far and as soon as possible from their old attachment to France was naturally and necessarily the primary purpose of Carleton's policy, and the Government's policy was simply Carleton's. It is true that Carleton and the Government recognized also from the outset that the active allegiance of the Canadians, could it be secured, might be of no little service to the Crown if the old colonies should carry their chronic discontent to the point of open rebellion. . . . The purpose of the Bill was to forestall the greater danger: it was an additional but quite secondary advantage in its authors' eyes that it carried with it an insurance policy, so to speak, against the lesser.

*   *   *   *   *

Did not the Quebec Act, like some ghastly injury of childhood, stunt and spoil the future life of Canada?

If the facts of that distant time have been truly stated in this essay, the first answer to such doubts and questions is evident. It is probable, in the highest degree, that, if the policy of the Quebec Act had not been adopted, Canada would have been lost to the British Empire in 1775, and no distinct Canadian nation could ever have come into being.

And the second answer is also clear. The contrary policy—the suppression of French-Canadian nationality—was in its essentials precluded by the terms of the Capitulations and the Treaty of Paris. The Roman Catholic religion and, in part at least, the French-Canadian civil law could not have been suppressed without a violation of public faith.

Apart, moreover, from the antecedent treaty rights and apart from the subsequent dangers of the American invasion, it is difficult to believe that the policy of suppression was really practicable. The French Canadians might have been deprived of their law, their Church of its legalized tithes, and their language of all official recognition. But would such measures, would even harsher measures, have succeeded in destroying French-Canadian nationality? . . . For nationality is at root a spiritual thing and difficult to kill. Nor was it in New France in 1774 a young and tender growth: the French Canadians had been rooted there for a century and a half. Nor, again, were they, like the French of Louisiana when it was annexed to the United States, a small minority in a great English-speaking state: the position was precisely the reverse . . . so long as their Church survived, the mainspring of their nationality would have remained unbroken. Forcible fusion, in fact, would have proved, if it had ever been adopted, a futile policy.

Reginald Coupland, The Quebec Act: A Study in Statesmanship
(Oxford, 1925), pp. 116–17, 194–5.

Or British Fair Play?

Thomas Chapais, conservative French-Canadian historian, suggests that the Quebec Act was no more than simple justice to the reasonable demands of French Canada for separation from the other British American colonies.

I have tried to retrace the genesis of the Quebec Act for you. You have seen it elaborated slowly in the thought of statesmen and civilians. You have been able to see the work by which it was prepared, the testing, the considerations, the reasoning, and the experiences by which it was built up step by step. You have been able to convince yourself that it was the end product of a long series of consultations, gropings, and deliberations. A currently accepted opinion is that it had as almost its only determining cause the imminence of the American Revolution and the necessity of satisfying ourselves, for whatever it may be worth, in order to ensure our loyalty in the coming conflict. Does the study which we have undertaken together in the course of these last lectures allow us to accept this theory? For my part I do not find it supported by the direct observation of the events. The warning signs of the American crisis may have had some usefulness to our cause, but only as a secondary consideration. Let us not forget that it was only at a later date that England came to believe in the reality of the American danger. The fundamental principles of the Quebec Act were approved of by British jurists and ministers long before that danger became apparent. The germ of that Act was in the report of Yorke and de Grey in 1766, in the letters from Carleton to Shelburne after 1767, and in those of Hillsborough to Carleton after 1768. I know very well that this last person sometimes used the American argument to support his arguments. But he had other points, and when we look at the mass of reports, of communications, of confidential notes relating to Canadian affairs to which we now have access, nothing indicates that that argument had had a preponderant influence in the solution adopted, except for the refusal to institute a legislative assembly.

No, the Quebec Act was due principally to our demands, to the doctrines and principles of natural law and of human law professed by the great English jurists. . . . Finally it was due to the persistent action of one man who, among British officials, could do more than any other to vindicate honour. That man was Carleton. For eight years he had pleaded in favour of French laws and the ending of religious disabilities. He saw his views adopted and his advice followed. Our victory was his victory. And that is why he will never cease to be in the forefront of those whose words and actions have weighed in our balance scale where the destiny of the French Canadian nationality fluctuated so long.

Thomas Chapais, *Cours d'Histoire du Canada* (Quebec, 1919),
Vol. I, pp. 168–72 (translation).

The Quebec Act in Its Imperial Setting

A. L. Burt, a Canadian who spent most of his teaching years in the United States, examines the Quebec Act in the context of a total imperial policy.

The conclusions drawn by the Americans at the time have since been supported by an appeal to the way in which the measure was passed. The government rushed it through parliament at the fag end of the session and withheld all the official papers which had been connected with its preparation. The opposition called for the reports of the governor and of the law officers, but their motions were rejected by a two to one vote. . . .

Against these arguments of the Americans then and of others later there is a good deal to be said. The imagination of the old colonists was already so disordered by their own resistance and the home government's retaliation that they were sure to see wild visions in anything that Britain did short of yielding to their every demand. Their nervousness might have been less had they known that, after the passage of the Quebec Act, Carleton was sent back to the colony without permission to raise one Canadian regiment, the object of his prayers for seven long years. Moreover, the main character of the act was mostly determined before people in England heard of the tea party that suddenly brought on the American crisis. The new boundary line, foreshadowed in a letter which Dartmouth wrote Cramahé on December 1, 1773, had long been an obvious necessity. An assembly seems to have been out of the question from the beginning of 1771, and any doubts lingering in Maseres' mind were removed by a statement which he received from Lord North in the summer of 1773.

The feudal system was restored to its full vigour in 1771 as an earnest of legal concessions repeatedly promised. The only major questions that had not been settled were the extent of the legal restoration and what should be the regulations for the church. . . .

The way in which the bill was railroaded through parliament is no proof of any evil motive on the part of its sponsors. It simply proves beyond all shadow of doubt that the coming of the Revolution merely precipitated the birth of the Quebec Act. The foundations of the British Empire in America were shaking. Canada might be swallowed up in an earthquake unless her constitution were immediately established on a firm basis. When not a moment was to be lost, can the government be blamed for withholding the preliminary papers that would have enabled the opposition to prolong the debate indefinitely? This was reason enough for the majority to defeat the motions for the production of the reports, and it was reinforced by the fatigue which they were suffering at the close of an exhausting session. There is no justification for saying that they voted under orders. The opposition's taunts that the government had some concealed purpose in framing the bill need not be taken seriously. Parliament had eagerly passed four penal statutes against the old colonies, and if the government designed this as a fifth, its supporters could have advanced no stronger argument for hurrying it through the House.

That the Quebec Act was not designed as a blow at the old colonies is the conclusion one draws . . .

A. L. Burt, *The Old Province of Quebec* (Toronto, 1933), pp. 184–6.

Further Reading

Quebec, the Revolutionary Age, 1760–1791 (Toronto, McClelland & Stewart, 1966) by Hilda Neatby provides a background survey of this period. Elizabeth Arthur, in "French-Canadian Participation in the Government of Canada, 1775–1785", *Canadian Historical Review*, XXXII (December 1951), suggests that the French Canadians gained practically no political power by the Quebec Act, that Carleton kept power to himself. Michel Brunet, *French Canada and the Early Decades of British Rule, 1760–1791* (Canadian Historical Association Booklet No. 13) emphasizes Carleton's "paternal despotism" and the increase in the power of the governor after the Quebec Act. The author is critical of both the motives and results of the Act. Marcel Trudel, "La Servitude de l'Eglise Catholique sous le régime anglais", Canadian Historical Association, *Report*, *1963*, examines the ways in which the Catholic Church was used to promote British governmental policies.

Problem 6

The Loyalist Tradition — Fact or Fancy?

The "patriot" tradition in the United States and the Loyalist tradition in Canada are both results of the same event—the American Revolution. This problem is intended to introduce the Canadian attitude of loyalism—of which the Loyalist tradition is an epitome. Loyalism consists of a fervent and sometimes highly emotional faith in the superiority of things British, particularly monarchy, the English constitution, and British justice. This faith is usually contrasted to the "American dream" of egalitarian republicanism, yet in Canada it is more a matter of admiration for British ideals than an understanding of British realities. Loyalism, then, is an ill-defined frame of reference consisting of vague but widely accepted ideals. However ill-defined those ideals may be in fact, the vitality of loyalism in Canada remains indisputable as any examination of the arguments over adopting a Canadian flag will show. It is a sentiment that in one sense is almost as much anti-Canadian as it is anti-American. Thus Joseph Pemberton rhymed in the *British Colonist* of Victoria, B.C., in 1870:

> True Loyalty's to Motherland
> And not to Canada,
> The love we bear is second-hand
> To any step-mama.

This strong grip of British ideals in Canada was noted early by Lord Selkirk, when he accused John Graves Simcoe of trying to ape English ways in frontier Upper Canada. The appeal of these British ideals to non-British Canadians was suggested in this century by Stephen Leacock's quip, "Leave them alone and pretty soon the Ukranians will think they won the battle of Trafalgar."

Who were the Loyalists with whom this tradition of loyalism seems to have originated? Simply stated, the Loyalist tradition describes the migration to Canada after the American Revolution of thousands of colonists who preferred British institutions to democracy and republicanism, whose migration involved terrorism and confiscation of property at the hands of the victorious rebels, who were victims of American perfidy in the matter of promised compensation, and whose settlement in the remaining provinces of British North America meant for them sacrifice and unspeakable hardships. The Loyalists were North Americans who preferred to be British at any price. Such is the tradition, but why is it so much stronger in Ontario than in the Maritimes where five times as many Loyalists settled? That there were significant differences between the Loyalist settlers in the Maritimes and those in Upper Canada soon becomes apparent. It also becomes apparent that the Loyalist *tradition* is more the product of the War of 1812 than of the War of Independence. Who recorded the Loyalist tradition if in fact the bulk of the Upper Canadian Loyalists were inarticulate or even illiterate? Is there not a hint of Anglo-Saxon racism in these expressions of the Loyalist tradition?

These are questions concerning the Loyalist traditions—of the Loyalists themselves the historian has other queries. Did the Loyalists come to Canada because of loyalty or land? Did they come of their own volition or were they, in modern parlance, displaced persons? Were the Loyalists simply making a virtue of necessity when they demanded special treatment in their new homeland? Finally, we must ask what contribution the Loyalists made to Canadian history and what is the place of the Loyalist tradition—whether fact or fancy—in Canada's development.

The Loyalists Demand Their Rights

As frontier farmers the Upper Canadian Loyalists were intensely concerned with land, the major asset of their new homeland. By 1783, 3.2 million acres had been distributed to them. That they were not diffident about using their loyalism as a claim to consideration is shown by their petition of 1785 for separation from the province of Quebec and the instituting of freehold instead of seigneurial tenure.

The Inhabitants of this Territory, already amounting to several Thousands, conceive with all Humility that they have the strongest Grounds to hope for such an exempt Jurisdiction as they ask for; They were born British Subjects, and have ever been accustomed to the Government and Laws of England. It was to restore that Government, and to be restored to those Laws, for which from Husbandmen they became Soldiers, animated with the Hope, even in the most gloomy Aspect of Public Affairs, that should they fail in their Attempts to recover their former Habitations by a Restoration of Your Majesty's Government, they would still find a Resource in some Parts of the British Dominions, where they might enjoy the Blessings of British Laws and of the British Government; and they still possess the greatest Confidence, that by Your Majesty's Gracious Interposition they will be exempted from the Burthens of French Tenures, which, however congenial they may be to Men born and bred under them, would be in the highest Degree exceptionable to Englishmen.

The Petitioners have the more Confidence in the Success of their Application, from reflecting that they do not ask for more than has already been granted to their Fellow Sufferers in Nova Scotia, for less indeed than is enjoyed by those who are settled in the Province of New Brunswick, and only to be in the same situation with the Settlers in the Island of Cape Breton. . . .

> A. Shortt and A. G. Doughty, eds., *Documents Relating to the Constitutional History of Canada, 1759–1791* (Ottawa, 1918), Pt. II, p. 775.

A Loyalist Settlement in Nova Scotia

The diversity and maturity of the Loyalist settlements in the Maritimes is reflected in the report by Nova Scotia's Governor John Parr of a visit to the boom—and bust—town of Shelburne, which initially received several thousand Loyalists but dwindled in a few years to a hamlet. Disheartened by the poor economic prospects of their new home, some Loyalists dubbed the colony "Nova Scarcity".

The Town stands upon a gentle rising Ground, the situation most beautifull, the Land good, with a prospect of its being very fertile, some good Timber, the Streets of Shelburne are laid out very regular at Right Angles, the Houses in great forwardness, Industry is seen in every Quarter. my being so particular may seem trifling, but it proceeds from the joy and pleasure I felt, at the universal satisfaction that appeard, upon my naming Your Lordship aloud, and the immediate firing of the Guns in the Town, the Fort, and the Sophie Frigate &c, &c, I then swore in the Magistrates and other Civil Officers. the next day they gave me *a Ball*, and the Ladys danc'd 'till nearly five, the whole went off exceeding well. I have since had my hands full of business, not of the most agreable nature, as Your Lordship may well imagine from the variety of

Characters, and different Interests of People who compose this Emigration, some of them not very easy to manage. . . .

John Parr to Lord Shelburne, 25 July 1783
Public Archives of Canada, *Report, 1921*, Appendix E, p. 3.

Loyalists and "Late Loyalists"

John Graves Simcoe, first Lieutenant-Governor of the new province of Upper Canada, counted on a combination of British institutions and the Loyalists' anti-Americanism not merely to preserve Upper Canada within the Empire but also to convert subsequent non-Loyalist American settlers into faithful subjects of King George III. Between the Loyalists and the later American arrivals came the "late Loyalists"—persons who had not fought for the cause of Empire and had not been active rebels.

It appears to me that . . . the utmost Attention should be paid that British Customs, Manners, & Principles in the most trivial as well as serious matters should be promoted & inculcated to obtain their due Ascendancy to assimilate the Colony with the parent state & to bear insensibly all their habitual Influence in the Support of that British Constitution which has been so wisely extended to that Country. . . .

I hold it to *be determined* upon & incontrovertible that Great Britain is to maintain her Possession of Canada. . . .

It being obvious that from such [late Loyalist] Emigrants, their Descendants (& in some measure all classes of People) will adopt that habitual attachment to the British Nation which is a great bond of Union between the Subjects of any State & a powerful Barrier against any attempts which may be made to overthrow or undermine the existing form of Government, nor let it be supposed that this aversion from Congress, so advantageous to the new Colony, if rightly improved on, has or is near dying away; the contest of the natives of Great Britain with the Subjects of the American States was decided by Arms & terminated by Treaty.

That of the American with the American still exists under all the injurious Remembrances of open or covert Vexation under the Taunts of triumph, taxes, & family Confiscations.

Other classes of Americans will emigrate to better their fortunes & whose Indifference to any form of Government may be converted into zealous attachment to that under which they shall live, whenever they shall feel the advantages of its beneficence & Wisdom, of the Equality of its Laws & its protection from the *probability* of *foreign Invasion.*

> J. G. Simcoe to Henry Dundas, Colonial Secretary, 30 June 1791
> E. A. Cruikshank, ed., *The Correspondence of Lieut.-Governor John Graves Simcoe, . . .* (Toronto, 1923–31), Vol. I, p. 27.

The Loyalists Prosper in Upper Canada

In 1787 Colonel Thomas Dundas, a commissioner investigating Loyalist claims for losses during the Revolution, commented on the nature of the Upper Canadian settlements and on the possible basis of their continued loyalty. Compare his description of the Loyalists with that of Governor Parr.

. . . we came to Canada in the month of May, and have been employed all this summer in examining the claims of persons resident in this extensive country. They are very numerous—I think from 1100 to 1200—but are in amount very small, being mostly farmers from the back parts of New York Province. These people have been settled since the peace in the upper part of Canada, beginning 50 miles above Montreal, and extending to Niagara. They find the soil excellent and the climate good. They are mostly thriving, in so much that already they have been able to supply the King's posts with bread, and very soon they will be able to be a good saving to Great Britain, as the expense of transporting provisions and stores to the upper posts is immense; it will likewise be a market for those farmers, and make it much their interest to remain attached to Great Britain.

> Thomas Dundas to Lord Cornwallis, 3 October 1787
> Ontario Bureau of Archives, *Report, 1904*, p. 22.

A Loyalist Criticizes Immigration Policies

Richard Cartwright, Loyalist soldier, successful merchant, and respected judge, explained to Lieutenant-Governor General Hunter how Loyalists reacted to the coming of American settlers at Simcoe's invitation. That other Loyalists did not speak out publicly against these developments can be taken as evidence of widespread illiteracy and preoccupation with the practical problems of pioneering. After noting the admission of "late Loyalists" beginning in 1788, Cartwright, in 1799, discusses the impact of the other Americans.

. . . In this train affairs continued till this country was made a separate Province, and General Simcoe sent over to govern it. He appears to have thought that the immediate peopling of the country was an object of sufficient importance to supersede the regulations which had been hitherto observed in distributing the waste lands of the Crown. A proclamation was immediately issued for the purpose of inviting emigrants, and the speculations in lands being about this time at their height in the American States, jobbers flocked in from every quarter, proposing to bring a large number of settlers, and the Loyalists heard, with astonishment and indignation, persons spoken of as proprietors of townships whom they had encountered in the field under the banners of rebellion, or who had been otherwise notoriously active in promoting the American revolution.

. . . a considerable number of people were brought into the country of a very different description from the original settlers, and the functions of the Land Boards having been put an end to in the year 1794, every application for lands was afterwards made immediately to the Executive Council, who of course exercised a discretion with respect to the character of the applicant, and the quantum of the grant that the Boards were not competent to, and it has so happened that a great portion of the population of that part of the Province which extends from the head of the Bay of Kenty [Quinte] upwards is composed of persons who have evidently no claim to the appellation of Loyalists. I will not disguise from your Excellency the opinion which I have always entertained, and on every proper occasion expressed, that this ought never to have been permitted. One necessary consequence has been to dispel the opinion fondly cherished by the Loyalists, that the donation of lands to them in this country was intended as a mark of peculiar favour and a reward for their attachment to their Sovereign, for how could such an idea remain upon their minds, when they afterwards saw them lavished upon persons who had such pretentions?

This, however, is not the greatest evil. . . . It must be admitted that the Americans understood the mode of agriculture proper for a new country better than any other people, and being, from necessity, in the habit of providing with their own hands many things which in other countries the artizan is always at hand to supply, they possess resources in themselves which other people are usually strangers to; and boldly began their operations in a wilderness, when the dreary novelty of the situation would appal an European. But their political notions in general are as exceptionable as their intelligence and hardihood are deserving of praise. I am not, however, inclined to impute to such of them as emigrate to this Province either hostile or treacherous views; but it would be an error equally as great to suppose that they are induced by any preference they entertain for our government. They come probably with no other intent than to better their circumstances, by acquiring lands upon easy terms.

C. E. Cartwright, ed., *Life and Letters of the Late Hon. Richard Cartwright* (Toronto, 1876), pp. 95-6.

A Visitor Comments on the Loyalists and Loyalism

The Duke de la Rochefoucault-Liancourt, a refugee from revolutionary France who toured North America, noted the anti-
Americanism of the Upper Canadian Loyalists and contrasted it
to the attitudes of Loyalists in the Maritimes. The Duke's impressions were, however, formed during a very brief visit to Upper
Canada. Incidentally, he notes here that some Maritime Loyalists
were moving into Upper Canada.

. . . the American loyalists, who have actually suffered by the war, still
harbour enmity and hatred against their native land and countrymen. These
sentiments however are daily decreasing, and are not shared by the far greater
number of emigrants, who arrive from the United States, Nova Scotia, and
New Brunswick. There are mal-contents in this country; but their number is
small. Several new settlers, who migrate into this province from the United
States, falsely profess an attachment to the British Monarch, and curse the
government of the Union, for the mere purpose of thus wheedling themselves
into the possession of lands. The high price of provision, the prohibition of a
commercial intercourse, and the protracted delivery of the deeds by which the
property of granted lands is conveyed to the occupiers, form, indeed, grounds
of much discontent; but this is by no means of a nature to cause uneasiness to
the government, which seems even to doubt its existence, though, in case of a
war with the United States, it might render its situation extremely critical.

W. R. Riddell, ed., *La Rochefoucault-Liancourt's Travels in Canada, 1785*
(Thirteenth Report of the Bureau of Archives for the Province of Ontario, 1916.
Toronto, 1917), p. 58.

The Loyalist Tradition Is Born

A Nationalist's Statement of the Case

Popular interest in Upper Canada history began in the late 1850's
when, in response to historical activities in French Canada, the
Canadian Parliament granted money for the collecting of Upper
Canadian historical materials. In 1861 the Historical Society of
Upper Canada was formed, and William Canniff, professor of
medicine, was encouraged to write the earliest history of pioneer
Ontario. Canniff prepared his book during the tense years of the
American Civil War and Fenian activities, and refused to excuse his
obvious anti-American bias or his patent Canadian nationalism.
The following selection, entitled "Patriotism", exemplifies a nation-

alist's use of the Loyalist tradition and is significant as being probably the first widely read exposition of this theme in Canada.

... In no country upon the face of the Globe, and at no period in the history of any country, has appeared a higher or purer order of patriotism, than is written upon the pages of the history of British America. British connection is to mostly every son of the land dearer even than life itself. At least it has been so in respect to those of whom we write, the U. E. Loyalists. Co-equal with the love they have to the British Crown, is the hearty aversion they bear to Republicanism. Neither the overtures of annexation, nor the direct and indirect attempts to coerce, has produced a momentary wavering on the part of the descendants of the ancient stock. Americans in our midst have vainly tried to inoculate the minds of the people with the principles of Republican Government; but the Canadian mind was too free, the body politic too healthy, the system too strong to imbibe any lasting feeling of desire to change the tried for the untried. The few annexationists who have, from time to time, existed, were but the fungoid offshoot of a healthy plant. . . . The U. E. Loyalists have been as a barrier of rock against which the waves of Republicanism have dashed in vain. It has been the refugee-settlers and their descendants, who prevented the Province from being engulfed in its dark waters. In 1812, in '37, and at all times, their loyalty has never wavered. It has been elsewhere stated, that settlers from the States came in at a later date. Those were found likewise truly loyal. Says McMullen, speaking of the war of 1812, "But comparatively few Canadians joined the American standard in the war, and throughout which none were more gallant in rolling back the tide of unprincipled avarice than the emigrant from New England and New York, who aside from the U. E. Loyalist, had settled in the country." There were a few renegades who forsook the country, not so much to join the enemy as because they had no soul to fight.

William Canniff, *A History of the Settlement of Upper Canada*
(Toronto, 1869), pp. 633–4

The Loyalists — Forgotten Americans?

Egerton Ryerson, Loyalist by descent and loyalist by conviction, began his study of the Loyalists in the 1850's at the suggestion of George Brown's *Globe* but did not finish his writing until after his retirement in 1876 from thirty years' service as superintendent of education in Ontario. Ryerson's work had been preceded by the American Lorenzo Sabine's more readable and detailed two volumes, *Biographical Sketches of Loyalists of the American Revolution*

(1864). W. Stewart Wallace in his *United Empire Loyalists* (1915) describes Ryerson's *Loyalists* as "written in a spirit of undiscriminating admiration". Ryerson explains in his Preface that his purpose is to rescue those forgotten Canadians from obscurity and to elevate them to their rightful place as founding fathers of British North America.

As no Indian pen has ever traced the history of the aborigines of America, or recorded the deeds of their chieftains, their "prowess and their wrongs"—their enemies and spoilers being their historians; so the history of the Loyalists of America has never been written except by their enemies and spoilers, and those English historians who have not troubled themselves with examining original authorities, but have adopted the authorities, and in some instances imbibed the spirit, of American historians, who have never tired in eulogizing Americans and everything American, and deprecating everything English, and all who have loyally adhered to the unity of the British Empire.

I have thought that the other side of the story should be written; or, in other words, the true history of the relations, disputes, and contests between Great Britain and her American colonies and the United States of America.

The United Empire Loyalists were the losing party; their history has been written by their adversaries, and strangely misrepresented. In the vindication of their character, I have not opposed assertion against assertion; but, in correction of unjust and untrue assertions, I have offered the records and documents of the actors themselves, and in their own words.

> Egerton Ryerson, *The Loyalists of America and Their Times*
> (Toronto, 1880), Vol. I, p. iii.

"Our Fathers that Begat Us" — Celebrating a Century

Inspired, or provoked, by American celebrations of a century of Independence, descendants and admirers of the Upper Canadian Loyalists organized centennial celebrations of the 1784 migration to be held at Adolphustown, Toronto, and Niagara, at each of which the Loyalist tradition was revived and refurbished. These celebrations coincided with the Canadian minority's agitation for annexation to the United States, a suggestion that inflamed the orators' patriotism. Typical of the speakers at Adolphustown, Senator George W. Allan emphasizes the physical hardships of the Loyalists and ends with a burst of emotional appeal to Canadian nationalism.

However much we may admire their courage and fortitude in braving the rigours of Canadian winters, and the difficulties of making homes for themselves and their posterity in the Canadian forests, we have met to-day more particularly to admire the spirit which brought them hither, and if possible to catch something of their devotion to principles which through the medium of the British Constitution, Heaven itself, in their estimation, had bestowed upon them.

We go back in thought a little farther, to those days when the older Colonies of Britain on this continent, decided to dishonour the flag, under whose ægis they had received all that is excellent in their present political system. I do not stop now to question the motives of those who excited the colonists to rebellion. It is enough for the present to say that, the men whom Canada delights to honour, regarded the course of the insurgents as a most unrighteous one, and rather than give it their consent and aid, chose to begin anew in this northern part of our great continent, where even amid cold and poverty and hardships of various kinds they might still live under the free flag of Britain, and enjoy the blessings of which that flag is the emblem. . . .

Talk of annexation to the United States. That is impossible. The institutions of the two peoples are too diverse to admit of a political amalgamation.

Talk of independence in the sense of separation from the old land! This is quite as impossible with the Canadian people. For this is our pride and our boast, we are a part of the great British Empire. Like that angel which John saw standing in the sun, I see standing in the earth a mighty giant, made mighty by the King of Heaven. Upon his head are those wonderful and glorious British Isles, his feet resting on the golden sands of Australia; his left arm, India, now being redeemed from the wheels of the Juggernaut and the superstitions of past ages; his right arm, Canada, now being redeemed from the growl of the wild beast and the war whoop of the savage.

Centennial of the Settlement of Upper Canada by the United Empire Loyalists
(Toronto, 1885), p. 57.

These speeches were relieved by patriotic songs and poetry readings, of which the following verses from "The United Empire Loyalists" ("specially written for the occasion by the Rev. LeRoy Hooker of Kingston") are a typical sample.

* * * * *

What did they then, those loyal men,
When Britain's cause was lost?
Did they consent,
And dwell content

Where Crown, and Law, and Parliament
    Were trampled in the dust.

Dear were their homes where they were born;
    Where slept their honoured dead:
        And rich and wide
        On every side
    The fruitful acres spread;
But dearer to their faithful hearts
    Than home, or gold, or lands,
Were Britain's laws, and Britain's crown,
And Britain's flag of long renown,
    And grip of British hands.

They would not spurn the glorious old
    To grasp the gaudy new.
Of yesterday's rebellion born
They held the upstart power in scorn—
    To Britain they stood true.

With high resolve they looked their last
    On home and native land;
        And sore they wept,
        O'er those that slept
In honoured graves that must be kept
    By grace of stranger's hand.

They looked their last and got them out
    Into the wilderness,
    The stern old wilderness!
        All dark and rude
        And unsubdued;
    The savage wilderness!

Ibid., p. 63.

At Niagara, the third place of celebration, Lt.-Col. George T. Denison, a Toronto magistrate and militant imperialist, made the inevitable and oft-repeated contrast between British-Canadian virtues and American "liberty". Like the previous speakers, Denison concluded that Canada is what the Loyalists made it.

The arrival of the U. E. Loyalists in this Province one hundred years ago, was an event which has had a lasting effect upon the history of this country, and was, to a great extent, the cause of our being to-day a portion of the greatest Empire in the world. I need not say here on this historic ground, teeming with recollections of hard fought fights, or to the descendants of those who preserved our liberties in 1812, that to the U. E. Loyalists we owe the fact that we enjoy to-day the true liberty that is to be found under a limited monarchy. Those early settlers who came here one hundred years ago were the very best of the old colonists. They were the law-abiding, God-fearing classes, and this was remarkably shown by the fact that in the early years of this country crime was almost unknown, the settlers being an orderly, peaceable, well-behaved people. They gave a start to this country, the benefits of which we are continually feeling year after year.

* * * * *

From British Columbia to Cape Breton we, Canadians, can proudly point to one of the largest and finest countries in the world, with as well-behaved and law-abiding a population as can be found anywhere, while south of us, the lawlessness is wide-spread, and the crimes of violence almost without number. Can any one say that the arrival of the U. E. Loyalists here in 1784 did not start this Province well, and that their maintenance of our freedom in 1812 did not preserve a system of government which is a great boon and blessing to us to-day.

Ibid., pp. 95–7.

THE VIEWS OF LATER COMMENTATORS

Loyalism or Land Hunger?

The interpretation of the Loyalist tradition popularized by such writers as Canniff and Ryerson was first challenged by a scholarly historian when R. O. MacFarlane offered a revisionist view in 1937 that took account of social and economic factors in the Loyalists' background.

. . . The decision to support the Crown, whether it originated in inherent ideals, in simple loyalty, in a desire to maintain law and order, in a traditional conservatism, or whether it developed from force of circumstances during the war, almost invariably forced the Tory along a road on which there was no turning back, and which frequently terminated in exile. Toryism then led to a series of social and economic conditions which made migration a necessity. The distinction between the traditional view of the causes of the Loyalist migration, and the argument presented in this paper, may seem trifling, since loyalty is basic in each case. Nevertheless it is submitted that the theory of social and economic necessity explains more rationally, especially to those untouched by the Loyalist tradition, why so many people left the comparative comforts of a settled region to face the rigours of pioneer life in the bush, than does the usual case based on sentiment alone. It also explains why those persons who joined the Tory camp for reasons other than loyalty, were so often found among the exiles.

R. O. MacFarlane, "The Loyalist Migrations: A Social and Economic Movement", *Manitoba Essays* (Winnipeg, 1937), pp. 107–8.

Pointing to the inaccessibility of the American western lands, MacFarlane continues:

Under such circumstances it is not surprising to find "land hunger" an important cause of immigration into Upper Canada in the early years of that colony's history. Since land was made available on much easier terms to Loyalists than to any other settlers, as many newcomers as could possibly do so, regardless of their background, claimed to be Loyalists. In fact after 1784 it is very difficult to separate "land hunger" from "loyalty" as a cause for immigration to the region adjacent to Lakes Erie and Ontario, particularly with respect to the "late Loyalists". This situation prevailed even after a great effort had been made to purge these peoples' names from the Loyalist lists.

*   *   *   *   *

. . . To maintain that these people left the American Colonies because they disliked republican institutions and loved monarchial ones, that they hated the Republic and loved the Motherland, is to support a half truth. Because of their ideals, and because of their loyalties, they had placed themselves in a position which was untenable once the victory had gone to the Whigs.

Many of these loyal people had been so active in the defence of the Royal Cause that after the peace they could not be tolerated in the Republic, regardless of what views they professed to hold. They had been, and were still regarded as being, enemies of the state, and hence were not only objectionable but positively dangerous people. This group was harried out of the land. Many of them came to Canada and the Maritime Provinces because there was nowhere else to go. This is not to disparage the sacrifices of the Loyalists, but merely to point out that their loyalty to Britain forced them into a position which was not compatible with the success of the Revolution. Loyalty was the basis of this cause of the migration, rather than the cause itself. The Loyalists migrated because their cause was lost; their bet was on the wrong horse. . . .

There was also an economic situation corresponding to this social one. Many Tories lost their living and it was quite impossible for them to keep body and soul together if they remained in their old homes. If a move to a new community was necessary, and life was to be begun anew, then many preferred the remaining British territory in North America, rather than some other part of the revolting colonies, but some chose the latter alternative.

*   *   *   *   *

In presenting what might on the surface appear to be a case against the Loyalists, one would point out that "simple loyalty" undoubtedly brought some people to British North America during and immediately after the American Revolutionary War. There has been no intention of glossing over this factor. It has not been dwelt on at length, only because it is so well known. Nevertheless there were many who migrated unwillingly because they could not carry on in their old homes. In addition there was around the genuine Loyalist group a fringe of people who managed to have themselves classed as Loyalists, for land grants or other purposes. This fringe did not reflect credit on the Loyalists proper, or their ideals.

Some Loyalists came to Canada and the Maritime Provinces for no other reason than to live under the Union Jack. Many more came, especially to Upper Canada, to better their economic position through the acquisition of free or cheap land. But the majority came because they had, for whatever reason, joined the Tory forces; in so doing they burnt their bridges behind them, placed themselves in an impossible social and economic position from which migration was the only exit.

Ibid., pp. 111–12, 114–15, 120–1.

A Defence of the Tradition

James J. Talman, in his Introduction to *Loyalist Narratives from Upper Canada*, replies to MacFarlane with a restatement of the traditional interpretation that again emphasizes the factor of political motivation. At the same time, however, Talman documents the limited political influence of the Loyalists themselves, as opposed to the political influence of the Loyalist tradition.

In Canada there is no clearly defined attitude toward the United Empire Loyalists. On one side, interest in them is purely patriotic and genealogical, and they are "regarded with an uncritical veneration which has in it something of the spirit of primitive ancestor-worship." On the other side, the "Loyalist tradition" is referred to in disparaging terms. A competent article with the revisionist approach is that by Professor R. O. MacFarlane, *The Loyalist migrations: A social and economic movement.* In support of the "Loyalist tradition," it may be said that no scholar will deny the contribution which the Loyalists made to Canada.

*   *   *   *   *

. . . But surely tarring and feathering and land hunger were completely unrelated causes. In fairness to the Loyalists it must be said that it was their support of Britain which brought them into the position of finding themselves astride a rail or unable to remain in their own communities. . . .

Generalizations regarding the motives of the Loyalists are dangerous: but it seems fair to say that the great majority of the first emigrants from the thirteen colonies went to Canada because their actions or words had made it impossible for them to remain in, or return to, their pre-revolutionary homes. The later emigrants followed where the Loyalists had led. One movement merged into the other; and it is almost impossible to say when the later movement became large enough to be recognizable, and the earlier had diminished sufficiently to be said to have disappeared. . . .

Migration actuated wholly or in part by loyalism may be taken . . . to have ended in the year 1798.

*   *   *   *   *

If it was difficult to distinguish between Loyalists and other loyal Canadians during the war of 1812, it became almost impossible to identify Loyalists with any group in the troubles of the thirties. The personnel of the "Family Compact," it has been shown, is to be found in the members of the legislative and executive councils of Upper Canada. Between 1791 and 1841 thirty-six persons were appointed to the executive council. At most, seven were United Empire Loyalists. During the same period sixty-nine legislative councillors were appointed. Of these at most twenty-one were Loyalists. Six of these were also in the executive council. So from 1791 to 1841 only twenty-two individual Loyalists served in the appointed councils. Some of these almost unquestionably owed their selection to their friendship with the Reverend (later Bishop) John Strachan rather than to their status as Loyalists. . . . The absence of such obvious names as Johnson, Grass, Butler, and Van Alstine from the councils is further evidence of the fact that Loyalists were not prominent in the "Family Compact." However, those Loyalists who were on the councils certainly made their presence felt. For example, in·1814 Claus and Cartwright, two Loyalists, and the Speaker, carried on the business of the council regularly for a season when no other members attended.

James J. Talman, ed., *Loyalist Narratives from Upper Canada*
(Toronto, 1946), pp. xx, xxvii, lxiii.

Did the Empire Desert Its Loyalists?

Viewing the Loyalist tradition within a total imperial context, A. L. Burt examines the claim of American bad faith toward the Loyalists in the matter of confiscations and places the blame on the imperial government rather than on the United States.

Most of the sufferings of the Loyalists had nothing to do with any violation of the treaty. The treaty simply did not protect them. For this defect, the opposition blamed the government when the latter submitted the preliminaries to Parliament. But the government had done its best to make protection of the Loyalists a corner stone of the treaty. It is doubtful if the effort could have succeeded without Britain's threatening to resume the war, and the government could not risk committing the country by such a move. Though Parliament rejected Shelburne, it accepted his peace in spite of this defect. Britain would compensate her own suffering children. This British acceptance of the treaty without the desired provision for the Loyalists thus offers a certain parallel with the acceptance by the American commissioners knowing that the treaty as worded would probably be interpreted to delay the surrender of the posts. Each side preferred a defective peace to the danger of renewing the war.

More fundamental was another reason which explains the American violation of the treaty as well as its defect from a British standpoint. Here debts and Loyalists can be lumped together. This treaty was peculiar in that only one of its two signatories possessed the attributes of sovereignty. America could bind Britain, but Britain could not bind America. The American party to the treaty was Congress, and Congress had only a limited power delegated by the thirteen sovereign states. It had no authority to bind them, and not one of them incurred a single legal obligation under the Treaty of Paris. The American peace commissioners did not try to conceal this fact. They rather emphasized it, because it was a shield against British demands. Yet some Canadians who should know better still blame the sad fate of the Loyalists upon the bad faith of the United States.

> A. L. Burt, *The United States, Great Britain and British North America, from the Revolution to the Establishment of Peace after the War of 1812* (New York, 1961), p. 97.

The Hardships of the Loyalists — Fact or Myth?

G. M. Craig in his recent scholarly history of Upper Canada offers a modern and critical view of the Loyalist tradition and of its evolution, indicating the degree of nationalist mythology that encrusts this problem.

The hardships of the Loyalists should not be forgotten; certainly there is little danger of this happening in Canada. Yet these refugees experienced a kinder fate than have most exiles in the long sad tale of humanity uprooted. (And perhaps few tears should be shed for men who would certainly have wreaked a stern vengeance of their own had they been on the winning side.) They came to a new country, but it was not a far country; sometimes they went back to their old homes to visit friends and relatives, and occasionally they even quietly remained there. Much of the bitterness died down with the passing years, and it was not equally intense among all the Loyalists. It took later events, especially the War of 1812, to revive the old memories, and it was not until the rising Canadian nationalism of the mid-nineteenth century that a Loyalist cult began to form.

Moreover, the tasks awaiting the Loyalists, although burdensome and, for many of them, depressing to contemplate, were by no means unfamiliar. Nearly all those who came into Upper Canada had been farmers in the old colonies. The accidents of war and revolution had thrown into the northern province just the kind of people needed for its development. The ability to attack and conquer the North American wilderness, to reduce it to orderly farms and settled communities, was a hard-earned skill, but it was one the Loyalists possessed. And they did not face the wilderness unaided. Apart from the free land grants promised to them by the British government, and the prospect of compensation for losses of property suffered through loyalty to the king's cause, they were also assured of the food, tools, and other supplies needed for beginning their new life.

Gerald M. Craig, *Upper Canada: The Formative Years* (Toronto, 1963), p. 7.

The Loyalist Impact in the Maritimes

In contrast to the Ontario experience, the absence of a strong political Loyalist tradition is implicit in W. S. MacNutt's description of the political growth of the Atlantic colonies in the post-Loyalist era.

The legislatures of New Brunswick and Nova Scotia carried on their work in the advanced political procedures and traditions of the lost thirteen colonies. In spite of all the propaganda that flowed about Lord Sydney at London, no changes of an authoritarian kind had been made in the structure and operation of provincial government. Though loyalty and harmony were watchwords in 1783–84, the provincial governors were to be subjected to the same strains that had finally destroyed the first British Empire. Loyalists and pre-Loyalists were indistinguishable from one another in their capacity for rivalry and dissension, in the scramble for office and patronage under the new regime. Replicas of the constitutional struggles that had made so large a part of the histories of New York and Massachusetts were to be the common lot of the two provinces. There was a great deal of talk about the mystic union between Crown and people, but the British government had produced no new formula to make the lot of colonial governors easier, no blueprints by which popular assemblies were assigned limits.

In Nova Scotia the constitutional contest at first took the form of a struggle between Loyalists and pre-Loyalists, between newcomers and "old-comers," as the popular prints said. The antagonistic feeling of 1783 welled up to a fight for mastery as the Loyalists gained a bloc of seats in the Assembly during the election of 1785. The British government had promised them preferment in the filling of vacancies to office, but the waiting was long. . . . Private vendettas mingled with public causes when the House of Assembly met in 1789 and the Loyalist attack was directed against the council. Isaac Wilkins, a leading apostle of moderation in Pennsylvania in 1775 who had asked the House of Assembly to abstain from sending delegates to Congress, urged that the Lieutenant-Governor's "privy council," who were "evil and pernicious," should be removed. Thomas Barclay, a leading Loyalist from New York, spoke equally warmly, pressing British precedents for the dismissal of ministers on address from representatives of the people. In this debate, which vividly anticipated the dilemmas of Durham's era and attacked heavily the Achilles' heel of colonial government, the Loyalists were accused of rebellion.

> W. S. MacNutt, *The Atlantic Provinces: The Emergence of Colonial Society, 1712–1857* (Toronto, 1965), pp. 123–4.

Further Reading

Very little recent writing on this Problem has appeared beyond those items included in THE VIEWS OF LATER COMMENTATORS. W. S. Wallace, *The United Empire Loyalists* (reprinted, Toronto, University of Toronto Press, 1964) is a brief, balanced, and readable account of the whole migration. E. A. Cruikshank, *The Settlement of the United Empire Loyalists on the Upper St. Lawrence and Bay of Quinte in 1784* (reprinted, Toronto, Ontario Historical Society, 1966) is a documentary study illustrating the social aspects of one phase of the movement. Esther Clarke Wright, *The Loyalists of New Brunswick* (Ottawa, the author, 1955) is an examination of settlement in another area.

Problem 7

The War of 1812 — Seed-Bed of Canadian Nationalism?

Popular historians have hailed the War of 1812–1814 as the true beginnings of a Canadian nationalism. That war has been depicted and accepted by Canadians as an example of naked aggression by a large and powerful country against a small and inoffensive neighbour. In this interpretation the crime is compounded by the fact that the United States was supporting Napoleon's unholy efforts to destroy freedom and Britain. The war has also been denounced as a renewed persecution of the Loyalists and the ideals they embodied. Yet it was that war more than the Loyalist migration that ensured the continuing presence of Britain in North America.

What were the prospects for survival of British North America when the war began in 1812? Geographic factors determined that the struggle with the United States should take different courses and produce different effects in the various regions of British North America. Under the protective umbrella of the Royal Navy, the Maritime colonies passed through the time of trial relatively unscathed. For that region the war brought prosperity but no particular increase in a sense of identity. In Lower Canada the war also caused little hardship, and the defeat of the American invaders at Chateauguay was the only event that engendered a sentiment of defensive patriotism. But Upper Canada, as the major scene of hostilities, emerged from the war with a triumphant faith in its own powers and destiny, and bitter memories of lives and property destroyed.

Paradoxically Upper Canada, the main source of the Loyalist tradition, seemed the weakest link in the chain of British North American colonies. In the three decades since the War of Independence, large-scale American migration into the colony had swamped the original Loyalist element in the population. How would these American settlers react to a war with the United States? Was it their presence in Upper Canada that led the Americans to concentrate their war effort in futile invasions of that province when the capture of Montreal could have forced Upper Canada to capitulate without a shot?

Given the large potential fifth column in Upper Canada, how and why did it happen that Upper Canada remained loyal throughout the war and even drew from the struggle a new basis for loyalism? Was Upper Canada saved by the efforts of its gallant militia, or by a handful of regular troops, or by American military incompetence? Was the sense of patriotism and identity apparently planted in Upper Canada by the War of 1812–1814 the genuine seed of nationalism, or only of an Upper Canadian loyalty that could not be shared by its sister colonies? Whatever the answer, what specific results did the war have for future British colonial development in North America?

General Hull's Proclamation

For Upper Canada the opening blow of the war came on 12 July 1812, when Brigadier-General William Hull landed near Windsor with two thousand men. The next day Hull issued a Proclamation to the Canadians, explaining American objectives in a document that combines threats, promises, coaxing, and cajolery.

Inhabitants of Canada! After thirty years of peace and prosperity, the United States have been driven to arms. The injuries and aggressions, the insults and indignities of Great Britain, have once more left them no alternative but manly resistance or unconditional submission.

The army under my command has invaded your country, and the standard of Union now waves over the territory of Canada. To the peaceable, unoffending inhabitant it brings neither danger nor difficulty. I come to *find* enemies, not to *make* them. I come to protect, not to injure you.

Separated by an immense ocean and an extensive wilderness from Great Britain, you have no participation in her councils, no interest in her conduct. You have felt her tyranny, you have seen her injustice, but I do not ask you to avenge the one or redress the other. The United States are sufficiently powerful to afford you every security consistent with their rights and your expectations. I tender you the invaluable blessings of civil, political and religious liberty, and their necessary result, individual and general prosperity. . . .

In the name of my country, and by the authority of my Government, I promise protection to your persons, property and rights. Remain at your homes, pursue your peaceful and customary avocations, raise not your hands against your brethren. Many of your fathers fought for the freedom and independence which we now enjoy. Being children, therefore, of the same family with us, and heirs to the same heritage, the arrival of an army of friends must be hailed by you with a cordial welcome. You will be emancipated from tyranny and oppression and restored to the dignified station of freemen. Had I any doubt of eventual success I might ask your assistance, but I do not. I come prepared for every contingency. I have a force which will look down all opposition, and that force is but the vanguard of a much greater.

> D. B. Read, *Life and Times of Maior-General Sir Isaac Brock*, *K.B.*
> (Toronto, 1894), pp. 125–7.

General Brock's Reply

Brock replied to Hull on 22 July with a counter-Proclamation appealing to the loyalty and self-interest of the Canadians, an appeal that brought forth a flood of volunteers everywhere except in the western region around Windsor.

. . . Where is the Canadian subject who can truly affirm to himself that he has been injured by the Government in his person, his property or his liberty? Where is to be found, in any part of the world, a growth so rapid in prosperity and wealth as this colony exhibits? Settled not thirty years by a band of veterans exiled from their former possessions on account of their loyalty, not a descendant of these brave people is to be found who, under the fostering liberality of their Sovereign, has not acquired a property and means of enjoyment superior to what were possessed by their ancestors. . . .

. . . Are you prepared, inhabitants of Canada, to become willing subjects— or rather slaves—to the despot who rules the nations of continental Europe with a rod of iron? If not, arise in a body, exert your energies, co-operate cordially with the King's regular forces to repel the invader, and do not give cause to your children, when groaning under the oppression of a foreign master, to reproach you with having so easily parted with the richest inheritance of this earth—a participation in the name, character and freedom of Britons.

The same spirit of justice, which will make every reasonable allowance for the unsuccessful efforts of zeal and loyalty, will not fail to punish the defalcation of principle. Every Canadian freeholder is, by deliberate choice, bound by the most solemn oaths to defend the monarchy as well as his own property. To shrink from that engagement is a treason not to be forgiven. Let no man suppose that if, in this unexpected struggle, His Majesty's arms should be compelled to yield to an overwhelming force, the Province will be eventually abandoned; the endeared relation of its first settlers, the intrinsic value of its commerce, and the pretension of its powerful rival to repossess the Canadas, are pledges that no peace will be established between the United States and Great Britain and Ireland, of which the restoration of these provinces does not make the most prominent condition.

Ibid., pp. 131–3.

Brock's Private Doubts

In Brock's opinion the greatest threat to Upper Canada was not the American army but widespread defeatism in the province, a sentiment based on the obvious difficulty of defending such an extensive frontier. Privately, British military authorities were prepared to abandon Upper Canada if necessary and rely on the fortifications of Quebec city as a bridgehead for reconquest. Significantly, the following letter is not mentioned by the historian D. B. Read in either his biography of Brock or his *History of the War of 1812* (1901).

... My situation is most critical, not from any thing the enemy can do, but from the disposition of the people—The population, believe me is essentially bad—A full belief possesses them all that this Province must inevitably succumb. This prepossession is fatal to every exertion—Legislators, Magistrates, Militia Officers, all, have imbibed the idea, and are so sluggish and indifferent in their respective offices that the artful and active scoundrel is allowed to parade the Country without interruption, and commit all imaginable mischief. ...

What a change an additional regiment would make in this part of the Province!! Most of the people have lost all confidence. I however speak loud and look big. . . .

General Brock to Colonel Baynes, 29 July 1812
Public Archives of Canada, C.O. 676, p. 239.

John Strachan Appeals to Patriotism

Brock's easy capture of Hull's army at Detroit in August and his decisive though fatal victory at Queenston Heights in October turned the tide at least temporarily in favour of the British cause. More important, these events banished defeatism from Upper

Canada. John Strachan, Anglican rector of York (Toronto), expressed the new enthusiasm for the war in a speech at the dedication of colours for a militia unit in the autumn of 1812 and in a sermon delivered in November, in which, incidentally, he credits the militia with saving Upper Canada.

Gentlemen of the third Regiment of York Militia

Permit me to express the great satisfaction I feel in meeting you on this occasion. The inestimable gift conferred on us by the Young Ladies of York must awaken the most lively confidence in every breast, and suggest new motives for redoubled efforts in resisting the enemy. They rely on our conduct and courage not merely in defending the banner which they have presented, but in making it the admonisher of the most important services, in support of our king and country. And you are not to suppose that this religious dedication of your colours is an unmeaning ceremony for they become a token and pledge of a most solemn engagement, not only between us and our Sovereign who calls us to arms, but between us and our fellow subjects for whose protection we are employed, especially of that tender & most amiable sex, who have consigned them to our hands, and who zealously hope that we shall never abandon them, but with life. It is our part to realize these grateful expectations, and to shew that they have not been consecrated by words only, but by our hearts & by the noble & heroic spirits, which the sight of them shall always awaken in our breasts.

The enemy against whom we contend are loud in their threats & enraged at the unexpected resistance which they have already experienced in this province, they will wreak the bitterest vengeance upon us should they prove victorious, but they can never be victorious while we are united, on the contrary they shall continue daily to receive bloody proofs that a country is never more secure, than when defended by its faithful, loyal, and industrious inhabitants, who have constantly before their eyes the tenderest pledges of nature and are influenced by all that is dearest & most interesting to the human heart. March then under these colours inspired by that pure honour, which characterizes the Christian Soldier, which inspires him with reverence for religion and loyalty to his Sovereign makes him a devouring flame to his resisting enemy, and the humane protector of the fallen, and it will be the most pleasing joy of our declining years to remember that we have made a noble use of the opportunity now presented of contributing to the defence, the safety, and the glory of this highly favoured portion of the British Empire.

George W. Spragge, ed., *The John Strachan Letter Book: 1812–1834*
(Toronto, 1946), pp. 11–12.

Archdeacon Strachan Praises the Valour of the Militia

. . . It will be told by the future Historian, that the Province of Upper Canada, without the assistance of men or arms, except a handful of regular troops, repelled its invaders, slew or took them all prisoners, and captured from its enemies the greater part of the arms by which it was defended. . . . And never, surely, was greater activity shewn in any country, than our militia have exhibited, never greater valour, cooler resolution, and more approved conduct; they have emulated the choicest veterans, and they have twice saved the country.

> *The Report of the Loyal and Patriotic Society of Upper Canada* (Montreal, 1817), Appendix, entitled "York, 22d November 1812. An Exhortation pronounced after the Sermon, or rather in continuation of it, to induce the Inhabitants to contribute to the comfort of the Militia fighting upon the Lines. . . ."

A Veteran Assesses the War and Canadianism

Such victories as Queenston Heights, Stoney Creek, Crysler's Farm, and even the debatable results of Lundy's Lane inspired in Upper Canadians a sense of pride and of identity with the country. Writing a generation later, John Beverley Robinson, who had become acting Attorney-General of the province at the age of twenty-one, thanks to Queenston Heights, points to the war's contribution to Canadian nationalism and to the increased British character of Upper Canada.

Again, if we admit, as I think we must, that the circumstance of the older colonies having severed the connexion at so early a date, has been in fact the means of saving the present British provinces to the mother-country, it is scarcely less certain that the war of 1812, which was engaged in by the United States, mainly for the purpose of subjugating the Canadas, has had the effect of binding them, as well as Nova Scotia and New Brunswick, much more strongly to the crown. Before that war the United States were scarcely looked upon by the subjects of the British empire as a foreign country; the probability of hostilities was not anticipated, and of course not guarded against; the citizens of the republic came in numbers to settle, especially in Upper Canada, and, but for the war, in a few years thousands of those fertile acres, which have since afforded a home to loyal and grateful emigrants from England, Ireland, and Scotland, would have been occupied in a manner much less conducive to the maintenance of British connexion.

The war was happily undertaken at a time when the adjoining states of America were but thinly inhabited, and when the invasion of Canada was, in consequence, attended with many difficulties which time has removed. It has had the effect of calling the attention of England to a danger which Lord Selkirk, in his very able book on emigration, pointed out to the government so early as the year 1805; it has produced in the British colonists a national character and feeling, and has taught both countries to appreciate their position more correctly.

J. B. Robinson, *Canada and the Canada Bill* (London, 1840), p. 15.

The War Inspires Bicultural Nationalism

The first history book to be printed in Upper Canada was David Thompson's *History of the Late War Between Great Britain and the United States* (Niagara, 1832). Thompson's volume, however, makes only a few vague references to patriotic feelings, and it was not until the critical years of the American Civil War that the War of 1812–1814 was portrayed by William Coffin in emotional terms of Canada's destiny. In the first two excerpts, Coffin sees in the successful defence of the Canadas a victory for bicultural nationalism. In the third excerpt, an appendix of the same book, is reproduced a contemporary French-Canadian appeal by "Castor" to patriotism based on the events of the war.

1812—like the characters on the labarum of Constantine—is a sign of solemn import to the people of Canada. It carries with it the virtue of an incantation. Like the magic numerals of the Arabian sage, these words, in their utterance, quicken the pulse, and vibrate through the frame, summoning, from the pregnant past, memories of suffering and endurance and of honourable exertion. They are inscribed on the banner and stamped on the hearts of the Canadian people—a watchword, rather than a war-cry. With these words upon his lips, the loyal Canadian, as a vigilant sentinel, looks forth into the gloom, ready with his challenge, hopeful for a friendly response, but prepared for any other.

The people of Canada are proud of the men, and of the deeds, and of the recollections of those days. They feel that the war of 1812 is an episode in the story of a young people, glorious in itself and full of promise. They believe that the infant which, in its very cradle, could strangle invasion, struggle, and endure, bravely and without repining—is capable of a nobler development, if God wills further trial.

*   *   *   *   *

The French population of Lower Canada are very proud of the victory of Chateauguay, and with just reason. The British population of the Upper Province had achieved a like success over the common enemy at Queenston

Heights. It was gratifying to the natural pride of a great national origin, that the fortune of war should have thus equitably distributed her honourable distinctions. They had, moreover, a stronger motive, both for resentment and exultation. The American Government and democratic press, with unexampled effrontery, had cast upon a race "*sans peur et sans reproche,*" the dishonouring imputation of an easy political virtue. They had been charged with a readiness to violate plighted honour, and with disaffection to the British Crown. Truthful and generous in all relations, whether of peace or war, they resented this indignity, as a stain felt more keenly than a wound, and they gave the "*Bostonais*" their answer on the field of Chateauguay.

This noble and opportune service had the effect of twenty victories. Twenty days had hardly elapsed since the defeat of Proctor on the Thames. Muttered rumours of disaster had scarcely reached remote districts, ere the cloud of anxiety and doubt was dispelled by the exploit of Chateauguay, and the Red Cross Banner of England gleamed forth unsullied, in the light of that valour which it had so often encountered, proved, and respected, under the Lilies of France.

*   *   *   *   *

Fifty years ago 300 brave men gave to the whole world the spectacle of one of the finest feats of arms of which our young country can be proud. Filled with the knightly courage which their ancestors bequeathed to them and marching in the steps of their valorous leader, De Salaberry, they repulsed and put to flight on the frontier of their homeland an army infinitely superior in numbers and full of the pride that past victories inspired. No doubt Mister Editor, you have already understood, and the victorious name of "Chateauguay" has come involuntarily to your lips, that name filled with emotions and throbbing with interest, but alas! fallen into oblivion. What! a half-century has barely passed, we have still in our midst some of those aged veterans who saw the starry flag flee before the French bravery of our "Voltigeurs," and nevertheless the finest page of our history is unknown to a large part of Canadian youth. That memorable day, which gives the lie to the dishonest assertion that casts doubt on the bravery and courage of French Canadians, ought to be graven on the hearts of every good citizen, and its memory enshrined by some public mark that will transmit it to our most distant posterity. Several years ago, with great pomp, the first stone was laid for a monument to General Brock and to his aide-de-camp, Colonel McDonald. Why hasn't Lower Canada done as Upper Canada has? Why was no monument, an irrefutable witness to our veneration, raised over the tomb of the Canadian hero as over that of the Briton?

William F. Coffin, *1812: The War and Its Moral: A Canadian Chronicle* (Montreal, 1864), pp. xiv, 264-5; p. 286 (translation).

Memories and Memorials of the War

The Loyalist centennial celebrations in 1884 had been the occasion for strong expressions of patriotism and anti-Americanism. The War of 1812 was similarly celebrated in 1912 at the foot of Brock's monument on Queenston Heights. This event, coinciding with the Anglo-German naval rivalry and fears of general war in Europe, drew attention to Canada's relationship to the Empire and to imperial defence. Colonel G. S. Ryerson, soldier and doctor, grandson of a Loyalist and son of a battle-scarred veteran of 1812, echoed the patriotic feelings expressed earlier by his famous uncle, Egerton Ryerson, but went further in emphasizing the War of 1812–1814 as the seed-bed of a bicultural Canadianism.

. . . The United Empire Loyalists came to this country not as those who desired to better their condition in life, nor were they possessed by land hunger, nor by ideas of political and social aggrandisement. They came solely because of their devotion to the British Crown and Constitution, and because they preferred to live in peace and poverty under a monarchical government rather than in wealth and discord under republican institutions. . . .

Nor must it be supposed that the United Empire Loyalists and their children were the only men who responded to Brock's call to arms. Our gallant French-Canadian compatriots were not a whit behind in their hearty response. Coming from a brave and adventurous race, they performed deeds of valour and endurance equal to the best in the defence of our country. The hardy Highlanders of Glengarry, too, were rallied to the flag by the Macdonells.

> Alexander Fraser, ed., *Brock Centenary, 1812–1912: Account of the Celebration of Queenston Heights, Ontario, on the 12th October, 1912* (Toronto, 1913), p. 45.

Angus Claude Macdonell reiterated the theme of the militia's role in the war as a basis of Canadianism.

. . . There were of course some British regular troops in Canada, noticeably the Forty-ninth, Brock's own regiment, but during the earlier stages of the war, and while Brock lived, the men of the province, militia and yeomanry, had to be relied upon mainly; these chiefly were the men of the York, Glengarry, Norfolk and other militia regiments; every loyal man capable of bearing arms in the province turned out to fight, or to help those who fought. The York and Glengarry militia served with great distinction, and I may perhaps be permitted to refer to the fact that forty-three gentlemen of my own name and family connection held commissions in the various regiments in that war. . . . In these days of our prosperity we must protect and defend and develop this great country, this rich heritage which the heroism of our forefathers has preserved to us. We must not only conserve it, but we must better it and develop it, and make useful to man all these possessions which have been given us. Our ideals and ambitions must always be high, and if we find ourselves faltering let us look upon this splendid monument and think of the hero in honour of whom it was raised; and let us at all times remember that now as in 1812 in unity we possess our strength; we must become one people if we are to be a great people, with one great common country. We have many provinces but only one Canada.

Ibid., 47. p.

Dr. James L. Hughes, a school inspector, suggested the uses of the war's history and traditions in the education of young Canadians.

We do not wish to make our children quarrelsome or offensive, but we do wish them to be patriotic Canadians, full of loyalty to their flag, their Empire, and their King. We wish them to understand what their predecessors did in order that they may have faith in themselves and in their country; and we intend that they shall learn the achievements of the past in order that they may have a true basis for their own manhood and womanhood. True reverence for courage and self-sacrifice, fidelity to principle, and devotion to home and country in time of need, is a fundamental element of strong, true character. The facts of history may have little influence in developing character, but the noble deeds of our ancestors performed for high purposes are the surest sources for the development of the strong and true emotions that make human character vital instead of inert.

* * * * *

We should teach other lessons from the War of 1812. We should fill each child's life with a splendid courage that can never be dismayed, by telling how a few determined settlers scattered widely over a new country successfully repelled invading armies coming from a country with a population of twenty-fold larger. We should teach reverence not only for manhood but for womanhood by recounting the terrible hardships endured willingly by Canadian women generally, as well as by proudly relating the noble work done by individual women, of whom Laura Secord was so conspicuous an example.

A certain class of thoughtless people call us 'flag-wavers' if we strive to give our young people a true conception of the value of national life, and of their duty to have a true love for their country and for their Empire. If a flag-waver means one who is proud of a noble ancestry, and determined to prove worthy of the race from which he sprung; one who knows that his forefathers gave a wider meaning to freedom, and who intends to perpetuate liberty and aid in giving it a still broader and higher value; one who is grateful because his Empire represents the grandest revelation of unity yet made known to humanity and who accepts this revelation as a sacred trust—then I am a flag-waver, and I shall make every boy and girl whom I can ever influence a flag-waver who loves his flag and waves it because it represents freedom, and honour, and justice, and truth, and unity, and a glorious history, the most triumphantly progressive that has been achieved by any nation in the development of the world.

Ibid., pp. 53–4, 68–70.

The War and the Maritime Provinces

Relations on the St. Croix Border

Since the Maritime provinces were not invaded during the War of 1812–1814, the war's influences there were different in kind and quality from those in the Canadas. Generally speaking, Maritimers strove, with considerable success, to maintain an undeclared neutrality with their New England neighbours. Symptomatic (but not precisely typical) of this neutrality were the experiences of New Brunswick and Maine residents facing each other across the St. Croix River.

. . . News of the outbreak of hostilities was received by the collector of customs at Eastport and the commander of the Fort Sullivan garrison on June 25, a week after the declaration. The latter was instructed by Washington authorities to put the town in a state of defense but to act only on the defensive. On the following morning Eastporters held a public meeting and resolved unanimously to preserve as good an understanding as possible with their New Brunswick neighbors and to discountenance any attempts to seize the property of provincial people. Some prepared to move. On the same day an account of the declaration of war and of the proceedings at Eastport was forwarded by Robert Pagan of St. Andrews to President Smyth of the Executive Council of New Brunswick. The council ordered one third of the militia to be ready for call on the shortest notice and recommended to customs officers that unarmed American vessels laden with provisions be admitted to St. John which was short of provisions and that they be permitted to take away British goods except arms and naval stores.

Harold A. Davis, "An International Community on the St. Croix (1604–1930)", *The Maine Bulletin*, LII (12), April 1950 (University of Maine Studies, Second Series, No. 64), p. 103.

The Halifax Collector of Customs complained with cause that some residents of the St. Croix area were "much more disposed for smuggling than war", although the profession of smuggling was only one of the ways found to circumvent the inconvenience of war.

In many instances British and American vessels adopted foreign registry and carried British goods from colonial to U.S. ports without hindrance. In June 1813 Britain proclaimed a blockade of the entire Atlantic coast. Large quantities of British goods were landed at Campobello and Indian Island and carried by "neutral" vessels into Eastport or nearby points on the mainland and from there overland to the Penobscot, Portland, Boston, and even to New York.

Ibid., p. 108.

When Eastport was seized by the British in 1814, residents found life far from impossible under the "new management".

Residents who remained were required to take the oath of allegiance to the crown; the others were ordered to leave within seven days. The municipal law was to remain in force. The majority took the oath and stayed. The customs house property, including about $10,000 in currency and some customs bonds were seized. One Rogers, or Rodgers, of Kennebec grasped the collector of customs, Colonel Lemuel Trescott, by the collar as he was removing his papers and held him until the British arrived. The deputy collector, Corney, took the oath of allegiance and was continued in office.

*   *   *   *   *

Eastporters were not given the full rights of British subjects which many of them had hoped to receive. Martial law was in force; their meeting house became a barracks; the town was crowded; houses were occupied without ceremony; and there were many abuses. Numerous vessels and much private property were confiscated. Although the port could now trade freely with the British colonies, supplies became very scarce with pork selling for $53 per barrel. Many farmers from the neighbouring towns did a lucrative business in provisions with the island, but the garrison was their principal customer. There were sales of real estate to the British until this was stopped by proclamation.

*   *   *   *   *

Eastport was not evacuated until 1818, and the four years of occupation were decidedly uncomfortable. However, relations between the inhabitants, the soldiery, and the officers, were, on the whole, not too unsatisfactory. Communication with the states was difficult at first, but Eastporters who had taken the oath could leave the island provided that they carried passes signed by the town major, and farmers and boatmen were permitted to bring in provisions from the mainland. The occupation added a few touches of color to an otherwise dull scene. There were balls; a theatre was organized; and horse races were held. In spite of British jurisdiction Moose Islanders cast their votes for governor of Massachusetts in 1816. British soldiers deserted in considerable numbers. On one occasion several entire guards disappeared, and the officers themselves were compelled to stand guard duty.

Ibid., pp. 109, 110, 111–12.

THE VIEWS OF LATER COMMENTATORS

The War's Impact on the Maritimes

A modern and scholarly appraisal by W. S. MacNutt of the war as it affected the Maritimes emphasizes that its main impact was economic rather than ideological.

The War of 1812 with the United States had the effect of lifting the Atlantic colonies to a new feeling of self-confidence and self-importance. The redoubled movements of fleets and armies everywhere provided a martial glamour, swelling provincial revenues and increasing commercial prosperity. The five colonies became more conscious of a British kinship of their own and looked with sympathy to the hard-pressed Canadians as New Brunswick's 104th Regiment, gathered together from distant garrisons, made its celebrated winter march to their assistance. Injurious consequences of the war were casual and unimportant, and, whatever the general result, the feeling was one of victory. Merchants complained of losses at sea, but this was only because the ships of the Royal Navy were blockading New York and the ports of the Chesapeake. American privateersmen were forbidden to land on British shores, so that the coastlines were left almost untouched. The tidings of triumph from Spain swelled the lustre of victory along the frontier of the St. Lawrence and the lakes. It was a heyday for Halifax as the prosperous merchants, on these numerous occasions, adjourned to their reading-room across the street from the flat roof of the market-place where bands played selections from loyal airs and marches.

W. S. MacNutt, *The Atlantic Provinces: The Emergence of Colonial Society, 1712–1857* (Toronto, 1965), p. 150.

The War as a Source of Anti-Americanism

A. L. Burt links the war with the Loyalist tradition as twin sources of a negative Canadianism based on anti-Americanism. He also suggests that the vaunted Canadian-American undefended border was an outgrowth of the realization on all sides that 1812–1814 must be "the war to end war" in North America.

The effect of the War of 1812 upon British North America was most evident in Upper Canada. The war suddenly stopped the peaceful American invasion of that province, and it checked a renewal of this invasion afterward, for it opened British eyes to what had been happening. It also stifled the potentially American character of the Upper Canadian population by purging it of the small minority who were incorrigible republicans and by corraling within the British fold the great majority who were not. These changes draw added significance from the fact that the tide of British immigration to this province was relatively small until fifteen years or so after the outbreak of hostilities in America. Then it might have been too late for these newcomers, themselves not very self-conscious politically, to impress a British character upon Upper Canada if the war had not cut, as with a knife, its growing connection with the United States.

Taking British North America as a whole, the war accentuated its British spirit by reinforcing the anti-American prejudice that dates from the American Revolution and the settlement of the Loyalists. To this very day Canadians have not been able to forget the fight to save their country from the United States, and they react against the anti-British prejudice that American memories of this war have strengthened in the United States.

Nevertheless, the experience of the war brought into clear relief a fundamental condition that made another war between the British Empire and the American Republic something to be avoided at almost any cost. The American commissioners at Ghent pointed it out in a reply to the British demand, later withdrawn, for a drastic revision of the boundary. The British said they must have it in order to give security to British North America, exposed as it was to an American attack by land. The reply pointed out that this was not necessary because Britain already had ample security in her undoubted ability to strike a more damaging blow on the Atlantic seaboard of the United States. That this balance of vulnerability governed the relations of the United States with British North America and through it the relations between Washington and London, becomes more apparent if one glances at the relations between the United States and its neighbors on the southwest, where there was no such balance. Thus did the revelation of the War of 1812 dictate permanent peace between the British Empire and the United States until the latter became a world power, when world considerations confirmed it.

A. L. Burt, *The Evolution of the British Empire and Commonwealth from the American Revolution* (Boston, 1956), pp. 139–40.

The "Militia" Tradition of 1812 — A Criticism

The tradition of "the gallant and loyal militia", as an ingredient of the emotional nationalism engendered by the war in later generations, has recently been both criticized and defended by two leading Canadian military historians.

. . . One of the most durable of our legends is what I may call the Militia Legend of 1812. By that I mean the idea that during that war the country was defended by 'the Militia' with only a little help from regular troops. I think this idea is still pretty widespread, and I suspect you can still find it in some school textbooks; but it isn't in accordance with the facts. It's perfectly true that the militia played an essential part in the defence of Canada, but it was still a secondary part. The country was not saved in 1812 merely by youngsters fresh from the tail of the plough. It was scientifically defended by men trained for the job. The battles on the border, particularly in the early days, were essentially a contest between ill-organized numbers on the American side and professional skill on ours. You won't find this in the schoolbooks: but Upper Canada was saved in the campaign of 1812 because the province was actually better prepared for war than the United States. It was better prepared because the British taxpayer had provided in Canada the essentials for successful defence. These were a naval force on the Lakes; an efficient body of regular troops, small, it is true, but equal to the job; and trained officers who could provide skilful and energetic professional leadership.

The regulars did more than supply the leadership. They usually did the lion's share of the actual fighting. Take a look at the casualty lists for the fiercest battle of the war, Lundy's Lane. . . . I am not suggesting that Canadians did not play an important part in the defence of Canada. I am merely saying that the trained soldier was the key figure in the whole affair, and that the amateur soldier was much less important than he has been made out to be. . . .

All the same, let's give credit where it's due. And the chief credit for the saving of Canada in 1812 is due to British soldiers. No one can read the documents that tell the story of the events in Upper Canada in the summer of 1812 without realizing that this is so. It is at least possible that this province would be part of the United States today had it not been for the presence here in that year of one single battalion of British regular infantry—the 41st Foot, now The Welch Regiment—and an able and energetic British major-general, Isaac Brock. Every Ontario schoolboy, I hope, still knows the name of General Brock; but how many of them have heard of the Welch Regiment?

C. P. Stacey, "The War of 1812 in Canadian History", *Ontario History*, Summer 1958, L (3), pp. 154–5.

The "Militia" Tradition Defended

. . . Did the militia play a significant part? Did militiamen prove of any real value to the country in the days of its travail? The answer to both questions is yes. Not the dominant role, it is true; but an important and essential role for all that.

During the three years of the war militiamen transported and convoyed military supplies; they provided garrisons for towns and depots; they constructed fortifications; they furnished guards at various points along the many miles of frontier between Amherstburg in the west and Lacolle in the east. These were necessary and important tasks. Even more important was their contribution of fighting troops. During the first year of the war, when the regulars in Upper Canada were few in number, militiamen were a large part, and usually the major component of the forces which defeated the enemy at Detroit, Queenston Heights, Frenchman's Creek, and Ogdensburg. . . .

Of course the militia had its weaknesses as a military force. It lacked training and it lacked discipline, although both of these drawbacks became less significant as militiamen gained actual experience under war conditions. Much more serious was the fact that the militia was not a disposable nor a permanent force; that militiamen, being soldiers only for several weeks or months during the year, kept one eye upon their farms and their families, and were disposed to go home when either of these interests demanded their attention. It was to overcome this weakness that Prevost embodied six battalions of militia in Lower Canada and that the Volunteer Incorporated Militia Battalion was formed in Upper Canada. Nevertheless, the various commanding officers in both Upper and Lower Canada recognized the worth of the sedentary militia and utilized its services in virtually every operation of the war. . . . That the province was preserved, proves both the activity and the efficiency of the aid rendered.

> George F. G. Stanley, "The Contribution of the Canadian Militia During the War", in Philip P. Mason, ed., *After Tippecanoe: Some Aspects of the War of 1812* (Toronto, 1963), pp. 44–5.

The War and the Birth of the Family Compact

This final commentary on the War of 1812–1814 as the seed-bed of Canadian nationalism indicates the way in which that war affected subsequent political development in Upper Canada.

Our examination may offer the following tentative conclusions:
The Family Compact was a group principally of professional men and bureaucrats with only a few businessmen. At its centre was a small elite of like-

minded men who made the important decisions on policy in the province. The Compact recruited its members from among men who in the War of 1812 had proved themselves leaders of the Upper Canadian community. The principal qualifications by which one gained entry to the group were ideological, the possession of "correct" views and attitudes approved by the elite. The elite, and the Family Compact generally, were dominated to a large degree by one man [John Strachan]. This group "ran" the province. . . .

Two determining factors which caused both the Family Compact and the Chateau Clique to differ from other "colonial-frontier" governing groups were the French Revolution and the War of 1812. The first imparted to them a "tory" attitude towards change and reform, the second gave them an acute sense of leadership, loyalty to Britain and a strong anti-Americanism. Where the Family Compact differed from the Chateau Clique was that it was a quasi-aristocracy of bureaucrats and professional men (principally lawyers), and not the expression, as in Montreal, of an alliance of politics, big business and government.

> Robert Saunders, "What Was the Family Compact?", *Ontario History*,
> Autumn 1957, XLIX (4), p. 178.

Further Reading

A. L. Burt, *The United States, Great Britain and British North America from the Revolution to the Establishment of Peace after the War of 1812* (reprinted, Toronto, Ryerson, 1966)* devotes several chapters to analysing the causes, both remote and immediate, of the war, and suggests that the war kept Canada British by preventing a peaceful American takeover through mass migration. The one hundred and fiftieth anniversary of the war saw the publication of several narrative histories of the events, including Mack Hitsman, *The Incredible War* (Toronto, University of Toronto Press, 1965)*, but no new analytical works beyond those quoted in this Problem. For a collection of reprinted essays on various aspects of the War of 1812 as it affected Upper Canada, see *The Defended Border* (Toronto, Macmillan, 1964), edited by Morris Zaslow. This volume includes a modern assessment of the war's importance, "The War of 1812 in Canadian History", by C. P. Stacey.

Problem 8

From Reform to Rebellion — What Caused
the Conflicts of 1837?

Exactly sixty years after the British surrendered at Saratoga and France recognized the independence of the United States, armed revolts broke out in Lower and Upper Canada, the two largest colonies remaining in Britain's North American Empire. Were these rebellions caused by the same factors as the American Revolution? Had Britain failed to learn the lessons of 1776? By the 1830's demands for reform were being voiced in all the British North American colonies, yet only in the two Canadas did rebellions occur. What diverted the course of colonial political evolution into the channels of revolution?

Like most historical phenomena, the rebellions of 1837 in Lower and Upper Canada had several causes. Some, but not all, were common to the two provinces. In 1837, as in 1776, the greatest weakness of colonial government was the lack of any connecting link between the elected assemblies and the appointed governors and councils. Was the American practice of elective institutions from top to bottom the only alternative to "irresponsible" government? Any hint of American influences was enough to arouse the emotional loyalism of the conservative elements in both colonies. Also, in those years prior to the rebellions, both Canadas were suffering economic dislocations that pitted agricultural against mercantile interests. Can the rebellions be explained in terms of conflict between these economic classes?

In Lower Canada language was another symptom of discontent, for the oligarchic government was identified with the English minority whereas the French language provided the main cohesive element in the French-Canadian nationalism that had been growing steadily since the Conquest. This problem of language was absent in English-speaking Upper Canada, but there the Church of England's exclusive enjoyment of the income from one-seventh of the surveyed lands had aroused bitter denominational antipathies in the religiously pluralistic society.

What then was at the root of the two rebellions? Was it the constitutional deadlock inherent in the "old colonial system" of government? Was it the conflict of economic classes? Was it the growth of French-Canadian nationalism in Lower Canada and of religious privilege in Upper Canada? However the causes of the rebellions are evaluated, it must be remembered that the radicals did not win widespread support in the colonies. Strong as the sense of grievance might be, the traditions of loyalty and the rule of law were far stronger. Only a few hundreds actually joined in the revolts, and such unpopular and ill-led rebellions were doomed to failure. Yet their very failure led directly to Lord Durham's famous Report on colonial problems, and that Report in turn helped the moderate reformers to gain with ballots in 1847 many of the objectives that the rebels could not win with bullets in 1837.

Democracy Versus Privilege

At the heart of the reform movements in both Upper and Lower Canada was an attempt to build a society of the North American democratic type on Canadian soil. The radical reform leaders came to favour republican institutions because these seemed to promise a broad degree of popular control over the government and the magistrature. They also opposed privilege in its various forms— banks, land companies, the Established Church, the appointive councils—because privilege was incompatible with the egalitarian society which they sought to build.

Louis Joseph Papineau (1786–1871), the leading Lower Canadian reformer, was a democrat, but he was also the spokesman of French-Canadian nationalism. Because of this double dimension, his personality is more difficult to analyse than that of his Upper Canadian counterpart, William Lyon Mackenzie (1795–1861).

In the colonies the people need democratic institutions because they are less costly and less burdensome than more expensive institutions. A new country needs robust men accustomed to hard work, to privations, and to the tech-niques needed to exploit the forests. It is in the customs, the nature and the common interests of colony and mother country that government institutions should be economical, for everything that is taken from the enjoyment of luxury is an endowment for new families that will marry earlier, will clear new land, will create a new productive capital to buy the useful manufactured products of cloth and iron rather than silks and liquors. . . .

Give institutions where there is no cause for flattery, and national distinctions will cease. In the present situation the Government is reaping the fruits that it has sown. There is need, they say, of a council to defend one part of the population that can't be a majority in the Assembly. A party is needed in the House to support the Council. . . . The complaints of this country against the evils of the Council's composition are too unanimous to make it necessary to say more on this subject. The Constitutional Act has given the Council a disastrous preponderance that allows it to paralyze all the work of the House of Assembly. It had been desired to give the latter body influence, since the Province of Quebec had been divided so that the original population in Lower Canada could protect its own institutions. But the Constitutional Act provided an easy way to destroy that hope: that was by installing Upper Canada in the Legislative Council of Lower Canada. And so it was done.

Speech by Papineau on the Legislative Council, reported in *La Minerve'*
21 January 1833
F. Ouellet, *Papineau: Textes choisis et présentés* (Quebec, 1958), p. 54 (translation)·

Canadians! It has been said that we are on the verge of a revolution. We are in the midst of one; a bloodless one, I hope, but a revolution to which all those which have been will be counted mere child's play. Calm as society may seem to a superficial spectator, I know that it is moved to its very foundations, and is in universal agitation. . . . The question today is not between one reigning family and another, between one people and another, between one form of government and another, but a question between privilege and equal rights, between law sanctioned, law fenced in privilege, age consecrated privilege, and a hitherto unheard-of power, a new power just started from the darkness in which it has slumbered since creation day, *the Power of Honest Industry*. . . . The contest is now between the privileged and the unprivileged, and a terrible one it is. The slave snaps his fetters, the peasant feels an unwonted strength nerve in his arm, the *people* rise in stern and awful majesty, and demand in strange tones their ever despised and hitherto denied rights. They rise and swear in a deep and startling oath that *Justice Shall Reign*. . . .

The Constitution, 26 July 1837.
Margaret Fairley, ed., *The Selected Writings of William Lyon Mackenzie*
(Toronto, 1960), p. 218.

Oligarchy Château Clique

The Family Compact: A Colonial Oligarchy   *Family Compact*

The name "Family Compact", as applied to the group of men who occupied senior posts in the Upper Canadian public service, was popularized by Mackenzie in 1833. The Family Compact was, however, neither compact nor a family. It included many persons who had risen from humble stations in life because of their ability, as well as those who gained positions because of their birth and family connections. Unlike its Lower Canadian counterpart, the Château Clique, the Family Compact was significantly lacking in men from the mercantile class. It was an administrative rather than an economic elite. In the following reading Lord Durham discusses the unpopularity of this colonial oligarchy.

. . . Upper Canada, . . . has long been entirely governed by a party commonly designated throughout the Province as the 'family compact' . . . For a long time this body of men possessed almost all the highest public offices, by means of which, and of its influence in the Executive Council, it wielded all the powers of government; it maintained influence in the legislature by means of its pre-dominance in the Legislative Council; and it disposed of the large number of petty posts which are in the patronage of the Government all over the Province. Successive Governors, as they came in their turn, are said to have either sub-mitted quietly to its influence, or, after a short and unavailing struggle, to have yielded to this well-organized party the real conduct of affairs. The bench, the magistracy, the high offices of the Episcopal Church, and a great part of the legal profession, are filled by the adherents of this party . . . they have acquired nearly the whole of the waste lands of the Province; they are all-powerful in the chartered banks, and, till lately, shared among themselves almost exclusively all offices of trust and profit. The bulk of this party consists . . . of native-born inhabitants of the Colony, or of emigrants who settled in it before the last war with the United States; the principal members of it belong to the church of England, and the maintenance of the claims of that church has always been one of its distinguishing characteristics.

A monopoly of power so extensive and so lasting could not fail, in process of time, to excite envy, create dissatisfaction, and ultimately provoke attack; and an opposition consequently grew up in the Assembly which assailed the ruling party, by appealing to popular principles of government, by denouncing the alleged jobbing and profusion of the official body, and by instituting inquiries into abuses, for the purpose of promoting reform and especially economy. . . .

C. P. Lucas, ed., *Lord Durham's Report on the Affairs of British North America* (Oxford, 1912), Vol. II, pp. 148–9.

A Defence of the Family Compact

The Family Compact was not without able defenders. Lieutenant-Governor Sir George Arthur thought that the group was unpopular because it had fought for years against the introduction of measures tending to republicanism. Before him, Lieutenant-Governor Sir Francis Bond Head had also praised the character and ability of the members.

It appears, then, from Lord Durham's own shewing, that this "FAMILY COMPACT," which his Lordship deems it so advisable that the Queen should destroy, is nothing more nor less than that "social fabric" which characterizes every civilized community in the world. It is that social fabric, or rather fortress, within which the British yeoman, farmer, and manufacturer is enabled to repel the extortionate demands of his labourers; and to preserve from pillage and robbery the harvest of his industry after he has reaped it!

*   *   *   *   *

The "*family compact*" of Upper Canada is composed of those members of its society who, either by their abilities and character have been honoured by the confidence of the executive government, or who, by their industry and intelligence, have amassed wealth. The party, I own, is comparatively a small one; but to put the multitude at the top and the few at the bottom is a radical reversion of the pyramid of society which every reflecting man must foresee can end only by its downfall.

Sir F. B. Head, *A Narrative* (London, 1839), pp. 464–5.

In Defence of the Church Establishment

In his early years as a teacher John Strachan (1776–1867) had educated most members of the Family Compact. Although the Church of England comprised only a minority of the Upper Canadian population, it contrived, thanks to Strachan, to monopolize the income from the Clergy Reserves and to control most educational institutions in the province, particularly King's College, nucleus of the present-day University of Toronto.

The Church of England may legally have been the state religion, but in fact it never possessed the rights of an establishment—such as the right to collect tithes from all citizens. It possessed privileges but not real power. The North American preference for separation of church and state that was echoed in the religio-political conflicts of Upper Canada was simply one more complicating factor in the

Reform Movement. Yet the privileged position of the Church of England was opposed with much more bitterness in Upper Canada than in either Nova Scotia or New Brunswick. Was the reason for this the greater extent of Clergy Reserves, or the proximity of Upper Canada to the United States?

In 1824 John Strachan, already a member of the Upper Canadian Executive and Legislative councils and soon to be made Archdeacon of York (Toronto), reported to the Colonial Office his conviction that the province needed a real as well as a nominal church establishment if loyalty was to be preserved.

That the Canadas might be attached to the Parent State by religious as well as political feelings was the intention of the great William Pitt when in forming a constitution for the Canadas he provided for the religious instruction of the people. For it was well known to this illustrious Statesman that almost all the Episcopal Clergy and their congregations remained during the American Rebellion loyal and faithful to the King proving by their conduct that had proper care been taken to promote a religious Establishment in Union with that of England the Colonies would never have been separated. The same wise policy is still maintained by His Majesty's government and the great Bond of attachment between the Colonies and Great Britain depends entirely upon the progress and influence of Church principles. Were two or three hundred Clergymen for example living in the Canadas amidst their Congregations and paid through the munificent arrangements of the British Government, they would infuse into the population a tone and feeling entirely English and acquiring by degrees the direction of Education which the Clergy at home have always possessed the very first feelings and opinions of the youth would be British.

> George W. Spragge, ed., *The John Strachan Letter Book: 1812–1834*
> (Toronto, 1946), pp. xiv–xv.

A Demand for Religious Liberty

Although some Presbyterians had already asked for money from the Protestant Clergy Reserves, the real attack on Anglican church establishment in Upper Canada dates from 1826, when Strachan aroused the ire of dissenters by publishing a sermon impugning their loyalty. The next year he gave the Colonial Office an "Ecclesiastical Chart" purporting to show that most Upper Canadians were either Anglicans or at least sympathetic to the established church. The Chart caused so much religious controversy that a

Select Committee of the Upper Canadian Assembly investigated and reported on the whole question of religious privileges in the colony in 1828.

There can be no doubt that in addition to the Methodists there are, in the Province, several denominations of Christians who are more numerous than the members of the Church of England. Besides these there are probably many other persons who are not attached to any particular church or form of worship: compared with the whole population, the members of the Church of England must therefore constitute an extremely small proportion. It would be unjust and impolitic to exalt this church, by exclusive and peculiar rights, above all others of His Majesty's Subjects who are equally loyal, conscientious and deserving. A country in where there is an established church from which a vast majority of the subjects are dissenters, must be in a lamentable state: the Committee hope that this Province will never present such a spectacle. . . . There is besides no necessity for such an establishment. It cannot be necessary for the security of the Government; the loyalty of the people is deep and enthusiastic, and it may be doubted how far it would be improved or increased by any state establishment of clergymen. Religious instruction, it is true, will promote and strengthen loyalty and all other virtues; but no more when communicated by clergymen of the Church of England than by those of other sects, and probably less if they are or appear to be political teachers and servants of the state, rather than ministers of the Gospel. It cannot be necessary for the ends of religion; other denominations of course will not be benefited by it; and the church itself will derive probably but little if any real advantage. The piety and religious prosperity of a church can gain but little from men who are induced by secular motives to assume the sacred functions of the clerical office. . . .

A. G. Doughty and N. Story, eds., *Documents Relating to the Constitutional History of Canada, 1819–1828* (Ottawa, 1935), pp. 379–80.

The Reform Movement in Lower Canada Interpreted as an Expression of French-Canadian Nationalism

The Reform Movement in Lower Canada began during the administration of Sir James Craig. According to Craig, the agitation was not caused by any defect in British policy but by the racial animosities of the French Canadians.

. . . I speak of a Colony, the population of which . . . I myself believe to exceed 250,000. Of these 250,000 souls about 20,000 or 25,000 may be English or Americans, the remainder are French. I use the term designedly My Lord, because I mean to say, that they are in Language, in religion, in manner and in attachment completely French—bound to us by no one tie, but that of a Com-

mon Government, and on the contrary viewing us with sentiments of mistrust
& jealousy, with envy, and I believe I should not go too far, were I to say with
hatred.

                    *   *   *   *   *

In considering the probability of these people having in view their return to
their own Government, it may be urged that they have been hitherto quiet &
faithful subjects, during the long lapse of 50 years, in which it would rather be
to be supposed that their old attachment should have gradually decreased, so
that there should be the less likelihood of their assuming now a disposition, of
which they have hitherto shown no indication; to all this however it may be
replied, that no circumstance whatever has occurred to awaken their attachment to their Mother Country, nor have any pains ever been taken to produce
such a change, their habits, language and religion, have remained as distinct
from ours as they were before the Conquest. Indeed it seems to be a favourite
object with them to be considered as [a] separate Nation; *La Nation Canadienne*
is their constant expression, and with regard to their having been hitherto quiet
& faithful subjects, it need only be observed that no opportunity has presented
them an encouragement to shew themselves otherwise.

> Sir James Craig to the Earl of Liverpool, 1 May 1810
> W. P. M. Kennedy, ed., *Statutes, Treaties and Documents of the Canadian
> Constitution, 1713–1929* (Toronto, 1930), pp. 226, 229–30.

The English Mercantile Community in Lower Canada and the Reform Movement

Adam Thom, a Scottish schoolteacher and lawyer, was the
journalistic spokesman of the English mercantile community in
Lower Canada. From September 1835 to January 1836, in a series
of letters published in the *Montreal Herald* over the signature
Camillus, he violently attacked the conciliating policy of the
Governor, Lord Gosford, toward the French Canadians, and
warned that such a policy could cause a revolt of the English.

If, however, the French Canadians should be goaded into rebellion by the
specious falsehoods of shameless traitors, such a rebellion would be speedily
suppressed. If they should, in the first instance, shed the blood of every English
inhabitant of the seigniories, they would pave the way not for ultimate success
but for most awful retribution. They would be hemmed in by a gradually
closing circle of English breasts and English bayonets, and would, in a few
short months, become the hunted of all hunters, the enslaved of all enslavers,
the slain of all slayers. Their wretched leaders would wish, that they had never
been born.

An English insurrection, however, a conciliatory cabinet may wisely dread—an insurrection not against a British King but against a French Viceroy. Such an insurrection is to be dreaded, not only as comparatively probable, but as absolutely certain of ultimate success. The probable consequences of such an insurrection I shall detail in my next letter. . . .

. . . An English insurrection against any French Viceroy of Lower Canada would, most certainly, be ultimately successful . . . The loss of Lower Canada would necessarily involve the loss of all British America. The loss of British America would deprive England of her most productive fisheries, place her entirely at the mercy of foreigners for the main element of her maritime power, and leave her not a single port on this continent for sheltering her navy to the northward of Bermuda. . . .

> Adam Thom (pseudonym Camillus), *Anti-Gallic Letters; Addressed to His Excellency, the Earl of Gosford, Governor-in-chief of the Canadas* (Montreal, 1836), pp. 39–41.

Thom then considers what influence a policy of conciliation is likely to have on the prosperity of the colony.

Will the French faction, my lord, devote the public revenue to the improvement of the commercial facilities of the province? Will the demagogues deepen Lake St. Peter? Will they improve and extend the wharves of Montreal? Will they complete the magnificent line of communication so nobly undertaken by their tributary victim of Upper Canada? Will they make one effort to render Montreal, what nature destined her to be, the rival of New York? No, my lord; they will not do anything, that at all tends to inundate the sacred soil of a French province with British, or Irish or American foreigners. . . . They will appropriate [the funds] . . . to local objects, which ought to be accomplished by local assessments, and thus buy the support or at least the neutrality of individuals, who are too short-sighted to see the fatal consequences of French supremacy. . . .

> *Ibid.*, p. 42.

The Reform Movement in Upper Canada Blamed on American Influence

According to Robert Baldwin Sullivan, a cousin of Robert Baldwin but a member of the Family Compact, the uprising in Upper Canada had been inspired by American influences and was intended to establish an American-type republic. The following passage is taken from Sullivan's Report to Lieutenant-Governor Sir George Arthur on the condition of Upper Canada.

In this country unfortunately the settlement of American citizens has been too much permitted and encouraged, and thus in the bosom of this community there exists a treacherous foe. The vicinity of the arena for the discussion of extreme political fantasies, infects this population, many of the natural born subjects of the Crown are carried away by the plausibility of republican doctrines. . . . Personal disappointments, disarrangement of private affairs, want of success in political intrigue, in short every circumstance which does not fall out precisely as every man . . . desires, is made a ground for organic change in government, a reason for revolution.

In such a state of things it is not wonderful that a considerable portion of this community may be said to be disaffected, and indeed it is much to the honour of the Upper Canadian people that the great majority are truly loyal.

*   *   *   *   *

It is for the British nation to judge whether it is for the interests of the empire to abandon this colony, or to give up its loyal inhabitants to the mercies of a demoralized American rabble, or its fair and fertile territory to the rapacity and avidity of American politicians.

*   *   *   *   *

. . . In many parts of the province the teachers are Americans. For the sake of obtaining employment they have swallowed the oath of allegiance which agrees so ill with them that the rest of their lives is spent in attempts to disgorge it. These men are utterly ignorant of every thing English and could not if they tried instruct their pupils in any of the duties which the connection of the province with England casts upon them. The books they use are all American, filled with inflated accounts of American independence and the glorious wars with England. The exploits of General Jackson and the heroes of '76 fill the youthful mind to the exclusion of every thing glorious or interesting in English history. The young man grows up without a single prepossession in favor of his country; he looks upon a British soldier as a person whom it would be honorable and glorious to oppose with the rifle. . . .

R. B. Sullivan to Sir George Arthur [1838]
C. R. Sanderson, ed., *The Arthur Papers* (Toronto, 1957), Vol. I, pp. 134, 135, 151.

The Demands of the Lower Canadian Reformers

The Ninety-Two Resolutions constitute the manifesto of radical reform in Lower Canada. These Resolutions were adopted by the House of Assembly in 1834, and an address based on them was then forwarded to the British Parliament.

9. Resolved, That the most serious defect in the Constitutional Act, its radical fault, the most active principle of evil and discontent in the province; the most powerful and most frequent cause of abuses of power . . . is that injudicious enactment . . . which invests the Crown with that exorbitant power . . . of selecting and composing without any rule or limitation, or any predetermined qualification, an entire branch of the legislature, supposed by the nature of its attributions to be independent, but inevitably the servile tool of the authority which creates, composes and decomposes it, and can on any day modify it to suit the interests or the passions of the moment.

14. Resolved, That this House is nowise disposed to admit the excellence of the present Constitution of Canada . . . nor to reject the principle of extending the system of frequent elections much further than it is at present carried; and that this system ought especially to be extended to the Legislative Council. . . .

52. Resolved, That since a circumstance, which did not depend upon the choice of the majority of the people, their French origin and their use of the French language, has been made by the colonial authorities a pretext for abuse, for exclusion, for political inferiority, for a separation of rights and interests; this House now appeals to the justice of His Majesty's Government and of Parliament, and to the honour of the people of England; that the majority of the inhabitants of this country are in nowise disposed to repudiate any one of the advantages they derive from their origin and from their descent from the French nation. . . .

64. Resolved, That the claims which have for many years been set up by the Executive Government to that control over and power of appropriating a great portion of the revenues levied in this province, which belong of right to this House, are contrary to the rights and to the constitution of the country. . . .

75. Resolved, That the number of the inhabitants of the country being about 600,000, those of French origin are about 525,000, and those of British or other origin 75,000; and that the establishment of the civil government of Lower Canada for the year 1832 . . . contained the names of 157 officers and others receiving salaries, who are apparently of British or foreign origin, and the names of 47 who are apparently natives of the country, of French origin . . . the latter class being for the most part appointed to the inferior and less lucrative offices . . . that the accumulation of many of the best paid and most influential, and at the same time incompatible offices, in the same person, which is forbidden by the laws and by sound policy, exists especially for the benefit of the former class. . . .

84. Resolved, That besides the grievances and abuses above mentioned, there exist in this province a great number of others . . .

1stly. The vicious composition and the irresponsibility of the Executive Council, the members of which are at the same time Judges of the Court of Appeals, and the secrecy with which not only the functions, but even the names of the members of that body have been kept from the knowledge of this House. . . .

4thly. The cumulation of public places and offices in the same persons, and the efforts made by a number of families connected with the administration, to perpetuate this state of things for their own advantage, and for the sake of domineering forever, with interested views and in the spirit of party, over the people and their representatives.

> Kennedy, ed., *Statutes, Treaties and Documents* . . . , pp. 271, 272, 280–1, 283, 285, 287.

Mackenzie's Declaration of Independence

When the rebellion at Toronto failed in December 1837, Mackenzie fled to Navy Island in the Niagara River, and from there issued a proclamation to the inhabitants of Upper Canada explaining the aims of the rebels. The document is largely a recapitulation of the grievances that Mackenzie had been attacking for more than a decade.

We have planted the Standard of Liberty in Canada, for the attainment of the following objects:

Perpetual Peace, founded on a government of equal rights to all, secured by a written constitution, sanctioned by yourselves in a convention to be called as early as circumstances will permit.

Civil and Religious Liberty, in its fullest extent, that in all laws made, or to be made, every person be bound alike. . . .

The Abolition of Hereditary Honors, of the laws of Entail and Primogeniture, and of hosts of pensioners who devour our substance.

A Legislature, composed of a Senate and Assembly chosen by the people.

An Executive, to be composed of a Governor and other officers elected by the public voice.

A Judiciary, to be chosen by the Governor and Senate, and composed of the most learned, honorable, and trustworthy, of our citizens. The laws to be rendered cheap and expeditious.

A Free Trial by Jury—Sheriffs chosen by you, and not to hold office, as now, at the pleasure of our tyrants. The freedom of the press. Alas for it, now! The free presses in the Canadas are trampled down by the hand of arbitrary power.

The Vote by Ballot—free and peaceful township elections.

The people to elect their Court of Request Commissioners and Justices of the Peace—and also their Militia Officers, in all cases whatsoever.

Freedom of Trade—every man to be allowed to buy at the cheapest market, and sell at the dearest.

No man to be compelled to give military service, unless it be his choice.

Ample funds to be reserved from the vast natural resources of our country to secure the blessings of education to every citizen.

A frugal and economical Government, in order that the people may be prosperous and free from difficulty.

An end forever to the wearisome prayers, supplications, and mockeries attendant upon our connection with the lordlings of the Colonial Office, Downing Street, London.

The opening of the St. Lawrence to the trade of the world, so that the largest ships might pass up to Lake Superior, and the distribution of the wild lands of the country to the industry, capital, skill, and enterprise of worthy men of all nations.

Charles Lindsay, *Life and Times of William Lyon Mackenzie* (Toronto, 1862), Vol. I, pp. 364–5.

A Moderate Upper Canadian Point of View

While Papineau, Mackenzie, and their followers were pressing for republican reforms, a group of moderates led by Robert Baldwin saw the remedy for colonial difficulties in the application of the British principle of responsible government. Believing that the imperial connection was in danger, Baldwin explained his doctrine to Lord Glenelg, the Colonial Secretary, in 1836. He first discussed and rejected three remedies as inexpedient or inadequate: making the Legislative Council elective, abolishing it altogether, or conceding isolated points as they arose.

I now come to the consideration of the fourth remedy, which consists of nothing more than having the provincial Government as far as regards the internal affairs of the Province, conducted by the Lieutenant Governor ... with the advice and assistance of the Executive Council, acting as a Provincial Cabinet, and composed of Men possessed of the public confidence, whose opinions and policy would be in harmony with the opinions and policy of the Representatives of the People. This, as I have before said, I look upon not only as an efficient remedy, but as the only efficient one that can be applied to the evils under which the Province is at present suffering.

*   *   *   *   *

That the adoption of this principle would without vesting the Election of the Executive Council in the People place in their hands such an indirect influence upon it, as would be sufficient to secure attention to their rights, feelings, and prejudices, is sufficiently evident; because if such attention were not paid by those in the confidence of the Lieutenant-Governor, the people have only to return to the next Parliament, men who would not give them parliamentary support, and they would necessarily have to resign; and the Lieutenant Governor to appoint others who possessed the confidence of the Representatives of the People.

> Robert Baldwin to Lord Glenelg, 13 July 1836
> Kennedy, ed., *Statutes, Treaties and Documents* . . . , pp. 338–39.

The Ten Resolutions — A Breaking Point?

Charged with administering a global empire, the Colonial Office was confused by the flood of petitions, counterpetitions, charges, and countercharges, arriving over the years from the two Canadas. Lord Gosford's mission to reconcile the differences in Lower Canada was frustrated by Sir Francis Bond Head, who published the secret instructions given Governor Lord Gosford ordering him to refuse any basic constitutional changes. The Lower Canadian Assembly then used its ultimate weapon, refusal to vote money for civil service salaries, in an attempt to force the government to meet its demands for an elective Legislative Council and a responsible Executive Council. Colonial Secretary Lord John Russell viewed this action as political blackmail and introduced resolutions in the imperial Parliament to allow Lord Gosford to break the financial deadlock. The passing of these Ten Resolutions reminded Lower Canadian radicals of the "taxation without representation" that preceded the American Revolution. They reacted to Russell's measures with cries of "robbery", "plunder", and "no surrender". Some historians have seen the Ten Resolutions as the breaking point in colonial relations—the immediate cause, if not a justification, for the armed revolt that broke out a few months later in Lower Canada.

Lord John Russell's Ten Resolutions, 6 March 1837

4. That in the existing state of Lower Canada, it is unadvisable to make the Legislative Council of that province an elective body. . . .
5. That while it is expedient to improve the composition of the Executive

Council in Lower Canada, it is unadvisable to subject it to the responsibility demanded by the House of Assembly. . . .

8. That for defraying the arrears due on account of the established and customary charges of the administration of justice, and of the civil government of the said province, it is expedient, that . . . the Governor of the said province be empowered to issue from and out of any other part of his Majesty's revenues, in the hands of the Receiver-General of the said province, such further sums as shall be necessary to effect the payment of the before-mentioned sum of £142,160. 14s. 6d.

9. That it is expedient that his Majesty be authorised to place at the disposal of the Legislature of the said province, the net proceeds of his Majesty's hereditary, territorial, and casual revenue arising within the same, in case the said Legislature shall see fit to grant to his Majesty a civil list. . . .

Ibid., pp. 342–3.

THE VIEWS OF LATER COMMENTATORS

A Nationalist Interpretation of the Lower Canadian Reform Movement

According to Gérard Filteau the Reform Movement was essentially a struggle for national self-determination. It aimed to destroy a colonial regime that it believed was keeping the French Canadians in a permanent state of subordination.

Never did the Patriotes propose reforms just from a love of change, or in a spirit of opposition or simply to satisfy theories. They were neither democrats nor reformers nor liberals: they were first and foremost nationalists. What they wanted was not the overthrow of existing institutions but simply their employment in the interests of the masses, according to the spirit that had erected them. . . .

The law of 1791 [the Constitutional Act] had the clearly proclaimed purpose of perpetuating French-Canadian national life. With rigorous logic the Patriotes wanted to put into practice that principle and develop it to its fullest extent: the formation within the body of the Empire of a French state endowed with all the freedoms—political, intellectual, and material—necessary for its life and compatible with the maintenance of allegiance to Britain. On the strength of the constitution of 1791 they postulated as an essential plank of their programme: Canadians ought to be masters of their own destiny, masters of their own Parliament, masters of their own affairs, masters of their legislation, masters of the natural resources of the country won by their ancestors. . . .

G. Filteau, *Histoire des Patriotes* (Montreal, 1938–9), Vol. I, p. 159 (translation).

An Economic Interpretation of the Reform Movement

Donald G. Creighton's view of the Reform Movement in Lower Canada differs considerably from Filteau's. According to Creighton, the causes of the quarrel lay in the different economic interests of the French and the English.

The quarrel had its origin in the rivalry of agriculture and commerce. It was continued and exasperated by the economic revolution which was gradually accentuating the social divisions of the country. Even in Lower Canada . . . the evidences of the new economy were conspicuous and unavoidable. In Quebec and Montreal, which were the nerve centres of the Canadian commercial system, lived a strong mercantile minority determined to break through all opposition and to realize the possibilities of the new age. The new settlements in the Eastern Townships, 5,000 strong according to the conservative estimate of Governor Milnes, were infected with the energy and initiative characteristic of the typical American frontier community.

*   *   *   *   *

The essential grievances of the merchants and their supporters can be seen clearly in the body of criticism which they began . . . to direct against French-Canadian culture. It was not the different religion or the different language of the French which exasperated the merchants . . . what goaded them to fury was the Canadians' lack of enterprise, their persistent failure to move with the swiftly moving times . . . To the commercial group, the chief sin of this spineless and unadventurous generation was its complete failure to conquer and exploit the country in the approved American way. As a settler and colonizer, the French-Canadian was despised.

To a very large extent, therefore—and the contestants were quite conscious of the fact—it was a battle between the new commercialism and the stiffened feudalism of the St. Lawrence. . . .

D. G. Creighton, *The Empire of the St. Lawrence, 1760–1850* (Toronto, 1956), pp. 157, 159. [First published in 1937 as *The Commercial Empire of the St. Lawrence.*]

A New Look at Unrest in Lower Canada

Unlike Filteau and Creighton, W. H. Parker, a geographer, emphasizes the internal problems of French-Canadian society as chiefly responsible for the Reform Movement and the uprising of 1837. According to Parker, these problems were the failure of wheat as a staple crop and the graduation from the classical colleges of a larger number of educated men than the country could absorb.

It may therefore be concluded that, by 1837, severe inroads had been made upon the traditional well-being of the French Canadian peasant, and that the main causes of this sharp deterioration in his condition were the failure of wheat as the staple crop and chief source of wealth, and the pressure of population upon the land, resulting in an excessive subdivision of holdings. Trying to support his large family on a smaller farm with reduced yields, yet still rendering the same tithes, and confronted with a seigneur who was no longer the friend and counsellor of earlier days but often an exacting alien, the habitant might be reduced to a misery which made him the easy prey of politicians. . . . It was . . . for the social and economic reasons adduced above that the habitants were willing to listen to agitators and ready to send fewer moderates and more extremists to the Assembly. The members were sometimes seigneurs, but more often professional and business men from the local villages, fired with zeal and devoted to Papineau. Dalhousie complained in 1828 that the new assembly was "a thousand degrees worse than the last—the lowest dregs of society, village surgeons, butchers, tavern keepers, and such. . . . I cannot give them my usual public dinner."

The village doctors, lawyers, butchers and innkeepers were not mere political opportunists preying upon the peasants' discontents; they had grievances of their own and had themselves developed a fierce hatred of the British that no concessions could appease. This resulted, in part, from the educational system. . . . Every year the Catholic colleges turned out two or three hundred men; almost all of them were the children of habitants selected by the village priest for their precocity. After leaving college they returned to their villages where, their education having unfitted them for agriculture which they now despised, they became *curés*, *avocats*, *notaires*, and *médecins*. But since there were too many of them to make a good living, their discontent dwelt upon the British office-holders whose places they coveted. Prominent among the grievances urged in the Ninety Two Resolutions . . . were the fewness and relative insignificance of the offices held by French Canadians.

> W. H. Parker, "A New Look at Unrest in Lower Canada in the 1830's",
> *Canadian Historical Review*, XL (September 1959), pp. 215–16.

The Question of American Influences on the Reform Movements

As proponents of "loyalism", colonial conservatives such as R. B. Sullivan (pp. 125 and 126) were ready to see every Reform complaint as proof of insidious American republican influences working to destroy the British connection. Gerald Craig suggests that the political unrest was really based on local conditions and reinforced by contemporary British and American politically liberal ideas.

. . . Like all the Tories in Upper Canada, Sullivan believed that the agitation of the Reformers had been inspired by a desire to destroy British government in the province, and replace it with republican institutions. Although this analysis of Sullivan's was far too simple, especially in its failure to see that the radical programme in Upper Canada had its deepest roots in local grievances and that much of its inspiration had derived from the contemporary reform movement in Britain, yet he had seen with great clarity a phase of the subject that has only recently received its fair share of attention from historians.

In one sense the peak of American influence in Upper Canada had already passed by the eighteen-twenties, since ties of population with the nearby states were far less close than they had been before the War of 1812. Furthermore, the growth of national feeling, both in the republic and in the province, the changing direction of the continental westward movement, the effect of the Erie Canal in depriving the St. Lawrence of the western trade—all helped to set off Upper Canada from the American community. On the other hand, the impact of the tremendous growth and expanding prosperity of the neighbouring states, and the contagious example of their democratic experiments, had an increasing effect after 1815 in determining the nature of the reform movement in Upper Canada. This province, as a small, predominantly rural community, with little intellectual life, was far less touched by British and European reform movements than it was by the developments taking place on its own doorstep. The American states of the Jacksonian period appeared to the Upper Canadians not as subordinate units of a vast centralized nation but as free, self-governing communities, grappling, on the whole successfully, with many of the problems facing their own province. The reform movement, as it gained strength in Upper Canada in the eighteen-thirties, depended heavily on the old American population that had entered the province during the previous generation, and received much inspiration and stimulus from the activities of democrats south of the lakes. The impetus motivating the Reformers was no narrowly conceived demand for a changed relationship of executive and legislature, but was rather a genuine democratic ferment, involving widespread discussion of a great variety of political and economic issues, a debate which crystallized the demand for self-government in the province.

> G. M. Craig, "The American Impact on the Upper Canadian Reform Movement before 1837", *Canadian Historical Review* XXIX (December 1948), pp. 333–4

The Clergy Reserves — Cause or Excuse for Unrest?

How much of the Upper Canadian opposition to the Clergy Reserves resulted from genuine economic difficulties caused by land policies? How much of it was simply a reflection of the popular dislike of religious privileges for a minority? Alan Wilson feels that the plan to support religion with land endowments was a reasonable developmental policy, that the Clergy Reserves did not impede economic development of the colony, and that the opposition to the existence of the Reserves stemmed from the secular and egalitarian spirit of North American society.

Undoubtedly, the Crown and Clergy Reserves assumed too large a proportion of the lands of a frontier province. Conflicts with other land schemes—private and public—were inevitable in view of the widespread speculation in lands. The ground plan of the Reserves might have been improved, but extensive changes in the current practices of private and governmental speculation would have remained necessary. Moreover, imperial interference would have to have been curtailed.

Despite serious and usually successful efforts to accommodate the Clergy Reserves to public needs for better communication and more intensified settlement, the government could not avoid censure or blunders. Private injury was perhaps slight. The worst abuse was certainly the sometimes heavy concentration of Reserves in back concessions, to which front reservations had been reassigned to facilitate prior development of the front.

Administrative weaknesses existed, but after 1830 they were being persistently attacked. By that decade, the advent of sales and the further progress of some areas in the secondary stage of their development relieved some of the worst pressures resulting partially from the Reserves and like lands. Indeed, R. B. Sullivan's report of March, 1837, suggests that the Reserves had become an effective instrument in furthering new settlement and in improving old.

The chief weakness of the Reserves system as an experiment in land endowment for a public object lay in the purpose to which they were devoted and in the failure to re-examine that purpose responsibly. The Clergy Reserves became the symbolic centre of a bitter politico-religious controversy. In several ways, the administration of the Reserves had kept abreast of the movement for Responsible Government, particularly as it affected the public service and administrative improvement. During two-thirds of the period of public controversy, the administration of the Reserves showed signs of steady improvement, even of public usefulness. The last period of their history, following the Sydenham régime, saw the virtual end of all but sectarian and secular arguments against them. These, however, were enough to bring an experiment of some merit to an end.

Alan Wilson, "The Clergy Reserves: 'Economical Mischiefs' or Sectarian Issue?", *Canadian Historical Review*, XLII (December 1961), p. 299.

British Responsibility for the Canadian Rebellions

Was the British Colonial Office really indifferent to the problems of the dependencies? Was it in fact unsympathetic to the aims of the Reform movements? Helen Taft Manning, an American expert on British imperial history, examines the popular opinion that the rebellions were caused by colonial frustrations with the conservative policies of the Colonial Office. She concludes that the Colonial Office was anxious to meet the desires of the colonists, but that its progressive policies were hampered as much by the bickering and the unco-operative attitude of the colonists themselves as by the constitutional limitations existing in Britain.

Although the Whigs certainly had no coherent plan of procedure, they did have firmly held principles. They really believed in giving the colonists control over their own internal affairs, and had the colonial assemblies been able to agree as to the form of self-government they wanted, they would probably have got it between 1835 and 1837.

*   *   *   *   *

The work of the Whig ministers during their first term of office may be described as exploratory and tentative, as far as the North American colonies were concerned, rather than decisive. It is easy to condemn them as faint-hearted reformers, subject to pressure from the die-hard reactionaries in colonial capitals, and to accept Mackenzie's verdict that the forces of reaction within the walls of the Colonial Office itself were still powerful. . . . It was the increasing bitterness of party strife in all four provinces after 1832 which rendered the later acts of the drama inevitable, and the existence of a reforming ministry in England was to a large extent responsible for the growing political consciousness that lay behind the party politics. When the Whigs returned to office in 1835 the situation overseas had passed beyond the control of conservative governors and councils, and the need for decisive measures was recognized.

*   *   *   *   *

. . . [The Colonial Office was] moving in a tentative way toward the goal of embryo cabinets which would be chosen and dismissed by governors as the political situation in the colony changed. It is too often forgotten that this was about as far as the ministers of the Crown in England could go at this time in the direction of "responsible government," without giving to colonial assemblies more power than was claimed by the House of Commons in England, and that the later steps had to be taken by the governors-general and the lieutenant-governors acting as the King's representatives. . . . it needs to be emphasized that the constitutional objections to conferring responsible government by any form of public pronouncement were fully as serious as the practical ones.

* * * * *

The British Government must bear a major part of the blame for permitting a situation to arise in North America in which the antagonism between racial, economic, and religious groups could reach such a white heat; and it was perhaps the most solid contribution of Whig ministers in the years under discussion that they undid some of the harm which was the result of the blind favouritism of earlier administrations, and laid a better foundation for the united efforts of the colonists in the forties. But it has been the purpose of this article to show that their aims after 1835 went beyond the mere redress of grievances, and that their failure to reach satisfactory settlements with the representatives of the colonists, at least in Nova Scotia and Upper Canada, was due to their ignorance of local political conditions and their lack of trustworthy emissaries far more than to any unwillingness on their part to make further concessions.

Helen Taft Manning, "The Colonial Policy of the Whig Ministers, 1830-37", *Canadian Historical Review*, XXXIII (September, December, 1952), pp. 203, 235-6, 355, 368.

Further Reading

The background of the revolts in the two Canadas is examined in two scholarly volumes, *Political Unrest in Upper Canada, 1815–1836* by Aileen Dunham (reprinted, Carleton Library No. 10, Toronto, McClelland & Stewart, 1963)* and *The Revolt of French Canada, 1800–1835* by Helen Taft Manning (Toronto, Macmillan, 1962). J. S. Moir, *Church and State in Canada, 1627–1867: Basic Documents* (Carleton Library No. 33, Toronto, McClelland & Stewart, 1967)* covers the religious controversy. C. B. Sissons, *Life and Letters of Egerton Ryerson*, Vol. 1 (Toronto, Clarke, Irwin, 1937) and Goldwin French, *Parsons & Politics* (Toronto, Ryerson, 1962), describe the Methodists' role. A modern interpretive biography of Mackenzie is *The Firebrand* by William Kilbourn (reprinted, Toronto, Clarke, Irwin, 1964)*. In "The Decided Policy of William Lyon Mackenzie", *Canadian Historical Review*, XL (September 1959), Lillian F. Gates argues that Mackenzie was more concerned about the quality of political leadership than about the form of political institutions. Fernand Ouellet's *Louis Joseph Papineau, A Divided Soul* (Canadian Historical Association Booklet No. 11) emphasizes Papineau's nationalism as being more important than his reformism. D. G. Creighton, "The Struggle for Financial Control in Lower Canada, 1818–1831", *Canadian Historical Review*, XII (March 1931), examines the conflicting economic aims of the agricultural and mercantile interests. J. J. Talman, "The Position of the Church of England in Upper Canada, 1791–1840", *Canadian Historical Review*, XV (December 1934), discusses Anglican privileges as opposed to church establishment. In the same issue of that quarterly A. H. Young, in "A Fallacy in Canadian History", asserts that the Church of England was never established in the Canadas. The Reform Movement in the Maritimes, omitted from this Problem because of space limitations, is discussed in J. S. Martell, "Some Editorial Opinions from the Newspapers of the Maritime Provinces in the 1830's", *Canadian Historical Review*, XIX (March 1938), and is documented for Nova Scotia in Murray Beck's *Joseph Howe: Voice of Nova Scotia* (Carleton Library No. 20, Toronto, McClelland & Stewart, 1964)*.

Problem 9

Responsible Government — Political Principle
or Political Patronage?

Some historians have suggested that the failure of the Rebellions in 1837 and the consequent reaction robbed Canada of a viable political radical tradition for all time and substituted for it a Whiggish tradition of colourless, middle-of-the-road moderation. This interpretation may be an oversimplification of Canada's complex political development, but it cannot be denied that the rebellions immediately stultified the evolutionary reform movement that was trying to solve the problem of combining colonial self-government with British constitutional practice as an alternative to adopting the American elective principle. Yet almost exactly a decade after the rebellions, the solution had been reached with the introduction of the cabinet system through the practice of colonial responsible government in Canada and Nova Scotia. Self-government in dependencies had been combined with imperial sovereignty, and the key to the evolution of the modern British Commonwealth had been found.

The method was deceptively simple—colonial executive councils were accepted as constituting cabinets in the parliamentary sense, with full control over *purely colonial matters*. Purely colonial matters were understood to exclude defence, and foreign relations both political and economic. Such a division of sovereignty between colony and mother country was a division based on a gentlemen's agreement that each would respect the sphere of the other. Inevitably such an artificial division could not be maintained—sovereignty in local matters gradually grew into sovereignty in the fullest sense, and a commonwealth of nations was then possible.

Such has been the historic result of responsible government in the colonies. But was this the expectation of its advocates? What did colonial Reformers mean by "responsible government"? Did they agree on a definition? Did they correctly interpret Lord Durham's idea of responsible government? Did French-Canadian Reformers seek responsible government for the same reasons as English-speaking Reformers? And what was the reaction of imperial statesmen to this novel doctrine?

An examination of the opinions of the three colonials most prominently connected with the achievement of responsible government in British North America—Robert Baldwin, Louis Hippolyte Lafontaine, and Joseph Howe—suggests wide divergencies in their motives but not in their understanding of the problem of dividing sovereignty. As for imperial governmental reaction, there is an unbridgeable gap in logic between, on the one hand, Russell, Lord Sydenham, Stanley, and Metcalfe, who denied the constitutional possibility of responsible government, and the *apparent* advocacy of responsible government by Lord Durham and its acceptance by Lord Elgin and Grey. How could Elgin and Grey in 1847 and 1848 have rationalized a practice that had seemed a logical impossibility for their predecessors during the previous decade?

Because of the limitation of space, the following documents are concerned primarily with the Province of Canada. There the meaning of responsible government was more widely and hotly debated than in Nova Scotia, where Joseph Howe's incisive exposition of the principle combined with the absence of the "race" question to simplify the responsible government issue to a question of implementation.

Lord Durham and Responsible Government

Lord Durham never used the term "responsible government" in his famous *Report*, but the following passages were seized upon by colonial Reformers as an exposition and justification of their own objectives.

. . . It needs no change in the principles of government, no invention of a new constitutional theory, to supply the remedy which would, in my opinion, completely remove the existing political disorders. It needs but to follow out consistently the principles of the British constitution, and introduce into the Government of these great Colonies those wise provisions, by which alone the working of the representative system can in any country be rendered harmonious and efficient. . . . I would not impair a single prerogative of the Crown. But the Crown must, on the other hand, submit to the necessary consequences of representative institutions; and if it has to carry on the Government in unison with a representative body, it must consent to carry it on by means of those in whom that representative body has confidence. . . . Every purpose of popular control might be combined with every advantage of vesting the immediate choice of advisers in the Crown, were the Colonial Governor to be instructed to secure the co-operation of the Assembly in his policy, by entrusting its administration to such men as could command a majority; and if he were given to understand that he need count on no aid from home in any difference with the Assembly, that should not directly involve the relations between the mother country and the Colony. This change might be effected by a single dispatch containing such instructions . . . Perfectly aware of the value of our colonial possessions, and strongly impressed with the necessity of maintaining our connexion with them, I know not in what respect it can be desirable that we should interfere with their internal legislation in matters which do not affect their relations with the mother country. The matters, which so concern us, are very few. The constitution of the form of government,—the regulation of foreign relations, and of trade with the mother country, the other British Colonies, and foreign nations,—and the disposal of the public lands, are the only points on which the mother country requires a control.

C. P. Lucas, ed., *Lord Durham's Report on the Affairs of British North America*
(Oxford, 1912), Vol. II, pp. 277–82.

Joseph Howe on Responsible Government

Nova Scotia had suffered no rebellion, and this undoubtedly facilitated Joseph Howe's efforts in his open letters to Colonial Secretary Lord John Russell to show that loyalty and responsible government were compatible in a colony.

I have ever held . . . that the population of British North America are sincerely attached to the present State; that they are proud of their origin, deeply interested in the integrity of the Empire and not anxious for the establishment of any other form of government here than that which you enjoy at home. . . . Why should we desire a severance of old ties that are more honourable than any new ones we can form? Why should we covet institutions more perfect than those which have worked so well and produced such admirable results?

*   *   *   *   *

The principle of responsibility to the popular branch must be introduced into all the colonies without delay. It is the only simple and safe remedy for an inveterate and very common disease. It is mere mockery to tell us that the Governor himself is responsible. He must carry on the government by and with the few officials whom he finds in possession when he arrives. He may flutter and struggle in the net, as some well-meaning Governors have done, but he must at last resign himself to his fate; and like a snared bird be content with the narrow limits assigned him by his keepers.

The Novascotian, 10 October 1839, quoted in Murray Beck, ed., *Joseph Howe: Voice of Nova Scotia* (Toronto, 1964. The Carleton Library), pp. 75–6.

Lord John Russell's Advice

When he sent Poulett Thomson (later Lord Sydenham) as Governor-General of British North America to execute policies based on Durham's recommendations, Lord John Russell warned him to beware of the pitfall of responsible government. He particularly warned Thomson of the basic problem facing any governor—the possibility that colonial councillors might want to implement policies that the imperial government had forbidden in the name of the Queen.

It appears from Sir George Arthur's despatches that you may encounter much difficulty in subduing the excitement which prevails on the question of what is called "Responsible Government." I have to instruct you, however, to refuse any explanation which may be construed to imply an acquiescence in the petitions and addresses upon this subject. . . . The Crown and the two houses of Lords and Commons having thus decisively pronounced a judgment upon the question, you will consider yourself precluded from entertaining any proposition on the subject. . . .

It may happen, therefore, that the Governor receives at one and the same time instructions from the Queen, and advice from his executive council, totally at variance with each other. If he is to obey his instructions from England, the parallel of constitutional responsibility entirely fails; if, on the other hand, he is to follow the advice of his council, he is no longer a subordinate officer, but an independent sovereign. . . .

While I thus see insuperable objections to the adoption of the principle as it has been stated, I see little or none to the practical views of colonial government recommended by Lord Durham, as I understand them.

Lord John Russell to Poulett Thomson, 14 October 1839
W. P. M. Kennedy, ed., *Statutes, Treaties and Documents of the Canadian Constitution, 1713–1929* (Toronto, 1930), pp. 421–2.

Tenure of Office

Two days after penning the above directions, Russell advised Thomson that as a result of developments in Australia the tenure of office in colonial administrations would be changed. Russell was unaware that this simple decision opened the way for the implementation of cabinet government in the colonies, but in Nova Scotia Joseph Howe saw clearly and immediately its implications. Henceforth, a simple vote of non-confidence could be used to force a governor to dismiss an unpopular minister or ministry.

You will understand, and will cause it to be made generally known, that hereafter the tenure of colonial offices held during Her Majesty's pleasure, will not be regarded as equivalent to a tenure during good behaviour; but that not only will such officers be called upon to retire from the public service as often as any sufficient motives of public policy may suggest the expediency of that measure, but that a change in the person of the governor will be considered as a sufficient reason for any alterations which his successor may deem it expedient to make in the list of public functionaries, subject of course to the future confirmation of the sovereign.

Russell to Thomson, 16 October 1839
Ibid., p. 423.

Lord Sydenham's Opinion

Thomson had no doubts in his own mind as to the meaning of responsible government or of the steps required to stop colonial agitation about the question.

... I am not a bit afraid of the responsible government cry. I have already done much to put it down in its inadmissible sense; namely, the demand that the council shall be responsible to the assembly, and that the governor shall take their advice, and be bound by it. In fact, this demand has been made much more *for* the people than *by* them. And I have not met with anyone who has not at once admitted the absurdity of claiming to put the council over the head of the governor. It is but fair, too, to say that every thing has in past times been done by the different governors to excite the feelings of the people on this question. First, the executive council has generally been composed of the persons most obnoxious to the majority of the assembly. And next, the governor has taken extreme care to make every act of his own go forth to the public *on the responsibility* of the executive council. So the people have been carefully taught to believe that the governor is nobody, and the executive council the real power, and that by the governor himself. At the same time they have seen that power placed in the hands of their opponents. Under such a system it is not to be wondered at if our argument founded on the responsibility of the governor to the home government falls to the ground. I have told the people plainly that, as I cannot get rid of my responsibility to the home government, I will place no responsibility on the council; that they are *a council* for the governor to consult, but no more. And I have yet met with no "responsible government" man who was not satisfied with the doctrine. In fact there is no other theory which has common sense. Either the governor is the sovereign or the minister.

> Thomson to an unnamed friend, 12 December 1839
> *Ibid.*, p. 430.

Francis Hincks Begins to Build a New Party

In April 1839, when reunion of the two Canadas seemed certain, the Upper Canadian Reformer, Francis Hincks, initiated a correspondence with L. H. Lafontaine, the Lower Canadian Reform leader, with a view to co-operation by their two parties in the united legislature.

You may depend that the Reformers of U.C. will in the United Legislature act towards you & your friends in *perfect good faith.* . . . Rely upon it, when we come to meet in Parliament *we will give you full satisfaction.* You must see the advantage of getting a Reform Majority in this Province as well as in yours so as to silence all cavilling on the score of national origins. I feel assured we shall have such, and by a little good management we shall get good men and true. . . . I observe what you say about the use of the French language in the proceedings of the Legislature. You do me and my friends no more than Justice when you express your conviction that we do not participate in the illiberal sentiments expressed by the Tories of both provinces. I am not prepared to say what course it may be desirable to adopt on the subject of the language. It will be difficult to get the Union bill repealed but not impracticable. You are of course aware that no obstacle exists *as to your speaking* French in the Legislature. . . . I feel assured however *that the desire of all my friends will be to meet your wishes in this as well as all other points and to act towards you with perfect sincerity and good faith.* Our object is similar. Why should we dispute on minor points? You must recollect that if *we as a party* had identified ourselves *prematurely* with your party in L.C. we would only have afforded a pretext to the Tories to make greater infringements on our liberties & God knows they have done enough. . . . I have already told you that I have always supported the Union without *reference to details* because *by it alone* I felt convinced we would have a majority *that would make our tyrants succumb.*

After what has taken place your countrymen would never obtain their rights in a Lower Canadian Legislature. You want our help as much as we do yours.

F. Hincks to L. H. Lafontaine, 17 June 1840
Public Archives of Canada [PAC], Lafontaine Papers,
Vol. 2, pp. 280–2.

Lafontaine Explains His Position

Lafontaine was convinced by Hincks that the union, intended to anglicize French Canada, could instead be used to preserve the French-Canadian way of life if responsible government were gained. Standing vainly for election in Terrebonne county, Lafontaine explained his policies to the voters.

But the means of obtaining this political liberty so essential to the peace and happiness of these colonies and to the development of their vast resources? . . . it is in a word the great question of the day: responsible government such as has been confessed and promised to the Assembly of Upper Canada to gain its consent for the principle of union, and not such perhaps as it is now explained in a certain quarter. . . .

The Reformers in the two provinces form an immense majority. There are those of Upper Canada, or at least their Representatives who have accepted the responsibility for the Union Act, and for all its unjust and tyrannical provisions, by leaving the decision for all the details to the discretion of the Governor General. They did not know, they could not have approved the treatment that that Act metes out to the residents of Lower Canada. . . . Nevertheless our cause is the same. It is in the interests of the Reformers of the two provinces to join on the floor of the Legislature, in a spirit of peace, of union, of friendship and brotherhood. Unity of action is more than ever necessary. . . .

Lafontaine to the Electors of Terrebonne County, 25 August 1840
M. Brunet, G. Frégault, M. Trudel, eds., *Histoire du Canada par les Textes*
(Montreal, 1952), pp. 168–9 (translation).

Definitions and Counter-Definitions

After accepting office under Lord Sydenham in 1840, Baldwin resigned in 1841 when Sydenham refused to dismiss conservative councillors, and introduced in the first parliamentary session a series of resolutions on responsible government. Sydenham countered with amendments (introduced by S. B. Harrison but probably

composed by Sydenham) that were deceptively similar to Baldwin's
but in fact obscured the basic issue of responsibility.

Baldwin's Resolutions

4. . . . advisers of the representative of the Sovereign, and constituting as
such the Provincial administration under him as the head of the Provincial
Government, ought always to be men possessed of the public confidence,
whose *opinions and policy harmonizing with those of the representatives of the
people*, would afford a guarantee that the well understood wishes and interests
of the people, which Our Gracious Sovereign has declared shall be the rule of
the Provincial Government, will at all times be faithfully represented to the
head of that Government, and through him to the Sovereign and Imperial
Parliament.
5. That as it is practically always optional with such advisers to continue in
or retire from office at pleasure, this House has the constitutional right of
holding such advisers politically responsible for every act of the Provincial
Government of a local character, sanctioned by such Government while such
advisers continue in office. . . .

Harrison's Amendments

3. . . . the chief advisers of the representative of the Sovereign, constituting a
Provincial administration under him, ought to be men possessed of the confidence of the representatives of the people, thus affording a guarantee that
the well understood wishes and interests of the people, which our Gracious
Sovereign has declared shall be the rule of the Provincial Government, will, on
all occasions, be faithfully represented and advocated.

> Resolutions of the Legislative Assembly of Canada, September 1841
> [italics added by editor].
> Kennedy, ed., *Statutes, Treaties and Documents* . . . , p. 458.

The Colonial Office Supports Minority Government

Lord Sydenham, the manager of men, died suddenly in 1841,
convinced that he had scotched Baldwin and Baldwin's interpretation of responsible government. His successor, the diplomat Sir
Charles Bagot, inherited Sydenham's "system", but soon found
difficulty in governing without any support from Lafontaine's
majority in Lower Canada. William Henry Draper, Attorney-
General and foremost member of the government, offered his own
resignation as a possible way to bring Lafontaine into the government, but Lord Stanley, the Colonial Secretary in the new Tory

cabinet in Britain, virtually ordered Bagot to make no concessions to the French bloc.

> . . . I can see all the temptation held out by the plan in the way of personal ease and comfort in carrying on your Government, yet I cannot think that it ought to be adopted—not adopted, that is, until all other means have been tried, and until it is manifest to this Country and manifest to the Conservatives, and the supporters of British influence in Canada generally, that you cannot carry on the Government without the French party, and that you can carry it on through & by them. Do not mistake me. When I say the French party, I mean that party conducted by its present Leaders, and headed by men more or less implicated in the late Rebellion. You may ultimately be *forced* to take these men; but do not take them till the World shall see that you are so forced; and my hope and belief is that that necessity will never arise.

Lord Stanley to Sir Charles Bagot, 1 September 1842
Ibid., p. 472.

Bagot's "Great Measure"

Stanley's advice to Bagot arrived too late. Lafontaine had already been taken into the government, along with Baldwin at Lafontaine's insistence.

> . . . I found however that I had no hope whatever of gaining the French party and people, who now seemed at my feet, unless I admitted him. I therefore consented to receive him upon the express understanding that he was to consider himself as brought in by the French Canadian party, admitted at their request, and for the sole purpose of enabling them to redeem their debt of gratitude to him. I declined to see him, or to have any communication with him, throughout the negotiation; he was of their nomination, and had no share in the construction of my Council, except so far as he might influence Mr. Lafontaine's opinion, of which I could be supposed to know nothing. . . . I was willing to make any reasonable sacrifice to gain the French Canadians, but none to propitiate Mr. Baldwin, still less to throw away the key stone of my policy, which was to admit the French as a part of, or an addition to my old Council, and not to reconstruct my Council with Mr. Baldwin and the French as the steeple of it.

Bagot to Stanley, 26 September 1842
Ibid., p. 480.

Metcalfe Attempts to Split the Alliance

Bagot died early in 1843. His successor, Sir Charles Metcalfe, who had served in the highest administrative posts in India, forecast a clash with his Reform advisers over their claim to control patronage as a prerequisite of office. Believing Sydenham's "system" was self-defeating and at the root of this continuing debate over the meaning of responsible government, Metcalfe provoked Lafontaine and Baldwin into resigning and later called an election on the responsible government issue in 1844, an election that produced only a slim majority for Metcalfe and his claim that no governor should be a "cypher" in the constitution. A year later, Metcalfe still faced the problem that had faced Bagot in 1842—inability to get any significant French-Canadian support. A new approach to Lafontaine was made by Draper through René Edouard Caron, Speaker of the Legislative Council, who believed that the alliance with Baldwin should be broken to ensure the French-Canadian majority a voice in government.

> I must tell you that I am of the opinion that the state that we are in now cannot last. Our party loses strength every day, we can no longer count on Upper Canada, the last Session showed us what we can expect from that quarter; we are sacrificed to Upper Canada, and it will be the same as long as we do not have anyone in the administration disposed to uphold our interests and capable of doing so. What we are offered is small enough, but it could be the beginning of something better.

> R. E. Caron to Lafontaine, 7 September 1845
> PAC, Lafontaine Papers, Vol. 6, p. 1150 (translation).

Lafontaine Refuses to Take Office Alone

The Union of 1841 had within a couple of years developed a dualistic or embryonic federal administration, with duplicate officials for the former Upper and Lower Canadas. Caron proposed this system as a basis for political action too, through double ministries and double majorities. In his reply to Draper's overtures Lafontaine accepted the principle of double majority and double ministry rule, yet rejected the offer of a coalition in which he believed the French Canadians would in fact be powerless. Like Caron, Lafontaine seemed to be asserting French-Canadian nationalism at the expense of responsible government.

> . . . in the circumstances of the country the majority of each Province should govern respectively in the sense that we attach to that idea—that is to say, that Upper Canada should be represented in the Administration of the day by

men possessing the confidence of the political party in that section of the province which has the majority in the House of Assembly, and that it should be the same for Lower Canada. . . . The present Administration, as far as regards U. C., is formed on this principle, but as regards L. C., its formation rests on an opposite principle. Why this distinction between the two sections of the Province? Is there not in this fact alone a manifestation of injustice, if not of oppression? . . . What is proposed to you is a repudiation of the principle of responsibility in so far as applies to Lower Canada. Since Mr. Draper admits that the Lower Canadian section of the ministry does not represent Lower Canada, why maintain it? Why, according to your principles, not form a new Administration for Lower Canada with the aid of some one constitutionally charged to do so? . . .

But it is said to you—We only wish to *join to us* some Canadians as French-Canadians. From that moment those who thus enter the Ministry enter it not in consequence of a constitutional right, not by the action of the opinion of their countrymen, but only by favour, by the good pleasure of a Governor. From that moment, as we learn by experience, they are without influence—they are no longer free agents; they are only instruments in the hands of the Governor, to do evil as to do good. . . . What such a state of things would bring us to, or rather what it would perpetuate, would be to accept office at any price. What French-Canadians should do above every thing is to remain united and to make themselves respected. They will thus make themselves respected in the Council, and will thence exercise the legitimate influence which is due to them, not when they are represented there only by the passive instruments of power, however numerous they may be, but when they shall be constitutionally represented there by a Lower Canadian Administration formed in harmony with principles which public opinion does not repudiate. . . . I arrive, then, at a conclusion regarding which you cannot misunderstand me. It is that, as regards the Administration, Lower Canada should have what is granted to Upper Canada—nothing more, but also nothing less. This is the sincere expression of my views. If I am mistaken, the error is mine.

Lafontaine to Caron, 10 September 1845
Sir Francis Hincks, *Reminiscences of His Public Life* (Montreal, 1884), pp. 150–3.

Baldwin Rejects the Double Majority Idea

Baldwin rejected the idea of double ministries and double majorities as inconsistent with party government, by which alone responsible government, as Baldwin conceived it, could be established. In the end, Lafontaine rejected the tempting offer of office, but the whole episode raised two basic questions—was the union in fact a federation, and if so how could responsible government be made to operate if such sectionalism was accepted as a political principle of action? For the historian, the documents also raise the question as to how far Lafontaine understood the meaning of responsible government.

. . . I fully concede that, assuming the principle of a double Cabinet to be supported by double majorities, you have put the matter upon the only footting [*sic*] upon which the formation of such, as I conceive it, anomalous political machine could be accomplished with any regard whatever even to the forms of Responsible Government. . . . But the principle itself is one that I conceive to be inadmissable and indeed wholly impracticable. I can well understand that in the practical work of legislation a certain deference should be paid to the Majorities from the respective sections of the Province in respect to such measures as are solely applicable to either. And that such measures should not be forced upon them against the decided opinion of a considerable majority of the representatives from such section. But this in my view of it is an entirely different principle from that of having a Double Cabinet the one half dependent for its existence on the confidence of the Representatives from Lower Canada and the others in the confidence of the Representatives from Upper Canada, which latter, I am satisfied, is essentially inconsistent with the basis upon which our political institutions not [*sic*] and one that in the end will prove in itself impracticable.

R. Baldwin to Lafontaine, 16 October 1845
PAC, Lafontaine Papers, Vol. 6, pp. 1215–16.

A New Governor and a New Approach

The arrival early in 1847 of the Earl of Elgin, Durham's son-in-law, as Governor-General produced another abortive attempt to win Lafontaine's separate support for the government. To Earl Grey, Colonial Secretary of the new Whig government and Lady Elgin's uncle, Lord Elgin stated his policy toward his council. Elgin was a Peelite—a practical politician who avoided theorizing—but this statement throws light on Elgin's understanding of the meaning of responsible government.

My course in these circumstances is I think clear & plain—It may be somewhat difficult to follow occasionally, but I feel no doubt as to the direction in which it lies. I give t[o] my Ministers all constitutional support frankly and without reserve, & the benefit of the best advice, such as it is, that I can afford them in their difficulties—In return for this, I expect that they will, in so far as it is possible for them to do so, carry out my views for the maintenance of the connexion with G^t Britain & the advancement of the interests of the Province. On this tacit understanding we have acted together harmoniously up to this time—Although I have never concealed from them that I intend to do nothing which may prevent me from working cordially with their opponents if they are forced upon me.

Lord Elgin to Earl Grey, 27 May 1847
Sir A. G. Doughty, ed., *The Elgin-Grey Papers, 1846–1852* (Ottawa, 1937), p. 46.

Lord Elgin's View of a Reform Government

The calling of a general election in December, 1847, coincided with the appointment of a Reform government in Nova Scotia. This government has been accepted by historians as the first responsible colonial government in the history of the Empire because it was composed exclusively from one party, assuming that previous conservative governments, such as Draper's, were coalitions. In Canada the elections returned a Reform majority and ensured a similar party government, yet Elgin did not consider this the beginning of responsible government. When, then, was responsible government granted, or won, in the colonies? Any answer depends on what is meant by responsible government.

The issue of our elections is no longer doubtful. Even in Upper Canada the Ministers have lost largely—and they have no chance whatsoever of maintaining themselves in the New Parliament— I do not think that they will even meet it, and in a few days I expect them to tender their resignations in a body.

I shall accept them, and at once address myself to the recognized leaders of the opposition La Fontaine Baldwin &c. How I shall get on with these Gentlemen remains to be seen. Looking to their antecedents and to the avowed sentiments of some of their supporters it is not improbable that I may have difficulties to encounter, but I trust that they will not prove insurmountable— One circumstance weighs on my mind in connexion with these changes— It is the position of M^[r] Daly. . . . He resigned a permanent office on the introduction of Responsible Government, at the request of the Governor for the time being— . . .

* * * * *

. . . with a certain class of the liberals of British origin, there exists a genuine preference for what they deem British or constitutional practise as opposed to Republicanism. Whether it will be possible to bring the views of these Gentlemen who look at our Institutions through an American medium into perfect harmony with those of British Statesmen sitting in Downing Street, may be doubtful— But there is obviously room for antagonism between those who hold that British Institutions, rightly interpreted, are the best in the World, and those who are pledged to prove that they are among the worst.—

Between these two political sections M. La Fontaine and his followers are now placed.— Circumstances, perhaps conviction, will induce them for the moment to take rank with the latter—

Elgin to Grey, 22 January 1848
Ibid., pp. 118–19.

Lord Grey Approves of Colonial Cabinet Government

Lord Grey, more than Lord Elgin, seemed to view the Canadian development as a point of departure, but also he seemed more concerned about possible extreme demands of the new ministers than about the abstract principle of responsible government. His comment to Lord Elgin is strikingly similar to Walter Bagehot's definition of the Crown's power fifteen years later in his *The English Constitution*—the right to be consulted, to advise, and to warn.

. . . I can have no doubt that you must accept such a Council as the newly elected Parl^t will support, & that however unwise as relates to the real interests of Canada their measures may be, they must be acquiesced in, until it shall pretty clearly appear that public opinion will support a resistance to them— There is no middle course between this line of policy, & that wh. involves in the last resort an appeal to Parl^t to over-rule the wishes of the Canadians, & this I agree with both Gladstone & Stanley in thinking impracticable— If we over-rule the Local Legislature we must be prepared to support our authority by force, & in the present state of the world & of Canada, he must in my opinion be an insane politician who w^d think of doing so— It does not however follow that you are by any means powerless if your advisers insist upon an improper course of proceeding the line to take is freely to place before them the objections to it, but to yield if they insist up to the point when they have put themselves so clearly in the wrong that public opinion will support you in resistance, . . .

Grey to Elgin, 22 February 1848
Ibid., p. 120.

Lafontaine Defends His Actions

At the beginning of the parliamentary session of 1849, Lafontaine's leadership of the French-Canadian Reformers was challenged publicly by the former rebel, L. J. Papineau, who accused Lafontaine of selling the interests of the French-Canadian nation for a mess of pottage called political office. Lafontaine's defence of his past policies throws another spotlight on the problem of why Lafontaine worked for the establishment of responsible government and his understanding of its meaning. One practical substantive answer to Papineau's accusations was the Rebellion Losses bill, a test of the good faith of Elgin and Grey regarding responsible government, and an excuse for violence on the part of frustrated Tory loyalists.

> ... Although as French Canadians we are in a minority position, our share of the representation [in Parliament] has been strong enough to allow us, even with the Act of Union, to make use of that instrument constructed to cause us harm, to make it produce a result exactly opposite to that intended by its author. ...
>
> It is by standing on the principle of recognizing in the Act of Union only a confederation of two provinces, as Upper Canada itself declared it to be in 1841, that I declare here emphatically that I will never consent to one of the sections of the province having in this House a greater number of members than the other does, regardless of the size of its population. To those who do not let themselves be blinded by their political feelings, it ought to be evident that before we are called upon to hold a new general election, Upper Canada will have a larger population than Lower Canada. And it is in the presence of this fact, the achievement of which is only too close, that the Honourable Member from St. Maurice County [Papineau] has just asked us to consecrate in fact and in law a principle that must place us forever in a position of inferiority and the adoption of which would be, more than that with which he charges us, a ratification, an irrevocable approval of that Act of Union which he pretends to condemn.
>
> Lafontaine, speech in the Legislative Assembly, 23 January 1849
Brunet, Frégault, Trudel, eds., *Histoire du Canada* ..., p. 181 (translation).

THE VIEWS OF LATER COMMENTATORS

The Traditional Meaning of Responsible Government

J. L. Morison, imperial historian and biographer of Lord Elgin, offers the traditional interpretation of the responsible government movement, an interpretation particularly popular with Canadian historians in the 1920's, when the country's leaders seemed obsessed by the idea of autonomy. To Morison and to Chester Martin, whose *Empire and Commonwealth* became the classic exposition in detail of the "responsible government to dominion status" theme, responsible government was the achievement of the single-minded Baldwin by his creation of a true political party, and of the wisdom of Elgin and Grey in accepting the inevitable with good grace. For this school of historians Sydenham appears as an evil genius and Metcalfe as a stubborn reactionary, neither of whom could or would try to fathom the meaning of responsible government as expounded by Baldwin.

It is now possible to summarize the movement towards autonomy so far as it was affected by the governors-general of the transition period.

The characteristic note in the earlier stages had been the domination of the governor-general's mind by a clear-cut theory—that of Lord John Russell. That theory was in itself consistent, and of a piece with the rest of the constitution; and its merits stood out more clearly because Canadian progressives had an unfortunate faculty for setting themselves in the wrong—making party really appear as faction, investing self-government with something of the menace of independence, and treating the responsibility they sought in the most irresponsible way. The British theory, too, as guaranteeing a definitely British predominance in Canada, brought into rather lurid relief the mistaken fervour of French-Canadian nationalism.

Yet Sydenham, who never consciously, or at least openly, surrendered one detail of the system entrusted to him by Russell, found events too much for him; and that which conquered Sydenham's resolution made short work of any resistance Bagot may have dreamed of offering. Metcalfe was wrong in suspecting a conscious intention in Sydenham's later measures, but he was absolutely right when he wrote, "Lord Sydenham, whether intending it or not, did concede Responsible Government practically, by the arrangements which he adopted, although the full extent of the concession was not so glaringly manifested during his administration as in that of his successor."

Canadian conditions were, in fact, evolving for themselves a new system— Home Rule with its limits and conditions left as vague as possible—and that new system contradicted the very postulates of Russell's doctrine. It was only when the system of Russell became incarnate in a governor, Lord Metcalfe, and when the opposing facts also took personal form in the La Fontaine-Baldwin ministry, that both in Canada and Britain men came to see that two contradictory policies faced each other, and that one or other alternative must be chosen. To Elgin fell the honour not merely of seeing the need to choose the Canadian alternative, but also of recognizing the conditions under which the new plan would bring a deeper loyalty, and a more lasting union with Britain, as well as political content to Canada.

J. L. Morison, *British Supremacy and Canadian Self-Government*
(Toronto, 1919), pp. 228–9.

The solid phalanx of French-Canadian Reformers under LaFontaine were the shock troops that won the most cherished of all Durham's recommendations. The ink was scarcely dry on the *Report* when Francis Hincks, the real architect of the party which won responsible government in Canada in 1848, opened a secret and confidential correspondence with LaFontaine designed to command a working majority in the legislature. The friendship which followed between Baldwin and LaFontaine was the sheet-anchor of the Reform cause. It was they who forced the Bagot incident in 1842; and when the Reformers were beaten in Canada West in 1844 LaFontaine had to find a constituency for Baldwin himself in Rimouski. It was LaFontaine in the greatest speech of his life and in the French language who carried the caucus of the Reform party against Papineau's bitter invective. It was LaFontaine to whom Elgin turned to form the first responsible ministry in the old province of Canada. . . . The long story of co-operation between Baldwin and LaFontaine, between Hincks himself and Morin, between Cartier and Macdonald is surely an ironical commentary upon Durham's prophecy: "never again will the present generation of French Canadians yield a loyal submission to a British Government." I should be inclined to say that the greatest achievement of the French race upon this continent was not before the conquest in 1763 but after it; not before but after the War of 1812; not before but after Lord Durham's *Report*.

Chester Martin, "Lord Durham's Report and Its Consequences",
Canadian Historical Review, XX (June 1939), pp. 185–6.

Principle or Patronage?

In a study that compares imperial and colonial practice in the matter of cabinet control of patronage, J. B. Brebner asserts that the Reformers were more intent on inaugurating the American "spoils" system than any British constitutional practice. Like Lord Metcalfe, the author ascribes Reform motives simply to a desire to monopolize the "fruits of office" for their own party.

Most of our Canadian histories treat the command of public offices as a mere symbol of the general principle of autonomy, whereas the reverse may well have been true. The mass of the unprivileged coveted the rewards of office, but they could only obtain those created by their own votes of funds or were pacified by mere crumbs from the rich man's table. Naturally they were quick to realize that to obtain the real prizes they must become masters of the executive. Joseph Howe was one of those who saw this most clearly and one sometimes wonders whether this frank and open realism on his part may not be one of the principal reasons why Canadian historians have tended to be rather coy and timid about describing him in the round, back as well as front.

*   *   *   *   *

Howe is valuable as a witness because he and Maritimers generally held themselves to be more British and more loyal than the turbulent French of Lower Canada and the Americanized British of Upper Canada. We should, therefore, perhaps be not too surprised to find Papineau, Mackenzie, Lafontaine, and Baldwin using the spoils system as the cornerstone of their constitutional edifices. After all, British governments and British governors had always primarily employed it against them and had been very frank about it too, as the records attest.

* * * * *

With Lafontaine and Baldwin we come to the men whose capacity to win majorities, and whose sheer stubbornness with governors who were aiming to play George III on them, won cabinet government for Canada just as the younger Pitt had won it for Great Britain sixty years before. Every serious student of Canadian history knows that the principle upon which they stood or fell, the yard-stick which they invariably used for victory or defeat in their quest, was control of the patronage.

* * * * *

Responsible government and patronage were indeed one matter, so inextricably amalgamated that they can seldom be found apart in the tangled party politics of 1841–47. Sir Allan MacNab said "that he would be damned if he would put any but friends into office if he was in power", and the Lafontaine-Baldwin alliance accepted or resigned office in accordance with governors' willingness or unwillingness to allow them to control dismissals and appointments. Metcalfe summed up the whole conflict as almost any Englishman would have seen it when he declared that it was not about any principle of government, but about the question as to whether "the patronage of the Crown should be surrendered to the Council for the purchase of Parliamentary support".

J. B. Brebner, "Patronage and Parliamentary Government", Canadian
Historical Association, *Report, 1938*, pp. 27, 28.

A Revisionist Interpretation

George Metcalf sees in the achievement of responsible government a more complex pattern of relationships than do the traditionalists, but he finds the key to Elgin's policy not in Canadian circumstances but in the accession to power in Britain of a Liberal government in 1846.

. . . If . . . the Canadians broke the British connection themselves—or as is much more likely, convinced the imperial government that the maintenance of the connection was no longer worth the effort—then the question would have been solved. Canada would have achieved self-government; but it would have taken the form of a right to send representatives to a Congress in Washington. For if Canada had cut the ties with Britain in the eighteen-forties, there can be no doubt that she would have ere long succumbed to either the blandishments or the force of her southern neighbour.

It was for all these reasons that it was so important that the irresistible force of the Reformers did not collide head on with the immovable object of Lord Metcalfe. Baldwin, of course, might claim sincerely that it was not the Reform principles at all, but the intransigent attitude of Metcalfe that endangered the connection. Indeed this attitude has been perpetuated by historians. Yet it ignores certain salient facts, particularly the stand of the imperial government. Metcalfe's only alternative to acting the way he did was the one—an inconceivable one for a man of the Governor's character—of deliberately disobeying the very clear and specific instructions of the Colonial Office. Stanley had sent Metcalfe to Canada under orders to conduct himself according to the principles contained in the despatch which Sir Charles Bagot had received too late to act upon—in other words the policy of extension, playing off all parties against each other. On the very day of the crisis with Baldwin and LaFontaine, Metcalfe had received from the Colonial Secretary a letter instructing him never, under any circumstances, to give up his power of bestowing patronage—the most powerful tool of a colonial governor. Historians have also been misled into blaming Metcalfe because of the fact that after the Governor's departure, Responsible Government was speedily realized. Yet the significant occurrence was not really Lord Metcalfe's resignation, but that the Conservative government in Britain had fallen and been replaced by an administration which was quite prepared to accept the new theory of colonial government.

George Metcalf, "Draper Conservatism and Responsible Government in the Canadas, 1836–1847", *Canadian Historical Review*, XLII (December 1961), pp. 323–4.

Survival or Separatism — The Meaning of Responsible Government for French Canada

Maurice Séguin of the Université de Montréal is the historian who formulated the neo-nationalist interpretation of French-Canadian history which was later taken up by Guy Frégault and Michel Brunet. According to Séguin, responsible government did not substantially improve French Canada's political position. When this constitutional principle was finally conceded, French-Canadians had already become mere "lodgers" in a British "house".

If in 1840 English Canada, which comprised 55% of the population, had a majority hold in the government and, thanks to aid from Great Britain, alone had the necessary capital for industrialization, in brief, if English Canada overrode French Canada in all sectors, it was nevertheless impossible to assimilate the latter. Relations between the two nationalities were frozen to a standstill. The legislative union which carried with it concessions of a federal character towards the minority functioned spontaneously from 1841 as a federation. Since that date French Canadians survive, annexed and provincialized, in a great British North American empire.

This solution, which nobody could refuse, Lafontaine and his successors easily accepted. They even accepted it with a certain amount of enthusiasm as they found in it the application of federalist principles which, they considered, did not carry any major inconveniences. The capitulation of Vaudreuil had infallibly led to the capitulation of Lafontaine, a necessary and explainable capitulation, but a capitulation all the same. A whole people was forced to live and accepted to live as a minority under a foreign majority, without being able to measure the gravity of the situation.

The political history of French Canada can only be properly understood by taking into account this inevitable disaster, which was split into two phases, the first being the English colonization in 1760, the second being the consolidation of English power by the union of 1840. In search of independence, of separatism, French Canadians became annexed under the legislative union, and it is from that position that they slowly rose to an annexation less confining under a federal union which was highly centralized. The Federal Union of 1867 was only the legislative union of 1840 ameliorated as far as local concessions made to French Canadians but also consolidated in that which concerned British preponderance in the exercise of higher power.

> Maurice Séguin, "Origin and Historical Record of the Separatist Idea in French Canada", (three talks on the CBC programme "Conference", March-April 1962), reproduced by the Department of History of the University of Waterloo, 1964, p. 12, from a translation by Paul Franklin.

Further Reading

The achievement of responsible government in British North America has probably attracted the attention of more historians than any other topic in Canadian history. Of the many books and articles dealing with the issue only those most relevant can be mentioned here. *Letters from Lord Sydenham, Governor-General of Canada, 1839–1841* (London, Allen and Unwin, 1931) edited by Paul Knaplund, and G. P. de T. Glazebrook, *Sir Charles Bagot in Canada* (Oxford, Oxford University Press, 1929), give an inside view of British policy. W. G. Ormsby, "Sir Charles Metcalfe and the Canadian Union",

Canadian Historical Association, *Report, 1961*, shows the reasonableness of Metcalfe's position on responsible government. "The Civil List Question in the Province of Canada", *Canadian Historical Review*, XXXVI (June 1954), by the same author, examines an attempt of the imperial authorities to circumvent the demand for responsible government. Jacques Monet, "French Canadian Nationalism and the Challenge of Ultramontanism", Canadian Historical Association, *Report, 1966*, explains that Lafontaine's party were more concerned with the church-state problem in French Canada than with responsible government. W. S. McNutt, "The Coming of Responsible Government in New Brunswick", *Canadian Historical Review*, XXXIV (June 1952), covers the movement in that Maritime province while Murray Beck, *Joseph Howe: Voice of Nova Scotia* (Carleton Library No. 20, Toronto, McClelland & Stewart, 1964)* gives the essential documents from Nova Scotia, where responsible government was introduced first. Chester Martin's *Empire and Commonwealth* (Oxford, Clarendon Press, 1929) traces the theme of colonial responsible government in British North America to show its role in the evolution of the modern Commonwealth.

Problem 10

The Sources of Sectionalism — *Survivance*
or Thwarted Ambition?

The legislative union of 1841 was intended to solve the "Canadian Question" by providing Upper Canada with a seaport and financial stability, and by anglicizing Lower Canada through enforced assimilation. To achieve this last objective the larger population of Lower Canada was given only equal representation with Upper Canada, English became the only official language of government, and the capital was fixed at Kingston in Upper Canada (although the capital was removed to Montreal in 1844 and French was restored as an official language in 1848). In its first decade the Union seemed to be successful in allaying the problems of the two Canadas. The major political interest of that period was responsible government, apparently achieved in 1848 through the co-operation of French and English Reformers. But once responsible government was acknowledged in practice, the age of harmony ended and the United Province of Canada was torn politically, socially, religiously, and economically. French Canadian was pitted against English Canadian, Roman Catholic against Protestant, Lower Canada against Upper Canada. One element of potential conflict—language —seems, however, never to have been involved in these sectional difficulties. What were the causes of this ever-widening rupture of the Union along sectional lines? Was its appearance immediately after the auspicious beginnings of responsible government merely accidental? How was the sectional conflict related to the industrial, communications, and transport revolutions created at that very moment in Canada by the steam engine? Did responsible government itself contribute to the growth of sectionalism? Were these tensions the result of genuine and irreconcilable differences between two ways of life or only the product of temporary frustrations? If the former, what were the real causes—"race", religion, cultural inheritance, or economic disparity? If the latter, how much was due to factors external to the province, such as the imperial commercial revolution or the serious depression of the late 1850's that began in the United States? The escape from sectional conflict and political deadlock was ultimately sought in Confederation, but it remains a matter of debate whether Confederation fulfilled those expectations or simply projected central Canadian sectionalism on a transcontinental stage.

The Union of 1841 — A Solution to Sectionalism?

Even before the Union's inception Chief Justice John Beverley Robinson of Upper Canada prophesied that the balanced number of Roman Catholics and Protestants would create friction, that no scheme for representation could do justice to the disparate interests of the two colonies in a *mariage de convenance*, and that the United Province would be too large for efficient administration.

... If the French Canadians are not to be disfranchised, which they certainly ought not to be, and which it is not intended they shall be, their representatives must bear some very considerable proportion in the Assembly. . . . With nearly universal suffrage, in a colony situated as that is, is it reasonable to count upon such a majority as will render innocuous the hostile feelings which are represented as pervading the whole French population? . . . [If] the two provinces shall be united upon any principle of representation which Parliament could think of proposing, it would not be long, I fear, before the British Government would find that their difficulties had, at least, not been diminished by the measure. And a few years experience would probably serve to convince the people of Upper Canada that they had not done wisely in balancing uncertain hopes of revenue and trade against the certain and peaceful enjoyment of blessings which they well know how to appreciate, and which, under their present system, they will become every day more capable of preserving.

The loyal British population in Lower Canada might also be compelled to acknowledge, on their part, when the mischief had been done, that it was to no purpose they had shut their eyes against dangers which there was no reasonable hope of escaping; for they would probably see themselves as decidedly as ever under the dominion of a majority, from whose principles and proceedings they could have nothing to hope, but everything to fear.

*   *   *   *   *

Coming to a more particular statement of objections, there is one mischievous consequence which I believe would be certain to follow the union of the provinces, and which it would be difficult to discuss fully without the danger of being misapprehended, or misconstrued. And yet it is the very last consideration that should be overlooked.

The religious distinction between Catholic and Protestant has never hitherto occasioned animosity or contention in the Legislature of either province of Canada.

* * * * *

But if the inhabitants of both provinces are to be represented in one Assembly, I consider it to be altogether doubtful whether that Assembly, when it shall meet for the first time, would contain within its walls a greater number of Roman Catholics, or of Protestants.

If the ascendancy of the one over the other should be found to be fluctuating and uncertain, and to depend mainly upon the exertions that may be used at elections, then I venture to foretell, that from that cause alone will soon inevitably spring a contention more fatal to the happiness of both classes, and probably to the security of the country, than would be likely to arise from all other causes whatever.

J. B. Robinson, *Canada and the Canada Bill* (London, 1840), pp. 124–8.

The Fate of French Canada Under the Union

Unlike Upper Canada where the Legislature approved the Union principle, the lower province was forced into the Union while its constitution was suspended. Lord Durham's strictures on the French Canadians were a spur to F. X. Garneau to publish his history recording for the first time the drama and achievement of French Canada's past, a work that became the "national Bible" of the French Canadians. The following paragraphs, expressing Garneau's faith in the destiny and distinctiveness of the French-Canadian "nation", were added to the Preface of the second edition which appeared in 1852 and carried his history down to the time of the Union.

The destiny of Canada is dependent on the cause which we vindicate in this work; namely, the conservation of our religion, our language, and our laws. By holding to the creed and maintaining the nationality of our forefathers, we perhaps are opponents of British policy, which has placed the two Canadas under one government, in view of causing the disappearance of those three great features of Canadian existence; and it even may be, that in taking our stand upon the old ways, we incur the censure of such of our compatriots as wish to fall in with British views on this matter. In any case, we can conscientiously declare, that in whatever we have related, with or without comment, we have been actuated by no feelings of party hostility. We have only obeyed the impulses of our heart, by favouring a cause founded on all that is (or should be) sacred in the eyes of Christians and patriots.

We are quite alive to the consequences which may result from our firm attachment to repudiated sympathies. We know that in reproving the decrees of an all-potent metropolitan state, we may be denounced on one hand, as propagators of pernicious opinions; and on the other, regarded as the purblind votaries of a separate nationality, which had best become extinct. Not discouraged by such repudiations as the latter, we are consoled by the conviction that we play an honourable part; and although our Province should never attain that prosperity, or make that progress in material civilisation, which some parties think would result from an amalgamation of races, they must still respect the motives which impel us to pursue the even tenor of our way.

> F. X. Garneau, *History of Canada, from the Time of Its Discovery till the Union Year (1840–1)* translated by Andrew Bell (Montreal, 1860), Vol. I, pp. viii–ix.

Lord Elgin Opposes Assimilation

On the morrow of the accession of the Baldwin-Lafontaine ministry, Governor-General Lord Elgin reported to Lord Grey his conviction that the achievement of power and equality rendered the primary purpose of the Union—the anglicizing of the French Canadians—both impracticable and impolitic.

I am very anxious to hear that you have taken steps for the repeal of so much of the Act of Union as imposes restrictions on the use of the French language. The delay which has taken place in giving effect to the promise made, I think by Gladstone, on this subject, is one of the points of which M. Papineau is availing himself for purposes of agitation. I must moreover confess that I for one am deeply convinced of the impolicy of all such attempts to denationalize the French. Generally speaking they produce the opposite effect from that intended, causing the flame of national prejudice and animosity to burn more fiercely—But suppose them to be successful what w^d be the result? You may perhaps *americanise*, but, depend upon it, by methods of this description, you will never *anglicise* the French inhabitants of the Province.—. Let them feel on the other hand that their religion, their habits, their prepossessions, their prejudices if you will, are more considered and respected here than in other portions of this vast continent which is being overrun by the most reckless, self-sufficient and dictatorial section of the Anglo Saxon race, and who will venture

to say that the last hand which waves the British flag on American ground may
not be that of a French Canadian?

Lord Elgin to Earl Grey, 4 May 1848
Sir A. G. Doughty, ed., *The Elgin-Grey Papers, 1846–1852*
(Ottawa, 1937), pp. 149–50.

The Sources of English-Canadian Frustrations

As early as 1849 radical Reformers of Upper Canada had criticized the conservatism of the Great Ministry of Lafontaine and
Baldwin, and when both these leaders resigned in 1850 the coalition
of English and French Reformers began to dissolve. Independent
of these radical Clear Grits, George Brown, editor of the influential
Toronto *Globe*, expressed Upper Canadian frustration with the
Union after his involvement in the religious controversy over
"papal aggression" caused his defeat in a by-election in 1851.

On almost every issue the ministerialists were obliged to take up the defensive; they acknowledged that it would be well if such views could be carried
out—but they voted as if they thought the contrary, and palliate their incon-
sistency on the unworthy plea of expediency. It would have been desirable,
they admit, to have had a vote of the Assembly in favour of secularizing the
Reserves—but the French Canadians were opposed to it, and it was dangerous
to insist on it. It would have been well to apply the 550,000 acres at once to
educational purposes—but the French Canadians thought it best to await the
settlement of the whole Reserve question. It would have been well to prevent
new incumbents being placed on the pension-list—but the French Canadians
were in the way. The Rectories were better settled by Act of Parliament—but
the French Canadians are immoveable on this question, and absurd as the
Lawsuit is, it has been commenced and had better go on. The accumulation of
real estate in the hands of Clerical corporators is evil in the extreme—but the
French Priests are indignant on this point, and we dare not meddle with it.
The Jesuit College Bill was indefensible, and we voted against it on the second
reading—but you saw the storm our votes drew down on us from the French
papers, and we had all to *reverse them* on the third reading. The Three Rivers
Tax Bill was highly improper, but what could we do?—the French Canadians
demanded it. The sectarian clause of the Upper Canada School Bill is a great
evil—but the Roman Catholics demand Separate Schools; the French Hierarchy
of Lower Canada have taken up their cause—and what can we do? The division
of the University funds among the petty sectarian Colleges is wrong, truly;
but there has been extravagance in the management of the Institution. The
sectarian money grants annually voted, are vicious in principle, but how can

we cut them off, when they have existed so long? Population is the only true basis for Parliamentary Representation; but it would swamp the French Canadians, and they will never consent to it.

* * * * *

Such is the attitude of the Ministerialists on the proceedings of the late session. What limit can be set to this strain of argument? Disguise it as they will, the sum and substance of it is simply this "If the Reformers of Upper Canada insist on their views being carried out, it will cause a disruption between us and the French Canadians—we must in that case go out of office, and the Tories will come in; we are not so foolish as to do this, and therefore Upper Canada principles of Reform and Progress must stand in abeyance."

* * * * *

And in what a contemptible attitude does all this place the Reformers of Upper Canada! Does it not confess them the abject vassals of the French Canadian priesthood? Mark the long list of important reforms from which we are debarred by the *fiat* of Popery. And mark, too, the humiliating draughts we have been compelled to swallow under compulsion of the same power. What has French Canadianism been denied? Nothing. It bars all it dislikes—it extorts all it demands—and it grows insolent over its victories. And is this a state of things to delight the Reformers of Upper Canada? All this humiliation, all this sacrifice of principle, all this iniquitous legislation under the sanction of Western liberalism—for the noble consideration that "*the party*" is in office! Shame, shame on such degradation! I do not wonder that the well-tried Reformers of your neighbourhood seek some means of giving vent to the indignation that such things excite within them. I do not wonder that they long to see their leaders stand upright before the world, as they once did, bold in the confidence of truth, and scorning to barter principle for the miserable pageant of office without power.

But the Tories would come in, if we acted honestly—and they might remain in for ten years! And what if they did? It is our duty to act uprightly and leave consequences in higher hands. Shall we do evil that good may come? And such a good! —a base vassalage to French Canadian Priestcraft.

The Globe, 30 December 1852

A. T. Galt Proposes Escape in Federalism

If the two Canadas could not live together under one union roof, perhaps the political answer was semi-detached houses. A. T. Galt's resolutions, passed by the Assembly in 1858 with the tacit support of J. A. Macdonald's Liberal-Conservative government, offered a new solution—confederation—to reconcile sectionalism with interdependence.

1. That in view of the rapid development of the population and resources of Western Canada, irreconcilable difficulties present themselves to the maintenance of that equality which formed the basis of the Union of Upper and Lower Canada, and require this House to consider the means whereby the progress which has so happily characterized this province may not be arrested through the occurrence of sectional jealousies and dissensions. It is, therefore, the opinion of this House that the Union of Upper and Lower Canada should be changed from a Legislative to a Federative Union by the subdivision of the province into two or more divisions, each governing itself in local and sectional matters, with a general legislative government for subjects of national and common interest. . . .

> O. D. Skelton, *The Life and Times of Sir Alexander Tilloch Galt*
> (Toronto, 1920), pp. 219-20.

George Cartier Rejects "Rep by Pop"

In the mid-1850's, with political parties in a state of flux, a series of incidents underlined the growing strength of sectional animosities in the Union. The passing of a separate school Act for Upper Canada by a Lower Canadian majority, the miscarriage of justice after the murder of a Protestant, Robert Corrigan, by Roman Catholics, the long delay in getting French-Canadian support for secularization of the Clergy Reserves, the depression that fell more heavily on Upper than on Lower Canada—all were incidents of sectional conflict. For all these troubles the Upper Canadian radicals proposed a simple solution—representation by population, or "rep by pop"—a proposal rejected by French Canadians who, as a minority since being surpassed by the Upper Canadian population in 1851, now became the staunch defenders of Union.

The speech of the honourable member for Toronto (Mr. George Brown) can hardly be taken seriously. This member has spoken as if it were a question concerning only Upper Canada, whereas it concerns Lower Canada just as much as Upper Canada.

Representation based on population is unknown in the world. If one were going to decree it, it would be necessary to guarantee an absolute majority of the votes of the electorate. Is this practicable? . . .

*   *   *   *   *

Did Upper Canada conquer Lower Canada? If not, by virtue of what right can it ask for representation based on population in the aim of governing us? Everyone knows that the union of the two provinces was imposed on Lower Canada which did not want it at any price. But Lower Canada has carried out the Union loyally and sincerely with the determination of upholding it on the present basis.

Mr. M. H. FOLEY (Waterloo-North)—Yes, you make it work in your way; Lower Canada governs Upper Canada with the help of ministers who represent a minority of the section of the province to which they belong.

SEVERAL VOICES—Hear! Hear!

Mr. CARTIER—Say rather that the Upper Canadians demand representation based on population in the aim of dominating Lower Canada.

Mr. FOLEY—That is exactly what you do to Upper Canada.

Mr. CARTIER—I have indeed ascertained the aim of the Honourable member from Toronto in proposing representation based on population. He demands it with great clamour because he hopes thereby to produce for himself enough supporters to control Lower Canada. . . .

*   *   *   *   *

I don't oppose this measure from unjust design towards Upper Canada, but because I wish to fulfil loyally the Act of Union, which has been a great source of benefit for the two sections of the province. What would Upper Canada be without the Union? An exceedingly backward country, which would not be able to collect its customs duties. It has drawn many advantages from the Union. Lower Canada had saved its money and when this system was imposed on it, it saved Upper Canada from bankruptcy. . . .

> George Cartier, speech to the Legislative Assembly, 9 June 1858
> J. Tassé, ed., *Discours de Sir Georges Cartier* (Montreal, 1893),
> pp. 148–9, 151 (translation).

The "Double Majority" as an Alternative

A political compromise on the issue of representation was offered by John Sandfield Macdonald, leader of the small group of moderate Liberals, in the form of Lafontaine's old idea of the double majority. John A. Macdonald explained why the double majority was no more acceptable than "rep by pop" for the operation of responsible government within the framework of the Union Act. Oliver Mowat, in reply, denounced the tyranny of the minority.

. . . With reference to the Double Majority, he had to say he held the principles of Responsible Government; and he believed these principles were the only ones that could be successfully carried out. (Hear) He believed the Double Majority was opposed in every respect to the principles of Responsible Government and as such he would always vote against it. . . . His opinions were that they should govern the country by a government having the confidence of the majority of the representatives of the people in Parliament. (Hear)

An Administration was principally occupied in the discussion of a legislation of a provincial importance, equally applying to both sections of the country. The whole or nearly the whole of the measures of any great importance equally affected the east and the west. And the only way in which this country could be governed on constitutional principles was by a government who agreed on these great questions and had the confidence of the people to carry out their legislation. If it were conceded that an Administration should be divided into sections, each having local interests, one for the east and one for the west, constitutional government was at once destroyed. . . .

Mr. MOWAT said the system which the Government was pursuing was one of tyranny towards Upper Canada. They were ruled by a minority of Upper Canadians. What was tyranny but government by a minority? They were not a free people so long as a system was sanctioned by which a mere fraction of the people could rule over them—by which they could not get a law passed, a single officer appointed, or a single resolution passed—unless a minority of their own people chose to grant it.

The Leader (Toronto), 20 July 1858

George Brown on Sectionalism and Nationalism

At a crucial Reform Party convention held in Toronto in 1859, George Brown outlined Upper Canada's complaints against the Union.

What is it that has most galled the people of Upper Canada in the working of the existing Union? Has it not been the injustice done to Upper Canada in local and sectional matters? Has it not been the expenditure of Provincial funds for local purposes of Lower Canada which here are defrayed from local taxation? Has it not been the control exercised by Lower Canada over matters purely pertaining to Upper Canada—the framing of our School laws, the selection of our ministers, the appointment of our local officials? Has it not been that the minority of Upper Canada rule here through Lower Canada votes—that extravagant expenditures are voted by men who have not to provide the means—that fresh taxes are continually imposed by those who have not to pay them? . . .

The Globe, 16 November 1859

Later in the same speech, Brown prophesied a transcontinental Canadian nation.

Now, Sir, I do place the question on the ground of nationality. I do hope there is not one Canadian in this assembly who does not look forward with high hope to the day when these northern countries shall stand out among the nations of the world as one great confederation. (Cheers.) What true Canadian can witness the tide of immigration now commencing to flow into the vast territories of the North-West without longing to have a share in the first settlement of that great and fertile country—who does not feel that to us rightfully belongs the right and the duty of carrying the blessings of civilization throughout those boundless regions, and making our own country the highway of traffic to the Pacific? (Cheers.)

Ibid.

The Clear Grits Adopt the Federal Principle

After an internal struggle between the group favouring simple separation for Upper Canada and that favouring the federal principle, the Convention adopted resolutions that echoed the opinions of the party leader, George Brown.

1. *Resolved,*—That the existing Legislative Union of Upper and Lower Canada has failed to realize the anticipations of its promoters, has resulted in a heavy public debt, burdensome taxation, great political abuses, and universal dissatisfaction throughout Upper Canada; and it is the matured conviction of this assembly, from the antagonisms developed through difference of origin, local interests, and other causes, that the Union, in its present form, can no longer be continued with advantage to the people.

2. *Resolved,*—That highly desirable as it would be, while the existing Union is maintained, that local legislation should not be forced on one section of the Province against the wishes of a majority of the representatives of that section —yet this assembly is of opinion that the plan of government known as the "Double Majority" would be no permanent remedy for existing evils.

5. *Resolved,*—That in the opinion of this assembly, the best practicable remedy for the evils now encountered in the government of Canada is to be found in the formation of two or more Local Governments, to which shall be committed the control of all matters of a local or sectional character, and some joint authority charged with such matters as are necessarily common to both sections of the Province.

Ibid

Sectionalism as a Cause for Confederation

Sectional strife plus equal representation in the United legislature led to political deadlock in the early 1860's, and that deadlock produced the Confederation movement that achieved the British North America Act. During the Confederation debates in the

Canadian Parliament the colonial politicians tried to explain to themselves the forces that had destroyed the Union as a political entity.

John A. Macdonald discussed deadlock.

. . . We had election after election,—we had ministry after ministry,—with the same result. Parties were so equally balanced, that the vote of one member might decide the fate of the Administration, and the course of legislation for a year or a series of years. This condition of things was well calculated to arouse the earnest consideration of every lover of his country, and I am happy to say it had that effect. None were more impressed by this momentous state of affairs, and the grave apprehensions that existed of a state of anarchy destroying our credit, destroying our prosperity, destroying our progress, than were the members of this present House; and the leading statesmen on both sides seemed to have come to the common conclusion, that some step must be taken to relieve the country from the deadlock and impending anarchy that hung over us—

. . . The gentlemen who compose this Government had for many years been engaged in political hostilities to such an extent that it affected even their social relations. But the crisis was great, the danger was imminent, and the gentlemen who now form the present Administration found it to be their duty to lay aside all personal feelings, to sacrifice in some degree their position, and even to run the risk of having their motives impugned, for the sake of arriving at some conclusion that would be satisfactory to the country in general. The present resolutions were the result.

Parliamentary Debates on the Subject of the Confederation of the British North American Provinces (Quebec, 1865), p. 26.

Christopher Dunkin explained why the Union had promoted rather than ended sectionalism.

. . . Indeed, until 1848, equality in the representation of the two sections of the province in the Cabinet was never seriously aimed at. In 1848, from considerations of a peculiar character—perhaps more personal than political—the usage was commenced, and it has since been persevered in, of having a Premier and a sub-Premier, and a Cabinet organized under them, respectively, in two sections—of course equal in numbers, or as nearly so as possible. And on this usage and in connection with it have developed themselves all those double majority and double ministry notions and practices which again of late have so constantly been leading us into all manner of constitutional difficulties. (Hear, hear.) It has been found again and again impossible to constitute a satisfactory ministry of two sections; because one or other of the two sections, if they came together on any basis of real political agreement, was so very likely not to be able to command a majority of its sectional representation in this House. It was, practically, a division of the House, as well as of the Government, into two sections—practically, all but a government by two ministries and with two Houses. We did not quite admit, to be sure, that there were two ministries; although, by the way, at one time—I refer to the time of the first proposed vote of want of confidence in the MACDONALD-DORION ministry—a motion was on the point of being made—notice of it was given—which positively did speak of a Lower Canadian ministry as contradistinguished from an Upper Canadian ministry. I go into this to shew that already, in Canada, the force of circumstances has been one too many for us, and has inflicted upon us a system more complex—less workable—than obtains in England. With us, as at home, the Constitution makes the whole Ministry, collectively, responsible for all the acts it performs; but it is well known that here, for all practical purposes, we have for years had our Ministry acting by two sections—each section with a chief of its own, to a large extent a policy of its own, and the responsibility of leading and governing a section of this House of its own. (Hear, hear.) We have been federalising our Constitution after a very new and anomalous fashion ever since 1848, and by that, more than by anything else, have been getting ourselves into that sort of difficulty in which we have latterly found ourselves. (Hear, hear.)

Ibid., p. 498.

J. Dufresne (Montcalm) foresaw Confederation as the guardian of French-Canadian identity.

In examining this question, and in order to express more clearly and fully my opinion of these resolutions, I may say that I accept them for many reasons, but chiefly as a means of obtaining the repeal of the present legislative union of Canada, and securing a peaceable settlement of our sectional difficulties. I accept them, in the second place, as a means of obtaining for Lower Canada the absolute and exclusive control of her own affairs. I accept them, thirdly, as a means of perpetuating French-Canadian nationality in this country. I accept them, fourthly, as a more effectual means of cementing our connection with the Mother Country, and avoiding annexation to the United States. I accept them, fifthly and lastly, as a means of administering the affairs of the country with greater economy. Such are my reasons for accepting the Confederation scheme submitted to us by the Government. (Hear, hear.)

Ibid., p. 922.

Clear Grittism and Agrarianism

Frank H. Underhill, one of the first historians to study the 1850's in depth, sees in the Clear Grits and Brown's *Globe* expressions of agrarian radicalism to which the religious controversy was only an incidental astringent.

Today the main thing that is remembered about the *Globe* of those times is its attacks upon the Catholic Church; and in view of its reputation for religious intolerance one is rather surprised to find how small a part religious controversies play in its editorials. Of course, attacks on the supposed superstitions of the Roman faith and on the pretensions of the Vatican or of the local hierarchy to be the repositories of final truth can easily be quoted. But from about 1857 on these become less and less frequent. It was the *political* activities of the hierarchy which roused the *Globe*'s ire; their interference in elections; their refusal to accept the complete separation of Church and State which the Upper Canada Reformers thought the only possible policy in a country of such diverse faiths as Canada; and especially their working alliance with the big business interests of Montreal which regularly delivered some fifty-odd French-Canadian "Moutons" in the Assembly under Cartier's leadership to vote for every job of the Grand Trunk, for tariffs that compelled Upper Canada to buy from Montreal instead of from the United States, or for the mere lack of action that prevented Canada from challenging the monopoly of the Hudson's Bay Company in the North-West. It is true, of course, that Brown was hypersensitive on religious questions; and one suspects that a little skilful baiting by his opponents was not infrequently resorted to in order to lead him to make an exhibition of himself on the subject. Certainly they found his vociferous Protestantism a very useful red herring to drag across the trail whenever he grew particularly hot in the pursuit of some unsavoury job perpetrated by the government or its friends. But I think that an attentive reading of the *Globe* itself will lead one to the conclusion that it was gradually dawning on Brown as the years went by that the real enemy was not the Catholic Church but big business.

For the essential thing about the *Globe* and the movement it led is that it represented the aspirations and the general outlook on life of the pioneer Upper Canadian farmer. The "Clear Grit" party in Upper Canada was an expression of the "frontier" in our Canadian politics just as Jacksonian Democracy or Lincoln Republicanism was in the politics of the United States. It was to "the intelligent yeomanry of Upper Canada" that the *Globe* consciously made its appeal. Though Brown himself sat for one of the Toronto seats from 1857 to 1861, the Grits never succeeded in capturing the main urban centres. Toronto, London, Hamilton and Kingston pretty steadily elected supporters of the Macdonald-Cartier coalition.

* * * * *

This essential connection between the Clear Grit movement and the western farmer is shown also by the nature of the opposition to it. The Brown Reformers never succeeded in making very deep inroads into the eastern corner of Upper Canada—the St. Lawrence below Kingston and the Ottawa valley. These districts were economically connected with Montreal and the St. Lawrence route and naturally supported a Montreal government. It was in the West, in the Peninsula, that the centre of Grit influence lay; and "the eternal restlessness of the Peninsula" of which the Toronto *Leader* once complained was a temper of mind which Brown found congenial. Eastern Protestants, under the guidance of the Montreal *Gazette*, seldom allowed religious sympathies to draw them towards the dangerous radicals of the West. The *Gazette* steadily preached to them that their community of economic interest with their fellow Easterners, the French Catholics, was of far more importance than any religious difference or than the memory of old feuds in the pre-Responsible Government days.

* * * * *

The essence of the struggle which produced the political deadlock of the 1860s was not that it was primarily a fight of Protestant against Catholic or of English against French, though both these elements entered into it and embittered it. It was primarily a struggle of West against East; the then West being, like the modern West, in its social structure largely agricultural and in its geographical position a long way from its markets; and the East, then as now, being dominated by the transportation, banking and manufacturing interests which centred in Montreal.

> F. H. Underhill, "Some Aspects of Upper Canadian Radical Opinion in the Decade before Confederation", Canadian Historical Association, *Report, 1927*, pp. 46–7, 48–9.

Clear Grittism and Metropolitanism

J. M. S. Careless, George Brown's biographer, agrees with Underhill's estimate of the religious factor in this sectional conflict but qualifies Clear Grittism by pointing to its limited success in agricultural areas, and suggests that Brown's influence transformed the farmer's unrest into a liberalism based on the mercantile ambitions of the Toronto business community. This is an application of the metropolitan thesis of historical development to the sectional conflict, and pits Toronto and Montreal against each other as rivals for control of the agricultural hinterland.

. . . Grittism under Brown's strong-minded direction turned increasingly from agrarian radicalism to an Upper Canadian version of mid-Victorian British Liberalism. Brown himself was no agrarian; and in his political thinking could hardly be called radical. He opposed fundamental change in government. He distrusted full-fledged democracy on the American plan of one man, one vote, and preferred to see qualifications maintained whereby political rights fell to those who had some stake in the community. At any rate, during his period of control the Grits changed from an idealistic farmers' movement to a much more empirical political party but little concerned with basic reform.

This may not seem to fit with the record of Brown's fierce onslaughts on the very constitution of the old Canadian union, demanding that the equal division of seats in Parliament between the two sections be done away with, and that representation by population be adopted instead. Undoubtedly, French-Canadian journals wrote of "the savage doctrines of Brownite radicalism" (see *Le Canadien,* January 27, 1858), as they contemplated his equally fiery onslaughts on Roman Catholic power in politics. Yet here George Brown was simply voicing the sectional and sectarian protests of Upper Canadians against what they termed "French Catholic domination." To insist that representation in the union be altered, or to condemn Roman Catholic influence on government might be disruptive or unjustified—but it was hardly revolutionary. These positions did not even originate with Brown. French Canadians had talked of representation by population in days when Lower Canada itself had held the greater number of inhabitants. Tories had been loudly anti-French and anti-Catholic in times before they joined the Liberal-Conservative coalition. Besides, Clear Grits had cried out against French Catholic power and advocated representation by population before Brown took up these themes and made them so characteristically his own. In sum, sectional and sectarian vehemence derived essentially from the unsatisfactory nature of the union and the general rise of religious issues during the 1850's, not inherently from Brown.

That decade saw French Canadians holding a balance of power in politics while Upper Canada's population steadily increased beyond Lower Canada's but its parliamentary membership did not. At the same time, the fifties witnessed legislation to enlarge Catholic separate school rights in Upper Canada— acts passed against the will of the Protestant majority of that section by virtue of the combined strength of the western Catholic minority and the eastern Catholic majority. The legislation might have been just and necessary; yet its passage virtually amounted to the coercion of Upper Canada. Small wonder, then, the fervour of the western Protestant outcry. It was not George Brown's doing, even though he most strongly associated it with his reconstructed Clear Grit party.

Furthermore, his opposition to Roman Catholic "threats" was not the simple anti-Popery of the Orange Order. It went back to his belief in the total separation of church and state, the epitome of his Free Church Presbyterianism. Churches should keep free of state entanglements, and neither accept public grants nor seek special legislation to support their own denominational schools. Still further, the principle of the separation of church and state was an integral part of Brown's political Liberalism. He held, as his father before him, that true individual liberty required that religious authority should not interfere with political expression, and that churches should have no link with government or public funds, so that sectarian quarrels and religious differences need not enter into politics. No doubt these tenets actually led him to sectarian strife; but he was no less arguing from principle than his Roman Catholic foes who repudiated the concept of a "godless" state and of citizenship unsanctified by religious ties.

In any case, the Liberal party which George Brown moulded found a more lasting character in mid-Victorian Liberalism than in Protestant sectarianism.

J. M. S. Careless, "George Brown", in Robert L. McDougall, ed., *Our Living Tradition: Second and Third Series* (Toronto, 1959), pp. 43–5.

Economic Sources of Sectionalism

In analyzing the sources of pre-Confederation sectionalism, Donald G. Creighton stresses the economic disparity between the two Canadas in a union that depended on political equality. Lower Canada had not shared in the revolutions in transportation, communications, and industry that began about 1850 to anything like the same extent as Upper Canada. No other Canadian historian has examined this idea of thwarted economic ambitions as a cause of tension in that period, although the theme is frequently cited in connection with today's "quiet revolution" in Quebec.

The prime social division which existed between the English-speaking and French-speaking inhabitants of the Province had taken the concrete form of an obvious sectional cleavage. This cleavage had inspired the creation of the two Provinces of Upper and Lower Canada; it led to their continuance as two virtually distinct entities even after the political consolidation of 1841. Canada, after the union of 1841, was in form a unitary state; in fact, it was an unacknowledged federal system; and the division of portfolios, moneys and parliamentary places between the people of Canada East and Canada West was the inevitable consequence of inward and fundamental social differences. Ministerial places were apportioned with fair equality between the members from the two sections of the Province. Certain government departments, such as that for education, were split into two distinct divisions, equipped with separate staffs and granted approximately equal appropriations. Legislation affecting one section of the Province only was passed at every session of the provincial parliament: and even when, as in setting up the Municipal Loan Funds, no essential differences of treatment were contemplated, separate statutes were often passed for Canada East and Canada West. Expenditures in one section of the Province could not go uncompensated by comparable expenditures in the other. On the extinction of the seigniorial tenure, by which the Province was committed to the payment of substantial sums, efforts had to be made to recompense the Eastern Township of Lower Canada and the Upper Canadian municipalities; and these indemnities increased the financial burdens of the Province and complicated its accounts, without really satisfying the demands of the western section.

These administrative difficulties, serious as they were, were only one aspect of a fundamental political problem. The political system of the time was suspended in uneasy balance; but the economic and social forces of the period threatened disequilibrium. The straining energies and ambitions of the western section of the Province could find no scope within the *de facto* federalism of the existing union; and the cultural interests of the eastern section were thought to be endangered by anything but a *de jure* unity. The demand of the Grit Party for representation by population, and the urgings of Canada West for expansion into the territories of the Hudson's Bay Company, were alike inadmissible for they would alike destroy that rough political equality by which alone the Union of 1841 had been made acceptable to the French. The social composition of the country seemed to necessitate a static political dualism; the economic ambitions of the St. Lawrence appeared to encourage an expanding political unity. It was certain that these two different though equally legitimate interests could not both find peaceful satisfaction within the existing political system. Burdened with debts, inhibited from expansion, and distracted by its sectional differences, the Province reached the end of its difficult and erratic course in the ministerial crisis of 1864.

*   *   *   *   *

Political deadlock was not the mainspring of the Confederation movement, for political deadlock was itself the result of the entanglement of social and regional interests. It was not to make possible a stable government, but to end the sectional troubles of Canada that Brown entered the coalition of 1864; but, at the same time, deadlock, if it was not a prime cause, was at least more than the occasion, of Confederation. Confederation, which was a political achievement, could only be realized with political machinery; and the final breakdown of Canadian government in June 1864 provided both the chance and the incentive to form a party union through which a new political system could be achieved. The pressure of an inadequate political system, the uncertainties of government and the irritating shifts and devices to which in consequence administrations were reduced, all helped to arouse an urgency for action which was peculiar to Canada.

D. G. Creighton, *British North America at Confederation: A Study Prepared for the Royal Commission on Dominion-Provincial Relations* (Ottawa, 1939), Appendix 2, pp. 21, 61.

Further Reading

The only large history of this period is the old but factually reliable *The Last Forty Years*, by J. C. Dent (2 vols., Toronto, 1881). There is no recent general study of the "Fiery Fifties", but a few specialized monographs have appeared in recent years. J. S. Moir, *Church and State in Canada West* (Toronto, University of Toronto Press, 1959) examines the religious background of sectionalism and P. G. Cornell, *The Alignment of Political Groups in Canada, 1841–1867* (Toronto, University of Toronto Press, 1962) analyses party relationships in the Union Parliament in terms of selected issues. D. G. Creighton's *John A. Macdonald:* Vol. I, *The Young Politician* (Toronto, Macmillan, 1966)* and J. M. S. Careless's *Brown of the Globe*, 2 vols., (Toronto, Macmillan, 1959, 1963)* describe the relation of these men to the sectional issues of their day. A. D. DeCelles' biographies of L. J. Papineau and Sir George Cartier in *The Makers of Canada* series (1926) are in need of expansion and revision but they do present the French-Canadian view of the sectional difficulties under the Union. Leon Pouliot, *Monseigneur Bourget et son temps* (2 vols. of 4, Montreal, Beauchemin, 1955–   ) is a biography of the bishop who promoted the alliance of Conservatives and Ultramontanes in Canada East.

Problem 11

Confederation — The Nature of the Agreement

One of the most widely known "facts" about Canadian history is that the Dominion of Canada came into existence on 1 July 1867. But what lay behind the passage of the British North America Act, 1867, and the Queen's Proclamation, which brought the new entity into being?

Historians, political scientists, lawyers, and politicians have debated the significance of the various events and agreements which make up the Confederation movement from the time that they took place until today. Was the whole project merely a scheme to solve the problem of political deadlock within the old Province of Canada? Was it something concocted by some British railway and land speculators and their Canadian collaborators? Were the leading figures motivated mainly by a desire to create a new nation? Were the terms under which the delegates of the several colonies agreed to commit their provinces to the project recognized at the time as a "pact" or "treaty", hence not subject to alteration without mutual consultation and agreement of the consenting parties? Commentators at the time and later have come up with differing answers to these questions.

The problem is complicated by the secrecy with which the actual negotiations were conducted, and by the absence later of full accounts of the deliberations by the chief participants. The historian, thus, has to reconstruct the events from rudimentary minutes of the conferences, not intended for publication, the accounts of enterprising (and occasionally imaginative) newspaper reporters, the public addresses and correspondence of the delegates, and the dispatches to the Colonial Office of the governors who attempted to be as fully informed as possible on the deliberations.*

---

* The problems facing the historian have been described by W. M. Whitelaw in "Reconstructing the Quebec Conference", *Canadian Historical Review*, XXX (June 1938), pp. 123–37.

George Brown Explains the Canadian Proposal of a Federal Union

The formal negotiations which resulted in the formation of the Dominion of Canada were launched by a delegation representing the coalition government of the Province of Canada, who obtained an invitation to appear at a conference at Charlottetown in September 1864. This conference had been called to consider the proposal of Maritime Union, which would combine the three provinces by the sea into one larger colony. As the negotiations were conducted in secret, the first opportunity that the delegates were given to explain to the public the proposition which the Canadian delegates put to the Maritimers occurred in Halifax on 12 September, when the delegates were entertained at a banquet. In proposing or responding to toasts, the principal delegates presented their views. The following excerpts from Brown's speech, and from that of John A. Macdonald, illustrate the Canadian case, and also suggest something of the different temperament and personalities of the two men.

. . . It has been said that we have had the opportunity before now of entering into closer union with Nova Scotia and New Brunswick, but we did not avail ourselves of it; . . . and that we only come now seeking union with these provinces to escape from our sectional difficulties at home. . . . In these Lower Provinces* you have had your political troubles, but we in Canada have had sectional difficulties to distract and embitter us, vastly more serious than any you have had to contend with. Our Constitution of 1840 brought together under one government two countries peopled by two races, with different languages, different creeds, and different laws and customs; and unfortunately, while making us nominally one people, it retained the line of demarcation between Upper and Lower Canada, and gave the same number of representatives in parliament to each section, without regard to their respective populations, their contributions to the general revenue, or any other consideration. . . . A systematic agitation for the redress of the great wrong was commenced in Upper Canada: and as the only means of enforcing justice, we [the Upper Canadian Reformers] resisted all large schemes of improvement, we refused to enter into any new undertakings involving an increase of our public debt until a reform of our constitutional system was obtained; and we knew what our future position as a people was to be. . . . Parties were nearly equally balanced, the wheels of government had nearly ceased to move, a deadlock was almost

---

* The common designation of the time for the Maritime Provinces.

inevitable, when Mr. Cartier, who wields great power in Lower Canada, boldly and manfully took the ground that this evil must be met, and he would meet it. On this basis, I and two political friends* joined the administration, and the existing coalition was formed expressly for the purpose of settling justly and permanently the constitutional relations between Upper and Lower Canada. . . . We are pledged as a government to place before parliament at its next session a bill giving effect to the conditions of our compact [a federal union of the two sections of Canada]; and should the union of the whole provinces not be proceeded with, our Canadian Reform Bill will go on and our grievances be redressed. You will therefore clearly perceive that we have not come here to seek relief from our trouble,—for the remedy of our grievances is already agreed upon, . . . Our sole object in coming here is to say to you: "We are about to amend our constitutions; and before finally doing so, we invite you to enter with us frankly and earnestly into the inquiry whether it would or would not be for the advantage of all the British American Colonies to be embraced under one political system. Let us look the whole question steadily in the face: if we find it advantageous let us act upon it; but if not, let the whole thing drop.

> Edward Whelan, compiler, *The Union of the British Provinces*
> (Toronto, 1927), pp. 29–30.
> [First published in Charlottetown, 1865.]

Macdonald Invites the Maritimers to Share in New Opportunities

Macdonald spoke later the same evening. In reading this and other quotations from the period before 1867 it is necessary to remember that the term "Canada" applies to the united province of that name, and not to the larger, but then still unnamed, confederation.

The question of "Colonial Union" . . . absorbs every idea as far as I am concerned. For twenty long years I have been dragging myself through the dreary waste of Colonial politics. I thought there was no end, nothing worthy of ambition; but now I see something which is well worthy of all I have suffered in the cause of my little country. . . . There may be obstructions, local difficulties may arise, disputes may occur, local jealousies may intervene, but it matters not, the wheel is now revolving and we are only the fly on the wheel, . . . we cannot delay it—the union of the colonies of the British America, under one sovereign, is a fixed fact.

> *Ibid.*, p. 45.

---

* William McDougall and Oliver Mowat.

Later in his address Macdonald refers to the dangers of states' rights, a major cause of the American Civil War then still being waged.

The dangers that have risen from this system we will avoid if we can agree upon forming a strong central government—a great central legislature—a constitution for a union which will have all the rights of sovereignty except those that are given to the local governments. Then we shall have taken a great step in advance of the American Republic. If we can only obtain that object—a vigorous general government—we shall not be New Brunswickers, nor Nova Scotians, nor Canadians, but British Americans, under the sway of the British Sovereign. . . . In the conference we have had [the Charlottetown Conference] we have been united as one man—there was no difference of feeling, no sectional prejudices or selfishness exhibited by any one;—we all approached the subject feeling its importance; feeling that in our hands were the destinies of a nation.

Ibid., p. 47.

Turning to the proposal of the intercolonial railway as a necessary product of the Confederation, Macdonald combines appeals to local economic self-interest, to the "new nation" and to imperial loyalty.

In the case of a union, this railway must be a national work, and Canada will cheerfully contribute to the utmost extent in order to make that important link, without which no political connection can be complete. What will be the consequence to this city [Halifax], prosperous as it is, from that communication? Montreal is at this moment competing with New York for the trade of the great West. Build the road and Halifax will soon become one of the great emporiums of the world. All the great resources of the West will come over the immense railways of Canada to the bosom of your harbour. But there are even greater advantages for us all in view. We will become a great nation; and God forbid that it should be one separate from the United Kingdom of Great Britain and Ireland.

* * * * *

Union must take place some time. I say now is the time. . . . I will feel that I shall not have served in public life without a reward if before I enter into private life, I am a subject of a great British American nation, under the government of Her Majesty, and in connection with the Empire of Great Britain and Ireland.

Ibid., pp. 48–50

Debate on the Quebec Resolutions

Definite terms of union emerged in the form of seventy-two resolutions agreed upon by the delegates at a conference held at Quebec between 10 and 27 October 1864, at which the provinces of Canada, New Brunswick, Nova Scotia, Prince Edward Island, and Newfoundland were represented. The "Quebec Terms" became the basis of all later discussion. The terms were formally approved after a lengthy debate in the Canadian legislature, by a three-to-one majority in both houses. They were rejected by similar majorities in the legislature of Prince Edward Island. No similar formal opportunities were provided to debate the terms in the legislatures of the other provinces, although the issue dominated the general elections in New Brunswick in 1865, when the supporters of the Quebec Terms were routed at the polls, and in the following year when the same voters reversed their earlier decision.

The question of whether the agreements reached at Quebec constitute a "compact" or a "treaty" stem from the words used by delegates in defending the terms in the Canadian legislature.

George Cartier Sees Confederation as a Means of Protecting and Preserving the Interests of Minorities

In drafting the proposed terms of Confederation, George Cartier, leader of *le parti bleu*,* argued against the desire of many of his English-speaking colleagues to concentrate all authority in the central government. Once the Quebec Terms were published, he sought to reassure his fellow French Canadians that their interests had been adequately guaranteed. It is noteworthy that these guarantees included the retention of the monarchy and the decision not to base the new confederation on democratic principles. This debate is reported in indirect speech.

We found ourselves at the present day discussing the question of the Federation of the British North American Provinces, while the great Federation of the United States of America was broken up and divided against itself. There was, however, this important difference to be observed in considering the action of

* The dominant and more conservative of the two major political groups in Lower Canada.

the two peoples. They had founded Federation for the purpose of carrying out and perpetuating democracy on this continent; but we, who had the benefit of being able to contemplate republicanism in action during a period of eighty years, saw its defects, and felt convinced that purely democratic institutions could not be conducive to the peace and prosperity of nations. We were not now discussing the great problem presented to our consideration, in order to propagate democratic principles. Our attempt was for the purpose of forming a Federation with a view of perpetuating the monarchical element. The distinction, therefore, between ourselves and our neighbours was just this:—In our Federation the monarchical principle would form the leading feature, while on the other side of the line, judging by the past history and present condition of the country, the ruling power was the will of the mob, the rule of the populace.

* * * * *

Objection had been taken to the scheme now under consideration, because of the words "new nationality". Now, when we were united together, if union were attained, we would form a political nationality with which neither the national origin, nor the religion of any individual, would interfere. It was lamented by some that we had this diversity of races, and hopes were expressed that this distinctive feature would cease. The idea of unity of races was utopian, . . . Dissimilarity, in fact, appeared to be the order of the physical world and of the moral world, as well as in the political world. . . .

* * * * *

We could not do away with the distinctions of race. We could not legislate for the disappearance of the French Canadians from American soil, but British and French Canadians alike could appreciate and understand their position relative to each other. . . . It was a benefit rather than otherwise that we had a diversity of races. Of course, the difficulty, it would be said, would be to deal fairly by the minority. In Upper Canada the Catholics would find themselves in a minority; in Lower Canada the Protestants would be in a minority, while the Lower Provinces were divided. Under such circumstances, would any one pretend that either the local or general governments would sanction any injustice? What would be the consequence, even supposing any such thing were attempted by any one of the local governments? It would be censured everywhere. Whether it came from Upper Canada or from Lower Canada, any attempt to deprive the minority of their rights would be at once thwarted. Under the Federation system, granting to the control of the General Government these large questions of general interest in which the differences of race or religion had no place, it could not be pretended that the rights of either race or religion could be invaded at all. We were to have a General Parliament to deal with the matters of defence, tariff, excise, public works, and these matters absorbed all individual interest. Now, he would ask those self-styled nationalists . . . under what supposition could they think it possible for any injustice to be done to the French Canadians by the Central Government? . . .

Parliamentary Debates on the Subject of the Confederation of the British North American Provinces (Quebec, 1865), pp. 59–61.

Macdonald Describes the Quebec Terms as a Treaty

Partly, at least, as a device to discourage amendments to the Quebec Resolutions, several supporters of the project described the terms agreed upon at the Quebec Conference as a "compact" or a "treaty".* The student might compare the case for Confederation, as Macdonald presented it to the members of the Canadian Parliament, in the excerpts below, with its stress on local self-interest, with the case he had presented earlier (above, pp. 180–1) to the Maritime audience in Halifax.

I say to this House, if you do not believe that the union of the colonies is for the advantage of the country, that the joining of these five peoples into one nation, under one sovereign, is for the benefit of all, then reject the scheme. . . . As I stated in the preliminary discussion, we must consider this scheme in the light of a treaty. By a happy coincidence of circumstances, just when an Administration had been formed in Canada for the purpose of attempting a solution of the difficulties under which we laboured, at the same time the Lower Provinces, actuated by a similar feeling, appointed a Conference with a view to a union among themselves, . . . If it had not been for this fortunate coincidence of events, never, perhaps, for a long series of years would we have been able to bring this scheme to a practical conclusion. But we did succeed. . . . and the deputations from the several governments represented at the Conference went back pledged to lay it before their governments, and to ask the legislatures and people of their respective provinces to assent to it. I trust the scheme will be assented to as a whole. I am sure this House will not seek to alter it in its unimportant details; and, if altered in any important provisions, the result must be that the whole will be set aside, and we must begin *de novo*. If any important changes are made, every one of the colonies will feel itself absolved from the implied obligation to deal with it as a Treaty, each province will feel itself at

* The most explicit statement of this type was made in the British House of Commons by the Parliamentary Under-Secretary of State for the Colonies, C. B. Adderley, who attempted to forestall Members of Parliament sympathetic to the aspirations of Nova Scotian opponents of the project by describing the bill for the British North America Act as constituting "a matter of the most delicate treaty and compact between the Provinces". Great Britain, *Parliamentary Debates*, 3rd series, Vol. 185, col. 1169, 28 February 1867.

liberty to amend it . . . and we will have to renew our negotiations with all the colonies for the purpose of establishing some new scheme. I hope the House will not adopt any such a course as will postpone, perhaps for ever, or at all events for a long period, all chances of union. . . . If we do not embrace this opportunity the present favourable time will pass away, and we may never have it again. Because, just so surely as this scheme is defeated, will be revived the original proposition for a union of the Maritime Provinces, irrespective of Canada; . . . and it will be then too late for us to attempt to strengthen ourselves by this scheme, . . . If we are not blind to our present position, we must see the hazardous situation in which all the great interests of Canada stand in respect to the United States. I am no alarmist. I do not believe in the prospect of immediate war. . . . We know that the United States at this moment are engaged in a war of enormous dimensions—that the occasion of a war with Great Britain has again and again arisen, . . . It would then be too late when war had commenced to think of measures for strengthening ourselves, or to begin negotiations for a union with the sister provinces. At this moment, . . . in consequence of the irritation which now exists, owing to the unhappy state of affairs on this continent, the Reciprocity Treaty, it seems probable, is about to be brought to an end—our trade is hampered by the passport system, and at any moment we may be deprived of permission to carry our goods through United States channels—the bonded goods system may be done away with, and the winter trade through the United States put an end to. . . . Ourselves already threatened, our trade interrupted, our intercourse, political and commercial, destroyed, if we do not take warning now when we have the opportunity, and while one avenue is threatened to be closed, open another by taking advantage of the present arrangement and the desire of the Lower Provinces to draw closer the alliance between us, we may suffer commercial and political disadvantages it may take long for us to overcome.

Ibid., pp. 31–2.

A. A. Dorion Suggests that Big Business Was Responsible for the Confederation Agreement

Antoine A. Dorion (M.L.A. Hochelaga) was one of the leading critics of the Confederation project in the Canadian Parliament. The following excerpt illustrates a technique frequently employed by a critic of any proposal: the suggestion that others will profit from the new arrangements at the expense of those to whom he is addressing his remarks.

There was then another cause for this Confederation scheme of which representation by population was made the pretext. It is not so well known, but far more powerful. In the year 1861, Mr. [E. W.] Watkin was sent from England by the Grand Trunk Railway Company. He came with the distinct view of making a large claim on the country for aid, but in the then temper of the people, he soon found that he could not expect to obtain that. Thinking that if he only could put some new scheme afloat which would give a decent pretext to a well disposed Government, he would quietly get the assistance required, he immediately started for the Lower Provinces, and came back after inducing people there to resuscitate the question of the Intercolonial Railway. Parties were readily found to advocate it, if Canada would only pay the piper. A meeting of delegates took place, resolutions were adopted, and an application was made to the Imperial Government for a large contribution to its costs, in the shape of an indemnity for carrying the troops over the road. . . . but the Imperial authorities were unwilling to grant the required assistance, . . . Mr. Watkin, although baffled in his expectations, did not give up his project. . . . At this meeting of delegates, which took place in September, 1862, a new scheme for building the Intercolonial was adopted, by which Canada was to pay five-twelfths and the Lower Provinces seven-twelfths. So unpopular was this arrangement that when its terms were made known, if a vote of the people had been taken upon it, not ten out of every hundred, from Sandwich to Gaspé, would have declared in its favour, although Canada was only to pay five-twelfths of its cost. This project having failed, some other scheme had to be concocted for bringing aid and relief to the unfortunate Grand Trunk—and the Confederation of all the British North American Provinces naturally suggested itself to the Grand Trunk officials as the surest means of bringing with it the construction of the Intercolonial Railway. Such was the origin of this Confederation scheme. The Grand Trunk people are at the bottom of it; . . .

Ibid., pp. 250–1.

A Maritimer Attacks "The Botheration Scheme"

Debate on the Quebec Resolutions in the Canadian legislature took place between 3 February and 13 March 1865. On January 11th of that year, the first of twelve leading editorials on "The Botheration Scheme" or "Botheration Issue" appeared in the Halifax *Morning Chronicle*, a paper whose proprietor had on the previous day announced the removal of its pro-Confederation editor, Joseph McCully. Later, on 22 February, the *Chronicle* announced that Joseph Howe, the hero of the battle for responsible government in Nova Scotia, leading Reformer, early advocate of imperial federation, and sometime prophet of a united British North America, was the author of the series. The excerpts from the first letter printed here raise points which struck responsive chords in many Nova Scotians, that Confederation was a solution for the problems of the

Province of Canada, in which the Maritimers need not become involved. The techniques referred to in the introduction to Dorion's address can also be noted here.

Before deciding to hand over to the Canadians the patronage and revenues of Nova Scotia, let us enquire whether there is anything in our present condition to compel us to make this transfer.

Prior to the introduction of Responsible Government into this Province, Downing Street claimed the authority which it is now proposed to erect at Ottawa. How did we like that? Why, so little that our best men gave the flower of their lives to the struggle by which the system was changed. Huntington and Howe, Young and Uniacke, Doyle and DesBarres, and all their sturdy compatriots, in two or three Parliaments, fought out the great battle by which the appointment of our own officers—the control of our own revenues—the management of our own affairs—was secured to Nova Scotians. We possess and exercise these high powers now, in as full and ample a measure as the freest people on the face of the earth. And shall it be said that the labours of these men were in vain—that their policy was unsound, and that their lives have been wasted?

* * * * *

Why should anything be done? Nova Scotia, secure of self-government, can even bear with serenity an Administration that certainly tries her patience at times, for a year or two longer. She has been blessed with a good crop, an abundant fishery, a healthy season; her mining interests are extending; her shipyards have been busy all the year; her railroads are beginning to pay, and her treasury is overflowing, affording ample means to push forward public improvements just as fast as it is wise to push them, with the little surplus labour we have.

We have not a question to create angry discussion with the mother country, with our neighbours in the United States, or with the Governments of the surrounding colonies. We have entirely reorganized our militia, and drilled every man liable to be called out under the law, within the year.

* * * * *

But it is said that the Canadians have outgrown their Constitution. Well, if they have, what of that? If they are in trouble let them get out of it; but don't let them involve us in distractions with which we have nothing to do. Are not the Canadians always in trouble? Did not Papineau keep Lower Canada in trouble for twenty years, and McKenzie [*sic*] disturb the Upper Province for about the same period? Then did not both Provinces break out into open rebellion, which it cost the British Government three or four millions sterling to suppress? What would have been the situation of the Maritime Provinces then, had they been controlled by the Canadians? Would they not have been compromised by these outbreaks, and might they not all have been made the theatres of civil war? But they were not under Canadian influence. They maintained their loyalty unsullied. . . .

Again, in 1849, the Canadians tried their hands at another insurrection. They burnt down their Parliament House; pelted Lord Elgin and his Lady through the streets; hung American flags out of their windows, and published a manifesto, to which the principal citizens of Montreal signed their names, demanding annexation to the United States. Novascotians must have short memories if these things are forgotten.

Then, are not the Canadas always disturbed by religious feuds and secret societies? . . .

*   *   *   *   *

Now, is this the country for Novascotians to unite with, and to whose entire control we should hand over the management of our affairs? Here we have peace and order, everybody worships God as he pleases, and everybody obeys the law. There are no armed midnight processions—no villains chalking our doors at night—no arms secreted—no Fenians drilling—and everybody sleeps in his bed securely, with no man to make him afraid. In the name of common sense, then, are we to peril all these blessings, and mix ourselves up with distractions, the end of which no living man can foresee?

If civil war breaks out in Canada, from the apparently irrespressible conflicts of her secret societies, let the Canadians settle it among themselves. If border wars break out, . . . let those who provoke these controversies fight them out. We have no secret societies to disturb us—no frontier to tempt raiders to commit outrages on our neighbours. We are surrounded by the sea, and can only be involved in a national war when proclaimed by our sovereign, and then we are within ten days' sail of the fleets and armies of England, which, aided by our own volunteers and militia, would soon give a good account of any expedition sent by sea to disturb us. . . .

. . . Even if the bargain was financially a good one, we would not accept it at the cost of internal and external peace—of institutions hallowed by a possession of a hundred years, improved and consolidated by twenty years' labour of our ablest statesmen. Of all the characters of ancient story, the poorest spirited creature that we know is Esau; but if Novascotians surrendered their powers of self-government and provincial independence for the precious mess of pottage brought hither from Quebec, we would forever after be held in deserved contempt even by those by whom our birthright was enjoyed.

Halifax *Morning Chronicle*, 11 January 1865

Nova Scotia and New Brunswick Agree to the Principle of Confederation

Spurred by such attacks, opposition to the Quebec Terms reached significant proportions in Nova Scotia. Dr. Charles Tupper's government avoided a direct debate and vote on the issue. Eventually, on 3 April 1866, an independent member of the legislature for Richmond, William Miller, suggested a way out of the dilemma—that the Assembly pass a resolution approving the principle of federation, and authorize the appointment of delegates to arrange for terms of union with the British government.

If the Government will publicly abandon the Quebec scheme, and introduce a resolution in favour of a Federal Union of British America—leaving the details of the measure to the arbitrament of the Imperial Government, properly advised by delegates from all the provinces, I promise them my cordial support. This would be commencing rightly. By getting the endorsement of the Legislature in the outset—of the principle of Union, and its authority to enter on the settlement of the details of a scheme, the friends of the measure would occupy a very different position from that occupied by the delegates to the Quebec Conference, who went to Canada in 1864 without any authority from Parliament.

* * * * *

The object of my present movement is—and I fearlessly avow it—to defeat the Quebec scheme. Before it is too late—before we are borne down by the powerful influences against which we are now contending—while yet we have a formidable army in the field—while our opponents respect our strength and hesitate at an engagement—is it not wise to seek the most advantageous terms of compromise?

Nova Scotia, House of Assembly, *Official Report of Debates*, 1866, p. 189.

Although recognizing that the Canadian Government might consider itself bound by the Canadian Legislature's acceptance of the Quebec Resolutions, Dr. Tupper accepted Miller's suggestion, and the following resolution, quite different from the Canadian one which called for union on the basis of the Quebec Terms, was accepted by the legislature on 19 April 1866. A similar resolution, with an additional phrase calling for the immediate construction of the intercolonial railway, was passed by the New Brunswick legislature on 30 June 1866.

Resolved, therefore, that his Excellency the Lieutenant-Governor be authorized to appoint delegates to arrange with the Imperial Government a scheme of union which will effectually ensure just provisions for the rights and interests of this Province, each Province to have an equal voice in such delegation, Upper and Lower Canada being for this purpose considered as separate Provinces.

Nova Scotia, House of Assembly, *Journal*, 1866, p. 60.

"The Compact Theory of Confederation": The Proposition Attacked

A forthright attack on the theory that a compact was entered into by the delegates who participated in the conferences leading up to the passage of the British North America Act appeared in 1931. Its author, Norman McL. Rogers, a professor of Political Economy at Queen's University, later became a cabinet minister under W. L. Mackenzie King. The purpose of the article was to demonstrate that no "compact" existed under which unanimous prior consent of all provinces, or of all original provinces, was required for amending the Canadian constitution.

The compact theory of federalism in its Canadian form of expression is the deferred result of a sin of omission on the part of the Fathers of Confederation, a sin which in scriptural fashion has now been visited upon their children even unto the third and fourth generation. Sometimes we are tempted to recall with pride that the great task of the Quebec Conference was accomplished in the brief period of sixteen days, and perhaps to congratulate ourselves that this achievement compares most favourably with the four months devoted to the framing of the Constitution of the United States and the much longer period spent upon the Constitution of the Commonwealth of Australia. No one can doubt that those who drafted the Quebec Resolutions performed a difficult task with a high degree of skill and a reasonable measure of foresight, but it is not easy to forgive them for their failure to realize the necessity of providing the means whereby the Constitution might be amended in future years without incurring needless friction between the Dominion and the provinces. Certainly they would be the more entitled to our gratitude today if they had continued their sessions another week if need be in order to erect safeguards against the misunderstandings which must arise when changing conditions and new currents of political and economic thought would lead to a demand for alterations of the original terms of union.

*   *   *   *   *

From [a] recital of the events which preceded and followed the Quebec Conference, it is clear that the Resolutions of that Conference were handicapped from the beginning by the bar sinister. Their birth, so far as the maritime provinces were concerned, was illegitimate and they were never accorded legal recognition. To recapitulate briefly, up to the meeting of the London Conference in 1866, the Quebec Resolutions had been accepted only by the Legislature of the United Provinces of Upper and Lower Canada. In Nova Scotia and New Brunswick they had been abandoned to all intents and purposes, and the only point upon which the legislatures of the provinces were of a common mind was the desirability of Confederation provided it could be effected on just and equitable terms. So far as there was any compact, consensus, or general agreement among the legislatures of the provinces, it was confined to the fact of union and did not extend to any specific terms by which that union was to be achieved. It is equally clear that the Legislatures of New Brunswick and Nova Scotia agreed to leave the final terms of Confederation to the arbitrament of the Imperial Government and Parliament, as advised by delegates from the provinces. Further confirmation of this view is found in the fact that the legislatures of these provinces rejected proposals whereby the scheme arranged at London should be referred back to the provincial legislatures for approval before being implemented in legislation by the Imperial Parliament. The true function of the provincial delegations at the London Conference was advisory in character. The details of the Act of Confederation were left to the imperial authorities with the counsel and assistance of representatives of the several provinces. It is true that the Quebec Resolutions were used at London as the basis of the proposals which were later submitted to the Imperial Government, but this was obviously a matter of convenience since the majority of the Quebec Resolutions were not objected to by the delegates from Nova Scotia and New Brunswick, and it was of tactical importance to Macdonald to be able to assert that the Quebec scheme was the true foundation of the Act of Confederation.

* * * * *

The Canadian Legislature had accepted the Quebec Resolutions, but was not given an opportunity to consider the changes made at the London Conference. The provinces of New Brunswick and Nova Scotia had expressed their desire to be federally united, but approval of the terms of union was expressed not by the legislatures or by the people, but by the Governments of these provinces. The only legislative authority or approval behind the Canadian Constitution was that of the Imperial Parliament. The only agreement of provincial legislatures was confined to the acceptance of the principle of a federal union. The so-called compact of the Quebec Resolutions is without historical or constitutional basis. The London Conference was an advisory body. . . .

But if the Quebec Resolutions did not constitute a treaty in form or fact, how are we to account for the repeated use of the word "treaty" by leading members of the Conference? Are we to conclude that regardless of the confusion of thought and language in the debates in the Canadian Legislature the resolutions were intended by the delegates to operate as a binding agreement and that the Constitution to be based upon them was not to be altered except with the unanimous consent of the contracting parties? . . . In the first place it is significant that the use of the term "treaty" as applied to the Quebec Resolutions is confined to the delegates from the United Provinces. I have examined the debates in New Brunswick and Nova Scotia with some care and nowhere do I find that the resolutions were presented in these provinces as a treaty. On the contrary, the subsequent actions of the delegates from New Brunswick and Nova Scotia are entirely inconsistent with the view that they were regarded in this light.

It would appear then that there had been no formal understanding at Quebec that the resolutions should be presented to the several legislatures as a treaty, but that their presentation in this form to the Legislature of the United Provinces was simply the result of a ministerial decision to adopt a manoeuvre which would ensure their passage with the least possible delay and a minimum of discussion with respect to details. If this view is correct, it deprives the use of the word "treaty" by Macdonald, Cartier and others of the significance attached to it by proponents of the compact theory. It is equally important to observe that the language of "treaty" and "compact" was introduced before the rejection of the Quebec scheme by New Brunswick and before it became apparent that the resolutions would have to be modified in important respects before the Nova Scotia Legislature would express approval. This being the case, it seems reasonable to conclude that the use of the word "treaty" as applied to the Quebec Resolutions in the Canadian Legislature was either purely rhetorical or was adopted as a means of confining discussion to the acceptance or rejection of the resolutions *in toto*.

N. McL. Rogers, "The Compact Theory of Confederation", Canadian Political Science Association, *Proceedings, 1931* (Jackson Press, Kingston), pp. 205–6, 216–17, 219–21.

A Defence of the Compact Theory

A belated rejoinder to the attack by Professor Rogers came in the form of a Presidential Address to the Canadian Historical Association in 1956. The speaker, Professor G. F. G. Stanley, Dean of Arts at the Royal Military College of Canada and author of two studies of Louis Riel and the Red River and Saskatchewan uprisings, amongst other works, reflects his concern with the problems arising from the dualistic nature of Canadian society.

It was at Quebec that the new constitution took form and shape. . . . This gathering at Quebec was the first and only constituent body in the whole of our constitutional history. All previous constitutions had been drafted, considered, and passed, by an outside authority; in 1864 the thirty-three representatives of the British North American provinces met, with the blessing and approval of the British Government, to do what had hitherto always been done for them.

. . . In summary form, what the Quebec Conference decided was that the new union should be federal in character; that its central parliament should comprise two houses, the upper based on representation by provinces, and the lower upon representation by population; that the powers of the central government should be of a general character and those of the provincial legislatures of a local nature. These powers were carefully enumerated, but the legislative residuum was given to the central parliament. The French and English languages were to enjoy equal status in the central parliament and courts and in the legislature and courts of the province of Lower Canada.

Georges [*sic*] Cartier, generally, was satisfied with what had been achieved. He felt that even though he had been obliged to yield much to the demands of Macdonald and Brown and other advocates of a strong central government, he had, nevertheless, succeeded in preserving the rights and privileges of his own people and of the province in which they lived. He had, moreover, succeeded in maintaining the fundamental principle of the entente between the two racial groups in Canada, equality of race, equality of religion, equality of language, equality of laws. . . . The new constitution might not be designed to be the most efficient, but it would, at least, be just.

The next step was as easy as it was logical. Since both races were equal, a decision taken, an agreement arrived at by the equal partners on the fundamental character of the new constitution, could not be changed without the consent of each. It was, in fact, a treaty, a compact binding upon both parties. This was a view which scarcely roused a dissenting voice in the Canada of 1865. Not one of the Canadians who fathered the resolutions at Quebec failed to stress the unalterable character of the agreement they had made. Macdonald said, "these resolutions were in the nature of a treaty, and if not adopted in their entirety, the proceedings would have to be commenced *de novo*".* McGee, in his high-pitched but not unmusical voice, cried:

And that there may be no doubt about our position in regard to that document, we say, question it you may, reject it you may, or accept it you may, but alter it you may not. (Hear, hear.) It is beyond your power, or our power, to alter it. There is not a sentence—ay, or even a word— you can alter without desiring to throw out the document. . . . On this point, I repeat after all my hon. friends who have already spoken, for one party to alter a treaty is, of course, to destroy it.†

Taché, Cartier, McDougall, Brown, all of them described the Quebec Resolutions as a "treaty" or as a "pact", and argued for adoption without amendment.

---

* *Ibid.*, p. 16. Macdonald repeated this idea several times throughout his speech; see pp. 31–2. [Original footnote. The reference is to *Confederation Debates.*]
† *Ibid.*, p. 136. [Original footnote.]

It is easy for the lawyer or the political scientist, three generations later, to reply that in 1865 there was no treaty really made at all, that the Compromise of Quebec could not possess the attributes of a treaty or of a legal contract. Nevertheless the historical fact remains that the men who used these terms were the men who drafted the Resolutions; they chose their words with deliberation; many of them were lawyers, they knew what they were saying. They were not, every one of them, trying to becloud the issue before the legislature or to confuse the legislators. . . . The idea of a compact between races was not a new one in 1865; it had already become a vital thing in our history. It influenced both the political thinking and the political vocabulary of the day; and it was already on the way to become a tradition and a convention of our constitution.

The idea of a compact as I have outlined it was essentially, in its origin, a racial concept. But the meeting of the maritime delegates with those of Canada at Charlottetown and at Quebec introduced a new interpretation which has had mighty impact upon the course of our later history, namely, the idea of a compact between the politico-geographic areas which go to make up Canada. Even before the conferences it had become the common practice to identify the racial groups with the areas from which they came. Almost without thought "Quebec" and "French Canadians", or "Ontario" and "Anglo-Canadians", become synonymous terms in the mouths of Canadians of both tongues. It is, of course, a slipshod way of thinking as well as of speaking, . . . However, the point which I really wish to make is this; once Canadians (as distinct from Maritimers) began to identify provinces with specific linguistic groups, the idea of a pact between races was transformed into the idea of a pact between provinces. And the Compromise of Quebec became a compact between the provinces which participated in the conference. . . .

However, the compact idea, was still, in 1865, peculiarly a Canadian one. It was not shared by the delegates of the several Maritime colonies who had journeyed to Quebec. From what I have seen of the debates in the legislatures and the speeches reported in the press of Nova Scotia and New Brunswick, the words so familiar in Canada, words like "pact", "treaty" or "compact" were rarely used in reference to what had been decided upon at Charlottetown or Quebec. There was never any idea in the minds of the Maritime representatives that the Seventy-Two Resolutions were sacrosanct. Thus, when Nova Scotia and New Brunswick resolved in 1866 to renew the negotiations for a federal union with Canada, they sent their representatives to London with full authority to make any changes and to conclude any new arrangement they might see fit.

*   *   *   *   *

The explanation why the pact idea has remained most vigorous in the two central provinces is to be found in their history. We need only recall . . . the fact that the pact was, in its origin, an entente between the two racial groups of Old Canada, between the two provinces which were each the focus of a distinctive culture. Only in the two provinces of Old Canada did the racial struggle play any real part in our history; only in . . . Old Canada did this struggle have any real meaning. The Maritimers' . . . interest in federal union was largely financial, in the recovery of a passing age of sea-going prosperity. The western provinces, with the exception of British Columbia which found its own version of a compact in the terms of union in 1871, were the offspring of the federal loins; their interest in federal union was in their maintenance and subsistence. But in Upper and Lower Canada federation was the solution of the politico-racial contest for supremacy and survival. . . . The identification of the racial pact, which was a very real thing in the 1850's and 1860's, with the compromise arrived at by the several provinces in 1864 and 1866, has tended to obscure the racial aspect of the bargain and to deprive it of some of its strength. The Canadian delegates to Quebec and London were thoroughly convinced that their bargain was a treaty or a pact; however, this conviction was always weaker among the Maritimers than among the Canadians, and especially the French Canadians, whose principal concern as a vital minority has been and must be the survival of their culture and the pact which is the constitutional assurance of that survival.

It is the racial aspect of the pact of Confederation which gives the pact its historicity and confirms its continued usage.

> G. F. G. Stanley, "Act or Pact: Another Look at Confederation", Canadian Historical Association, *Report, 1956*, pp. 11–14, 24–5.

Further Reading

W. L. Morton, *The Critical Years: The Union of British North America 1857–1873* (Toronto, McClelland & Stewart, 1964) and D. G. Creighton, *The Road to Confederation: The Emergence of Canada, 1863–1867* (Toronto, Macmillan, 1964) provide modern full treatments of the achievement of Confederation. P. B. Waite stresses the public commentary on the proposed union in *The Life and Times of Confederation 1864–1867: Politics, Newspapers and the Union of British North America* (Toronto, University of Toronto Press, 1961)[*]. Morton and Waite append useful bibliographies. Biographies of the Fathers of Confederation should be consulted, and also J. M. Beck, *Joseph Howe: Anti-Confeaerate* (Canadian Historical Association Booklet No. 17). A detailed look at the question of "Act or Pact" that cannot be ignored by any serious student was made by W. F. O'Connor, *Report Pursuant to Resolution of the Senate to the Honourable the Speaker by the Parliamentary Counsel* (Ottawa, King's Printer, 1939).

Problem 12

The National Policy — Did It Fulfil Its Aims? At What Cost?

Writing in *Canada and Its Provinces*, Professor O. D. Skelton identified the "National Policy" as "a phrase Rose devised, Hincks stamped with his approval, and Macdonald made current".* Various meanings have been given to the phrase. The most narrow definition is the policy of protective tariffs advocated by the Conservative party in opposition prior to the election of 1878. A broader definition links the attempt to stimulate industry through tariff protection with the development of east-west channels of communication, notably railway expansion and the settlement of the prairie west. This more comprehensive National Policy would seem to culminate in the wheat boom just prior to the outbreak of war in 1914.

The policy was popularized by Sir John A. Macdonald in 1878 while he was in opposition, and was implemented immediately on his return to office. Its utility was questioned by the Liberal party under the leadership of Wilfrid Laurier in 1891, who advocated as an alternative "Unrestricted Reciprocity" with the United States. Macdonald so exerted himself in the winter campaign to vindicate "The Old Flag, The Old Policy, The Old Leader" that his death followed closely upon his victory. Laurier and the Liberals did succeed to power in the next general election, that of 1896, fought on other issues. Thereafter the Liberals themselves adopted the National Policy, modified with Imperial Preference, and in the

* In Adam Shortt and A. G. Doughty, eds., *Canada and Its Provinces* (Toronto, 1913), Vol. IX, p. 146. The phrase is quoted in V. C. Fowke, "The National Policy—Old and New", in *The Canadian Journal of Economics and Political Science*, XVIII (August 1952), p. 271. John Rose served as Minister of Finance for the Dominion from 18 November 1867 to 30 September 1869. Sir Francis Hincks succeeded him and served until 21 February 1873.

prosperous years that followed, reaped more success from it than had its Conservative authors. The very success of the policy, however, resulted in the rapid growth in the prairie west of a community opposed to tariff protection. In 1911 the Liberal government of Prime Minister Sir Wilfrid Laurier negotiated a reciprocity agreement with the United States. Thus, twenty years after the election of 1891, Canadian voters again were called upon to choose between the National Policy's east-west channels of trade, which postulated the development of Canada's principal export markets beyond the North American continent, and a continental economy with greater north-south lines of trade. In 1911, as two decades earlier, the voters rejected the continental alternative following a campaign marked by anti-American slogans and appeals to imperial loyalty.

Commentators on Canadian history have generally assumed that the National Policy was a key factor in the development and maintenance of a separate Canadian political entity in North America.

Questions which are intended to be raised by the following excerpts include: Did the National Policy fulfil its original aims? At what cost? What can account for the changing attitude of the Liberal Party to the policy?

Macdonald Explains the Purpose of the "N.P."

The issues were being defined for the forthcoming general election when Sir John A. Macdonald launched a debate on the projected "National Policy" during the Budget debate of 1878 through the parliamentary device of offering the following amendment to the Liberal government motion to go into supply:

... but that this House is of opinion that the welfare of Canada requires the adoption of a National Policy, which, by a judicious readjustment of the Tariff, will benefit and foster the agricultural, the mining, the manufacturing and other interests of the Dominion; that such a policy will retain in Canada thousands of our fellow countrymen now obliged to expatriate themselves in search of employment denied them at home, will restore prosperity to our struggling industries, now so sadly depressed, will prevent Canada from being made a sacrifice market,* will encourage and develop an active interprovincial trade, and moving (as it ought to do) in the direction of a reciprocity of Tariffs with

* The contemporary term for an area where foreign goods are disposed of below normal selling prices, partly as a device to discourage the development of competitors in the market: a "dumping ground" in more modern parlance.

our neighbours, so far as the varied interests of Canada may demand, will greatly tend to procure for this country, eventually, a reciprocity of trade.

Canada, Parliament, *Debates of the House of Commons*, 1878, (Ottawa), p. 854.

The second part of the following excerpt from his speech, relating to reciprocity in tariffs or in trade, adumbrates the effective campaign slogan of the forthcoming election. That one of the professed purposes of the National Policy was to exact tariff concessions from the United States by retaliating against the American trade-protectionist policy is frequently forgotten.

. . . The resolution speaks not only of a reasonable readjustment of the tariff but of the encouragement and development of interprovincial trade. That is one of the great objects we should seek to attain. Formerly, we were a number of Provinces which had very little trade with each other, and very little connection, except a common allegiance to a common Sovereign, and it is of the greatest importance that we should be allied together. I believe that, by a fair readjustment of the tariff, we can increase the various industries which we can interchange one with another, and make this union a union in interest, a union in trade, and a union in feeling. We shall then grow up rapidly a good, steady and mature trade between the Provinces, rendering us independent of foreign trade, and not, as New Brunswick and Nova Scotia formerly did, look to the United States or to England for trade, but look to Ontario and Quebec, —sending their products west, and receiving the products of Quebec and Ontario in exchange. Thus the great policy, the National Policy, which we on this side are advocating, would be attained. Hon. gentlemen opposite laughed very much when they heard that part of the resolution relating to reciprocity of tariffs and reciprocity of trade; but I will tell them that, if there is one thing more than another in the minds of the people at the present time, it is this very subject. There is no mistake about it, for during the summer I had the opportunity of visiting all parts of the country,* and have met many who profess themselves to be Reformers, Grits, or Liberals, upon whose minds the idea has been impressed. It has taken fast hold of the people of Ontario. Hon. gentlemen may depend upon it that the country will have it. The country will not have the present unjust policy. The country will have fair play, and will not allow our markets to be made use of by the manufacturers of a neighbouring country when they can find no better market elsewhere, and at the same time have no access to their markets.

Ibid., p. 861.

---

* A reference to his campaign through "the picnic grounds of Ontario".

The Railway Construction and Settlement of the Northwest
Supplement the Protective Tariff

The intimate association of the construction of the east-west
railway lines, especially the Canadian Pacific Railway, and the
settlement of the northwest with the protective tariff of the National
Policy was clearly enunciated in a statement of administration
policy made in the House of Commons by Sir Charles Tupper,
Minister of Railways and Canals, on 15 April 1880.

After criticizing certain actions of the preceding Liberal Administration, he stated:

When we found ourselves brought face to face with this very serious question
what did we do? We reverted back, as far as possible, under the changed
circumstances to our former policy. Our policy was this: That the lands of the
North-West ought to build the Canadian Pacific Railway. That was the
principal plank in our platform. The late First Minister [Alexander Mackenzie,
Prime Minister 1873–8] in his address at Sarnia, covered the whole ground
when he said "that it was impossible ever to draw emigration into that great
country and settle it without the construction of a Canadian Pacific Railway."
We held that opinion, and we felt that, inasmuch as that great fertile North-
West must remain a barren waste until the Railway was constructed, and that
inasmuch as those lands were the most fair and fertile, and the richest to be
found on the face of the globe, and that they must remain useless to Canada
unless the Railway was constructed, we felt warranted in adopting the policy
which we have adopted.

*   *   *   *   *

No person can look abroad over the Dominion without feeling that the
Great North-West Territory is the district to which we must look for our
strength and development. Just as the older of the United States look to their
Great North-West, with its rapidly increasing population, adding hundreds of
thousands and millions to their strength, not only may we look for strength by
reason of an additional Customs Revenue from the increased population of
that Territory, but we must look upon that western country as a field for the
manufacturing industries of the older and more settled parts of Canada. Every
person acquainted with this country knows we have exhausted to some extent
its bread-growing power, but under the National Policy that Canada has
adopted, we must look forward not only to building up thriving centres of
industries and enterprise all over this portion of the country, but to obtaining
a market for those industries after they have been established; and I say where
is there a greater market than that magnificent granary of the North-West,
which, filled up with a thriving and prosperous population, will make its

demands upon Ontario, Quebec, Nova Scotia and New Brunswick for these
manufacturing products that we, for many years, will be so well able to supply?

*   *   *   *   *

. . . At this moment the eyes of a large portion of the civilised world are
centred upon the Great North-West of Canada, and hundreds of thousands
of people in every foreign country, as well as the British Empire, are studying
the question as to whether they shall come with their capital and industry and
build up Canada into a great, prosperous and progressive country.

Canada, Parliament, *Debates* . . . , 1880 (Ottawa), pp. 1408–9, 1424–5.

The National Policy Attacked

The implementation of the National Policy was followed by a
brief upward swing in the economy, but it was soon obvious that,
by itself, it had not provided the magic formula which would cause
the Canadian economic growth rate to equal that of the United
States. Few settlers, either from the old provinces or from overseas,
took up land in the Canadian prairies. Instead, Canadians continued to emigrate to the neighbouring republic. The phrase "the
Exodus", when used in the journals of the day, required no explanation. Investors continued to favour American, Australian, and
Argentinian offerings in the London and other European money
markets.

Understandably, voices critical of the National Policy were
raised throughout the Dominion. In 1886 Premier William Fielding
of Nova Scotia conducted a successful provincial election campaign
on the issue that the province should seek escape from the baneful
effects of the National Policy through secession. The two-way
interprovincial trade, which Macdonald had prophesied in 1878,
had not materialized.

An alternative policy emerged in 1887, when a bill was introduced
into the United States Congress providing for free entrance of
Canadian goods into the United States whenever American goods
were permitted free entrance into Canada. This project became
known as Commerical Union. It proved popular among farmers,
who were attracted by the possibilities of larger markets close at
hand, and by some manufacturers who welcomed the possibility of
competing in the larger market, but most of the latter group opposed

the idea. Commercial Union Clubs were organized in many centres, especially in Ontario.

The Attorney-General of Nova Scotia, J. W. Longley, a strong critic of the National Policy and a professed annexationist,* became an active advocate of Commercial Union. Before many audiences he expressed variations of these views.

Granting, for the moment, that under ordinary circumstances the National Policy is sound—in other words, that in a new country like Canada it is the true policy to build up domestic industries by imposing high tariffs against the products and manufactures of older countries, still, upon a careful examination into the peculiar circumstances of our position, it must strike any mind that is not prejudiced or dull, that such a policy is simple madness, and must sooner or later collapse. A political union of the several Provinces of British North America was effected in 1867, but not a commercial union, and the twenty years that have elapsed have served only to demonstrate how utterly impossible a commercial union between the several Provinces is.

I take the solid ground that naturally there is no trade between Ontario and the Maritime Provinces whatsoever. Without the aid or compulsion of tariffs scarcely a single article produced in Ontario would ever seek or find a market in Nova Scotia, or the other Maritime Provinces; in like manner, unless under similar compulsion, not a product of the Maritime Provinces would ever go to Ontario. Twenty years of political union and nine years of an inexorable protective policy designed to compel inter-Provincial trade have been powerless to create any large trade between these two sections, and what it has created has been unnatural, unhealthy, and consequently profitless.

* * * * *

Does any one ask why this state of things exists? The answer is simple. God and nature never designed a trade between Ontario and the Maritime Provinces. . . .

J. W. Longley, "Current Objections to Commercial Union Considered", in *Handbook of Commercial Union: a collection of papers read before the Commercial Union Club, Toronto* . . . (Toronto, 1888), pp. 111, 112, 113.

Edward Blake on the Effects of the National Policy

One variant of the Commercial Union proposal, "Unrestricted Reciprocity", provided for complete freedom of trade between Canada and her southern neighbour, but specifically permitted both

---

* One who advocated the incorporation of Canada into the United States.

countries to maintain their own tariff structures toward other countries. Unrestricted Reciprocity became the principal plank for the platform on which the Liberal Party campaigned in the election of 1891.

The campaign, Sir John A. Macdonald's last, was notable for the emotional appeals epitomized in the slogan, "The Old Flag, The Old Policy, The Old Leader", and the peroration of Sir John's address to the electors of Canada: "As for myself, my course is clear. A British subject I was born—a British subject I will die. With my utmost effort, with my latest breath, will I oppose the 'veiled treason' which attempts by sordid means and mercenary proffers to lure our people from their allegiance."*

One of the most telling indictments of the National Policy composed during the election was not published until the day following the polling. The former leader of the Liberal party, Edward Blake, was not a candidate in the election. Nevertheless, he composed a manifesto for the electors of his old constituency of West Durham in which he attacked the effects of the National Policy, and expressed reservations on the proposed remedy, Unrestricted Reciprocity. He was persuaded by Laurier, his successor as leader, to withhold publication until after the election. His views on the legacy of the National Policy, coloured as they inevitably were by the heat of election passions, remain a significant commentary of one of the most acute minds to have operated in Canadian politics.

It has left us with a small population, a scanty immigration, and a North‑West empty still; with enormous additions to our public debt and yearly charge, an extravagant system of expenditure, and an unjust and oppressive tariff . . . and with unfriendly relations and frowning tariff walls ever more and more estranging us from the mighty English-speaking nation to the south, our neighbours and relations, with whom we ought to be, as it was promised that we should be, living in generous amity and liberal intercourse. Worse, far worse! It has left us with lowered standards of public virtue and a death-like apathy in public opinion; with racial, religious and provincial animosities rather inflamed than soothed; with a subservient parliament, an autocratic executive, debauched constituencies, and corrupted and corrupting classes; with lessened self-reliance and increased dependence on the public chest and on legislative aids, and possessed withal by a boastful jingo spirit far enough

---

* Joseph Pope, *Memoirs of the Right Honourable Sir John Alexander Macdonald* (Toronto, 1930, revised edition), p. 777.

removed from true manliness, loudly proclaiming unreal conditions and exaggerated sentiments, while actual facts and genuine opinions are suppressed. It has left us with our hands tied, our future compromised, and in such a plight that, whether we stand or move, we must run some risks which else we might either have declined or encountered with greater promise of success.

O. D. Skelton, *Life and Letters of Sir Wilfrid Laurier* (Toronto, 1921), Vol. I, pp. 419–20.

Laurier Embraces the National Policy

When he was called to the Prime Ministership following the Liberal victory in 1896, Laurier selected William Fielding, the erstwhile secessionist premier of Nova Scotia, as Minister of Finance. The Finance Minister of the previous Liberal government, Sir Richard Cartwright, a doctrinaire free trader and long-time critic of the National Policy, was given a less sensitive portfolio.

Although the new administration made certain concessions to freer trade, notably the creation of special British Preference rates in the tariff of 1897, they generally accepted the inherited national policy. In the prosperous years which followed 1896, emigrants flooded into the prairies, two new transcontinental railway systems were undertaken with government sponsorship, and Canada's manufacturers at last found a profitable market.

Sir Wilfrid Laurier's changed attitude toward a policy which promised to make the twentieth century Canada's can be seen in his address to the Canadian Manufacturers' Association in 1905. By the end of the decade rumbling of discontent from the prairie west, where the settlers did not accept the position assigned them in this speech, had had its influence in persuading the Liberals to explore again the possibilities of a reciprocity agreement with the United States. The result was the agreement and the general election campaign of 1911.

They [the settlers filling up the Prairie West] will require clothes, they will require furniture, they will require implements, they will require shoes—and I hope you can furnish them to them . . . they will require everything that man has to be supplied with. It is your ambition, it is my ambition also, that this scientific tariff of ours will make it possible that every shoe that has to be worn in those prairies shall be a Canadian shoe; that every yard of cloth that can be marketed there shall be a yard of cloth produced in Canada; and so on and so on. It does not follow that I do not want to trade with other nations, and I still hope that our scientific tariff will not prevent the trade with other nations. I want to give a preference to Great Britain, but I do not hesitate to say that I have no hard feelings against the Americans, . . .

Canadian Annual Review, 1905 (Toronto, 1906), pp. 149–50.

THE VIEWS OF LATER COMMENTATORS

An Appraisal from the Close of the Laurier Boom

Reference was made in the introduction to this Problem to O.D. Skelton's contribution in *Canada and Its Provinces*, the large-scale co-operative venture in historical scholarship which was published just prior to the outbreak of the First World War. The following excerpts demonstrate the author's appreciation of the emotional element involved in the framing of the policy, and a recognition that there were favourable and unfavourable effects.

The demand for a higher tariff, finally, was not based solely on economic grounds; it professed to be a National Policy. No small measure of the strength of protection in Canada as elsewhere has lain in the readier appeal it makes to patriotism. Patriotism is ordinarily both positive and negative; it is composed in varying parts of love of one's own country and dislike of other lands. On the negative side protection made strong appeal to the anti-American feeling inherited from United Empire Loyalist days, and fostered by the repeated rejection of Canada's trade overtures. It scored equally on the positive side. It promised national self-sufficiency. It promised an industrial life varied enough to find places for all the boys who otherwise would be lost—absorbed by the United States. It promised to develop trade between the provinces, to create an east and west traffic fed by Nova Scotia's coal and Ontario's flour, and to cement national unity by the common interests thus established.

*   *   *   *   *

A generation after the adoption of the National Policy, it is still an open question whether protection has helped or hindered Canadian development. So far as the economic bearings of the case go, the fact that one-sided free trade would compel the Canadian manufacturer to share his small market with the United States manufacturer, while he himself would be barred from the larger market and from the economies that go with the larger field and scale of production, must never be left out of reckoning. It may be, again, that many of the scores of United States corporations which have established branch factories in Canada would have attempted to supply the Dominion from the other side of the border, but for the tariff wall. . . . So far as the political bearings of protection go, it is to be set down to its credit that in former days it helped to create a common national spirit, and on the debit side that it now [1912] is creating a dangerous sectional divergence, only to be ended by doing away with protection or by making the West as well an industrial district.

> O. D. Skelton, "General Economic History of the Dominion, 1867–1912", in *Canada and Its Provinces* (Toronto, 1913), Vol. IX, pp. 145, 204.

The National Policy: The Coping Stone of National Unity

In his paper, "The Contribution of Macdonald Conservatism to National Unity, 1854-78", read before a session of the Canadian Historical Association annual meeting, 1939, A. D. Lockhart implied an unqualified acceptance of the political value of the National Policy, while suggesting that its original advocacy by Macdonald involved an element of opportunism.

The coping stone which rounded off the services of Macdonald Conservatism to unity was its enunciation in 1878 of National Policy. Much has been said and written on the "insincerity" of Macdonald in advocating protection, while, on the other hand, an attenuated case can be made out for consistency. Possibly Macdonald's pragmatic attitude is best revealed in a letter written to D. L. MacPherson in 1872—the election year in which some of the constituencies were given a mild preview of N.P. "Mackenzie, Brown and Co. are thoroughly committed to free trade. Now you are, I know, a hot free-trader, so am I; but I quite agree with Patterson [of the Toronto *Mail*] that our game is to coquet with the protectionists. The word 'protection' itself must be taboo, but we can ring the changes on National Policy, paying U.S. in their own coin, etc."

A study of the origins of National Policy—as it appeared, full-dress, in 1878 —reveals that the Conservative leaders were not so much the sponsors, as the recipients of it. Hundreds of letters and press articles testify to this fact. Goldwin Smith remarked that national sentiment was ripe for protection and to refuse it was "to slam the door in the people's faces." Macdonald was amazed at the popularity of the demand, and proceeded hastily to educate himself in the finer points of "industrial politics". . . . Macdonald's own contribution to National Policy was to put behind it the vehicle of party and to present the case to the electors. It was significant that for the first time, a Dominion leader—backed by a united party—stumped not only Central Canada, but the Maritimes as well.

National Policy was in substance economic nationalism. As such, it tested the aspirations of Canadians and the degree to which the forces of cohesion had done their work. The acceptance of the policy in every province, except New Brunswick, marked a determinant achievement in national unity.

A. D. Lockhart, "The Contribution of Macdonald Conservatism to National Unity, 1854–78", Canadian Historical Association, *Report, 1939*, pp. 131–2.

The National Policy Is a Begetter of Sectional Discontent

The historian of the Progressive Movement, Professor W. L. Morton, then of the University of Manitoba, indicates the tendency toward sectional discontent inherent in the National Policy.

At the root of the sectional conflict, from which the Progressive Movement in part sprang, was the National Policy of 1878. Such conflict is partly the result of the hardships and imperfect adaptations of the frontier, but it also arises from the incidence of national policies. The sectional corn develops where the national shoe pinches. The National Policy, that brilliant improvisation of Sir John A. Macdonald, had grown under the master politician's hand, under the stimulus of depression and under the promptings of political appetite, until it had become a veritable Canadian System Henry Clay might have envied. Explicit in it was the promise that everybody should have something from its operation; implicit in it—its inarticulate major premise indeed—was the promise that when the infant industries it fostered had reached maturity, protection would be needed no more.

This, however, was but a graceful tribute to the laissez-faire doctrine of the day. This same doctrine it was which prevented the western wheat grower from demanding that he, too, should benefit directly from the operation of the National Policy. That he did benefit from the system as a whole, a complex of land settlement, railway construction, and moderate tariff protection, is not to be denied. But the wheat grower, building the wheat economy from homestead to terminal elevator in a few swift years, was caught in a complex of production and marketing costs, land values, railway rates, elevator charges, and interest rates. He fought to lower all these costs by economic organization and by political pressure. He saw them all as parts of a system which exploited him. . . . Accordingly, he hated and fought it as a whole. Of the National Policy, however, the tariff was politically the most conspicuous element. Hence the political battle was fought around the tariff; it became the symbol of the wheat growers' exploitation and frustration, alleged and actual. Like all symbols, it over-simplified the complexities it symbolized.

W. L. Morton, "The Western Progressive Movement, 1919–1921", Canadian Historical Association, *Report, 1946*, p. 41.

Is the Answer to the Problem to Be Found in Developments South of the Border?

Writing under the influence of the boom conditions of the 1950's, Professors W. T. Easterbrook of the University of Toronto and H. G. J. Aitken of the University of California, Riverside, assess the events in their textbook, *Canadian Economic History*.

As the vision of a commercial empire of the St. Lawrence faded, a larger vision took its place. This has come to bear the label "National Policy," a term which has been applied both to the programme of creating a Canadian nation and, in a much more restricted meaning, to the system of protective tariffs which was adopted in 1878. The broader use of the term is now widely accepted and for our purposes is preferable to its narrower application. This makes the problem of its exact definition more difficult, since it embraces a range of elements which by Confederation had not been woven into any clear-cut pattern. On the other hand, the main ingredients are easily discerned: the central place of the St. Lawrence area as the basis for continental expansion, the reliance on transportation improvements to provide the backbone of this expansion, the emphasis on a few staple products for export to European markets, the encouragement of developments in finance and secondary industries to support this structure, and finally the slow shift to tariffs to round out this broadly conceived policy of economic growth. . . . To link transportation, tariffs, land policy, banking and public finance in a more closely-knit pattern, to foster agriculture and industry in the St. Lawrence provinces and the lumbering and fisheries of the Maritimes, and to create in the process a larger and more unified economic structure—these were preliminary steps in the development of a national economy. A great area of internal free trade and a stronger bargaining position with other nations could be expected to result from the attainment of this objective.

* * * * *

Although there has been a tendency to underestimate the rate of progress of the Canadian economy over the period from 1874 to 1896, it is true that economic growth was much slower over these decades than had been anticipated. . . .

This disappointingly slow rate of progress has been attributed to a number of factors. Unfavourable world conditions have been held to explain Canada's inability to attract and hold population and capital in the volume anticipated. Yet other new countries, rich in resources and lacking in labour and capital, fared better than Canada. Bouts of depression in Europe made for a strong push of migration from that area, and the New World stood to gain in population from the difficulties of the Old. Canada's pulling power, however, was more than matched by that of Australia, Argentina, and the American West, . . . But the most decisive factor in relegating Canada to a very minor role in the world migration and capital movements of this period must be sought in the weight and momentum of United States expansion westward. The northern nation had to wait its turn until the twentieth century when the westward moving frontier swung north to the Canadian prairies. In contrast to the inter-war years of this century and the present [1956], a period whose tempo of economic growth is greatly increased by United States capital and enterprise, the later nineteenth century, so far as Canada was concerned, is best summed up as a period of consolidation and waiting until world interest, its capital and its labour, were attracted in volume to the hitherto neglected northern half of North America. . . .

It was only when the best lands in the United States had been alienated, her agricultural surplus reduced by her growing domestic market, and her forest resources nearly exhausted that Canada's national policy began to pay long-awaited dividends.

*   *   *   *   *

Indications of better times to come made their appearance as early as 1896. The prolonged downward movement of world prices gave way in that year to a moderate movement upward. Substantial additions to the world's gold stocks in a period in which the gold standard was operating effectively helped to bring about this change. This was only one of a number of highly favourable circumstances which appeared at this time to bring prosperity to the Canadian economy. Not only was the selling-price of Canadian exports moving upward, but the cost of transporting wheat, Canada's key staple, was dropping sharply.

The influx of capital was a basic element in an upward movement which, following the years of recovery, 1896–1901, achieved momentum in 1902–3 and took on the proportions of a boom in the years 1909–13. Funds reached the country through various channels; immigrants brought capital with them, investors in search of quick returns from land and other speculations were attracted, and, much the most important, Canadian securities were sold in very large volume in the London money market by governments and railway companies for developmental purposes. British and continental funds began to move on a scale sufficient to dominate this phase of the country's growth. The vast area of Canada and the bulky character of its products necessitated large supplies of capital for transportation and related improvements, and for agricultural, manufacturing and mining development. . . . Domestic supplies of capital were much too limited to provide the huge sums needed and it fell mainly to the British investor to meet the capital requirements of the Canadian economy of this period. . . .

*   *   *   *   *

In every respect conditions were favourable to a high level of prosperity in the Canadian economy of the early twentieth century. The spread of industrialism in Europe created a demand for Canada's export staples, a source of cheap manufactured goods for Canadian consumption, and a growing volume of capital for investment in Canadian expansion. In North America, the northward shift of the frontier to the Canadian prairies, the shrinking export surplus of the United States, and that country's declining demand for foreign capital helped to heighten European interest in Canada. Further, technological progress in agriculture, mining and manufacturing in the United States undoubtedly accelerated the rate of Canada's growth since there were few barriers to the entry of technical innovations, most of which could be readily applied to Canadian resource development. In Canada itself, the economic and political bases of expansion had been laid before the end of the century. A national policy based on the closely interrelated elements of railway construction, tariff policies and wheat production for the world markets had been formulated. It remained to implement more effectively the national design visualized by Confederation.

> W. T. Easterbrook and H. G. J. Aitken, *Canadian Economic History* (Toronto, 1956), pp. 388–9, 395, 396, 400, 401, 402.

The National Policy's Price: Corruption

Frank H. Underhill, the dean of liberal Canadian historians, discussed the National Policy and its alternatives in the third of his Massey Lectures on the C.B.C. radio network in 1963, a lecture entitled, "History against Geography". In the preceding lecture he examined the "Canada First Movement" (to which reference is made in the following Problem). He concluded that broadcast with the words:

There was developing a national sentiment in the new Dominion, but it was canalized along economic lines rather than political lines. It found expression in the National Policy tariff to protect native industries and in the building of the C.P.R. to tie the sections of the new Dominion together. The National Policy was, of course, a Declaration of Economic Independence. The first romantic phase of nationalism had passed quickly. Canada was living in the Bismarckian era. The realistic, practical politician, rebuilding one of the old parties after its downfall in the Pacific Scandal, had triumphed over the idealistic intellectuals.

> F. H. Underhill, *The Image of Confederation* (Toronto, 1964), pp. 22–3.

Early in his next lecture he remarked:

The nationalism that captured the support of the Canadian people was not that of Canada First or of Goldwin Smith or of Edward Blake, but that of John A. Macdonald—the nationalism of the protective tariff and the Pacific railway. To build up a national loyalty you must succeed in attaching some of the major groups in the country to the national government as the centre of their primary interest. The young men of Canada First lacked the basis of an effective political movement because they spoke for no particular social groups whose economic ambitions were to be furthered through the activity of the national government, and for no discontented groups who might form the basis of another Grit party. And, of course, they did not speak for the most solid group of all, the French Canadians.

What Macdonald did was to attach to the national government the interests of the ambitious, dynamic, speculative or entrepreneurial business groups, who aimed to make money out of the new national community or to install themselves in the strategic positions of power within it—the railway promoters, banks, manufacturers, land companies, contractors, and such people. They supplied the drive behind his so-called National Policy, and they stood to reap the greatest benefits from it. They also required the fostering care of a Hamiltonian government and the lavish expenditure of taxpayers' money in public capital investment if their ambitions were to be realized. In return, their support was necessary to keep the Conservative government in office. "The day that the C.P.R. busts, the Conservative party busts the day after" said a slightly inelegant cabinet minister in the Macdonald government of the 1880s. The actual, functioning nationalism, therefore, that emerged out of Confederation was based on a triple alliance of federal government, Conservative party, and big-business interests: government of the people, by lawyers, for big business.

The benefits of this nationalism were very unevenly distributed. As Norman Rogers pointed out in his Report on the Fiscal Disabilities of Nova Scotia, in 1934, the National Policy was the first step in making a national plan for Canada, and there should have been further steps to ensure that its benefits and costs were distributed equitably among the various classes and sections of the nations. . . .

The Macdonald system also involved a tremendous amount of corruption, which lowered the standards of our public life and has remained one of the heavy costs of this kind of nationalism ever since. For Macdonald's working principle was that every man has his price. "Generally I would charge against your party, as represented by the government in which you sat" wrote Sir John Willison to Sir Charles Tupper, as he looked back on this first generation of Confederation, "that it carried out a great constructive Canadian policy by bad political methods and gross corruption in the constituencies, and that the net result was to build up Canada and greatly to lower public morals." This seems to me to be a pretty good summing up of that first generation of Canadian nationalism. But Willison lived to see his own party, the Liberals, in power for fifteen years after 1896. And his final conclusion was that all that distinguished Liberals from Conservatives in nation-building was their "voluble virtue".

Ibid., pp. 24–6

An Economic Historian Reviews a Political Historian's Book on the Topic

The following excerpts are taken from a review article by Professor Melville Watkins of *Canada's National Policy: 1883–1900: A Study in Canadian-American Relations* (Princeton: Princeton University Press, 1964) by Robert Craig Brown, an American-born but Canadian-trained historian, who has pursued his academic career entirely in Canadian universities. The introduction and concluding chapters of this book would make appropriate supplementary reading for this topic. The author of the review article uses the book merely as a point of departure for an expression of his own considered opinions on the impact of the National Policy in Canadian history (the events in Canada's past) and in Canadian historiography (what historians and others have written about the past).

The most characteristic feature of Canadian nationalism may well be the persistent uncertainty felt by Canadians as to its existence. If this is so, the fault does not lie with the historians of Canada who, necessarily writing within the confines of a world of nation-states, have usually been prepared to embellish their documents with the unifying theme of the building and maintenance of Canada as a nation. The results have not always been convincing, and it is perhaps not surprising that there are those who appear to imagine that Canadian nationalism would go away if the historians would stop writing about it.

* * * * *

The interrelationship of economics and politics on the North American continent is the essence of the historical exercise in Canada; it is much too complex to be dealt with by simple immersion in the facts. Brown's conclusion —that economic nationalism was necessary to political independence—may be correct. Certainly no one has previously documented so well the case that the tariff was an invaluable instrument of nation-building and hence a political success. But how is one to know? Answers depend on the questions put and the methods used, with different disciplines giving conflicting answers to the same question. While Brown's view seems to be universally accepted by Canadian historians, there is a countercase argued by some economists (notably Harry

Johnson*) that lowering the standard of living—which is what the National Policy probably did—weakened the material base on which political independence must stand. That the latter conclusion is also too *simpliste* is clear, but that is only to argue that economic analysis *per se* is no more effective in providing an answer than is conventional historiography unadorned by any analysis whatsoever.

It is necessary to transcend the approaches of both disciplines. There is no presumption that it can be done here and now, but at least one can put down some cryptic comments that may suggest new approaches. While the National Policy was national in the sense of being nationalistic, it was not a native Canadian innovation; . . . it was, in every important respect, a carbon copy of prior American policy. Paradoxically, the National Policy was an early manifestation of the Americanization of Canada, a process that it then facilitated by encouraging the creation of a branch plant economy, . . . A policy of free trade might have genuinely distinguished Canada from the United States. Nor was the National Policy a planned and integrated set of policies. The tariff was a response to depression and American unwillingness to countenance reciprocity; it then created the vested interests necessary for its indefinite survival and the inefficiency that required its continuation. . . . Commitments to build railways were consistently made in periods of prosperity when imports overrode the tariff and created government surpluses, while a protective tariff was justified by the need to provide traffic for over-built railways in periods of stagnation. Immigration was needed in part to offset the emigration that resulted from a lowering of the standard of living consequent on the National Policy and the resulting widening of the differential between American and Canadian incomes. National support for the protective tariff was in part accidental, with the Maritime provinces not yet disabused of their hopes to industrialize around their coal, and the West not yet in existence. Both regions have complained of the tariff ever since, raising doubts as to whether economic nationalism has in fact contributed to national unity and nationalism.

While the National Policy helped to build Canada, as Brown shows, there is a serious danger of exaggerating its contribution. Successful nation-building requires firm foundations in geography and technology. The existence of Canada is attributable not to a defiant act of will, but rather to the St. Lawrence River and the potential of the canoe and the railway to extend its empire to the Pacific. The National Policy was the ideological content of the new technology of the railway wedded to the old fur economy of the St. Lawrence. Railway subsidies were justified as being necessary to obtain all-Canadian routes, and the tariff was defended as being necessary to provide traffic for the railways. . . .

---

* Prof. H. G. Johnson, Canadian-born economist, who has served on the faculties of the University of Chicago and The London School of Economics. Author of *The Canadian Quandary* (Toronto, 1963).

The National Policy was vulgar materialism writ large. . . . The major burden of economic nationalism is perhaps not the extent to which it lowers the standard of living—real though that is—but rather the extent to which, by monopolizing politics, it narrows vision and lowers the quality of national life. Brown follows in the tradition of Creighton,* whose work clearly demonstrates that the National Policy was more the imperialism of the St. Lawrence merchants than a broadly based nationalism. That the mob was sometimes allied with the elite . . . is hardly a cause for national self-congratulation.

* * * * *

Canada's National Policy emerged against the background of a wave of nationalism—and the new imperialism—of the late nineteenth century. In contrast with more rampant nationalisms, then and now, Canada's National Policy is tame, and therefore admirable. For the same reason it is innocent; the simple-minded pursuit of material gains has little to do with the horrors that lay just under the surface in the late nineteenth century and have since erupted with such violence and terror. Perpetual innocence soon becomes irrelevance, as the non-existence of American-Canadian relations demonstrates; it is probable that what Canada was doing in the late nineteenth century was setting out down a road which ultimately leads nowhere.

> Melville H. Watkins, "Economic Nationalism", *The Canadian Journal of Economics and Political Science*, XXXII (August 1966), pp. 388, 390–1, 392.

Further Reading

R. C. Brown, "The Nationalism of the National Policy" and John Dale, "Protection, Immigration and Canadian Nationalism", University League for Social Reform (Peter Russell, ed.), *Nationalism in Canada* (Toronto, McGraw-Hill, 1966) bear directly on this problem. D. G. Creighton, *John A. Macdonald:* Vol. II, *The Old Chieftain* (Toronto, Macmillan, 1955) notes (pp. 120–1) that the name and the three essential factors of the National Policy were advocated by Macdonald in 1872. This book provides an eloquent defence of the policy. E. Porritt, *Sixty Years of Protection in Canada, 1846–1907* (London, 1908), attacks the policy from a British free-trade viewpoint. V. C. Fowke, *The National Policy and the Wheat Economy* (Toronto, University of Toronto Press, 1955) discusses the culmination of the policy.

---

* Professor D. G. Creighton, of the University of Toronto, biographer of Sir John A. Macdonald, and also author of *The Empire of the St. Lawrence, 1760–1850* (Toronto, 1956), first published in 1937 as *The Commercial Empire of the St. Lawrence*.

Problem 13

The Focus of Loyalty — Nation? Province? Empire?

The constitutional means by which the Dominion of Canada came into being complicated the growth of national consciousness among the residents of a country. A comparison with the situation in the United States demonstrates the difference. The creation of the American republic can be traced through well-defined, dramatic events. These include: the Declaration of Independence, a successful armed revolution, formal recognition by the British Government of this independence in the Treaty of Paris, 1783, and the drafting and ratification by special state conventions of a federal constitution which came into effect in 1789. Following these events, most of which transpired on American soil, providing convenient patriotic shrines, only two political entities competed as the focus of loyalty for a "loyal" citizen: his state, and the "Union". At various times, most dramatically with the outbreak of the Civil War in 1861, individual Americans have been forced to decide which loyalty takes precedence, to their state, or to the Union. Fortunately, Canadians have never been faced with the same necessity to stand and be counted on an issue where the conflict of loyalties has led to an open rupture, but they have been faced with a three-fold, or greater, competition for their ultimate political loyalty rather than the American's choice of two contenders. This situation is a result of the peaceful, evolutionary (rather than revolutionary) process of political integration. Legally Canada was a creation of an outside authority. In passing the British North America Act, 1867, a simple statute, the British Parliament provided that "the Provinces of Canada, Nova Scotia and New Brunswick shall form and be one Dominion under the name of Canada". The exact day for the creation of the new political entity was set by Royal Proclamation. The legal instruments for the inclusion of other British North

American territories into the Dominion in the nineteenth century were also British. It was, therefore, quite respectable for residents of Canada to profess loyalty to the source of imperial authority which created Canada as well as to their colony-turned-province, or to Canada itself. Their external focus of loyalty might be Britain, or the wider, less clearly defined concept of "The Empire" or later "The Commonwealth". The problem is further confounded by professions of loyalty to the person of the monarch or to "The Crown", which, with no difficulty, can be combined with any of the loyalties mentioned above.

A different conflict of loyalty which troubled French Canada will be examined in Problem 14.

Views of the Founding Fathers

The speech given by John A. Macdonald to the Halifax audience on 12 September 1864* can profitably be reread at this point. The conviction that the claims of "new nationality" and imperial loyalty could be reconciled were held by all chief advocates of Confederation. The views of Arthur Rankin, M.L.A. for Essex, expressed in support of the Quebec Resolutions in the Confederation Debates in the Parliament of the Province of Canada, suggest that the claims of the province should take precedence over those of the mother country. Readers should remember that in 1865 the name, Canada, referred to the old province. The anti-American sentiment with which the excerpt closes is also significant, representing an important unifying factor for the different communities which were to make up the Dominion.

I am not disposed to insinuate that there is a solitary member of this House who entertains sentiments of disloyalty to Great Britain. We all have a right to express our views, and in fact it is our duty to do so since we are sent here to consider what is best for the interests of Canada *first*; for though we owe allegiance to England, Canada is *our* country, and has the strongest and best claims to our devotion. I, sir, am not one of those Canadians who place the interests of England first, and hold those of Canada in secondary estimation. . . . [W]e ought not to permit ourselves to lose sight of the fact, that with nations as with individuals, the time does arrive when it becomes each person to be responsible for himself, and when he can no longer look to his parents to give

* See above, pp. 180–1.

him a standing in the world. Sir, the time must come, sooner or later, when this country must cease to be a colony dependent on Great Britain; and whatever we do . . . we ought always to keep the fact plainly before our eyes, that passing events are calling upon us, either to commence the establishment of a nationality for ourselves, or make up our minds to be absorbed in the republic lying along our southern borders. Nothing could be more distasteful to me than to become what is called a citizen of the United States, though I admit the enterprise and intelligence which characterize the people of that country.

> *Parliamentary Debates on the Subject of the Confederation of the*
> *British North American Provinces* (Quebec, 1865), p. 916.
> [Italics as in the original.]

An Anti-Confederation Speaker Appeals to Colonial Loyalty

W. H. Needham, an opponent of the Confederation project, appealed to local New Brunswick loyalty in a speech delivered in the New Brunswick legislature on 3 April 1865 from which the following excerpt is taken. In order to appreciate the speaker's sarcasm the reader should bear in mind that the Parliament buildings were still under construction in Ottawa ("Westminster-in-the-bush" as critics of the new capital city had dubbed it) and that it was generally expected that a royal prince would take up residence as viceroy when the Union of Provinces came into being.

. . . I know there are men whose souls soar away beyond us, who are satiated with all that little New Brunswick can give them, and they reach forward to the celebrated towers and palaces of the far-off Ottawa; for this they would let New Brunswick go to the winds and be lost for ever. Bring us near to the darling of our souls, the far away Ottawa, with its miles of cornice and its acres of plaster and let us revel there in vice-regal glory. But there are loyal sons of New Brunswick who will not be carried away by all this splendor, and when the time comes, it will be seen that this splendor has been like a dissolving view to their eyes, become "the baseless fabric of a vision which leaves not a wreck behind."

*   *   *   *   *

I have shown . . . that I have a right to feel I am pursuing an honest and disinterested course in sustaining that Government, who have determined with me to resist to the political death any onslaught on the rights and liberties of this free people; . . .

When I forget my country so far as to sell it for Confederation, may my right hand forget its cunning, and if I do not prefer New Brunswick, as she is, to Canada with all her glory, then let my tongue cleave to the roof of my mouth. When the day comes when we shall have . . . Confederation deposited in the grave, those that will be there will not be there as mourners, but as glorifiers, and they will sing, with hearts elate with patriotic joy:

> Then safely moored, our perils o'er,
>> We'll sing the songs of Jubilee,
> For ever and for ever more,
>> New Brunswick, Land of Liberty.

New Brunswick, *Debates of the House of Assembly for 1866*, p. 89.

Newfoundlanders Express Their Sentiments in Song

Although Newfoundland was represented at the Quebec Conference in 1864, the colony did not enter Confederation until 1949. The question of participating in the union was hotly debated in the latter 1860's and was the leading issue in the election campaign of 1869. Appeals to the islanders' sense of independence and to their ties with Britain, similar to the appeals made by anti-Confederation leaders in the other "Lower Provinces", were common. One of the better known of the campaign ditties was the following:

> Hurrah for our own native isle, Newfoundland!
> Not a stranger shall hold one inch of its strand!
> Her face turns to Britain, her back to the Gulf.
> Come near at your peril, Canadian wolf!
>
> Ye brave Newfoundlanders who plough the salt sea
> With hearts like the eagle, so bold and so free,
> The time is at hand when you'll all have to say
> If Confederation will carry the day.

* * * * *

> Would you barter the rights that your fathers have won,
> Your freedom transmitted from father to son?
> For a few thousand dollars of Canadian gold,
> Don't let it be said that your birthright was sold.

* * * * *

From a collection of folk-songs published by Gerald Stanley Doyle.
Quoted in Edith Fowke, Alan Mills, and Helmut Blume, *Canada's Story in Song* (Toronto, 1960), pp. 106-7.

The "Nova Scotianess" of Nova Scotians Survives

Contrary to John A. Macdonald's hopes that the constitutional arrangements of the B.N.A. Act had forestalled the possibility of states' rights movements developing north of the border, such agitations broke out immediately upon the creation of the Dominion. The circumstances under which Nova Scotia entered Confederation provided a particularly fruitful seed-bed for such movements. An early, minor crisis pertained to the financing of a government building which was under construction in Halifax when the union was consummated. The building was designed to house a number of government departments, some of which had been transferred to the central government. The Dominion debited the subsidy paid to Nova Scotia with interest charges computed on the cost of this building pending its transfer to the federal authorities. In 1871 Dr. E. L. Brown (M.L.A., Kings) commented on the controversy in the following terms:

> Ever since this controversy commenced, I have steadily supported the claim of Nova Scotia to the balance referred to in the resolutions before the House. I have supported our claim, not only because we are rightly and justly entitled to it, but because I would prefer to have a dispute with our Canadian oppressors. I prefer war to peace, and I trust they will continue to be doing something to irritate and provoke the people of Nova Scotia. I don't wish to be on friendly terms with Canada. I hate her and her politicians, and all who sympathize with her in her accursed policy of enslaving a few [*sic*, free?] people. . . .

*   *   *   *   *

> Time was, Mr. Speaker, when I was proud of the name of Nova Scotian. I feel now that that name is debased and tarnished, and I am ashamed of it; and I am more ashamed of the man, Confederate as well as Anti-Confederate, who has not the manliness to resent the deadly wrong that has been inflicted on himself and his fellow men. . . .

> The claim of Canada is simply absurd and preposterous. But, Sir, this building is a mean and petty theme to engage the patriots of Nova Scotia. I wish the opportunity had occurred—the occasion had come to discuss with advantage and propriety that grander and nobler theme—"How shall we break the chains that bind us?"

> Sir, what has been the result of this annexion? Our revenues robbed, and used to corrupt our public men. What Ireland is to Britain—what Poland is to Russia,—that Nova Scotia will be to Canada,—a smoldering fire ready to burst out when the crisis comes.—And if I mistake not the signs of the times,

that crisis is approaching, and the time of our deliverance is near. May we not be wanting in our duty!

Nova Scotia, *Debates and Proceedings of the House of Assembly*
(Halifax, 1871), pp. 162–3.

Should Dominion Day Be a Compulsory School Holiday in Nova Scotia? (1896)

An indication that the wounds of 1867 long rankled in Nova Scotia occurred in 1896, when C. E. Tanner (M.L.A., Pictou) moved the second reading on his bill declaring Dominion Day a school holiday in the province. An amendment in effect nullifying the bill was promptly introduced and carried, 22 to 11. The final speech, from which the following excerpt was taken, was made by William Roche (Halifax).

Were there not now sufficient holidays? In the city of Halifax the aspirations and sentiments of the people cluster around another day, the 21st of June. That great statesman [Joseph Howe] whose portrait adorns these legislative walls said of that day:

> Hail to the day when the Britons came
>   over
> And planted their standard with sea foam
>   so [*sic*, still] wet,
> Around and above us their spirits will
>   hover,
> Rejoicing to know how we honour it yet.

That is the day Halifax honours, the day of the foundation of Halifax by the British government, the day which commemorated the time when the British government was expanding in all portions of the globe . . . and wherever Britain's standard was unfurled citizens honoured and revered that day in commemoration of the patriotism of the men who, despite adverse circumstances, went upon that adventurous voyage and constituted the province of Nova Scotia a colony of the British crown. The people of the province of Nova Scotia were loyal before confederation, just as they were to-day, and they rejoice to be connected with British institutions. But the day which found favour with the hon. mover of this bill was a day, instead of being commemorated as a day of rejoicing and bonfires, was rather the anniversary of a day of shame and humiliation, a dark page in the history of the province which would be more fittingly hung with crepe than marked by tokens of jubiliation.

Ibid., 1896, pp. 126-7.

The "Canada First" Movement

Recognition that the making of a new political entity, the Dominion of Canada, did not by itself produce a new national sentiment led some young idealists to organize the Canada First movement. Its genesis was described by one of its founders, George T. Denison, who, as was mentioned in Problem 6, later became one of the leading Canadian advocates of Imperial Federation.

It was at the period when these conditions existed that business took me to Ottawa from the 15th April to the 20th May, 1868. Wm. A. Foster of Toronto, a barrister, afterwards a leading Queen's Counsel, was there at the same time, and through our friend, Henry J. Morgan, we were introduced to Charles Mair, of Lanark, Ontario, and Robert J. Haliburton, eldest son of the celebrated author of "Sam Slick." We were five young men of about twenty-eight years of age, except Haliburton, who was four or five years older. We soon became warm friends, and spent most of our evenings together in Morgan's quarters.

                    *   *   *   *   *

These meetings were the origin of the "Canada First" party. Nothing could show more clearly the hold that confederation had taken of the imagination of young Canadians than the fact that, night after night, five young men should give up their time and their thoughts to discussing the higher interests of their country, and it ended in our making a solemn pledge to each other that we would do all we could to advance the interests of our native land; . . . Forty years have elapsed and I feel that every one of the five held true to the promise we then made to each other.

One point that we discussed constantly was the necessity, now that we had a great country, of encouraging in every possible way the growth of a strong national spirit. Ontario knew little of Nova Scotia or New Brunswick and they knew little of us. This was natural, for old Canada had been an almost unknown Province to the men who lived by the sea, and whose trade relations had been mainly with the United States, the West Indies, and foreign countries.

It was apparent that until there should grow, not only a feeling of unity, but also a national pride and devotion to Canada as a Dominion, no real progress could be made towards building up a strong and powerful community. We therefore considered it our first duty to work in that direction and to do everything possible to encourage national sentiment. History had taught us that every nation that had become great, and had exercised an important influence upon the world, had invariably been noted for a strong patriotic spirit, . . .

G. T. Denison, *The Struggle for Imperial Unity* (Toronto, 1909), pp. 10–12.

The Aims of Canada First

In the latter part of 1873 the leading spirits of the Canada First movement had decided to launch a new political party. The movement was unsuccessful, its supporters being divided on the question of the imperial connection. Nevertheless, the party's first manifesto provided the clearest summary of the group's aspirations.

CANADA FIRST

Address of the Canadian National Association to the People of Canada

FELLOW COUNTRYMEN

Our motto, "CANADA FIRST," is said to admit of various interpretations— fertile imaginations have almost proved that. Some profess to see in it, Annexation; others Independence; others Know-nothingism.*

*   *   *   *   *

It has been alleged that we desire to create antagonism between native born Canadians and Canadians by adoption. The contrary is the fact. Our earnest desire is to do away with all invidious distinctions of nationality, creed, locality or class, and to unite the people of the Dominion, as Canadians, through affection for and pride in Canada, their home. A serious impediment to our progress towards unity has been, and unfortunately still is, the hostility of *creed toward creed*, nationality toward nationality, class towards class, section towards section, which faction, for its own selfish temporary purposes, provokes, and political sharpers systematically use.†

> *Canada First: A Memorial of the late William A. Foster, Q.C.*
> (Toronto, 1890), pp. 48–9, 52. [Italics as in the original.]

Oliver Mowat on the Primacy of Ontario, 1884

Oliver (later Sir Oliver) Mowat was one of the two other Reformers who entered the Canadian coalition cabinet with George Brown in 1864. It was he who introduced the resolutions on the division of powers between the central and provincial governments

---

* The term refers to various anti-immigrant, anti-Roman Catholic groups which sprang up in the United States in the 1840's and '50's. Members of these groups were believed to have been instructed to answer "I know nothing" to any inquiry concerning their group's aims.

† Members of the Canada First movement had earlier disregarded these strictures by stirring up anti-French sentiments in Toronto over the issue of Louis Riel's "murder" of Thomas Scott in 1870. See G. T. Denison, *The Struggle for Imperial Unity*, pp. 41–3.

at the Quebec conference. In 1864 he left politics to assume the judicial post of Vice Chancellor of Upper Canada. He resigned this office in 1872 to take over the premiership of Ontario, a post which he held until 1896, when he joined Laurier's cabinet as Minister of Justice. During his long premiership he fought strenuously for provincial rights in opposition to Sir John A. Macdonald's efforts to retain the primacy of Dominion authority. One of the more dramatic confrontations of the two leaders took place over the question of the definition of the western boundary of Ontario. Mowat personally argued the case before the Judicial Committee of the Privy Council in London, the final court of appeal for the Empire. The committee's decision was in favour of Ontario, establishing the present southwestern boundary between the province and Manitoba, whose claimed area was diminished by the award. Mowat received a hero's welcome on his return to Ontario. The following excerpt comes from his response to a mass reception at Queen's Park, Toronto, on 16 September 1884.

We have been engaged lately in a great battle (Cries of "And we won it.") Yes, and we won it. We won it for you, and we won it for every part of our country. The addresses which you have presented to me come from every part of our province: from Algoma on the north—which thanks to the decision of the Privy Council, is now nearly as large as all the rest of Ontario together— and from the Ottawa River on the east, and from Sarnia on the west, as well as all along the Great Lakes and the interior parts of the country. I cannot doubt, therefore, the interest taken by the people of Upper Canada in this great subject. You are here representing all classes of our fellow-citizens, and I rejoice to know that among you there are not Reformers only, but Conservatives also.

Now, why is it that we are so anxious that the limits of our province shall not be curtailed? First, and foremost, is because we love Ontario, we believe in Ontario, and we know from past experience that it is in the interest of the Dominion, as well as of the provinces composing the Dominion that the limits of Ontario should not be restricted. Ontario is, in fact, the "back-bone" of the Dominion; and we desire that that should continue to be the position of our province; that it should not be brought down to be one of the least of the great provinces; that there should be an extent of country ample enough to admit of its development, so that, as the other provinces develop, Ontario should develop also.

C. R. W. Biggar, *Sir Oliver Mowat . . . a biographical sketch*
(Toronto, 1905), Vol. 1, p. 428.

John S. Ewart and the Kingdom of Canada

One of the most persistent advocates of Canadian independence in the first third of the twentieth century was John S. Ewart, a lawyer who expounded his views on the platform, in the periodical press, and in booklets published at his own expense and mailed free of charge to anyone who requested them. These papers were paged consecutively and were bound as *The Kingdom Papers* (Vol. 1, 1911–12; Vol. 2, 1912–17). His main theme was that Canada could achieve and maintain complete independence as a Kingdom sharing a common monarch with Britain. He was more ambivalent on the constitutional question in his later and less influential series, *The Independence Papers* (Vol. 1, 1925; Vol. 2, 1930).

The following excerpts, taken from the first two papers, published in 1911, reflect a nationalist's evaluation of the prevailing priority of loyalties at that time. The first paper was based on an address given at a number of Canadian Clubs and before a class in Political Economy at Queen's University, Kingston.

I am a Canadian nationalist. I may be doing you an injustice, but I assume that the majority of you are not, that you would call yourselves Imperialists. And the question I now wish to discuss is, whether there is any substantial difference between us? Or, perhaps, the better question would be: Is there any reason why an imperialist should not be a Canadian nationalist? I am firmly persuaded that there is no such reason. And I feel certain that, if I can but clearly state the case, you will all agree with me. I do not mean that I shall be able to persuade any imperialist to abandon his desire for imperial federation or any other form of imperial political union; but I do believe that I can offer good reasons why such a desire should not, meanwhile, be permitted to obstruct Canada's upward progress to nationalism. . . .

* * * * *

And first let me point out that we are learning to speak—and to speak with pride—of Canada as a "nation." We do not like the word "colony." It connotes subordination and subjection and humiliation. We do not like that. We feel that we are big enough to manage our own affairs. Moreover we do manage them without interference from anybody. . . . And I submit to you that every man is a Canadian nationalist who asserts, with pride, that Canada is, or ought to be, a nation.

Kingdom Papers, No. 1, March 1911, pp. 1–2.

In the next paper Ewart took a stronger line against imperialism.

We have a difficult problem here in Canada . . . We have to unify and nation-
alize a people—several peoples—whose geographic and ethnographic conditions make for separation. . . . Add to all this the divergence in interest caused
by the difference in situation; add also the similarity of interest between the
various parts and corresponding portions of the United States, and the magnitude of our difficulty may be, to some extent perceived. But only partially, for
other disintegrating influences are in operation, amongst which perhaps the
chief is the growing tendency in provincial legislation (1) to discriminate in
favor of Canadians who reside within the province as against Canadians who
reside in other provinces; and (2) to encroach upon federal control of purely
federal affairs.

We are terribly disunited now. I fear that the tendency is toward further
disunion. We have had frank, and I am afraid, perfectly sincere warnings
from the prairie provinces that they refuse to be dominated by the east. . . . The
prairies have always had a feeling of resentment against the east. It commenced
with our bungling over premature exercise of authority there; it was intensified
by the disallowance of all attempts by Manitoba to establish railway communication with the United States;* it has been perpetuated by tariff arrangements; and unfortunately the policy of one of the political parties in the west
(each in turn) has been to protest against Ottawa injustice and patriotically to
fight for "Provincial Rights".

How are we to unify Canada? There is but one possible way: Make her a
nation in name as well as in fact. Let her throw off her mean colonial wrappings,
and let her assume her rightful place among the nations of the world. Give
us a common pride.

. . . I . . . intreat [the imperialists] to lend their aid in the great work of the
consolidation of Canada; the developing of a unifying and elevating Canadian
sentiment; and the creation of a true Canadian nation, always in close sympathy
with the other members of the Associated Kingdoms, and, always, with the
same Sovereign as theirs.

Kingdom Papers No. 2, June 1911, pp. 54–6.

British Columbians View Union with Canada

In 1870 the Legislative Council of British Columbia conducted
its own version of the Confederation Debates. Following the incorporation of the Northwest Territories into the Dominion, a land

---

* The reference is to the actions of the Federal government in the 1880's to preserve
the so-called "monopoly clause" of the original Canadian Pacific Railway contract.

frontier existed between the Pacific colony and Canada. The Dominion government was thus in a position to consider generous terms of union with an impoverished British Columbia, where the short-lived gold rush boom had subsided. The debates reflect the attitude of representatives of some ten thousand colonists who were aware that a choice of alternatives was open to them: incorporation as a territory into the United States (which following the purchase of Alaska provided their neighbours both to the north and south) or premature provincial status in the Dominion. There was in the legislature a "Canadian party", a group who either leaned toward incorporation in the United States or who saw this eventuality as inevitable, and a group of expatriate Britons. The two speakers quoted here represent the last two elements.

J. S. Helmcken of Victoria saw the union as, at best, a marriage of convenience.

No union between this Colony and Canada can permanently exist, unless it be to the material and pecuniary advantage of this Colony to remain in the union. The sum of the interests of the inhabitants is the interest of the Colony. The people of this Colony have, generally speaking, no love for Canada; they care, as a rule, little or nothing about the creation of another Empire, Kingdom, or Republic; they have but little sentimentality, and care little about the distinctions between the form of Government of Canada and the United States.

British Columbia, Legislative Council, *Debate on the subject of Confederation with Canada: reprinted from the Government Gazette Extraordinary of March, 1870* (Victoria, 1912), p. 13.

Thomas Lett Wood, J.P., an official (non-elected) member of the Council, contrasted the relationship between colony and mother country with the projected new association.

The bond of union between Canada and the other Provinces bears no resemblance to the union between England and her Colonial Possessions. There is no natural love and original feeling of loyalty. The feeling of loyalty towards England is a feeling blind, instinctive, strong, born with us and impossible to be shaken off; and I believe that it is impossible to transfer a feeling of loyalty and fealty at will. . . . There is no direct conflict between the Mother Country and a Colony in these days; but it cannot be supposed that any British Province will submit patiently to injustice at the hands of a Canadian Ministry or a Canadian House of Commons.

Ibid., pp. 28, 29.

THE VIEWS OF LATER COMMENTATORS

The Growth of Canadian Nationalism
Is an Appropriate Subject for Study (1920)

"The Growth of Canadian National Feeling" appeared in the second issue of the *Canadian Historical Review*. Its author, W. S. Wallace, editor of the *Canadian Historical Review* and later librarian of the University of Toronto, represents the school of Upper Canadian historians who have been most influential in shaping English-Canadian historiography. The article ignores completely the protest movements of the Maritimes and of western Canada and presents Canadian development as something which took place entirely within the context of the old province of Canada. It is noteworthy that Wallace regarded the existence of the feeling of nationality as beyond dispute.

The growth of Canadian national feeling might reasonably be regarded as the central fact in Canadian history. Yet, apart from a pamphlet entitled *Canadian Nationality, its Growth and Development*, published by William Canniff, the historian of Upper Canada, as long ago as 1875, there has been hitherto—so far as would appear—no attempt to trace in a connected way the process whereby Canadian national feeling has grown to what it is today.

One of the chief reasons for this neglect is, no doubt, the fact—of which Canadians nowadays are apt to be forgetful—that Canadian national feeling is a phenomenon of very recent growth. Certainly its recognition has not been of long standing. As recently as the Confederation epoch, there were many able and distinguished men in Canada who refused to recognize the existence of what was called at that time "the new nationality".

*   *   *   *   *

To-day however, he would be a bold man who would deny to Canada the existence of a distinctive national feeling—a national feeling not French-Canadian or British-Canadian, but all-Canadian. Since 1892 Canada has had her own national flag, the union ensign of Canada, the outward and visible sign of an inward and invisible unity. She has travelled so far along the road to autonomy that she is now on the point of creating the germ of a Canadian diplomatic service. . . . In the Great War the maple leaf badge came to be recognized as the symbol of a strong national spirit which never failed before any task with which it was confronted.

W. S. Wallace, "The Growth of Canadian National Feeling",
Canadian Historical Review, I (June 1920), pp. 136, 138.

Wallace traces the growth of nationalism through geographic isolation from first France, then Britain, the American Revolution, the War of 1812, the rebellions of 1837, the Durham Report, and the Confederation movement, coming next to the Canada First movement.

The name, "Canada First," seems to have originated with [J. D.] Edgar and [G. T.] Denison. . . . But the name did not obtain general currency until the publication of [W. A.] Foster's now famous lecture entitled *Canada First; or Our New Nationality.* . . . Read in cold blood to-day, it may seem, as Goldwin Smith said, to belong "to the heyday of Confederation and of youth", but its effect at the time was great. It embodied in passionate phrases a growing sentiment, it gave coherent shape to a floating idea, and it provided the Canadian nationalists with a rallying point.

*   *   *   *   *

To attempt to measure the growth of national feeling since the days of Canada First is impossible. There is no gauge for the things of the spirit. But that growth is written all over the political and economic history of Canada since 1875 and in particular it is seen in the development of Canadian autonomy within the Empire and in the triumph of the National Policy.

*   *   *   *   *

The triumph of Canadian national autonomy and the impregnability of the National Policy are monuments to the growth of a national feeling in Canada. Without a strong national feeling these things could not have come to pass, and he would be a man of some temerity today [1920] who, in view of these developments, denied to Canada either a national feeling or a national status.

*   *   *   *   *

Canadian nationalism, moreover, is far from absolute, since it contains within it two subordinate nationalisms, the British-Canadian and the French-Canadian, each based mainly on the element of language. There is in this fact itself nothing deplorable; for . . . two or more subordinate nationalisms may well exist within a single supernationalism. Indeed, a state which contains within it two or more varieties of national feeling is in some respects . . . in a more advantageous position than a state which contains within it only one type of nationalism. In the latter state nationalism is apt to become intolerant, to regard itself as the sole basis of citizenship; whereas in a composite national state, people are likely to be forced to learn the lesson of toleration. . . . It has taken the world many centuries of religious wars to learn the lesson of religious toleration; and it is apparently going to take it some centuries of national wars to learn the lesson of national toleration. But once the lesson is learnt there is no reason why two nationalisms based on language should not continue to exist within a larger nationalism in which language is not a necessary ingredient.

From this point of view Canadians are particularly fortunate in that they have at the source of their national history a federal compact itself founded on the principle of toleration. The Confederation compromise is the sheet-anchor of an all-Canadian national feeling, and as long as the spirit underlying that compromise is not forgotten, the continued existence and growth of an all-Canadian nationalism should be assured.

Ibid., pp. 152, 153, 157, 162–3.

A Broader and Less Sanguine View of the Problem (1940)

The Royal Commission on Dominion-Provincial Relations was appointed by federal order-in-council on 14 August 1937. The Commissioners were charged to undertake "a re-examination of the economic and financial basis of Confederation and of the distribution of legislative powers in the light of economic and social developments in the last seventy years". The Commissioners, work-ing under the chairmanship first of N. W. Rowell and, after his death, of Joseph Sirois, and assisted by an extremely able staff of civil servants and academics who were commissioned to undertake special studies, conducted a thorough investigation of the problem, received submissions and testimony from all sections of the country, and presented their report on 3 May 1940. Book I of the report consisted of a history of the development of the federal system couched in impersonal, economic terms, which has earned itself a significant place in Canadian historiography. The following excerpts indicate that the Commissioners were aware of the prevailing dis-content with the federal government's centralizing tendency, and of the vitality of provincial loyalties, both of which the author of the preceding piece had ignored. The excerpts also reveal that provincial loyalties had reasserted themselves after 1920.

The enactment of the British North America Act did not of itself assure that balance between national loyalties and interests and provincial loyalties and interests which an effective federal system requires. The Act merely pro-vided a framework within which such a balance might be established. During the first thirty years, Canada had to search for an equilibrium between these two sets of forces. . . .

*   *   *   *   *

Between 1868 and 1874, Dominion revenues nearly doubled. . . . This buoyant financial condition enabled the new Federal Government to consolidate the union and assume the dominant and aggressive role which the Fathers of Confederation had assigned to it. . . .

The Dominion Government not only asserted its leadership in economic development; in its attitude toward the provinces, there was much of the old paternalism which had marked the actions of the Imperial Government in colonial days. . . .

It was prepared to veto legislation which, according to its view, conflicted with imperial treaties or policies, or with Dominion interests and policy.

It was quite in harmony with this theory of its superior position that the Dominion maintained its sole right to supplement the original financial arrangements of 1867 or to fix the terms of admission of new provinces. . . .

However, the forces which made this Dominion leadership and predominance possible waned rapidly after 1870. In that year the Red River Rebellion ended and the last Fenian Raid failed. In 1871, with the entrance of British Columbia, the Dominion tightened its hold on the West. The outstanding disputes between the United States and Great Britain were settled by the Washington Treaty in the same year, and the Republic accepted, by implication, the accomplished fact of a transcontinental Dominion. . . . The Dominion was not compelled, after all, to battle for its existence. The political and military purposes which had helped to justify its creation slipped from the minds of a pacific and unapprehensive people.

> D. V. Smiley, ed., *The Rowell-Sirois Report: An Abridgement of Book I of the Royal Commission on Dominion-Provincial Relations* (Toronto, 1963. The Carleton Library), pp. 58, 62–3.

A discussion of the Great Depression of 1873–1896 follows.

A bald statement of the length of the depression gives little hint of its effect on the lives of the people. Federal policies had burdened them with debt and failed to bring prosperity. . . . The failure of the Dominion's economic policies, which formed such important elements in the new national interest, discouraged the growth of a strong, national sentiment; and local loyalties and interests began to reassert themselves.

Indeed there had never been any large transfer of loyalty from the older communities to the new Dominion created for urgent common purposes. The achievement of Confederation and the spectacular activity of the Federal Government in the early years had merely overshadowed or, at most, temporarily subordinated the separate interests of the distinct regions and communities. From the very date of the union, there had been a widespread and burning conviction in Nova Scotia that it had been manoeuvred into a bargain prejudicial to its vital interests. . . . The new [provincial] Government tried desperately to extricate the Province from the bonds of the union. Although these efforts were unavailing, the sentiment against Confederation remained strong in Nova Scotia and was significant in New Brunswick.

*   *   *   *   *

Such Dominion-provincial friction was not limited to cases of the resurgence of loyalties antedating Confederation. The problems of the Pacific railway embittered the relations of British Columbia and the Federal Government during the seventies; and in the eighties the requirements of federal railway policy brought Manitoba and the Dominion into sharp conflict. . . .

British Columbia was irritated by federal tariff policy and its long controversy with the Dominion over Oriental immigration. . . . Large sections of opinion in the Maritimes were antagonized by the introduction of the National Policy in 1879. In 1886 a series of resolutions was introduced into the Legislature of Nova Scotia advocating secession on the ground that the commercial and financial interests of the Province had been vitally injured by Dominion policies. . . . Ontario clashed with the Dominion over the location of the Ontario-Manitoba boundary and the ownership of its northern natural resources.

*   *   *   *   *

The common efforts of all regions in building up the country between 1896 and 1913 cemented the political union of 1867 and Canadians became conscious of themselves as a nation. The growing sense of community was accompanied by increasing economic interdependence. The national policies of all-Canadian transportation and protective tariffs were effective in making the wheat boom the basis of a general economic expansion in which the manufacturing industry of Eastern Canada became heavily dependent on the agricultural export region of the Prairies. With the exception of the Maritimes, which were affected by but did not share generally in the expansion, the wheat boom brought prosperity to the whole country. . . .

Ibid., pp. 70–2, 106–7.

On the impact of the War of 1914–1918 the authors observed:

Canada had never before seen such a demonstration of national unity. . . . The evidence of a single national purpose was unmistakable and sufficed to give the Federal Government immense moral authority in keeping with its sweeping legal powers.

*   *   *   *   *

Provincial politics and provincial interests were overshadowed by the magnitude of the common national purpose. . . . The conscious nationalism which accounted for the temporary eclipse of provincialism made itself felt in external relations. It disposed the Dominion Government to regard Canada's participation in the War as that of a principal combatant and not merely as that of a satellite of Great Britain.

Ibid., pp. 110-11.

Following an account of the Conscription crisis, the authors turned to the developments of the 1920's and 1930's, where, they noted, provincial self-consciousness was again in the ascendant.

[In the 1920's] The provinces were not affected by war weariness and there were many things to be done in the provincial sphere which solid majorities would support. . . . The provinces owned the natural resources which had become immensely valuable through the development of new techniques. . . . Moreover provincial governments assumed a larger importance in the daily lives of the people. . . . From the point of view of the recipients, they became the donors of old age pensions; they provided mothers' allowances and minimum wage legislation. The popular basis of provincial political power was being solidly laid at a time when the Dominion was losing its intimate touch with the people. . . .

*   *   *   *   *

Throughout this period the provinces were politically aggressive. . . . In their difficulties, in their ambitions and opportunities, as well as in the disparities between them, several sets of common interests of a regional character emerged. These regional forces served to weaken the common interest in a national integration. . . .

But the great depression which began at the end of the period . . . was to widen greatly the disparities, and to reveal both the insecurity of the foundation on which the prosperity had been based, and differences of interest which were extremely difficult to reconcile under conditions of sharply falling revenues. These differences of interest were to assume a new significance in an era of depression, when weaker provinces, overwhelmed in the struggle to carry new and old responsibilities, were to become financial wards of the Dominion, and the strongest stood to gain by enlargement of provincial autonomy.

Ibid., pp. 153, 159.

Further Reading

This theme has not been thoroughly examined by historians as yet. Book 1 of the Royal Commission on Dominion-Provincial Relations still provides the fullest analytical statement, but a number of articles have illuminated various facets of the problem. Archibald MacMechan, "The Nova Scotia-ness of Nova Scotia", *Canadian Magazine*, XXV (June 1905), pp. 163–5 provides a whimsical statement by an assimilated Upper Canadian. A. G. Bailey, "The Basis and Persistence of Opposition to Confederation in New Brunswick", *Canadian Historical Review*, XXIII (December 1942), pp. 374–97 covers the early suspicions of the neighbouring province. The rejection of Confederation by the Newfoundlanders is discussed by H. B. Mayo in "Newfoundland and Confederation in the Eighteen-Sixties", *Canadian Historical Review*, XXIX (June 1948), pp. 125–42. K. A. MacKirdy has examined a number of manifestations of the phenomenon in "Conflict of Loyalties: The Problem of Assimilating the Far Wests into the Canadian and Australian Federations", *Canadian Historical Review*, XXX (December 1951), pp. 337–55; "Problems of Adjustment in Nation Building: The Maritimes and Tasmania", *The Canadian Journal of Economics and Political Science*, XX (February 1954), pp. 27–43; and "National vs. Provincial Loyalty: The Ontario Western Boundary Dispute, 1883–1884", *Ontario History*, LI (Summer 1959), pp. 191–8. N. McL. Rogers, "The Genesis of Provincial Rights", *Canadian Historical Review*, XIV (March 1933), pp. 9–23 focuses on the constitutional and political issues. The Hon. C. H. Cahan's "Canadian and/or Commonwealth Loyalty", *United Empire*, XXIX, (January 1938), pp. 25–9 and G. G. Sedgwick's "A Note on Anglo-Canadian Relations", *ibid.* (February 1938), pp. 60–2 are comments inspired by Governor-General Lord Tweedsmuir's then controversial address of 12 October 1937, in which he stated that a Canadian's first loyalty was to Canada, not to the Commonwealth.

Problem 14

The Struggle for *La Survivance* — Misguided Effort
or Source of Permanence?

The principal and, some will add, heroic theme of the history of French Canada is the struggle for survival. Its roots go back to the British Conquest of 1760, but it was only after the implementation of the Act of Union of 1840 that it became a conscious exercise of the collective will. The French Canadians had now become a minority in the United Province of Canada; they knew that British policy, based on the recommendations of Lord Durham's *Report*, aimed at their assimilation. The community responded strongly to this challenge to its national existence. Through its political and religious leaders as well as through its literary figures it asserted its will to survive.

A long period of harmonious Anglo-French relations might have ultimately convinced the French Canadians that their survival was assured and that they could safely discard what has aptly been described as their siege mentality. But instead, a fresh series of incidents strengthened their defensive outlook. First there was Confederation, which aggravated their minority status. Then the execution of Louis Riel was regarded as proof of English Canada's refusal to recognize French rights outside the province of Quebec. Afterwards came the school questions in Manitoba, Saskatchewan, Alberta, and Ontario, which involved a denial of public funds to separate schools in some cases or discrimination against French as a language of instruction in others. World War I and conscription constituted the final blow. In the Union government of 1917 it seemed that all of English Canada had come together to impose its will brutally on the French Canadians, and to force the sons of Quebec to shed their blood and to lay down their lives in the defence of the British Empire.

These successive crises caused French Canadians to take a close look at Confederation and to formulate programmes to ensure the respect of their rights. Three persons, Jules-Paul Tardivel, Honoré Mercier, and Henri Bourassa, made particularly meaningful suggestions on this subject. Born in the United States, Tardivel came to Quebec at the age of sixteen not knowing any French, and with this unlikely background became the first person to expound a systematic doctrine of separatism. Briefly, Tardivel construed each assault on his adopted nationality as proof that Freemasons and "English" Canadians were conspiring together to extinguish the liberties of the Roman Catholic Church and to assimilate the French Canadians. In his newspaper *La Vérité* he maintained that separatism alone could defeat this threat and ensure the survival of French Canada and its institutions. Honoré Mercier, premier of Quebec from 1887 to 1891, looked back to the period of Union for his political doctrine. By rallying as a nation behind a single leader, Lafontaine, French Canadians had then defeated the designs of Durham and had conquered self-government. Therefore, to prevent the repetition of such "outrages" as the execution of Louis Riel, they should again lay aside party divisions and follow one leader. Mercier, however, was not a narrow provincialist, for he also demanded that French and English co-operate, as in the days of Baldwin and Lafontaine, to build a greater Canada. The third figure, Henri Bourassa, was also principally interested in ensuring the survival of French Canada, but the programme he devised to achieve this end was more original and more profound than either Tardivel's separatism or Mercier's racial blocs. Bourassa saw the French and the English in Canada not as a minority and a majority but as free and equal partners who should show mutual respect for each others' rights and judge all questions and issues from a purely Canadian standpoint.

The struggle for survival also had a profound effect on the type of society French Canadians were building for themselves inside Quebec. Survival meant primarily the safeguarding of the French language, the Roman Catholic religion, a school system heavily orientated towards the classics, and a traditional economy based on the small farm. To preserve these traditional institutions and values, French-Canadian leaders exerted themselves to stem the progress of the alien force of industry, to prevent the rise of the secular liberal state, and to amplify the prestige of their Church. Thus would their people resist the de-Christianizing and de-nationalizing influences of materialistic North America and retain their traditional organization and outlook in an alien world. Such an ultra-conservative programme was not accepted by everyone. Dissenters claimed that instead of trying to hold off the modern world, French Canadians should seek to control it and use it for national purposes. They should therefore accept the separation of Church and State and the modernization of the school system, and take a greater interest in industry. These apostles of modernization, however, could not make their views prevail. "It is not necessary that we possess industry and money," retorted Tardivel. "We will no longer be French Canadians but Americans almost like the others. Our mission is to possess the earth and spread ideas. To cling to the soil, to raise large families, to maintain the hearths of intellectual and spiritual life, that must be our role in America."*

French Canadians have today outgrown their conservatism and are in the process of creating the institutions and acquiring the outlook of a typical North American liberal democratic society. Even if the old ideology of survival long acted as a brake on the progress of Quebec, the historian should not simply condemn it out of hand as the work of misguided enthusiasts and reactionary churchmen. He should also ask himself if French-Canadian society would still survive today if its past generations had not looked upon themselves as a special people in North America. In view of the progressive assimilation of English Canada into the civilization of the United States, which is largely due to the absence of a compelling national ideology, the question is not without relevance.

The Providential Mission of the French Canadians

Louis-François Laflèche, bishop of Trois-Rivières from 1870 until his death in 1898, was a very prominent figure in the politics of his age. He waged a relentless war against liberalism, which he considered an impious and dangerous doctrine, and was also one of the most forceful exponents of a French-Canadian nationalism based on language, race, and religion.

---

* R. Cook, *Canada and the French Canadian Question* (Toronto, 1966), p. 86.

The formation of nations is not the work of chance but of a Providence infinitely wise, who has a purpose for everything He creates. God then had a goal when He made us a nation . . . That goal is our mission. If we agree that we have a mission we must also agree that we have the means of carrying it out. To speak otherwise would be to accuse the Lord and to utter a horrible blasphemy. . . .

But what is our mission? That is the greatest question we can ask as a people, and to find the answer we must look back to history. . . .

You have chosen St. Jean Baptiste as a patron and protector. You have done well. In studying this model we find striking similarities between his mission and that of the Canadian people. The high priest Zachary, speaking when inspired by God, told St. Jean Baptiste . . . "And you, little child, shall be called Prophet of the Most High and you shall prepare the way of the Lord. Go and bring light to those who sit in darkness, in the shadow of death." . . .

* * * * *

Our fathers brought the word of God to the Indian tribes. They thus accomplished their mission which was the beginning of ours.

* * * * *

So as not to prolong unduly these reflections, be profoundly convinced of this, my brethren. Our mission, as that of our fathers, is entirely religious. It consists of working for the propagation of truth and for the expansion of the Kingdom of God on this continent. So that we may accomplish this purpose, we shall become a great people.

> A speech by Bishop Laflèche given in Ottawa on 25 June 1866, on the occasion of the feast of St. Jean Baptiste.
> A. Savaète, *Oeuvres oratoires de Mgr. Louis-François Laflèche* (Paris, n.d.), pp. 59–62 (translation).

The French-Canadian Nation and Agriculture

According to Bishop Laflèche, the ideal economic basis for French Canada was agriculture. The farm would protect the French Canadians from the corrupting influences of the city and the factories and place them in close relationship with God.

I do not hesitate to say, gentlemen, that agricultural work is the normal state of man on this earth and the one to which is called the great mass of mankind. It is also the one which most favours the development of man's moral, physical, and intellectual faculties and which places him in the most direct relationship with God. Do not fail to repeat to the farmers that agriculture is the most noble occupation because it is necessarily carried out with the assistance of the Almighty.

Have you ever stopped to ask who made the sheafs of wheat that are gathered at harvest time? You know as well as I that they are the product of the efforts of two workers: man and God. If the farmer had not gone to his field in springtime, if he had not cleared the land of weeds and thorns, if he had not ploughed deeply to plant his seed, there would certainly have been no wheat. That is the work of the farmer, that is what God asks of him. When he has finished his labour he leaves his field and encloses it carefully so that nothing may disturb the divine work which will succeed to his own arduous labour. His field becomes something sacred, something over which he must watch with great care, because it is now God's turn to continue the work begun. The Lord will send the light of dawn and the morning dew, the heat of midday and the evening rain, and after a few days germination will begin. . . . There are but two men who thus work jointly with God: the priest in the supernatural order and the farmer in the natural.

* * * * *

Yes, the prosperity and the future of the French Canadians are to be found in the farmland and grazing grounds of their rich territory. May they understand this important truth and never lose sight of it if they wish to fulfil the great destinies which Providence has no doubt prepared for them.

> A speech by Bishop Laflèche given at an agricultural convention at Oka, Quebec, on 9 August 1895.
> *Ibid.*, pp. 429–30 (translation).

Survivance and Separatism

Unlike today, separatism was not a significant factor in the Quebec politics of the late nineteenth century. Jules-Paul Tardivel, who became a separatist after the execution of Louis Riel in 1885, was an isolated figure. But by means of his newspaper, *La Vérité*, which was widely read in classical colleges and by the clergy, he was able to exercise a certain influence on public opinion. The following reading is one of the clearest exposés of Tardivel's political philosophy.

Since our newspaper began we have often stated our hope of seeing a French Canada, a New France, emerge on the shores of the St. Lawrence River. Confederation never appeared to us as the final state of our national destinies. It is too vast and contains too many jarring and even hostile elements to become a true fatherland. It is large enough to permit the formation and peaceful co-existence of several independent nations. Our ambitions, as French Canadians, must be to establish solidly in this St. Lawrence Valley, cradle of our race, a new fatherland, French, and let us not fear to add, Catholic.

How and when will the French-Canadian people assume the place to which they are so evidently called among the autonomous nations of the earth? That is God's secret. But sooner or later that hour will certainly strike if we remain true to the Providential mission which He has assigned to us. This mission consists of carrying on in North America the work of Christianization and civilization which Catholic France accomplished through so many centuries and which she might still accomplish today if only she returned to what in the past were her sources of strength and glory.

This providential hour will strike, be certain of it, for it is inconceivable that God could not have willed to make a true nation of the French-Canadian people whose birth and youth he has so visibly protected. It is folly to believe that the destiny of this prolific and vigorous race, which has acquired such strong roots in the St. Lawrence Valley, is to merge with its surrounding elements or to remain eternally in this violently unnatural state of a race distinct but not independent.

For despite all one might say or do, the French Canadians do form a people apart in Confederation and unless they are renegades to their mission they will never allow themselves to be assimilated. Once this principle is admitted, political union with people with whom they have nothing in common will always appear as an abomination . . .

Some will perhaps say that the withdrawal of Quebec from Confederation is today impossible. We do admit that it is difficult, but difficult or even very difficult is not the same as impossible.

What appears to be manifestly impossible is the continuation of the present political régime for any length of time, unless the French-Canadian race accepts collective suicide and disappearance as a distinct entity. Change appears inevitable. Some speak of annexation, others of independence. . . .

Annexation to the United States would mean a struggle for national existence against 65,000,000 people. And we already find this struggle difficult against three or four million.

As for the independence of Canada, it would in no way ensure the independence of French Canada. We would still be riveted to a people who hate us and who yearn for our disappearance.

Confederation was perhaps necessary twenty-five years ago to avoid a civil war. But it was a transitory form of government and it has now run its course. It has become a threat both to French Canada and to public peace and order. What was supposed to avoid a racial war is today the cause of worsening clashes and must necessarily end in catastrophe.

[J.-P. Tardivel,] *La Vérité*, 18 March 1893 (translation).

Canadian Dualism Is a Myth

The following passage was written by Tardivel in the course of a celebrated newspaper debate with Henri Bourassa over the nature of the Canadian nation. Bourassa had stated that the nation which he wished to see develop was the Canadian nation, composed of French and English Canadians. Tardivel soon replied that such an ideal was an impossible one.

Just as M. Bourassa distrusts those who wish to establish a great British Empire, we are constantly on guard against those who work to create a great Canadian entity.

Yet the dream of Mr. Chamberlain [the British Colonial Secretary] is not lacking in grandeur. It is of a nature to seduce those minds which are attracted by what is powerful and colossal. However, M. Bourassa is opposed to this dream because he rightly sees that its realization would be a great danger to colonial autonomy.

The goal of those who hope to create a great homogeneous Canadian entity from the Atlantic to the Pacific, composed of all the British North American colonies, also has some captivating aspects. Nonetheless, we find this object frightening and horrifying because we see all too clearly that its achievement would be detrimental to French Canada.

M. Bourassa distrusts the colonial tie because the imperialists would use it to build the Empire of their dreams. We share those feelings. But does he share our mistrust of the provincial connection which is the instrument used by those who hope to build a great Canadian entity while stifling little by little the autonomy of French Canada? We shall not answer this question, but we deem it necessary to define clearly our position and feelings.

Our position toward the provincial connection and the architects of the great Canadian entity is exactly that of M. Bourassa towards the colonial tie and the architects of the British Empire . . . The danger for our nationality that we see in the provincial connection is very real; we would have liked it never to have been formed. However, because it exists, we must take it into account, but only to prevent it from harming us French Canadians. And we must be prepared to proclaim loudly: Perish the provincial connection! Perish Confederation! rather than let French Canada suffer from either of them. . . .

* * * * *

M. Bourassa is working to promote the development of Canadian patriotism based on the duality of races. But even as he is devoting himself to this task, the great Canadian entity is trampling underfoot on the Prairies the sacred rights of one of the races and consequently destroying the very foundations of the political monument which the Member for Labelle [Bourassa) wishes to erect. And we have no guarantees against the future mischiefs of this harmful Colossus.

[J.-P. Tardivel,] *La Vérité*, 15 May 1904 (translation).

Voices of Dissent

The three readings that follow have been selected to illustrate the points of view of those French Canadians who did not agree with the particular brand of nationalism expounded by Bishop Laflèche and J.-P. Tardivel. The first is from an editorial that appeared in the newspaper *Le Pays*, the principal organ of the Liberal party in Montreal. The second is from an article written by L. O. David, a liberal nationalist, for the newspaper *L'Opinion Publique*. David is perhaps best known as the author of the pamphlet *Le Clergé canadien, sa mission, son oeuvre*, published in 1896, which the Roman Catholic Church placed on its Index of forbidden books. In it the author had bitterly criticized the French-Canadian clergy for having opposed Wilfrid Laurier in the elections held that year. The third is by Arthur Buies (1840–1901), one of the most turbulent figures in the history of French Canada. In the 1860's and 1870's, Buies belonged to the small group of radical Liberals known as the *Rouges*. He earned his living as a writer and journalist.

Education! There is the great question.

A new classical college is being planned. We wish to speak out with all our strength against this superabundant way of producing inutilities. The province is flooded with classical colleges, and not only is there no need for others but we should even convert a number of the existing ones into schools that are more suited to our economic position, our resources, and our future.

Until now the principal and avowed purpose of classical colleges has been to prepare young men for the priesthood. This is an excellent thing but it must have limits for all our young men cannot become priests . . . It is not only farmers and workmen who flee their native land but also the youth of our colleges, who have no future with their impedimenta of bad Latin and worse French and with their complete ignorance of English and all other practical subjects, which alone can open up lucrative careers. What we need are engineers, geologists, miners, and industrialists. Let there be classical colleges. They are worthy institutions; but only if they maintain a balance and not if they have a monopoly on education . . . We also want at their side schools that dispense knowledge of those arts and sciences which today engross almost all the attention as well as the intellectual vigour of civilized people.

Unless we soon take measures to have some of these schools we will become a miserable people, relegated to the background, outclassed, deprived of all legitimate influence. We will have famous doctors and lawyers, priests who are learned theologians, but what will the rest of us amount to?

Le Pays, 20 June 1868 (translation).

Have you ever stopped to think how wealthy and populous our beautiful country would be if the money spent abroad were used to supply us with industries? If we produced all that we are capable of producing we would see the face of the land change in a few years. Cities and villages would spring up on our rivers and streams, our forests would be populated by a vigorous people, workers, businessmen, and professionals would enrich themselves. We would finally see the emergence of national [French-Canadian] fortunes. . . .

Public opinion as well as all political parties must rally around this idea— the progress of Lower Canada by industry. The first and only important thing at the present hour is to take possession of the land's natural wealth before it is taken from us by outsiders.

[L. O. David], *L'Opinion Publique*, 26 October 1871 (translation).

Canada, over and above all, is an industrial country. As long as we lack factories we will lose our sons and our brothers. Why do they emigrate to the United States? to work on the farms? Never. They rush into the factories and can be counted there in hundreds of thousands. Hundreds of thousands whom we miss. Before this number I stop in despair. . . . Confederation, which was supposed to cure everything and make everyone rich, has been but a coalition of miseries and of provinces being bled of their populations.

Poor people! They have been reduced to abandoning, en masse, whole parishes at a time, those lands granted two hundred years ago, those long fields of thirty and forty *arpents* . . . They must flee this Eden, this ignored paradise, because in it they die before having known life, because they have no fertilizers, because seven months lost every year are more than even the strongest races can bear; because money is needed today to settle in cash what could formerly be paid after a quarter of a century; because there are all kinds of new needs, none of which can be satisfied with barley, oats, and buckwheat; because factories, manufactures, and all sorts of occupations are needed to avoid unemployment and misery and to enable one to look to tomorrow with something besides fear.

A. Buies, *Chroniques canadiennes, humeurs et caprices* (Quebec, 1873).
L. Lamontagne, *Arthur Buies* (Ottawa, 1959), pp. 54–5 (translation).

The Political Views of Honoré Mercier

The political views of Honoré Mercier form the subject of the next two readings. The first consists of extracts from the famous speech he gave at the mass rally held on the Champ de Mars in Montreal on 22 November 1885, to protest the execution of Louis Riel. The second has been taken from a speech on patriotism given between 1878 and 1883. These documents suggest that, for Mercier, French Canada's *survivance* did not lie in isolationism but in a just and equitable Anglo-French partnership.

Riel, our brother, is dead, the victim of his devotion to the Métis cause whose leader he was, the victim of fanaticism and treason: the fanaticism of Sir John [A. Macdonald] and of a few of his friends; the treason of three of our own [the three French Canadians in the Macdonald cabinet] who sold their brother to save their portfolios.

In killing Riel, Sir John not only struck our race at the heart but also struck the cause of justice and humanity which, represented by all languages and sanctified by all religious beliefs, demanded mercy for the prisoner of Regina, our poor brother of the Northwest.

We are here 50,000 free citizens, gathered according to our constitutional rights, in the name of humanity that cries for vengeance, in the name of all the friends of justice trampled underfoot, in the name of 2,000,000 French citizens in tears. . . .

In the face of this crime, in the presence of these falterings, what is our duty? We have three things to do. Unite to punish the culprits; break the alliance which our deputies concluded with Orangeism; and seek in another alliance, more natural and less dangerous, the protection of our national interests.

To unite! Oh, how I feel at ease in uttering these words. For twenty years I have called for a union of all the living forces of the nation. For twenty years I have asked my brothers to sacrifice on the altar of the threatened fatherland the hatreds that blinded us and the divisions that killed us. This rallying cry that came from a patriotic heart was answered with insults, recriminations and slander. One of our brothers had to die, a national calamity had to happen, before it was heeded. . . .

All those joining together on this day of atonement are of the same race, speak the same language, and kneel at the same altars. The same blood courses in their veins; they are all brothers. May heaven grant that this time they will listen to the call of their blood. . . .

But this union, gentlemen, which we have concluded and which we ask you to bless in the name of the fatherland which you represent, is not a union of one race against another, of one religion against other religions.

*   *   *   *   *

We do not ignore that in the neighbouring province and in other parts of Canada there are generous souls who are prepared to devote themselves to the common cause, to the cause of justice and humanity. . . .

It is not therefore a racial war which we want; it is not an exclusively French party which we demand; but it is the union of all the friends of justice and humanity whose sacred cause has been outraged by the death of Riel. . . .

In the evil days of yore, when even the strongest souls were crushed by memories of the gallows of 1837, when the same fanaticism as today asked for the blood of those who demanded liberty, two men appeared to grant the liberty and refuse the blood; they were Baldwin and Lafontaine, Ontario and Quebec. . . .

Again today Ontario offers us a Baldwin [Edward Blake]. Search in the other two parties and find a Lafontaine. The Liberals think that they have him in their ranks, but if you so wish and if you can find him there, take him from the Conservatives. We will hail him joyfully and serve him faithfully.

> J. O. Pelland, ed., *Biographie, discours, conférences, etc. de l'Honorable Honoré Mercier* (Montreal, 1890), pp. 328–33 (translation).

We have a right to our national existence as a race apart, and woe to any man who will try to deprive us of it. But we must not in any way molest our brothers whose racial origins or religious creed differ from our own. We must claim our rights with firmness, but not aggressively. We must energetically oppose everything which tends to destroy our national character, but we must respect in others the rights that we demand for ourselves. There is no longer any question of fighting enemies weapon in hand, but of competing as a race with brothers in the fields of education, labour, and honesty.

* * * * *

Tied together as the branches of the same tree, the various races that dwell in Canada today must accept this community of existence. The interests of Canada, our common fatherland, must dominate interests of race and caste. We must not forget, we the citizens of this country who are called upon to become a great people, that if we are French, English, Scots, and Irish, we are also Canadians, and that this title must satisfy our pride as well as our legitimate ambition. We descend from the world's strongest races. Our destiny is not to perpetuate antiquated hatreds on this continent, but to build here a great nation whose future is bright in the designs of Providence.

> *Ibid.*, pp. 689–91 (translation).

The Political Views of Henri Bourassa

Henri Bourassa attempted to formulate a political programme for French Canada in a period of rapid and perplexing changes.

The settlement of the western prairies by a heterogeneous immigrant population had rendered obsolete the type of dualism envisaged by Mercier. *Survivance* was also being threatened by the emergence of a new British imperialism which seemed likely to undermine Canadian autonomy and to absorb the Dominion into a great Anglo-Saxon empire. Finally, the growing importance of the city and of industry was eroding French Canada's traditional value system. Given below are some of Bourassa's answers to these problems.

From the presence of the two races in Canada, there is no reason, I believe, to dread any danger or even any additional troubles, if only our politicians be willing, instead of pandering to sectional prejudices, to appeal to the best sentiments of both elements.

A mutual regard for racial sympathies on both sides, and a proper discharge of our exclusive duty to this land of ours, such is the only ground upon which it is possible for us to meet, so as to work out our national problems. There are here neither masters nor valets; there are neither conquerors nor conquered ones: there are two partners whose partnership was entered into upon fair and well defined lines. We do not ask that our English-speaking fellow-countrymen should help us to draw closer to France; but, on the other hand, they have no right to take advantage of their overwhelming majority to infringe on the treaty of alliance, and induce us to assume, however freely and spontaneously, additional burdens in defence of Great Britain.

The Canadian soil, with its blood and its wealth, with its past, its present and its future, in short, our whole national inheritance is ours only to be handed down unimpaired to our descendants. I, for one, respect and admire in my English-speaking fellow-countryman his love for his dear old and glorious motherland; and I am bound to say that he would be beneath my contempt the man who, in her hours of trial, did not tingle in sympathy with his Mother country. I have a right to expect that he should reciprocate that feeling by showing the same regard for his fellow-countrymen who still keep in their hearts an undying love for France, the land of their origin. But, apart from all such considerations within the province of the heart or of the mind, I say that the only sure way of obviating fatal misunderstandings lies in a determination that we shall, both of us, French and English alike, look at all constitutional and political questions from a purely Canadian standpoint.

H. Bourassa, *Great Britain and Canada* (Montreal, 1901), p. 45.

Our own nationalism is a Canadian nationalism founded upon the duality of races and on the particular traditions which this duality involves. We work for the development of a Canadian patriotism which is in our eyes the best guaranty of the existence of the two races and of the mutual respect they owe each other. For us, as for M. Tardivel, our compatriots are the French Canadians; but the English Canadians are not foreigners, and we regard as allies all those among them who respect us and who desire like us the maintenance of Canadian autonomy. For us, the fatherland is all Canada, that is, a federation of distinct races and autonomous provinces. The nation that we wish to see develop is the Canadian nation, composed of French Canadians and English Canadians, that is of two elements separated by language and religion . . . but united in a feeling of brotherhood, in a common attachment to the common fatherland.

> This statement was made by Bourassa during his debate with J.-P. Tardivel.
> From *Le Nationaliste*, 3 April 1904.
> Mason Wade, *The French Canadians 1760–1945* (Toronto, 1956), pp. 524–5.

A Test Case for the Doctrine of "Mutual Regard"

In 1905 the Autonomy bills, conferring provincial status upon the settled parts of the Northwest Territories, were introduced into the House of Commons by Sir Wilfrid Laurier. Article 16 of the original legislation stipulated that Catholic and Protestant ratepayers in the new provinces of Alberta and Saskatchewan would enjoy the right to establish separate schools "as they think fit". The Prime Minister, however, was forced to modify this clause when it caused a revolt in his cabinet. In its final form, Article 16 severely restricted both the number of separate schools and their conditions of operation. It was now the turn of Bourassa, who then represented the riding of Labelle in the federal Parliament, to argue forcefully that the Catholics of Alberta and Saskatchewan should enjoy full liberty to establish separate schools supported by public funds.

The question that today occupies the attention of Parliament is perhaps the most solemn that our nation's representatives have had to consider since the British colonies of North America were united under the same constitutional regime.

Our Legislature is being asked to bestow a constitution upon the vast regions of the West which, before the passing of another century, or perhaps even fifty years, will hold half of the Canadian population. What will be the national character of those new provinces of Alberta and Saskatchewan which sooner or later will dominate Confederation? Will they be cosmopolitan or Canadian?

Yesterday the kingdom of Indian tribes and buffalo herds, shall we hand them over to foreigners tomorrow: Galicians, Doukhobors, Mennonites, Americans, Frenchmen, and Englishmen, without safeguarding the acquired rights, the liberties, the very existence of those who were the pioneers of Christian civilization and of the Canadian nationality in those regions?

If we want this mighty flood of human beings, so different in race, customs, and aspirations, to become an element of force and unity instead of a cause of disintegration, we must make a compact whole of them and infuse into them some other common ideal than the thirst for riches and the sole desire to increase their material well-being.

In other words, we must give a body to this population, we must above all give it a soul; and that soul must unite it with the fundamental races that inhabit eastern Canada.

H. Bourassa, *Les Ecoles du Nord-Ouest* (Montreal, 1905), p. 1 (translation)

A Novelist Views *La Survivance*

The man who perhaps came nearest to capturing the quintessence of the spirit of *la survivance* was a novelist, Louis Hémon (1880–1913), in his famous work *Maria Chapdelaine*. Hémon had been born and raised in France and had spent eight years in England before coming to Canada in 1911. His work was based on impressions he had gathered during a stay in the Lake St. John country in 1912.

The following passage comes near the end of the book when the heroine, Maria Chapdelaine, must decide whether to emigrate to a city in the United States or remain in Quebec, on the land of her fathers. In a dream she hears the voice of her province:

Then it was that a third voice, mightier than the others, lifted itself up in the silence: the voice of Quebec—now the song of a woman, now the exhortation of a priest. It came to her with the sound of a church bell, with the majesty of an organ's tones, like a plaintive love-song, like the long high call of woodsmen in the forest. For verily there was in it all that makes the soul of the Province: the loved solemnities of the ancestral faith; the lilt of that old speech guarded with jealous care, the grandeur and the barbaric strength of this new land where an ancient race has again found its youth.

Thus spake the voice:—'Three hundred years ago we came, and we have remained. . . . They who led us hither might return among us without knowing shame or sorrow, for if it be true that we have little learned, most surely nothing is forgot.'

'We bore overseas our prayers and our songs; they are ever the same. We carried in our bosoms the hearts of the men of our fatherland, brave and merry, easily moved to pity as to laughter, of all human hearts the most human; nor have they changed. We traced the boundaries of a new continent, from Gaspé to Montreal, from St. Jean d'Iberville to Ungava, saying as we did it: Within these limits all we brought with us, our faith, our tongue, our virtues, our very weaknesses are henceforth hallowed things which no hand may touch, which shall endure to the end.'

'Strangers have surrounded us whom it is our pleasure to call foreigners; they have taken into their hands most of the rule, they have gathered to themselves much of the wealth; but in this land of Quebec nothing has changed. Nor shall anything change for we are the pledge of it. Concerning ourselves and our destiny, but one duty we have clearly understood: that we should hold fast—should endure. And we have held fast, so that, it may be, many centuries hence the world will look upon us and say: — These people are of a race that knows not how to perish . . . We are a testimony.'

'For this it is that we must abide in that Province where our fathers dwelt, living as they have lived, so to obey the unwritten command that once shaped itself in their hearts, that passed to ours, which we in turn must hand on to descendants innumerable:—In this land of Quebec naught shall die and naught shall suffer change. . . .'

L. Hémon, *Maria Chapdelaine* (Paris, 1921). Translation by W. H. Blake
(Toronto, 1921), pp. 258–60.

THE VIEWS OF LATER COMMENTATORS

Why French Canadians Think the Way They Do

Examples have been given in this problem of the Messianic and agrarian traditions on which French-Canadian nationalism is so largely based. In the following readings Michel Brunet, an historian, and Pierre-Elliot Trudeau, trained in law and economics, give their opinions on the origins and nature of this type of thought.

The historian of French-Canadian thought is faced with a difficult task, for he is studying a society whose historical development has not been normal. Such is the case with all groups subjected to a foreign domination and the French-Canadian nationality is no exception to the rule.

* * * * *

After a total military defeat Canada, a country founded by France, was conquered by England . . .

* * * * *

A Canadian society was reduced to a miserable state of survival . . .

*   *   *   *   *

It had been completely disorganized and placed in a position of permanent inferiority. It could no longer assure its own progress by self-action. The British cadres had taken the place of the Canadian ones. The St. Lawrence Valley was no longer a French colony. The conquerors had founded there a new colonial society. Between 1760 and 1790 the Canadians, vanquished, conquered, and occupied, lost control of their destinies. Since that tragic era, whether they admit it or not . . . they have lived a diminished existence.

Those are the facts. No one can deny them.

Under such conditions the evolution of French-Canadian thought necessarily differed from that of societies whose situation favoured their full development. The result: an incomplete, truncated, often puerile type of thinking, towed along by foreign influences or seeking refuge in a sterile isolationism, unable to grasp the complex problems of the environment and unable to define them, likely to feed on illusions and on vast syntheses divorced from daily reality, showing all the symptoms of an infancy unduly prolonged. To stress the weaknesses and contradictions of this thinking without taking into account the terrible consequences of the conquest is to be guilty of a grave injustice. The historian who fails or neglects to regard the conquest as the principal fact of the history of French Canada, as the event which completely transformed its development, either lacks objectivity or does not know his craft.

*   *   *   *   *

French Canadians believed in the psychology of nations and based themselves on this so-called science to explain why their historical development differed from that of their Anglo-Saxon fellow-citizens. Their weaknesses became qualities and their inadequacies secret signs of predestination. Whoever questioned the superiority, the virtues, and the genius of the French-Canadian nation was anathematized. A Messianic nationalism of romantic and romanesque inspiration gave birth to a sonorous and impotent patriotism.

*   *   *   *   *

For a century one school of thought has dominated and orientated the whole of French-Canadian society: agrarianism.

How can we define agrarianism? To describe it as an inordinate love of agriculture remains an incomplete definition. Agrarianism is first of all a way of thinking, a philosophy of life that idealizes the past, condemns the present and distrusts the future. It is a rejection, based on a static view of society, of the contemporary industrial age. The agrarians maintain that the world went astray when it entered the age of the machine and of technology. They denounce the materialism of our time and declare that past generations lived in a spiritual environment. According to them, the golden age of humanity was a time when tilling the soil was the occupation of the great majority of mankind.

> M. Brunet, "Trois dominantes de la pensée canadienne-française: l'agriculturisme, l'anti-étatisme et le messianisme", in *La Présence anglaise et les Canadiens* (Montreal, 1958), pp. 114–19 (translation)

In Quebec, during the first half of the twentieth century, our social thought was so idealistic, so *a priori*, so foreign to the facts and, to say everything, so futile, that it never succeeded in animating dynamic and living institutions. . . .

A whole people, by the force of things, was being obliged to live at one level [that of an urban industrial civilization] while their moral and intellectual disciplines were encouraging them to live at another.

Nationalism has been, until the end of the period studied in this book [1950], the principal axis around which has gravitated the entire social thought of French Canadians. This fact, which no one will question, need not be explained here. For a people who had been vanquished, occupied, decapitated, evicted from commerce, pushed out of the cities, and reduced gradually to a minority in the land which they had discovered, explored, and colonized, there were not many mental attitudes that could enable them to preserve their identity. They created a defensive system for themselves which, by a process of hypertrophy, caused them to attach excessive importance to everything which differentiated them from others, and to consider with hostility all changes (be it progress) if these were suggested by outsiders.

That is why, against an environment that was English, Protestant, democratic, materialistic, commercial, and later industrial, our nationalism developed a system of defence dominated by the opposite forces—the French language, Catholicism, authoritarianism, idealism, rural life, and later the return to the soil.

> P.-E. Trudeau, *La Grève de l'Amiante* (Montreal, 1956), pp. 11–12 (translation)

The Canadianism of Henri Bourassa

The following readings have been selected from two outstanding short studies of Henri Bourassa. The first is by André Laurendeau, co-chairman of the Royal Commission on Bilingualism and Biculturalism and previously one of the chief editorial writers for *Le Devoir*, the newspaper founded by Bourassa in 1910. The other is by M. P. O'Connell, a political scientist.

When Bourassa proclaims that he is first a Canadian, his Canadianism, it must be noted, does not float between heaven and earth. There were simply for him two ways of living it: one French and one English. He does not advocate a fusion; he is clearsighted enough to see that any fusion would favour the group that is stronger in number and wealth. "La patrie" is for him "le Canada tout entier"; but Canada is "une fédération de races distinctes et de provinces autonomes". He believes in the Canadian nation but sees it composed of French Canadians and English Canadians—"c'est-à-dire de deux éléments séparés [the word is strong] par la langue et la religion, et par les dispositions légales nécessaires à la conservation de leurs traditions". Canadian patriotism is therefore not a renunciation but an extension of the love one bears one's own. Canadian patriotism unites two entities which differ from one another, but which join again "dans un commun attachement à la patrie commune". In a word, Bourassa proclaims himself a Canadian first, but not merely a Canadian. He believes in a hyphenated patriotism, and in this kind of patriotism only. The word "Canadian" is the common denominator for people who are not in themselves common denominators. Canadian and French Canadian, Canadian and English Canadian are realities that are organically linked to each other. "Canadian" means, above all else, the acceptance of one group by the other, with the legitimate sacrifices that any marriage must entail.

> A. Laurendeau, "Henri Bourassa", in Robert L. McDougall, ed., *Our Living Tradition: Fourth Series* (Toronto, 1962), pp. 143–4.

A concept of Canadian nationality was basic to Bourassa's nationalism. It was designed to provide security and expansion for French-Canadian nationality throughout Canada, and to equate this with a broad national interest. Its essence was an integral dualism, which he hoped to see taken up by all Canadians, not simply as something to be endured, but as a positive goal giving the nation its unique character. Indeed, for Bourassa, the fundamental condition for having a Canadian nation at all in North America was that cultural and ethnic dualism be extended everywhere and in a concrete manner.

His idea of a "broad Canadian nationality" thus repudiates the concept of a "Quebec reservation"; that is, the view of 1867 that Quebec would be the French province and that the other provinces would be English in character. For him integral dualism meant the spread of French-speaking settlements, as distinct communities, as "little provinces of Quebec", into the English-speaking provinces and the surrounding of them, as he said in 1905, with an "atmosphere preservative of their native character and original qualities". To settle French Canadians in the West would make that country "homogeneous"; that is, give it a "double mentality" without which a Canadian nation would with difficulty emerge. French-speaking groups in the West would serve to "unify" the country and to stand as the only permanent barrier to absorption—mental, economic, and social—by the United States.

Essential to this design of dualism were separate schools for Catholic education and a system of bilingual instruction, together with related arrangements, such as the general use of French in business and government. French Catholics, in effect, must find as minorities and not as individual citizens the "same liberty that the Anglo-Protestant minority finds in the province of Quebec".

M. P. O'Connell, "The Ideas of Henri Bourassa", *The Canadian Journal of Economics and Political Science*, XIX (February 1953), pp. 372–3.

Further Reading

The history of French Canada during the period covered by this problem is given in M. Wade, *The French Canadians 1760–1945* (Toronto, Macmillan, 1956), Chapters VII to XII. Two popular biographies by R. Rumilly can be profitably consulted: *Mercier* (Montreal, Editions du Zodiaque, 1936) and *Monseigneur Laflèche et son temps* (Montreal, Editions du Zodiaque, n.d.). The first presents an image of Mercier that is overly romantic, but the volume on Bishop Laflèche succeeds in recreating the spirit of the period. For the biography of a man at the other political extreme, see L. Lamontagne, *Arthur Buies, homme de lettres* (Quebec, les Presses Universitaires Laval, 1957). M. Ayearst, "The Parti Rouge and the Clergy", *Canadian Historical Review*, XV (December 1934), pp. 390–405, is a good account of the conflict between the Church and the Liberal party in Quebec.

In recent years, several analytical essays have been written on the economic and social evolution and intellectual tradition of French Canada. The first notable collection of such papers was J. C. Falardeau, ed., *Essais sur le Québec, contemporain/Essays on Contemporary Quebec* (Quebec, les Presses Universitaires Laval, 1953), now regrettably out of print. Several of these essays, however, have been reprinted in M. Rioux and Y. Martin, *French-Canadian Society*, Vol. I (Carleton Library No. 18, Toronto, McClelland & Stewart, 1964)*. This volume, which brings together the works of geographers, economists, and sociologists, should be required reading for everyone interested in French Canada. R. Cook, *Canada and the French-Canadian Question* (Toronto, Macmillan, 1966)* is a useful collection of articles and essays. The one entitled "Quebec: the Ideology of Survival" is particularly relevant to this Problem. Professor Cook argues that French Canada's unending struggle for survival has consumed energies that might otherwise have been devoted to internal problems of social and economic reform.

Problem 15

Colony to Kingdom — Acquiring Sovereign Status by Evolution

How does a political entity cease to be a colony and gain recognition as a sovereign state? Prior to the gradual emergence of Canada and the other dominions on the international scene, the only recognized process was that followed by the United States and the former American possessions of Spain and Portugal: a formal declaration of independence, generally followed by an armed struggle and the eventual recognition of the new status by other states, including the former "mother country".

Canada's gradual acquisition of the badges of sovereignty, participation of her statesmen in top-level conferences as fully accredited diplomats, the making of treaties, and the committing of the country to peace or war by decision of her own government and Parliament, the sending and receiving of permanent diplomatic missions, pose a number of questions to the historian.

Was there an inevitability about the process? Were these concessions wrested from a reluctant British government? Did the country's leaders foresee the consequences of their actions? These are but a few of the questions that can be raised from the readings which follow.

Representation on British Teams

In 1871 a Canadian for the first time participated as a principal in formal diplomatic negotiations. The British and American governments agreed to refer the disputes which had brought the two nations to the verge of war to a ten-member International Joint Commission, five chosen by each government. Sir John A. Macdonald was selected as one of the British team, a recognition of the interest Canadians had in the negotiations. Charles Sumner, Chairman of the Foreign Affairs Committee of the U.S. Senate, had suggested, for instance, that all British North America be ceded to the United States as partial compensation for the "indirect claims" arising from the ravages of British-built Confederate commerce raiders.

In a private letter dated 21 March 1871 to his cabinet colleague, Charles Tupper, Macdonald described his unenviable position as part of the British team, defending the interests of Canada, which were often at variance with British interests. One such point was the coastal fisheries of the Maritime provinces, from which the Canadians wished to exclude American competitors while retaining an open American market for their produce.

The result of Lord de Grey's communication with Lord Granville . . . was an instruction to proceed with the negotiations for the settlement of the Fisheries, but to insert a clause in the Treaty that its provisions would be subject to ratification by the Canadian Parliament.

This instruction, though satisfactory in some respects, places me in an exceedingly embarrassing position.

If a majority of my colleagues should at any time conclude to accept terms which I do not approve of, I must, of course, either protest and withdraw, or remain on the Commission and trust to the non-ratification of the Treaty by Canada.

If I take the first course it will disclose to the Americans the fact of a difference of opinion, a conflict in fact, between Canada and England. This the Americans are anxious to establish, in order to get up a sort of quarrel between the two, and strengthen that party in England who desire to get rid of the Colonies as a burden.

If I continue to act on the Commission, I will be attacked for making an un-worthy sacrifice of Canada's right, and may be compelled to vote in Parliament against a Treaty which I had a share in making. I must arrange matters, however, as best I can as circumstances arise.

Public Archives of Canada microfilm. Macdonald Letterbook, Vol. 14.

Britain's Wars Are Not Necessarily Canada's

During Macdonald's lifetime a number of significant further steps toward participation in diplomatic affairs were taken by the Canadian government. They included the creation of the office of High Commissioner for Canada at London in 1880, the issuing of credentials to the high commissioner to participate in international technical conferences (starting with one on submarine cables in Paris in 1883), and to act as a plenipotentiary to negotiate trade treaties, first granted in 1884. Not until 1893 did a Canadian (along with a British colleague) sign a trade treaty, one between the Dominion and France.

Meanwhile Macdonald was confronted with the problem of Canadian participation in British wars. In 1885 an expedition was being raised for the Sudan to "avenge Gordon" (Charles C. "Chinese" Gordon, the popular hero who died when Khartoum fell to Mahdist forces in November 1884). On 18 February 1885 Sir Charles Tupper, the Canadian High Commissioner, had written from London, urging the Canadian government to offer troops as the Australian colonies had, and requesting that he be kept better informed of the views of the government.

Macdonald replied on 12 March, 1885:

> I have your notes of the 18th and 27th on the subject of sending Canadian troops to the Soudan. I . . . have . . . talked it over with my colleagues, and we think the time has not arrived, nor the occasion, for our volunteering military aid to the Mother Country.
>
> We do not stand at all in the same position as Australasia. The Suez Canal is nothing to us, and we do not ask England to quarrel with France or Germany for our sakes. The offer of those Colonies is a good move on their part, and somewhat like Cavour's sending Sardinian troops to the Crimea. Why should we waste money and men in this wretched business? England is not at war, but merely helping the Khedive [ruler of Egypt] to put down an insurrection, and now that Gordon is gone, the motive of aiding in the rescue of our countrymen is gone with him. Our men and money would therefore be sacrificed to get Gladstone and Co. out of the hole they have plunged themselves into by their own imbecility.
>
> Again, the reciprocal aid to be given by the Colonies and England should be a matter of treaty, deliberately entered into and settled on a permanent basis. The spasmodic offers of our Militia Colonels, anxious for excitement or notoriety, have roused unreasonable expectations in England, and are so far unfortunate. I dare say that a battalion or two of venturous spirits might be enlisted, but 7d. a day will cool most men's warlike ardour.

Joseph Pope, *Correspondence of Sir John Macdonald* (Toronto, n.d.), pp. 337–8.

Imperial Federation as a Way to Full Citizenship

Macdonald was well aware of the different and conflicting inter-ests of the component parts of the British Empire. There were

Canadians, however, who saw their countrymen shaping their destiny through the reorganization of Great Britain and the self-governing colonies into a federation in which colonists would participate, through their federal delegates, in the framing of a single imperial foreign policy. One of the most active and wide ranging of the Canadian proponents of Imperial Federation was George R. Parkin, headmaster of the Collegiate School, Fredericton, who resigned in 1889 to join the staff of the Imperial Federation League as a travelling lecturer.

In 1892 he published *Imperial Federation: The Problem of National Unity.* The subtitle suggests that his concept of "nation" differed from that of Macdonald. He argued that only by assuming a share of the full responsibilities of Britain's world role would the citizens of the self-governing colonies acquire full enfranchisement.

The concession of Responsible Government to the colonies was an important, but by no means a final step in political development. From some points of view the change seemed to superficial observers very closely akin to the concession of independence. It gave the absolute control of local affairs, the power of levying taxes, and of applying the proceeds; but the higher functions of government, it must be remembered, still remained with the central power. Not only was this so, but the responsibilities of independence were clearly not imposed in the same proportion that its privileges were granted.

In the minds of some colonists and more Englishmen I have found a belief, ... that any closer union ... could only be effected by taking away from the colonies some of the self-governing powers which they now possess. That this is necessary is clearly a mistake, and one which probably arises from the erroneous impression about the degree of self-government which a colony enjoys. Not the resignation of old powers, but the assumption of new ones, must be the result of Federal union. A colony has now no power of making peace or war; no voice, save by the courtesy of the mother-country, in making treaties; no direct influence on the exercise of national diplomacy. Admitted to an organic union, its voice would be heard and its influence felt in the decision of these questions. To the Imperial Parliament, that is, as things now stand, to the Parliament of the United Kingdom, is reserved the right to override the legislation of a colony, just as, for example, the Parliament of the Dominion has the right to override the legislation of a Canadian Province. But as the Canadian feels in this no sense of injustice or tyranny, since he is represented in the superior as well as in the inferior Legislature, so the colonist would feel no loss of political dignity if he had his true place in the higher as well as in the lower representative body. With enlarged powers, it is true, the colony would have to accept enlarged responsibilities. In human affairs the two invariably and rightly go together.

G. R. Parkin, *Imperial Federation: The Problem of National Unity*
(London, 1892), pp. 55–8.

The Boer War — To Participate or Not?

The summoning of the governments of the self-governing colonies to "Colonial Conferences", a practice which started in 1887 when many colonial statesmen attended the London ceremonies marking the fiftieth anniversary of Queen Victoria's accession to the throne, provided a forum for both the advocates and opponents of further unification of policy within the Empire. The full-fledged federation advocated by Parkin found few supporters among practical politicians. The advocates of greater unification looked to the creation of a trading community, *Zollverein* (to use the German term fashionable at the time), or a military community or *Kriegsverein*.

These questions were still being widely debated when the Boer War broke out in 1899, forcing Sir Wilfrid Laurier's government to decide on the extent of active Canadian participation in the hostilities. They had the precedent of Macdonald's reaction to the Sudan expedition, noted above, but the desire on the part of a large and articulate portion of English-speaking Canadians was much greater. There was also greater pressure from British authorities for the offer of troops.

The government's solution was a compromise. Volunteers would be recruited, equipped, and transported by the Canadian government, but would be paid and commanded in South Africa by the British Army. The decision was ratified by order-in-council rather than by a vote in Parliament. The action of the government was criticized in and out of Parliament by a former supporter of Laurier, Henri Bourassa, whose reputation as a Canadian nationalist stemmed from his stand on this issue.

. . . wrong as I think it for us to participate in . . . [the war] without having had the right to pronounce upon the causes of it, I repeat that I do not oppose these resolutions, for one reason. I feel disposed to take the same stand that the English Liberals have taken upon this question. It has been said in this House that we should not discuss the merits of the war of to-day, because the time has passed for discussing them. Well, Sir, when was that time or when shall come the time to discuss them? In England, in all the Australian colonies, in all the British constitutional countries except Canada, the representatives of the people were called together and given the opportunity of expressing their views and casting their votes upon the constitutional question as well as upon the merits of that war. In Canada, however, we have been treated differently.

. . . England is at war with the South African Republic but we are not. I do not admit that we are, because I do not admit that Canada, any more than any other free country, can be plunged into war by an Order in Council without obtaining the opinion of the representatives of the people.

Canada, Parliament, *Debates of the House of Commons*, 1900, (Ottawa), p. 394.

Repercussions of the Alaska Boundary Decision, 1903

The story of the Alaska Boundary Dispute is frequently cited by Canadian historians as an example of Canadian interests being sacrificed "on the altar of Anglo-American friendship".* The British nominee on the six-man tribunal had abandoned his two Canadian colleagues by voting with the three Americans for a settlement that favoured United States' territorial claims. This aroused widespread public resentment in Canada, which was reflected in Prime Minister Sir Wilfrid Laurier's comments in Parliament.

I have often regretted, Mr. Speaker, and never more than on the present occasion, that we are living beside a great neighbour who I believe I can say without being deemed unfriendly to them, are very grasping in their national actions, and who are determined on every occasion to get the best in any agreement which they make. I have often regretted also that while they are a great and powerful nation, we are only a small colony, a growing colony, but still a colony. I have often regretted also that we have not in our own hands the treaty-making power which would enable us to dispose of our own affairs. But in this matter we are dealing with a position that was forced upon us—we have not the treaty-making power. . . . Our hands are tied to a large extent, owing to the fact of our connection—which has its benefits, but which has also its disadvantages—the fact of our connection with the mother country making us not free agents and obliging us to deal with questions affecting ourselves through the instrumentality of British ambassadors . . . The difficulty as I conceive it to be, is that so long as Canada remains a dependency of the British

* D. G. Creighton, *Dominion of the North: A History of Canada* (Toronto, 1957), pp. 403–10; A. R. M. Lower, *Colony to Nation* (Toronto, 1957), p. 438; W. L. Morton, *The Kingdom of Canada* (Toronto, 1963), pp. 395–7.

Crown the present powers that we have are not sufficient for the maintenance of our rights. It is important that we should ask the British parliament for more extensive powers so that if ever we have to deal with matters of a similar nature again, we shall deal with them in our own way, in our own fashion, according to the best light that we have.

Canada, Parliament, *Debates* . . . , 1903, col. 14814–17.

The Formation of a Department of External Affairs

The creation of a Department of External Affairs by the Canadian Parliament in 1909 was not a direct result of the disenchantment expressed above. The need for such an office was revealed in the chaos resulting from the absence of any clearing house or repository for documents relating to affairs outside Canada. Joseph Pope, the Under-Secretary of State, described the existing situation and recommended the creation of a new department in a memorandum he submitted to the Royal Commission on the Civil Service on 25 May 1907.

All communications which reach the Secretary of State [the Canadian Cabinet minister] for transmission to England or to a foreign country, are forwarded by him to the Governor General with a recommendation that he would be pleased to transmit the same to their destination. All despatches from the Colonial Office are addressed to the Governor General and by His Excellency are sent, for the most part, to the Privy Council where they are referred to the heads of those departments which they particularly concern. . . . Much bears upon what I have called external affairs, that is to say, questions touching our relations with foreign countries, as the Behring Sea Seal question, the Alaska Boundary, the Atlantic Fisheries, International boundaries, and other pending controversies with the United States; or, it may be, with questions whose scope and bearing, though within the empire, extend beyond the bounds of the Dominion; such, for example, as the difference with Newfoundland over the boundary in Labrador. . . .

It may happen; it must sometimes happen; that the official to whom these Imperial despatches are referred, while fully competent to deal with the merits of the question in its present aspect, is not familiar with the past history of the controversy or skilled in the framing of State papers. There are moreover certain questions which relate partly to one department and partly to another, so that it may not be easy to tell at first sight to whom a new despatch should be referred. The earlier communication may have related to one department, and a later despatch on the same subject to another. Neither department having any knowledge of what has been referred to the other, the consequence is that both departments, . . . are working more or less in the dark.

*   *   *   *   *

The practical result of the system in vogue is that there does not exist to-day in any department a complete record of the correspondence to which I have alluded. It has been so scattered, and passed through so many hands that there is no approach to continuity in any of the departmental files. . . . As the Dominion grows this state of things must always be getting worse. . . . Even now, I am of opinion that it would be an extremely difficult task to construct from our official files anything approaching to a complete record of any of the international questions in which Canada has been concerned during the past fifty years. . . .

My suggestion is, that all despatches relating to external affairs should be referred by the Privy Council to one department, whose staff should contain men trained in the study of these questions, and in the conduct of diplomatic correspondence. . . .

I recommend that a small staff of young men, well educated and carefully selected, . . . be specially trained in the knowledge and treatment of these subjects. In this way we shall acquire an organized method of dealing with international questions which at present we wholly lack.

> Quoted in James Eayrs, "The Origins of Canada's Department of External Affairs", *The Canadian Journal of Economics and Political Science*, XXV (May 1959), pp. 112–13.

Separate Representation at the Peace Conference, 1919

The First World War provided the cause or occasion for a number of developments which now are seen as milestones on Canada's road to sovereignty. These include: the prompt summoning of Parliament, whose members agreed to active Canadian participation, the creation of a distinctive Canadian Army Corps, the stationing of a Canadian cabinet minister in London to deal with the political consequences of the employment of the Canadian forces, and the Dominion Prime Ministers' participation in framing imperial policy through the Imperial War Cabinet in 1917. These developments represented domestic arrangements within the British Empire.

For Canada and the other dominions to be permitted separate representation at the peace conference required the consent of the allied and associated powers, essentially a recognition by other sovereign states that the dominions had graduated from conventional colonial status. The exchange of telegrams from which the following samples have been selected illustrate the arguments presented by the Canadian government to gain this status.

Sir Robert Borden to David Lloyd George, 29 October 1918

There is need of serious consideration as to representation of the Dominions in the peace negotiations. The press and people of this country take it for granted that Canada will be represented at the Peace Conference. I appreciate possible difficulties as to representation of the Dominions, but I hope you will keep in mind that certainly a very unfortunate impression would be created and possibly a dangerous feeling might be aroused if these difficulties are not overcome by some solution which will meet the national spirit of the Canadian people. . . .

Lloyd George to Borden, 3 November 1918

. . . I fully understand the importance of the question that you raise. It makes me impressed all the more with the importance of your coming immediately to Europe, for practically it is impossible to solve by correspondence the many difficult problems which it raises and which you fully appreciate. . . .

Newton W. Rowell (Acting Prime Minister) to Borden in London, 4 December 1918

Council to-day further considered Canadian representation at Peace Conference and is even more strongly of opinion than when you left, that Canada should be represented. Council is of opinion that in view of war efforts of Dominion other nations entitled to representation at Conference should recognize unique character of British Commonwealth composed of group of free nations under one sovereign and that provision should be made for special representation of these nations at Conference, . . . Should not representation be to some extent commensurate with war efforts? Would you like Order in Council passed or any other official action taken declaring attitude of Government on question of Canadian representation at Conference? . . .

Borden to Acting Prime Minister, 2 January 1919

In [Imperial War] Cabinet to-day I took up question of representation of the Dominion and spoke very frankly and firmly as to Canada's attitude. My proposal which I consider the most satisfactory solution that is practicable and which was accepted by the Cabinet is as follows:—

First, Canada and the other Dominions shall each have the same representation as Belgium and other small allied nations at the Peace Conference.

Second, as it is proposed to admit representatives of Belgium and other small allied nations only when their special interests are under consideration,

I urged that some of the representatives of British Empire should be drawn from a panel on which each Dominion Prime Minister shall have a place. . . . It is anticipated that the British Empire will have five representatives entitled to be present at all meetings of Conference. I expressed my strong opinion that it would be most unfortunate if these were all selected from the British Islands. Probably three will be named and two others selected from the panel for each meeting. The panel will comprise both British and Dominion Ministers. No public announcement can be made until these proposals have been communicated to Allied Governments and accepted. . . . My proposal really gives to Dominions fuller representation than that accorded to small allied nations such as Belgium.

Canada, Parliament, *Sessional Papers*, No. 41, Special Session 1919, pp. 1–3.

Does British Association Imply Involvement?

As a result of the separate representation in the Paris Peace Conference, Canada, the other dominions, and India became charter members of the League of Nations, with the right to be elected as non-permanent members of its Council (as Canada was in 1927). A further opportunity for Canada to participate in diplomacy came with the agreement to accredit a Canadian minister to Washington negotiated during 1919 and 1920. The need for such an official had been recognized before the outbreak of war. Any doubts had been removed during the struggle by the volume and nature of the business performed by the Canadian War Mission. In order to emphasize that distinctive Canadian representation at Washington did not imply a Canadian foreign policy separate from that of the British Empire, the British and Canadian governments agreed that the Canadian minister plenipotentiary should reside with his staff in the British Embassy. The Canadian minister would handle all Canadian business with the American officials, and, as the second ranking officer in the Embassy, would be in charge of all business when the ambassador was absent.* Certain of the members of the opposition in the Canadian Parliament expressed concern at this arrangement. The following exchange between Ernest Lapointe, future chief lieutenant of W. L. Mackenzie King, and Prime

---

* Documents illustrating these negotiations are to be found in Walter A. Riddell, *Documents on Canadian Foreign Policy 1917–1939* (Toronto, 1962), pp. 265–9.

Minister Arthur Meighen on 21 April 1921, presents the differing viewpoints of what have been called the "Smuts-Borden" and "King-Hertzog" concepts of Commonwealth relations.*

Mr. LAPOINTE: . . . Any questions I ask are more by way of constructive criticism, because I do not object to the principle. Anything which is a step in the road to nationhood has my full approval. I would like to know whether the people of Canada will be responsible for the actions of their own appointee when he acts as British ambassador, transacting purely British affairs as distinct from Canadian affairs.

Mr. MEIGHEN: Inasmuch as he is named on the advice of the Canadian people he would be responsible, I think, in the same way as any other ambassador to his own country. I do not know what his responsibility to Canada would be in respect to matters purely British. It would appear to me that he would owe direct responsibility in that regard more to Great Britain. He is our direct appointee, and for his general conduct he is responsible to us, but if there are matters which he may be called upon to discharge in this contingency which may never arise, matters in which Canada has no interest but which are purely British, it would appear to me that he would be responsible more directly to the people of Great Britain. They are ready to accept that.

Mr. LAPOINTE: What purpose is served by this arrangement? Why should it have been agreed that the Canadian representative will act for the British ambassador in his absence?

Mr. MEIGHEN: The idea is to give him rank such as he should have. He is in the position second in authority there, and naturally would be first in authority in the absence of the first in authority. . . . and if the British government is ready to accept it, I cannot see what we have to risk in that regard.

W. A. Riddell, *Documents on Canadian Foreign Policy* 1917–1939
(Toronto, 1962), pp. 273–4.

A Specific Disclaimer of Canadian Commitment to British-Negotiated Obligations (1924)

Partly as a result of the confused domestic political situation in Canada in the early 1920's, no Canadian minister was accredited to Washington until 1927, by which date the idea of associating

---

* The conflicting ideals of unified ("Smuts-Borden") and highly decentralized ("King-Hertzog") concepts of the Commonwealth are set forth in F. H. Underhill, *The British Commonwealth: An Experiment in Co-operation Among Nations*, (Durham, 1956), pp. 54–9.

him with the British Embassy was abandoned. Further Canadian legations* were established at Paris in 1928 and Tokyo in 1929.

The difficulties inherent in developing and carrying out a common imperial foreign policy were demonstrated in the negotiations at the Imperial Conference of 1921 concerning the renewal or abrogation of the Anglo-Japanese alliance. The cause of separate diplomacy was furthered by the signing of the North Pacific Halibut Treaty with the United States by a Canadian plenipotentiary (Ernest Lapointe) with no British counter-signature in 1923.† Earlier that year the Canadian government had received an enquiry from the British to the dominions whether they separately would supply contingents to a threatened war with resurgent Turkish nationalists who were confronting the British at Chanak, on the Dardenelles. Canadian newspapers had published news of the enquiry before the cabled dispatch had reached Prime Minister W. L. M. King. The cabinet agreed that parliament must be consulted before troops could be committed.

No war followed the Chanak crisis, but when the peace treaty between Turkey and the allied powers was renegotiated, the Canadian government did not participate. When the new treaty was ready for ratification, an exchange of cables took place between the British government and the Governor-General, who was still the official channel of communication between a dominion government and London.

From the Secretary of State for the Colonies to the Governor-General

London, March 21, 1924

My telegram dated February 22. Peace Treaty with Turkey. Bill has now been read third time House of Lords and hoped to introduce it into House of Commons March 28th, and to secure passage within very short period thereafter. It is considered extremely important that His Majesty's ratification should take place at the earliest possible moment after passage of Bill. In the

---

* A diplomatic mission headed by an official with the rank of minister. An embassy is a mission headed by an ambassador. The first Canadian legation raised to embassy status was Washington in 1943.

† The right and propriety of the signing of a treaty applying solely to Canada rather that signing it for the Empire as a whole raised a number of questions in the Empire and in the United States Senate. See Riddell, *op cit.*, pp. 78–86.

circumstances hoped that your Ministers may be in a position to reply to my telegram at very early date and if possible by the end of March.

From the Governor-General to the Secretary of State for the Colonies

Ottawa, March 24, 1924

. The Government of Canada not having been invited to send a representative to the Lausanne Conference and not having participated in the proceedings of the Conference either directly or indirectly, and not being for this reason a signatory to the Treaty on behalf of Canada . . . my Ministers do not feel that they are in a position to recommend to Parliament the approval of the peace Treaty with Turkey and the Conventions thereto. Without the approval of Parliament they feel they are not warranted in signifying concurrence in ratification of the Treaty and Conventions. . . .

Canada, Parliament, *Sessional Papers*, No. 232, 1924, pp. 10, 11.

A Footnote to the Balfour Committee's Definition of Dominion Status

The use of the Governor-General's Office as the channel of communication between dominion and British governments was terminated shortly after the acceptance by the Imperial Conference of 1926 of the Report of the Inter-Imperial Relations Committee chaired by Lord Balfour. A British High Commission was established in Ottawa in 1928 to serve, in common with the long-established Canadian High Commission in London, as a channel of communications between the governments.

The text of the key passages of the Balfour Report, particularly the definition of dominion status normally reproduced in italics, have been reproduced too frequently to require being quoted here. The following selections from the memoirs of L. S. Amery, the Secretary of State for Dominion Affairs,* provide some background to the drafting and presentation of the passage.

When the Balfour Committee met on 27th October . . . We were unanimous at the outset in considering that our task was not to try and evolve any kind of Empire constitution, but only to see how far we were agreed on what the

---

* A Dominions Office separate from the Colonial Office was established in 1925. L. S. Amery held both portfolios, but different parliamentary and permanent under-secretaries were appointed from the inception of the new office.

constitutional position, in fact, was, and how far there was anything in existing forms or arrangements which required adjustment to that position.

I had rather hoped that we might then begin with some of the more detailed practical issues in order to see how we got on together. But Hertzog, with the deductive mind of a jurist trained in Roman Law, insisted on raising at once the necessity for a precise definition of our relationship to govern the rest of our discussion. He promptly produced his own formula, which began by referring to the Dominions as independent States equal in status and separately entitled to international recognition, but went on to describe them as united by the common bond of allegiance to the Crown and freely associated as members of the British Commonwealth of Nations. Mackenzie King, while agreeing with the substance, demurred to the word independence on the ground that in Canada it might be held to mean the same as in the American Declaration of Independence—the very thing from which Canada had dissociated herself.

* * * * *

The idea had been that the agreed definition should serve as a prefix or preamble to a more general statement on the nature of our Commonwealth relationship. But Balfour had a much happier solution, that of incorporating it in the body of the statement itself. In this way he was able, without detracting from the importance of the definition, to put it into its proper perspective, and balance the somewhat negative impression it might otherwise have created. Taking it home with him that Friday afternoon he sat down rapidly filling sheet after sheet of the loose-leaf notebook which he habitually used for his original drafts. . . . When we met on Monday we unanimously applauded Balfour's draft as a masterpiece of balanced expression, and approved it as it stood. Every line of it still holds good today [1952].

* * * * *

This now became the opening passage of our Report, . . . But on 19th November the Report was adopted by the full Imperial Conference. In the roneoed [duplicated] copies circulated to the Committee the defining sentence had been underlined in order to show where it dovetailed in. By an oversight this was reproduced by the printer in italics, thus to some extent undoing Balfour's effort, which was to deprive the sentence of its unduly negative emphasis. . . . A pity, for it has been habitually quoted out of its context ever since.

L. S. Amery, *My Political Life* (London, 1953), pp. 384–92.

Canada Declares War, 1939 and 1941

After the passage of the Statute of Westminster by the British Parliament in 1931, any remaining limitations on the autonomy of the dominions were self-imposed. For instance, Section 7(1) of the Statute, "Nothing in this Act shall be deemed to apply to the repeal, amendment or alteration of the British North America Acts, 1867 to 1930, or any order, rule or regulation made thereunder." was added at Canadian request. The autonomy thus acquired by Canada and the other dominions was still qualified by ambiguity surrounding the concept of the members of the Commonwealth being "united by a common allegiance to the Crown". Was the Crown divisible? Could the King of the United Kingdom be at war with a foreign country while the King of Canada remained at peace with the same country?

The test came in September 1939. On September 3rd a state of war between Great Britain and Germany was declared to exist. The Australian and New Zealand governments, by executive action, promptly declared that their countries were automatically, by virtue of the British Act, at war with Germany. In the Union of South Africa the question of remaining neutral was referred to Parliament, which happened to be in session, when the cabinet split on the issue. Upon the rejection of the neutrality resolution a new government was formed, and relations with Germany were severed.

On September 1st, when the outbreak of war appeared inevitable, the Canadian Prime Minister, W. L. Mackenzie King, had summoned a special session of Parliament which convened on September 7th. A formal declaration of war was not issued until Parliament had endorsed the government's policy of co-operation with Britain and France by accepting the Speech from the Throne on September 9th.

International recognition of the right of the dominions to declare war individually was contained in the Proclamation of Neutrality, which the President of the United States issued on 5 September 1939. It listed Britain, Australia, New Zealand, and India as belligerents, but not Canada or South Africa.

The Canadian government's position on its policy of committing Canada to war by action of the Canadian Parliament is summarized in the following extract from the Prime Minister's opening speech.

　　. . . The action we are taking to-day, and such further action as this parliament may authorize, are being and will be taken by this country voluntarily, not because of any colonial or inferior status vis-à-vis Great Britain, but because of an equality of status. We are a nation in the fullest sense, a member of the British commonwealth of nations, sharing like freedom with Britain herself, a freedom which we believe we must all combine to save.

Let me repeat: [he quotes from a statement of September 1st]

> In the event of the United Kingdom becoming engaged in war in the effort to resist aggression, the government of Canada have unanimously decided, as soon as parliament meets, to seek its authority for effective cooperation by Canada at the side of Britain.

We did not decide we would have to go into war willy-nilly; we decided that the policy as therein set forth was what we believed the Canadian people wished to have given effect; and we have summoned parliament to express here, as representing the Canadian people, its will and its wish in the matter of this country entering this war voluntarily and of its own decision and right.

Canada, Parliament, Debates . . . , Second Session 1939, p. 30.

When Japanese forces struck at British and American installations in the Pacific on 7 December 1941, Canadian army units stationed at Hong Kong were immediately involved. In contrast to the policy followed in 1939, the Canadian declaration of war was issued as an executive action and was in effect before either its British or American counterparts. The Canadian Parliament was in recess from 14 November 1941 to 21 January 1942. Only on the latter date was the House of Commons formally notified of the executive action.

THE VIEWS OF LATER COMMENTATORS

A Canadian Survey History's View of the Inter-War Developments

Of the standard one-volume surveys of Canadian history used in introductory university courses, A. R. M. Lower's *Colony to Nation* reflects most clearly a Canadian autonomist's views.

In 1928 no one was disposed to dispute Canadian claims to autonomy. The intervening decade had virtually completed the evolution and all that remained was to work out the details. In external affairs here was the significant development of the period. The Imperial Conference resolution of 1917 had declared for a revision of the constitution of the Empire when time permitted. The Prime Ministers' meeting of 1921, owing to its preoccupation with the Japanese alliance and to the gathering sentiment in Canada and South Africa against giving fixed form to inter-imperial relationships, did not undertake the task. If Arthur Meighen was not prepared to work out a constitution for the Empire, Mackenzie King could hardly be expected to be, . . . What would be expected of him would be stress on Canada's separate legal personality, that is, on autonomy, and that is exactly what occurred.

The indirect refusal to assist Great Britain over the Chanak incident, 1922, was the first notice given that Canada would make up her own mind about foreign affairs. It was followed by the still more emphatic show of independence involved in the way in which the Halibut Treaty of 1923 with the United States was signed. No Dominion had previously claimed complete diplomatic independence and treaties, if negotiated by Dominions representatives, had been signed by the appropriate British diplomat as the King's plenipotentiary. But in 1923 Mr. Ernest Lapointe went to Washington furnished with full powers from the King and when the British ambassador, Sir Auckland Geddes, turned up to sign the treaty, he was politely informed that that would not be necessary. The name of the King's Canadian plenipotentiary alone appeared on the document.

The manner of signing the Halibut Treaty practically established diplomatic autonomy, although a rearguard action was fought by certain constitutional metaphysicians who contended that since the King had to furnish full powers to the Canadian representative and since he must act on advice and this advice must be that of his British ministers, little change had occurred. If the British nations were to remain together, the position attained had become impossible. The Halibut Treaty had been accepted by the American senate only with many objections, for that body could not discern Canada as an independent state. In the Imperial Conference of 1926, therefore, an attempt was made to straighten the matter out.

*   *   *   *   *

The Conference of 1926 solved the great problems of inter-imperial relationships in principle but left a good many details to be worked out. This process was completed at the next Conference, in 1930, but previously heavy pressure had been put upon the Prime Minister, Mr. R. B. Bennett, by Howard Ferguson, the Conservative premier of Ontario, to secure consultation before the Committee's report was accepted. Mr. Ferguson's case was based upon that specious conception, the Compact theory of Confederation. Mr. Bennett yielded and the proposed constitutional and defining statute was changed to prevent any possibility of its being made a basis for altering Dominion-provincial relations as defined in the British North America Act. With this modification the act was passed in 1931 under the title of The Statute of Westminster.

*   *   *   *   *

The Statute of Westminster came as close as was practicable without revolutionary scissors to legislating the independence of the 'Dominions'. There is good ground for holding December 11, 1931 as Canada's Independence Day, for on that day she became a sovereign state. It was still possible to make a debating contention that the authority which had enacted a statute must be superior to those existing under such statutes, that the British Parliament having constituted Canada by the British North America Act and clarified its position by the Statute of Westminster, must be a superior body to the Canadian Parliament and that under certain circumstances, it could prove its superiority by repealing these acts. But the British Parliament had also long ago passed an act acknowledging the Independence of the United States: could it reduce the United States to a group of colonies again by repealing that act? The only means by which independence could have been more sharply defined would have been a declaration of independence from the people of Canada themselves. . . . There was no hint of desire for such a course: Canadians followed the road to which they had become so thoroughly habituated, the well-tried road of legal tradition.

A. R. M. Lower, *Colony to Nation* (Toronto, 1946), pp. 481–5.

Status Without Responsibility Does Not Equal Independence

A. R. M. Lower's appraisal of the significance of the interwar period, especially of the importance of the Statute of Westminster, contrasts with that of A. P. Thornton, the British-born and British-trained author of *The Imperial Idea and Its Enemies*. Thornton is now a professor at the University of Toronto, but he was still viewing Canada from a trans-Atlantic vantage point when he wrote the following lines.

. . . The United States could not be relied upon by anybody except Canada. It was because of this hard fact of geography, which had been as valid in Laurier's day as now, that Canada got more annoyed than any other Dominion at the many suggestions that she should contribute to the naval defence of the Empire. The many carefully-worked-out tables that were drawn up by amateur statisticians and strategists, . . . drew the irritated reply from Ottawa that it was pointless to pretend that the British Navy existed in order to protect Canada. If Canada had not been there, the Navy would still have to be paid for. To be sure it was true, that British sea-power protected Canadian shipping and commerce, but equally was it true that it also protected the oceanic trade of such countries as Sweden and Belgium—and no suggestion had yet been made to Swedes and Belgians that they should have an immediate whipround among themselves to cover the costs of the British Navy. Such an argument struck the *Round Table** as particularly ungracious. It was a farce, it declared, that Dominions which made so much to-do about claiming independent status through the League of Nations—and with it the right to negotiate treaties—should nevertheless continue to expect Great Britain to provide the force without which treaties were scraps of paper. This was true, but the Canadians were facing truths that lay in a different direction, and had ideas about them that would never square with *Round Table* imperialist preconceptions. In this new age it was the imperialist preconception that had to give ground.

The British Government thus geared itself to its somewhat thankless task of meeting the Dominion claims for status. To those foreign Governments that troubled to watch this process in operation, the task seemed more than a little academic, for what would come of all these nice readjustments and fresh juxtapositions of constitutional convention within the British imperial structure? The structure might find for itself a new facade as a result, but behind it would stretch the old imperial building and its outhouses. Canada's Mackenzie King was himself prepared to admit that status was not the same thing as stature. Nobody in Europe supposed it was. Thus, while devising formulae to soothe Canadian, Irish, or South African *amours-propres* was doubtless an occupation worthy of the attention of an intellectual statesman like Balfour, could these ever alter the fact that the control of imperial defence, and therefore the ultimate decisions in foreign policy, still lay where they had always lain, in the hands of the Cabinet of the Government of the United Kingdom? The average American's belief that King George V governed Canada as King George III had once governed the thirteen American colonies was of course absurd, but was not this very absurdity only a truth perceived in a distorting glass? . . . French diplomats continued on their part to incline to the opinion that the whole notion of the 'independence' of the Dominions, their separate status and their right to have their say in British policy as it affected the affairs of Europe, was one of those subtler inventions of the devious Lloyd George—whose efficacy his successors, although admittedly less astute, were still determined to exploit. . . .

From within the imperial structure this problem of status, as it confronted its inmates, seemed much less clear-cut. The Imperial Conference of 1923 had recognised that on each part of the Commonwealth fell the responsibility for its own local defence, but emphasized, too, that there were certain routes and areas whose security was vital to the whole group. . . . The Conference did not state whose task it was to guard and maintain these lines of imperial communication, but in fact, as everyone knew, there was only one 'partner' who had the means to carry this out, and that was the United Kingdom. The Conference of 1926 affirmed this point. The principles of equality and simi-

---

* A journal advocating closer imperial ties.

larity appropriate to status, it was now declared, did not universally extend to *function*.

* * * * *

Thus the great Conference of 1926, while indeed it did serve to assure the Dominions that their status as independent, equal, and autonomous powers was all that they wanted it to be, was not such a landmark in the evolution of both human and imperial affairs as the admiring press of the day, constitutional historians later, and all the theorists . . . have combined to make it appear and no doubt genuinely assumed it to be. It did not stress the facts of power and the necessity for action, or with whom lay the ultimate responsibility for the security of that status to which so much publicity was being given: but these facts remained, which could be ignored over dinner-tables but had to be coped with in Dominion Cabinets. . . .

A. P. Thornton, *The Imperial Idea and Its Enemies* (London, 1959), pp. 195–201.

Further Reading

An interesting early source is the "Postscriptum" in W. Sanford Evans, *The Canadian Contingents and Canadian Imperialism* (London, 1901). Here an ardent imperialist advocated the creation of a distinct Canadian ministry of "Imperial and Foreign Affairs" before any Canadian autonomist, apparently, had suggested such a portfolio. On the general theme of imperial federation see J. E. Tyler, *The Struggle for Imperial Unity (1868–1895)* (London, Longmans Green, 1938), in addition to the book by G. T. Denison mentioned on p. 220, and that by G. R. Parkin on p. 256.

The pioneer scholarly study of the development of Canadian foreign policy is R. A. MacKay and E. B. Rogers, *Canada Looks Abroad* (Toronto, Oxford University Press, 1938). For most purposes this book is now superseded by G. P. de T. Glazebrook, *A History of Canadian External Relations* (Carleton Library No. 27, Toronto, McClelland & Stewart, 1966)*. R. M. Dawson, *The Development of Dominion Status, 1900–1936* (London, Oxford University Press, 1937) and K. C. Wheare, *The Statute of Westminster and Dominion Status* (London, Oxford University Press, 5th ed., 1953) remain the standard references on the theme stressed in their titles. Another study which places Canadian inter-war aspirations toward autonomy within the wider context too frequently neglected by Canadian historians is W. K. (later Sir Keith) Hancock, *Survey of British Commonwealth Affairs*, Vol. 1, *Problems of Nationality, 1918–1936* (London, Oxford University Press, 1937, reprinted 1964).

R. L. Borden, *Canada in the Commonwealth: From Conflict to Co-operation* (Oxford, Clarendon Press, 1929) gives an account of the emergence of Canada onto the international scene by the chief Canadian agent of the development.

H. B. Neatby, *William Lyon Mackenzie King*, Vol. 2, *The Lonely Heights* (Toronto, University of Toronto Press, 1963) covers the 1926 Imperial Conference and other landmarks on the Canadian road to autonomy. Vincent Massey, *What's Past is Prologue* (Toronto, Macmillan, 1963) casts light on many points raised in this Problem.

The manuscript for *Public Servant: the Memoirs of Sir Joseph Pope*, edited and completed by Maurice Pope (Toronto, Oxford University Press, 1960) was completed by the son of the Dominion's first Deputy Minister of External Affairs some thirty years before its ultimate publication date. Hence this anecdotal narrative reflects the pre-Statute of Westminster atmosphere in which it was written. Ramsay Cook, *The Politics of John W. Dafoe and the Free Press* (Toronto, University of Toronto Press, 1963) deals with one of the persons who was highly instrumental in converting Canadian leaders and electors to the desirability of a distinctively Canadian foreign policy. He served at the Peace Conference of 1919 as an adviser to Sir Robert Borden and at the Imperial Conference of 1923 in a similar capacity to W. L. M. King. Although he was not present at the 1926 Conference he was kept well informed, as is demonstrated in Ramsay Cook, "A Canadian Account of the 1926 Imperial Conference", *Journal of Commonwealth Political Studies* III (March 1965) pp. 50–63. It contains the text of three letters to Dafoe from D. B. MacRae, of the *Free Press* staff.

James Eayrs, *In Defence of Canada*, Vol. 1, *From the Great War to the Great Depression* (Toronto, University of Toronto Press, 1963)* and Vol. 2, *Appeasement and Rearmament* (1965)* are studies in what the author calls "national security policy", a term comprehending both foreign policy and defence policy. These two volumes (a third is promised) bring the story down to 1940. By that date the problem of asserting a Canadian identity in a world at war was becoming more complicated. A helpful American viewpoint on these problems is presented in Stanley W. Dziuban, *Military Relations Between the United States and Canada, 1939–1945* (The United States Army in World War II, Special Studies. Washington, Department of the Army, 1959).

Problem 16

Sectional Protests of the 1920's — How Can Prosperity Be Shared?

As was indicated in W. S. Wallace's "Growth of National Feeling",* English-speaking Canadians, at least, emerged from World War I with an enhanced feeling of national consciousness. During the following decade this sense of identity was blurred by the growth of strong regional protest movements in the newly settled Prairies and in the long-established Maritimes. Before remedial measures proposed in the 1920's to rectify these situations had time to take effect, the entire country was plunged into the Depression of the 1930's.

In this Problem our attention is focused first on the causes and consequences of the discontent on the prairies which is associated with the rise of the Progressive movement. We then turn our attention to the eruption of the Maritime Rights agitation in the small provinces by the sea. While examining and pondering over the statements of grievances and proposed remedies outlined in the readings which follow, the student might imagine himself in the position of a national statesman being confronted with this situation. Are the disabilities complained of as real as the grievances they give rise to? Are they the result, in whole or in significant part, of policies undertaken by the national government? What practical solutions could be offered? Would concessions to one region provoke additional demands elsewhere?

The Revolt in the Prairies

Rumblings of discontent from the wheat lands were heard in Ottawa a decade before prairie voters registered their disillusion

* See above, pp. 226–8.

with the two traditional Canadian parties by returning Progressives at the general election of 1921. In mid-September 1910 about 500 representatives of the grain growers' associations of the three Prairie Provinces, together with some 300 other farmers, converged on Parliament Hill in the so-called "siege of Ottawa" and presented a farmers' case which had a strong western flavour.* Lower tariffs, including reciprocal free trade with the United States and increased British preference providing for free trade with Britain within ten years, were stressed.

Although Laurier's Liberals lost the 1911 General Election (in which the Reciprocity Agreement with the United States, negotiated partly in response to western demands, was a major issue), it is noteworthy that the Liberals captured all but two of the seventeen seats in Saskatchewan and Alberta.

The Farmers' Platform

Neither the election results of 1911 nor the outbreak of war in 1914 stilled western demands for tariff reform. In the 19 January 1916 issue of *The Grain Growers' Guide*, the organ of western agrarianism, an editorial calling for "Independent Political Action" observed: "The biggest question in the west today is that of Free Trade."

A Farmers' Platform† was drafted by the Canadian Council of Agriculture in 1916 and endorsed by the Manitoba Grain Growers' Association, the Saskatchewan Grain Growers' Association, the United Farmers of Alberta, and the United Farmers of Ontario. The platform was revised in 1918, renamed, significantly, "The New National Policy", accepted by the member organizations in 1919, and then updated for the general election of 1921. The following excerpts are from the latest of these drafts.

---

* Chipman, G. F., ed., *The Siege of Ottawa: being the story of the 800 farmers . . . who met the Government and members of Parliament in the House of Commons chamber on December 16, 1910 and demanded more equitable legislation* (Winnipeg, Grain Growers' Guide, n.d.), p. 64.

† "The Farmers' Platform", reproduced in W. L. Morton, *The Progressive Party in Canada* (Toronto, 1950), pp. 300–1.

2. We believe that the further development of the British Empire should be sought along the lines of partnership between nations free and equal, under the present governmental system of British constitutional authority. We are strongly opposed to any attempt to centralize imperial control.

The Tariff

3. Whereas Canada is now confronted with a huge national war debt and other greatly increased financial obligations, which can be most readily and effectively reduced by the development of our natural resources, chief of which is agricultural lands; . . . And whereas the war has revealed the amazing financial strength of Great Britain, which has enabled her to finance, not only her own part in the struggle, but also to assist in financing her Allies . . . , this enviable position being due to the free trade policy which has enabled her to draw her supplies freely from every quarter of the globe and consequently to undersell her competitors on the world's market, . . . we believe that the best interests of the Empire and of Canada would be served by reciprocal action on the part of Canada through gradual reductions of the tariff on British imports, having for its objects closer union and a better understanding between Canada and the Motherland and at the same time bring about a great reduction in the cost of living to our Canadian people; . . .

* * * * *

Definite Tariff Demands

Therefore be it resolved that . . . as a means of remedying these evils and bringing about much-needed social and economic reforms, our tariff laws should be amended as follows:

(a) By an immediate and substantial all-round reduction of the customs tariff.

(b) By reducing the customs duty on goods imported from Great Britain to one-half the rates charged under the general tariff, and that further gradual, uniform reductions be made in the remaining tariff on British imports that will ensure complete Free Trade between Great Britain and Canada in five years.

(c) By endeavouring to secure unrestricted reciprocal trade in natural products with the United States along the lines of the Reciprocity Agreement of 1911.

(d) By placing all foodstuffs on the free list.

(e) That agricultural implements, farm and household machinery, vehicles, fertilizers, coal, lumber, cement, gasoline, illuminating fuel and lubricating oils be placed on the free list, and that all raw materials and machinery used in their manufacture also be placed on the free list.

(f) That all tariff concessions granted to other countries be immediately extended to Great Britain.

(g) That all corporations engaged in the manufacture of products protected by the customs tariff be obliged to publish annually comprehensive and accurate statements of their earnings.

(h) That every claim for tariff protection by any industry should be heard publicly before a special committee of parliament.

> "The Farmers' Platform", reproduced in W. L. Morton, *The Progressive Party in Canada* (Toronto, 1950), pp. 302–4.

Taxation Proposals

The drafters of the platform agreed that the tariff reductions they proposed would reduce national revenue. They proposed the following direct taxes: on unimproved land values, including natural resources; a graduated personal income tax, succession duties "on large estates"; graduated corporation income tax. In future, natural resources were not to be alienated from the Crown, but developed under short-term leases granted at public auction.

Free Trade or Protection of Local Interests?

The General Election of 1921 saw 65 Progressives elected, making them the second largest political group in Parliament, the Liberals having returned 116 members and the Conservatives 50. In the three Prairie Provinces the Liberals had returned 2 members, the Conservatives none. The remaining 38 seats were held by Progressives.* In Parliament the Progressives did not organize themselves along the normal lines of a political party, declining the role of official opposition. By 1925, the date of the next election, the Progressives' support had dropped to the point where only 24 members were returned, although 22 of these were from the Prairies. They lost two of these seats in the general election of 1926.

One factor in the disintegration of the movement was its members' attitude toward Protection. Although the stand taken in the Farmers' Platform appeared clear-cut, the issues on which the principles involved in the question of free trade vs. protection were encoun-

---

* 24 Progressives were returned from Ontario, 2 from British Columbia, and 1 from New Brunswick. The quick fall-off of Progressive support in these other provinces (only 2 were returned from Ontario in 1925, and none from the other provinces) suggests that the nature of Progressive support outside of the Prairies was quite different.

tered in Parliament could assume embarrassing forms. One such issue, debated in 1923, concerned the prohibition of oleomargarine. On a free vote on a resolution calling for the prohibition of the importation, manufacture, or sale of oleomargarine, 45 Progressives became practising protectionists. The Rev. T. W. Bird (Nelson, Man.), one of 15 members of the party who voted to permit free trade in the butter substitute, expressed sympathy to his colleagues.

I have a great deal of sympathy with some hon. members on my own side of the House who imagine that by prohibiting oleomargarine they are doing a service to the cause of agriculture. However, . . . it seems to me that the farmers of this country are beginning to nose around the protection trough, . . . They have seen other people in it for fifty years and they have been shoved aside or have been persuaded to keep aside. But tonight the farmers of Canada . . . are beginning to see the attractions of that trough and some of their old time prejudices are being held less firmly than before. Will any man stand up in this House and say that they are to be blamed for that, that they are swallowing their principles? Why, what are principles for but to be swallowed. . . ?

It is not the swallowing that is wrong; it is the inopportune time that we choose to swallow. . . . I want to point out this, and I hope I do not need to point it out because everybody with his eyes open will have seen it before now, . . . we have seen the British farmer go to his government with the plea for protection; we have seen the United States farmer go to his government with the plea for protection, and we have seen the Canadian farmer to-night not exactly asking the government for protection but just hovering around and trying to hint to the government that they would like some protection if they dared give it to them. That is the position. Now where are we coming to? . . . we are just beginning to get in the thin end of the wedge and by and by you are going to have a Farmers' party in Canada that will be one hundred per cent protectionist. They will all be in the trough then.

Canada, Parliament, *Debates of the House of Commons*, 1923, p. 3568.

Other Prairie Grievances

The prohibition of oleomargarine represented a normal protectionist device for the assistance of a producer for the domestic market. The wheat farmer, however, disposed of the bulk of his produce overseas. During the 1920's his spokesmen sought compensation for his inability to shelter under the conventional protectionist umbrella by securing a return and extension of freight rates embodied in the "Crowsnest Pass Agreement"* under which he could ship grain to export terminals at a lower rate per mile than could his competitors in other nations.

A reaction of the Prairie spokesmen to the granting of lower freight rates to the Maritimers during this period will be quoted later.

The third major grievance of Prairie spokesmen during the 1920's concerned the control of the natural resources in the three Prairie Provinces. Whereas the original provinces retained control of Crown lands (lands whose ownership is still vested in the state) this control was retained by the federal government over the territory obtained from the Hudson's Bay Company, out of which Manitoba, Saskatchewan, and Alberta were carved. Control over natural resources was handed over to the three Prairie Provinces in 1930, and compensation in addition to earlier subsidies paid to the three provinces "in lieu of lands" was arranged. As Chester Martin, then professor of history at the University of Manitoba, wrote in 1920, the Prairie Provinces were, in effect, second-class members of the Canadian federation.

> Indeed there is a sense in which the provincial control of the public domain served an even more fundamental purpose. It is more than the cornerstone of Confederation. It was part of the foundation, the very bed-rock upon which the whole edifice was built, for without responsible government and its first corollary, the 'grant of full rights over the land,' the provinces which entered into Confederation in 1867 would never have been in a position to aspire to a British and trans-continental Dominion.
>
> Now while it is seldom that a great principle has been so discerningly built into the foundations of a nation, it is doubtful if a parallel can be found to the half-century of devious expedience during which this fundamental principle has remained in abeyance in the case of Manitoba. Beyond a doubt this Province has been the Cinderella of Confederation; it has been her misfortune for fifty years to sit among the ashes and aspire only to the commonplace rights and privileges of the more fortunate provinces of the Dominion. She inherited from the Riel Insurrection an unenviable prejudice from the rest of Canada that was as meaningless as it was unjust. Within her boundaries for fifty years have been fought out the bitter controveries of Quebec and Ontario. . . . Railway communications east and west were a by-product of the terms of union with British Columbia, and the public domain was withheld

---

* See below, p. 282.

because the Canadian Pacific Railway 'must be built by means of the land through which it had to pass.'

With regard to 'land revenues' it was twelve years before any fiscal concessions were made to alleviate the poverty in that respect which had been imposed upon the province 'for the purposes of the Dominion.'

*   *   *   *   *

It is submitted that the time has come to right this half-century of vested wrong by an Imperial amendment . . . which shall leave this province like the other provinces of the Dominion 'supreme' over its own lands 'directly under the Crown as its head.' . . . 'The Natural Resources Question' may thus be said, without false modesty, to constitute one of the most important problems of the Dominion. Its settlement would set the seal of full provincial status under the *British North America Act* of 1867 upon three Canadian 'colonies,' and would enable the Dominion, with its house in order, to move forward discerningly among the British nations of the Empire and the other nations of the world.

> Chester Martin, *The Natural Resources Question* (Winnipeg, 1920),
> pp. 121–2, 123, 124.

Maritime Rights

The eruption of Maritime Rights agitation in the mid-1920's is significant both in the reversal of approach employed by the Maritimers and by co-operation displayed in the three provinces. Earlier Maritimers had agitated for freer trade with their "natural trading partners" in the Atlantic area, with the Liberal Party usually serving as their political vehicle.

In the mid-1920's the advocates of Maritime Rights, who became most effective within the Conservative Party, were demanding an extension of the advantages of Protection to the Maritimes.

The case for Maritime Rights was stated concisely in a covering letter which was sent out by members of the Nova Scotian cabinet to influential citizens in other parts of Canada with copies of the brief prepared by the Government of Nova Scotia for submission to a Dominion Royal Commission on Maritime Claims ("The Duncan Commission").

You will appreciate that Confederation was not sought by the Maritime Provinces, but that an appeal had been made to them to join the movement, primarily for the benefit of Quebec and Ontario, then united as the Province of Canada, the ultimate object being to build up a great Canadian nation upon the territory to the north of the American boundary, stretching from coast to coast.

At that time the Province of Nova Scotia was working out its own destiny as a self-contained and prosperous Crown Colony. The natural misgivings felt by our public men in the face of this drastic constitutional change were met by the statesmen of Canada with assurances that this Province would benefit materially by entering the federation; that free trade among the Provinces would be effective under one national flag, with the advantage of unification of the major public services of transportation, tariff, trade and commerce, immigration and postal service.

*   *   *   *   *

Following the trend of conditions since that time, you will note the gradual growth of disabilities which have so depressed these Provinces as to render them economically unhealthy and drive their population from their shores. You will see how funds contributed in part by this Province were utilized for the acquisition of new lands and territories, out of which have arisen provinces peopled largely by those without knowledge of the original aims of Confederation and now inclined to be unsympathetic towards maritime claims. You will observe that the Maritime Provinces have borne their share of the cost of the great transportation systems of the Dominion, systems constructed with the avowed purpose of creating the necessary facilities for the development of the nation as a whole, and yet have benefited little or nothing from that contribution. You will perceive how that into the general revenues of the Dominion . . . have gone from this Province moneys which have been used to finance various undertakings for the upbuilding of our Canadian West and the Dominion in general, while no corresponding effort has been made for the benefit of Nova Scotia. You will notice that, while other sections of the Dominion have received special consideration in the matter of freight rates, the entire freight rate structure of the Dominion has oppressed this Province almost to the point of strangulation. You will observe how the general fiscal policies adopted by the Dominion in large measure force the Maritime Provinces to buy many commodities in a highly protected market in Canada, while, especially in later years, the market in Canada, which was supposed to be available for the Maritimes, has been gradually thrown more and more open to world competition, with the general tendency to make us buy in the highest market and sell in the lowest.

*   *   *   *   *

Just as . . . statesmen in other countries adopted unusual or artificial measures to overcome natural conditions, that their country in whole or in part might benefit, so Canada is asked to take the steps necessary to place the Maritime

Provinces in that position of equality with the rest of the Dominion which they deserve to occupy, . . .

Circular letter "Maritime Rights", dated "Province Building,
Halifax, N.S., 23 Sept. 1926".

A Westerner's Reaction to a Reduction of Maritime Freight Rates

One of the principal recommendations of the Duncan Commission was a reduction on freight rates from the Maritimes to make their products more competitive in the larger central Canadian market. When a bill incorporating this provision was introduced into Parliament, it was opposed by the Prairie Progressives.

A speech by John Evans (Rosetown, Sask.) provides a sample of the arguments. Note his assumption that the Maritimers should find their market abroad, a solution which the Maritimers had found impractical over the previous half-century. The belief that both the Maritimers and Western Canada were being exploited in the industrial East provides one bond of sympathy.

The legislation to equalize freight rates was enacted, in my opinion, to find an excuse for robbing western Canada of statutory protection against the skyrocketing of freight rates, . . . Now added to that, we have to bear one-fifth of the rate charged in a part of Canada which lies by the sea, and which, from an export country like Canada, should find a market for its products overseas. The maritimes also have the advantage of having a line of boats running below cost to their most prolific market, under the West India agreement, and the deficit on that service will have to be met every year by the country at large.

*   *   *   *   *

But let us look at this matter from another angle. When the maritime provinces, by agitation and threats of secession, can obtain a free gift of one-fifth of its rail rates, which are lower now by fifteen to twenty per cent than in some other parts of the Dominion, is it not natural that western Canada may ask herself if she is not paying too high a price to remain in confederation, and there will be more excuse for complaint than has ever been in the maritime provinces. Further than that, what will the industrial areas of Ontario and Quebec care how much they pay in taxes to meet their subsidy each year, as long as they can pass it on in the price of the goods they manufacture down here, and compel us to buy at their own price? . . . I am in sympathy with the maritime provinces as they are, but I want to meet conditions as they exist and go to the root of the evil now.

. . . I contend the difficulty is common to every province and parts of provinces throughout Canada, with the exception of those towns and cities in central Canada which have thrived by the adversity in other parts, of which adversity they have been the cause.

Canada, Parliament, *Debates* . . . , 1926–7, pp. 1845, 1846–7.

THE VIEWS OF LATER COMMENTATORS

Interrelationship of Tariff, Freight Rates, and the Progressive Movement

A student of the Canadian freight rates structure has provided a concise account of the interrelationship of the three factors in an article which appeared in the *Canadian Historical Review* in 1940.

The railway was the key which unlocked the economic resources of the Canadian West. The story of how the Canadian Pacific, the first important railway in the West, was built has frequently been told. It is important to note, however, that it was the customs tariff which was to provide the government with revenue to help finance the road. . . .

Even after the Canadian Pacific was completed, however, the expansion of the West was disappointingly slow. Among the reasons for this backwardness, high freight rates were prominent not only in the minds of the settlers themselves, as evidenced by frequent and bitter complaints in Parliament and press, but also in the opinions of impartial observers. . . . In extenuation . . . it should be pointed out that freight rates on grain in Canada were slightly lower than the charges for corresponding distances on American lines. Also . . . the company was in no financial position to stand the possible reduction in revenue which might be occasioned by the lower charges. . . .

The first real reduction in rates came in 1897 with the famous Crowsnest Pass Agreement. Under the terms of this agreement the Dominion government granted the Canadian Pacific a cash bonus amounting eventually to slightly over $3,400,000 for the construction of a railway from Lethbridge through the Crowsnest Pass to Nelson, B.C. In return the company undertook by September 1, 1899, to reduce by three cents per hundred pounds the then existing rates on grain and flour from all points in the West to Fort William, Port Arthur, and points east thereof. From Brandon . . . this reduction amounted to about 19 per cent. In addition the railway cut by 15 per cent the rates then applicable to fruits, coal oil, cordage, implements, various building materials, and furniture from eastern Canada west-bound. . . . In brief, in return for a cash subsidy, the Canadian Pacific reduced the freight rates on the chief export of the region and on settlers' requirements inbound. The concessions were made without limit of time.

*   *   *   *   *

. . . The subsidy enabled the construction at once of a line of railway which the Canadian Pacific had planned for some time. The branch would open up the mineral regions of southern British Columbia and would prevent the area from becoming economically tributary to the American lines which were entering from the south. Moreover, development of the district would provide a welcome nearby market for farmers in the far West.

*   *   *   *   *

During the first decade of the twentieth century western Canada enjoyed unexampled prosperity. Good crops, rising prices, the inflow of capital and settlers, the mechanization of agriculture and many other factors contributed to this development. It is significant, too, that the cost of transference of grain from the West to Liverpool was reduced at almost every stage . . . These lower costs gave the farmer a relatively higher net return than previously. . . . In one or two crop years there were complaints that railway equipment was insufficient to handle the grain traffic expeditiously but on the whole the service, as well as the freight rates, was considered satisfactory.

*   *   *   *   *

The significance of the 1911 election on the subsequent freight rate development in Canada has been considerable. The West is fundamentally interested in two objectives: selling its grain abroad at the highest possible price and buying personal necessities, farm equipment, and supplies at the lowest price. To achieve the first, it needs low freight rates; to obtain the second, it desires a low tariff. The defeat of reciprocity cut off the West from its natural market in the United States and by putting the traditionally high tariff party in power prevented any hope of abandonment of a high protective system. Accordingly the West was thrown back on its first objective, that of obtaining lower freight rates. Canadian railways opposed reciprocity as being inimical to their own interests: now they were to be faced with the insistent demand for low rates from the western grain-grower so that he might more easily reach the distant European market. It is not suggested that the farmer determined the connection between freight rates and tariffs in any logical way. He turned for help in the direction which at the moment seemed to promise the greatest relief from his economic problems. For him the matter was one of expedience but the underlying factors were definite.

The country had scarcely settled down after the excitement of the reciprocity campaign when it was caught up in the throes of the Great War. During the conflict the West enjoyed a fictitious prosperity with acreage expanding and prices rising. At the same time railway operating costs were increasing. . . . The government, by an executive order under the provisions of the War Measures Act, exempted the Board from its legal restrictions. Thus for the first time since 1899 grain rates were set above the level of the Crowsnest Pass Agreement. . . .

While these events were occurring . . . the rise of a farmers' party was a significant development in the political life of the country. In the parliament elected in 1921 this group held the balance of power. The new Liberal government traditionally stood for lower tariffs but its practical policy was strongly influenced by post-war economic nationalism in the rest of the world and by the fact that Liberals from Quebec and most of those from Ontario were opposed to drastic reductions in tariff schedules. Thus the West was again frustrated in its efforts to cut tariffs. In 1922, in view of the approaching expiration of the suspension of the Crowsnest Pass Agreement, the government, instead of doing the logical thing of referring the matter to the Board of Railway Commissioners, appointed a "Special Committee of the House on Railway Transportation Costs." The personnel of the Committee was impressive but the practice of referring such complicated technical matters as freight rates to an unskilled political body cannot be too strongly condemned. The only reason it was done in this case was that the West had completely lost faith in the Railway Commission . . .

*   *   *   *   *

The result of this long series of enactments by Parliament and rulings by the Board of Railway Commissioners is that freight rates on grain for export from the West are held down to the level existing in September, 1899. This principle applies whether the grain originates on branch or main lines and whether it moves east through Fort William, Port Arthur, and even by rail to Quebec or west through Vancouver. Rates on grain in Canada are from 40 to 50 per cent lower than those for the corresponding distances on railways in northern United States operating under substantially similar traffic conditions. Undoubtedly part of Canada's present [1940] railway difficulty is due to the unusually low statutory rates on grain. Nevertheless these rates may be justified on the ground that they permit Canadian growers to export wheat from the heart of a continent to the world market in competition with producers in Australia and the Argentine who have a long but relatively inexpensive water journey and only a short haul by rail where rates per mile are much higher than by sea. In any event the Western farmer is convinced that low grain rates are essential to his existence and . . . he realizes too that his favourable freight rates are a partial offset to the burden of the tariff.

*   *   *   *   *

To a considerable extent the Canadian rate-making problem has become a matter of satisfying diverging regional interests without completely ruining both railways in the process.

> A. W. Currie, "Freight Rates on Grain in Western Canada", *Canadian Historical Review*, XXI (March 1940), pp. 40–1, 44–7, 54–5.

A Prairie Economist Compares Prairie and Maritime Complaints

The following excerpts come from an article written in 1935. It was inspired in part by the publication of a Nova Scotian brief prepared for another Royal Commission enquiry into the problems of the Maritime Provinces.

There is an important difference, however, between the case for Nova Scotia, as it was presented to the Royal Commission and the case for the Prairie Provinces. A great part of the brief for Nova Scotia is concerned with negotiations preliminary to the passing of the British North America Act and many of the grievances rightly go back to that period. The Prairie Provinces entered a Confederation already in existence with a lively sense of benefits to be obtained. The alternative was not, as for Nova Scotia, of coming into Confederation or of remaining a separate colony, but of coming in or of remaining a territory of the Dominion. We were not beguiled into Confederation with the connivance of the secretary of state for the colonies. Nor have we since coming into Confederation seen our formerly prospering industries languish and die. We are not obsessed with the memory of a glory that has departed. On the contrary, our growth was steadily upward, interrupted only by disturbances that were common to the whole country. Our protest is not concerning what we once were and now are but rather about what we are now and what we might be,—but this does not mean that the protest is any the less real. The protest of to-day is not new in anything except its vigour and yet it manifests a difference in degree that is equivalent to a change in quality.

*   *   *   *   *

The West is not prepared to put the custody of its future in the hands of railway executives. Nova Scotian experience with the working of the 1926 reduction in its rates merely reinforces the West in this opinion.

The more realistic politicians known to be supporters of a tariff unpopular in the West, have usually argued that, while the tariff could not but be a burden on the prairies, lower freight rates could be used as a device to offset it. . . . For this reason the West regards the railway deficits of Canada with almost complete equanimity. They are regarded as an offset to the cost of the tariff and the West will continue so to regard them.

R. McQueen, "Economic Aspects of Federalism—A Prairie View", *The Canadian Journal of Economics and Political Science*, I (August 1935), pp. 352–8.

The Problem as Reported in a Survey History

Although concern with Prairie and Maritime Rights preoccupied the citizens of those areas in the 1920's, their impact on the consciousness of the inhabitants of the St. Lawrence-Great Lakes area was less profound.

D. G. Creighton's summary of events in the 1920's stresses the general prosperity of the period. Although the problems of the wheat growers and maritimers are recognized, they are briefly disposed of. He stressed the centrifugal tendencies of the enhanced prestige of the provincial governments at the expense of the Dominion.

Ever since the 1890's Great Britain had been the chief market for Canadian exports; the flow of goods from Canada to the United Kingdom had been exceptionally high during the War of 1914–18; but in 1921, by a slight margin, the United States regained its old position as Canada's best customer. The . . . tariff of 1922, . . . seriously interfered with several valuable Canadian trades with the Republic; but a number of important staple products—newsprint, base metals, gold—continued to enter in large and increasing quantities. The United States became the principal purchaser of the new staples of the post-war period, while Great Britain remained the chief customer of the traditional agricultural products of the past.

The effects of these changes on the Canadian economy as a whole—on the economic integration and political unity which had been achieved in the war and the pre-war periods—were varied and somewhat contradictory. Without any question, Canada was in many ways a more favoured and stronger country in an age of electricity, alloys, and airways than she had been in the era of steam, steel, and rail. And yet, though the economic life of the whole country unquestionably grew richer and more varied, the bounty of the post-war period seemed unequal in its distribution, partial in its rewards, disintegrating in some of its consequences. Wheat had proved itself to be a force in favour of national unity; but the new staples almost seemed to encourage the unfortunate process of regional division. In the pre-war age, wheat had been the one great export staple, round which the whole economic life of the country had centred; but now there were half a dozen distinct staple-producing regions, each with its own important export specialty or specialties, each with its individual successes and misfortunes. While some provinces, such as Ontario, Quebec, and British Columbia, profited superlatively from the new enterprises, others, like Manitoba and Alberta, benefited only moderately, and still others, like Saskatchewan and the Maritime Provinces, gained little advantage at all. Saskatchewan depended largely on the old staple, wheat; Nova Scotia's coal and steel industry was linked with the bygone railway-building age and her fisheries with the ancient sugar-producing markets of the West Indies. These regions were relatively untouched by the new industries and trades; but there were other, lucky places upon which the post-war economic energies seemed almost to converge. The development of northern Ontario strengthened Toronto as a financial centre of central Canada. The opening of the Panama Canal helped to make Vancouver a great ocean port, with a hinterland stretching far back into the prairies.

One of the most important effects of the post-war age and its regional tendencies lay in the rapidly changing relations of the Dominion and the provinces. . . . For a whole generation . . . the influence and authority of the federal power in Canada had risen steadily toward its pinnacle in the War of 1914–18. Now the movement was halted, then reversed; and the importance of the provinces began unmistakably to ascend. There were a number of reasons for this; but prominent among them was the close association of the provincial governments . . . with the new sources of economic power and the new problems of social welfare. . . . During the age of western development and European war, the Dominion had retained its leadership; but, amid the post-war problems of regional expansion and social security, its preeminence began to decline.

> D. G. Creighton, *Dominion of the North: A History of Canada*
> (Toronto, 1957), pp. 476–8.

A Party Leader Confronts the Problem

Arthur Meighen was the leader of the Conservative Party during the period under review. Although he had grown up in the west and had entered Parliament as the member for the Manitoba constituency of Portage la Prairie (where he had been defeated in the Progressive sweep of 1921) he was a firm supporter of the protective tariff.

Meighen's biographer, Professor Roger Graham, comments on the problem Meighen faced as the leader of the opposition on the eve of a general election.

Although . . . Meighen refused to countenance any suggestion that some issue other than the tariff be given first place in the Conservative programme, he did begin during 1924 to work his way towards a restatement of fiscal policy, . . . which he hoped would meet objections to the protective system. It was more than simply a matter of satisfying his own disquieted followers with some vote-catching promise, nor was it merely the West which objected. As on the prairies so in the Maritimes there was widespread and deeply rooted dissatisfaction with the effects, not of the protective tariff alone, but of national economic policies in general, in short with Confederation itself. It was such discontent that had given rise to the Progressive movement; although that movement was now losing its impetus as an organized political force the sentiment behind it was still very much alive. It was also this discontent that had inspired the recurring agitations for Maritime rights, most markedly in Nova Scotia, which had led on occasion to demands for secession from the Dominion. The difficulties of the Maritimes were more profound and complex than those of the West: the economy of the Atlantic provinces was stagnating, their industries languished, their port facilities lay mostly idle, their people left for greener fields. But like the prairie West they felt themselves to be in bondage to the central provinces, economically as well as politically, believed that they were being forced to pay high taxes, high consumer prices, high freight rates, in brief to bear the costs of national policies of which Ontario and Quebec were the chief, if not the sole, beneficiaries.

The problem, then, a fundamental, chronic Canadian problem, was to find some way of distributing more equitably among the various sections of the country the burden of maintaining and developing a largely unnatural, artificial national economy. There was no way, in Meighen's opinion, of getting rid of these burdens altogether if Canada were to remain one country and not be absorbed by the United States; certainly there was no possibility of discarding the protective system. But political leaders were in duty bound to present what human intelligence must be capable of devising—appropriate measures to lessen the disparities of costs and benefits falling upon the different regions of Canada as a result of the operation of basic economic policies. The search for such means had begun in Meighen's mind long before Cahan* had referred . . . to the importance of "reconciling divergencies of political opinion" between the two central provinces and the aggrieved, unhappy regions to east and to west.

> Roger Graham, *Arthur Meighen*: Vol. II, *And Fortune Fled*
> (Toronto, 1963), pp. 301–2.

---

* C. H. Cahan, a Montreal Conservative who had criticized Meighen's continued stress on tariff issue in a letter published in the Montreal *Gazette*, 10 December 1924. He later served in the cabinet of R. B. Bennett, 1930–35.

Further Reading

An entire series of studies, "Social Credit in Alberta: Its Background and Development", has been devoted to the development of Western particularism and discontent during the period under review. W. L. Morton, *The Progressive Party in Canada* (Toronto, University of Toronto Press, 1967)* mentioned in this Problem, is part of the series. An American scholar, Paul F. Sharp, examined the phenomenon of the Progressive Movement from another vantage point in *The Agrarian Revolt in Western Canada: A Survey Showing American Parallels* (Minneapolis, University of Minnesota Press, [c. 1953]). W. K. Rolph, *Henry Wise Wood of Alberta* (Toronto, University of Toronto Press, 1950) studies the activities of a leading advocate of the co-operative movement as a solution to the plight of the western grain grower.

Files of the *Grain Growers' Guide* are rarely held in Canadian academic libraries, yet this organ of the wheat farmer should be studied by those who wish to understand the alienation of the prairies during this period.

A brief but helpful account of the culmination of Maritime discontent is provided by W. A. Craik, "The Maritime Rights Movement: Its Progress in 1925–26", in *The Canadian Annual Review 1925–26* (Toronto, 1926), pp. 395–9. A pamphlet of an address delivered by F. B. McCurdy before the Canadian Club of Toronto on 27 April 1925, *A Statement of Nova Scotia's Position* (n.p., n.d.), was widely distributed at the time. A number of Maritime Rightists seized the opportunity granted them by the Address in Reply to the Speech from the Throne in the Dominion Parliament of 1926 to vent their region's grievances. One of the most effective was Robert K. Smith (Cumberland, N.S.) *Debates* . . . 1926, pp. 225–30.

Regional grievances have generally been most forcibly stated and thoroughly investigated in submissions to and studies commissioned by royal commissions. Copies are often available in legislative libraries and in the libraries of some of the older universities. Fortunately a study for the Royal Commission on Dominion-Provincial Relations which bears on the Problem under review has been republished: W. A. Mackintosh, *The Economic Background of Dominion-Provincial Relations* (Carleton Library No. 13, Toronto, McClelland & Stewart, 1964)*.

Problem 17

The Depression — Should the Existing System
Be Revised or Scrapped?

Although the Great Depression of the 1930's was basically an economic phenomenon, its impact on the Canadian scene had far ranging social, political, and constitutional repercussions. As was indicated in the preceding problem, not all sections of Canada shared in the prosperity of the 1920's. Unlike the prosperity of the Laurier period, that of the 1920's did not coincide with the initiation of nation-welding projects which could capture the popular imagination, such as the rapid peopling of the West and the launching of two new transcontinental railway systems, notable features of the Laurier era. Instead, as Professor Creighton explained in the excerpt quoted in the preceding problem, the role and prestige of the provinces grew at the expense of those of the federal government during this period. The prosperous provinces expanded their welfare services, casting their governments in the attractive role of Lady Bountiful in the eyes of their beneficiaries. This arrangement was possible only so long as tax revenues remained buoyant and demands for assistance were relatively light.

The Depression descended upon a Canada ill-prepared to face such a prolonged and serious crisis.

Because the existing constitutional framework was unable to cope with the problem, the Royal Commission on Dominion-Provincial Relations* was established to report on the nature of the problem and recommend reforms. The dispassionate statement of the causes and effects of the depression in Book I of the Report provides a useful introduction to the topic.

---

* See above, p. 228.

The Rowell-Sirois Commission States the Problem

The implications of the nature and extent of the world depression to Canada are obvious. The effects upon this nation, which obtains over one-third of its national income directly from abroad and two-thirds of whose exports consist of raw materials, were extremely drastic. For upwards of thirty years external influences and technical changes had played favourably upon Canada's resources and produced an era of almost unbroken expansion and prosperity. The Canadian economy had become delicately geared to the increasing foreign markets for foodstuffs, newsprint, lumber and minerals. For the production of these commodities a large and expensive transportation system was built and huge amounts were invested in power projects, processing plants, implements and machines. Much of the capital required for the provision of this immense equipment was borrowed from other countries. The application of this capital and of advanced techniques to virgin resources became the principal basis of our economic life. It involved a narrow specialization in the production of a few export staples, heavy fixed charges, and a precarious dependence upon the commercial policies of other countries.

As long as the conditions of international trade were favourable, specialization yielded a high standard of living. . . . Our social and economic institutions became closely related to the nature of the economy and rested on the condition of continuous expansion. When the bases for progress along the old lines disappeared and the full force of the world depression fell upon our specialized exports, the problems of adjustment were extremely difficult. Canada's political, public finance and economic organizations were not adapted to deal with sharp and prolonged economic reverses. . . .

. . . The market situation for the two leading exports, wheat and newsprint, was especially weak. . . . Since Canada supplied 40 per cent of the world exports of wheat and 65 per cent of the world exports of newsprint, she would suffer the full impact of unfavourable developments.

* * * * *

The Canadian manufacturing industry, except that portion of it engaged in the processing of export staples and certain naturally sheltered branches, grew up behind a protective tariff. The steep increase in duties during 1930 and 1931 and the intensification of administrative restrictions greatly widened the scope for the maintenance of prices. . . .

. . . Consequently the Canadian manufacturer had a considerable cushion against the contracting market. Total salaries and wages in the tariff-protected manufacturing industry fell proportionately much less than earnings in many other occupational classifications.

The naturally sheltered industries and occupations were even more thoroughly shielded against the losses of the slump. The costs of many professional and personal services, and of the distributive and administrative overhead of the country, could not be sharply reduced. With the decline in the cost of living, most of those engaged in these services were better off in 1933 than in 1929. Far from assuming any considerable part of the depression burdens, they received a considerable increment in their share of the national income.

The incidence of the depression on the various regions and provinces was determined by their relations to the factors discussed above. . . . [T]here was no reason to expect anything approaching a uniform distribution of losses.

The depression burdens, which could be shifted only with great difficulty, in the end fell almost completely on the exporters, the unemployed, the investors in defaulted farm mortgages, and the receivers of income from equities. In Central Canada and Nova Scotia, where the amounts obtained from salaries and wages in tariff-protected and naturally sheltered occupations and from fixed interest investments were relatively the greatest, the total incomes fell least. In Western Canada, where the proportions of the receipts from export production were the highest, the total incomes fell most. The Prairie Provinces, almost wholly dependent upon the export of wheat, suffered the most severe declines.

THE DECLINE IN PROVINCIAL PER CAPITA INCOMES,
1928-29 TO 1933

	1928-29 average $ per capita	1933 $ per capita	Percentage Decrease
Saskatchewan	478	135	72
Alberta	548	212	61
Manitoba	466	240	49
Canada	471	247	48
British Columbia	594	314	47
Prince Edward Island	278	154	45
Ontario	549	310	44
Quebec	391	220	44
New Brunswick	292	180	39
Nova Scotia	322	207	36

The large disparities shown in the above table are striking testimony of the extreme differences in the incidence of the depression and of the great problems of public finance and economic policy which they created.

*   *   *   *   *

The policies of Western settlement, all-Canadian transportation, and industrialization by protective tariffs had been designed to promote, and to function under the influences of, expansion. They had set the stage and in some measure had provided the incentives for the activities of private enterprise which were counted on to bring general prosperity and build an economically integrated and united nation. The success of the whole scheme depended upon the availability of extensive virgin resources and expanding foreign markets. In 1930 when the external influences became extremely unfavourable and the supply of new land suitable for agriculture had become virtually exhausted, the old policies became largely negative. They were important conditions under which the economy had grown up and under which individuals had obtained their opportunities and produced their incomes and thus could not be sharply reversed without severe repercussions. On the other hand, the nation's prosperity could no longer be maintained simply by settling immigrants and subsidizing the construction of railways.

The depression brought a set of problems almost entirely new in Canadian experience. Their solution or amelioration required new departures in federal policy. Broadly there were two alternatives. One was to try to *counteract the factors which were responsible for the slump* by attempting to maintain export values, to keep up activity in construction, and to prevent prices and costs from getting too far out of line. This would have involved what then appeared to be risky and unorthodox monetary measures. The other was carefully *to avoid risky and unorthodox monetary measures and to endeavour to maintain income in the sheltered and protected sectors of the economy* by drastic restrictions against imports, by following "sound" financial policies which would maintain confidence, preserve the public credit both internally and abroad, and thus facilitate the operation of the natural forces of recovery. While there could be no absolute certainty about which course would hold the total national income at the higher level, the latter would widen the disparities in the losses falling on the various groups . . . and hence would greatly increase the transfers of income which would have to be made through the public finance system to support the casualties of the unequal incidence of the depression. The second alternative describes briefly the policies which were actually adopted by the Dominion.

> "The Depression", *Report of the Royal Commission on Dominion-Provincial Relations*, Book I, *Canada: 1867–1939* (Ottawa, 1940), pp. 143–4, 149, 150–1.
> [Italics as in the original.]

The Impact of the Depression on Individuals

The statistics quoted above fail to convey to anyone who did not live through the Depression the soul-destroying frustrations and confusion that arose when a supposedly well-organized world economy suddenly went awry. Skilled workmen were being laid off by companies who had no contracts on which to employ them. Youths were leaving school only to find no employment, and no opportunity to acquire skills. In the prairie west the collapse of farm prices coincided with years of drought and plagues of grasshoppers, which turned the world's bread basket into a dust bowl.

A brief suggestion of the attitude of the era is conveyed in the following lines written a few years later by M. J. Coldwell, a Regina school principal who was one of the founders of the Co-operative Commonwealth Federation.

This was a time of drought, of grasshoppers, of crop failure, when people had no money and poverty was extreme. In these years vast accumulations of unsold and almost worthless grain filled the elevators and granaries on the farms. Wheat dropped to less than twenty cents a bushel at prairie points; eggs were traded in the country stores for two and one-half cents a dozen; horses, cattle and hogs were almost worthless. Yet in the cities long lines of unemployed sought relief. The man on the land could not dispose of foodstuffs which the man in the city could not buy.

M. J. Coldwell, *Left Turn, Canada* (London, 1945), pp. 19–20.

Parliamentarians and the Dilemma of the Depression

By early 1930 the provincial governments were hard pressed to cope with the requests from municipalites to assist them in alleviating the unemployment crisis. When the provincial governments, in turn, sought assistance from the federal authorities, Prime Minister Mackenzie King stated in Parliament in April that he would not give a five-cent piece to any province with a Tory government, arguing that subsidizing provincial coffers with federal funds was a vicious principle. Public reaction to this comment, well publicized by the Conservatives, possibly helped bring about the Liberal government's defeat in the general election held in July that year.

The new Conservative Prime Minister, R. B. Bennett, summoned a special session of Parliament in September 1930. His hope that the problem could be solved by raising tariffs was revealed in the operative paragraph of the brief Speech from the Throne with which the session opened.

The necessity for dealing with exceptional economic conditions and with the resultant unemployment has induced me to summon you at an earlier date than

would otherwise be necessary. Measures will be submitted for your consideration, including amendments to the Customs Act and the Customs Tariff which
it is anticipated will do much to meet the unusual conditions which now prevail.

Canada, Parliament, *Debates of the House of Commons*, Special Session 1930,
(Ottawa), p. 4.

The relatively modest scope of the proposals is indicated by the
Prime Minister's estimate of the new employment opportunities
that might be developed by the higher tariffs.

. . . And we have very definite assurances from the producers in this country
that as a result of the action we are taking they will increase the number of men
and women in their mills and factories. I said the other day, Mr. Speaker, that
the number might be estimated at 25,000 within a reasonable time.

Ibid., p. 239.

In the special session W. L. Mackenzie King, as leader of the
opposition, continued to question whether the unemployment situation was as serious as the Conservatives had painted.

The preamble of the bill . . . sets forth that unemployment is primarily a
provincial and a municipal responsibility. That has been the position that has
been taken, so far as I am aware, at all times in this parliament by all parties
herein. The government, of course, assumes the responsibility of stating that
the problem is at the present time a national problem, and also responsibility
for the grounds on which it has reached that conclusion. My hon. friend [the
Prime Minister] has not given to me in the correspondence respecting unemployment that I asked for any information which would indicate that he has received
from the governments of any of the provinces direct information to the effect
that the situation within its borders with respect to unemployment has become
such that the province itself is unable to cope with it.

Ibid., p. 141.

Threats of Secession

The prescience of Helmcken and Wood in the British Columbian
version of the Confederation Debates* was confirmed in the rash
of threats of secession (even from landlocked Saskatchewan) that
marked the 1930's. "The only bond of union," Dr. Helmcken had

---

* See above, p. 225.

observed in 1870, "will be the material advantage of the country and the pecuniary benefit of the inhabitants." Neither were readily apparent in the 1930's. The dislocation of the Pacific province's trading patterns, stemming partly from the attempt of the federal government to induce prosperity through higher protection, encouraged the *Vancouver Sun* to publish a front page editorial entitled

A DOMINION OF BRITISH COLUMBIA

What is the political and economic future of people in this province? That is a question which is being asked in every store and club in Vancouver and throughout the country. The question is hardly a party one, it is not a new one, but events of the last few days have forcibly brought it before our people.

Premier [R. B.] Bennett's refusal to extend to the Government of British Columbia the same credit help that was given to the C.P.R. was one incident. The other, Ottawa's disclosure* that an outside owned tobacco monopoly had, in 5 years, paid out some 32 million dollars in dividends while at the same time reducing to Canadian growers a tobacco price per pound from 30¢ down to 15¢.

These are only samples of a series of events which show British Columbians how they and their rich province are being exploited.

*   *   *   *   *

Our ability to produce and pay is openly admitted. President Beatty, at the recent annual meeting of the C.P.R., stated that 50% of the freight revenue came from the West; . . . But when it comes to sharing emoluments and control and executive position, we are not on the map. Hardly an executive salary or ranking directorship in any Canadian institution is now held by men west of the Lakes.

The centralizing policy of the East may have been all right in the growing, building, prosperous days of Canada, but to allow this exploiting and unequal sharing to settle down into a permanent policy and economy for CANADA is, to independent-minded, social-minded, British-minded, British Columbians, unthinkable.

*   *   *   *   *

The cruel exploitation of tobacco growers in Eastern Canada is only a mild sample of what has been done to Western holders of Turner Valley oil properties by Canada's oil monopoly; to Peace River and Pacific development, and generally in preventing British Columbians from sharing their rightful heritage.

*   *   *   *   *

---

* A reference to the Royal Commission on Price Spreads hearings then in progress.

Confederation was formed on a basis of very low tariffs. This province could, on a basis of the B.N.A. Act, buy and sell and trade unhampered with the world. A scheming, exploiting East has changed all this.

Now we must try and sell our lumber and minerals and wheat and fruits in world markets, but are compelled to buy all our goods from and do all our business with Eastern Canada.

Although there are markets for tens of millions worth of our Western products in England and Japan and China, we British Columbians cannot exchange a seagrass rug with Japan without paying several hundred per cent duty; we cannot bring in a bamboo chair from China; we cannot exchange cotton or woollen goods or machinery with England without being taxed unpayably high duty.

The financial and industrial manipulators in St. James Street do not seem to realize that they are building up in England an antagonism against Canadian products that is reducing to peonage the people who live in this Western half of Canada.

* * * * *

The Okanagan and Fraser Valley fruit farmer is not the docile habitant of Quebec; our loggers and miners in this province are real men; while the great middle classes in our British Columbia cities average up a people unequalled on earth.

If we are forced to it by Eastern Canada, we can separate and pay our own way and go it alone; and we can be sure we will have 100 per cent British support.

Victoria and Vancouver are world seaports. This province is a great hunting and sporting country. And regardless of the tongues and races in the rest of Canada, we are and propose to remain, a British people.

There must be a more equitable sharing among Canadians of things Canadian, or else this province must look about in self-defence to find ways and means to federate these parts into a DOMINION OF BRITISH COLUMBIA.

Vancouver Sun, 14 May 1934, p. 1.

Discontent Spawns New Parties

The apparent failure of the economic system encouraged many Canadians to consider alternative systems. In Alberta William Aberhart, a high school principal and popular radio evangelist, preached his version of the Social Credit doctrines of Major C. H. Douglas. With the promise to provide a "basic dividend" (he cited $25.00 a month as an example) to every citizen of the province, he and his followers were swept into power in 1935. In 1936 the reins of power in Quebec passed over to Maurice Duplessis and his newly organized *Union Nationale,* which also campaigned on a platform calling for radical economic reform through state action.

A party which in later years remained more faithful to its founding principles, though it was less successful in its immediate quest for office, was the Co-operative Commonwealth Federation. The C.C.F. was founded in Calgary in 1932 as a federation of three distinct interests: farmers' groups surviving from the Progressive movement of the 1920's, labour and socialist organizations, and the League for Social Reconstruction, which was an association of radically oriented academic and professional people residing in Toronto and Montreal. A platform and constitution for the new party was agreed on at a national convention in Regina in July 1933. The following excerpts from the preamble of "The Regina Manifesto" suggest the temper of the time.

We aim to replace the present capitalist system, with its inherent injustice and inhumanity, by a social order from which the domination and exploitation of one class by another will be eliminated, in which economic planning will supersede unregulated private enterprise and competition, and in which genuine democratic self-government, based upon economic equality will be possible. The present order is marked by glaring inequalities of wealth and opportunity, by chaotic waste and instability; and in an age of plenty it condemns the great mass of the people to poverty and insecurity. Power has become more and more concentrated into the hands of a small irresponsible minority of financiers and industrialists and to their predatory interests the majority are habitually sacrificed. When private profit is the main stimulus to economic effort, our society oscillates between periods of feverish prosperity in which the main benefits go to speculators and profiteers, and of catastrophic depression, in which the common man's normal state of insecurity and hardship is accentuated. We believe that these evils can be removed only in a planned and socialized economy in which our natural resources and the principal means of production and distribution are owned, controlled and operated by the people.

*   *   *   *   *

This social and economic transformation can be brought about by political action, . . . We do not believe in change by violence.

"The Co-operative Commonwealth Federation Platform" as quoted in
Kenneth McNaught, *A Prophet in Politics: A Biography of J. S. Woodsworth*
(Toronto, 1959), p. 321.

Unemployed Canadians Riot

Major riots have been sufficiently rare in Canada that such events remain newsworthy. Hence, although there was but a single death in the disturbances on Dominion Day, 1935, in Regina, "The Regina Riots" had a profound impact across Canada. The following summary of the events appeared in the *Canadian Annual Review*.

During the Spring and early Summer discontent had been growing in the relief camps for unemployed in British Columbia and on June 3 some 900 men broke camp and started eastward with the avowed intention of proceeding to Ottawa to place their grievances before the Dominion Government. Travelling by freight train, their ranks were swelled along the way by recruits from other camps and other unemployed individuals. At Calgary on June 7 they were reported to be 1,300 strong. This number increased at each city or camp on their forward march. On June 12, with the "army" at Swift Current, the Dominion authorities issued orders to the Royal Canadian Mounted Police that the march must be stopped at Regina. Two days later the men, now reported to number nearly 2,000, were at Regina. They threatened to defy the order. The relief strikers raised about $1,500 by a "Tag Day" in Regina, and on June 17 the Hon. R. J. Manion and the Hon. Robert Wier of the Dominion Cabinet arrived from Ottawa to confer with their leaders; following this, it was arranged that a delegation from the strikers should go to Ottawa to lay their case before the Cabinet. On June 22 the leaders of the strikers presented certain "demands" to Prime Minister R. B. Bennett and his Government, which were rejected. Subsequently the Ottawa Government proposed to take care of the men at a temporary camp at Lumsden, Saskatchewan, near Regina. On June 26 the strikers refused to accept this provision and decided to continue on to Ottawa. The next day on orders from Ottawa the R.C.M.P. mobilized to prevent the strikers moving eastward from Regina. An attempt by some of the men to move out by trucks was thwarted, and five men, including a Regina clergyman, were arrested and charged the next day under Section 98 of the Criminal Code dealing with unlawful associations. The R.C.M.P. warned citizens not to aid the strikers, announcing that no police action would be taken if the men would go to the Lumsden camp from where the Dominion authorities would provide them with transportation back to their relief camps or their homes.

Leaders of the relief strikers called a mass meeting of their followers and sympathizers in the market square of Regina for the evening of July 1 and in addition to the strikers thousands of Regina citizens attended. The R.C.M.P. and the Regina city police decided on this meeting as a suitable occasion for the arrest of leaders. Shortly after eight o'clock in the evening, forces of both bodies marched into the square as the meeting was in progress. Panic ensued. The police were attacked and fighting and rioting developed and continued for some three hours. Detective Charles Millar of the Regina city police lost his life, being beaten to death by rioters using sticks and other weapons. Approximately 100 persons, including several members of the R.C.M.P. and city police, were injured, several seriously. Much property damage was caused. In the course of the attacks on the police shots were fired by the city police although the R.C.M.P. did not use guns. The police brought the situation under control, some 80 men being arrested. The next day the Provincial Government intervened. In telegrams to Prime Minister Bennett and the Hon. Hugh Guthrie, Minister of Justice, the Provincial Prime Minister, the Hon. J. G. Gardiner and the Provincial Attorney-General, the Hon. T. C. Davis, K.C., protested against the course taken by the Dominion authorities, Mr. Davis claiming it was an invasion of Provincial jurisdiction. Mr. Gardiner protested that the police had acted on orders from Ottawa while the Provincial Government was considering proposals of the strikers that they should undertake their return to their camps and homes. He informed the Dominion Prime Minister (Mr. Bennett) that the Provincial Government was prepared to disband the men and send them back without sending them to the Lumsden camp. The Provincial Government proceeded to take charge of the situation. In negotiations with representatives of the strikers they obtained their consent to return to their camps and homes. On July 5 about 1,500 were moving westward on special trains engaged by the Provincial Government.

On July 5 the Government of Saskatchewan announced the appointment of a Commission to inquire into the riot, . . .

The Commission's Report was made public on May 16 [1936]. The Commission found the organized conduct of the relief strikers was a menace to "peace, order and good government" and the action of the Dominion authorities in halting the march to Ottawa to have been justified. The Commission was of opinion that had the strikers reached Ottawa their numbers probably would have reached 5,000 and a more serious riot might have occurred there.

Canadian Annual Review, 1935–6 (Toronto, 1939), pp. 312–13.

Has the Dominion the Constitutional Authority to Help Combat a Depression?

In 1935 the Conservative administration of R. B. Bennett sponsored a broad programme of New Deal-like legislation. The question of how and why the Prime Minister was converted to more active state intervention in the economy at this date is still a matter of debate. The extent of the conversion can be seen by comparing the excerpts of the Speech from the Throne with which the 1935 session of Parliament opened with those from the Speech which opened the 1930 Special Session.

Better provision will be made for the security of the worker during unemployment, in sickness, and in old age.

*   *   *   *   *

Action will be taken to ameliorate the conditions of labour, to provide a better and more assured standard of living for the worker, to secure minimum wages and a maximum working week, and to alter the incidence of taxation so that it will more directly conform to capacity to pay.

You will be invited to enact measures designed to safeguard the consumer and primary producer against unfair trading practices and to regulate, in the public interest, concentrations in production and distribution. . . .

. . . New conditions prevail. These require modifications of the capitalist system more effectively to serve the people. . . .

You will be invited to authorize the constitution of an economic council, the functions of which will be to advise my ministers upon all economic questions which concern the national welfare. . . .

Canada, Parliament, *Debates of the House of Commons*, 1935, (Ottawa), pp. 3–4.

During the debates on the bills which the government introduced to implement this programme, the legislative competence of the federal parliament to deal with subjects which would entrench on the right given the provinces by Section 92 (13) of the British North America Act to legislate on matters pertaining to "Property and Civil Rights in the Province" was frequently questioned. The trend of decisions by the Judicial Committee of the Privy Council, the highest court of appeal of the Empire-Commonwealth, had so eroded the right of the Dominion "to make Laws for the Peace, Order and Good Government of Canada in relation to all Matters not coming within the Classes of Subjects by this Act assigned exclusively to the Legislatures of the Provinces" that Section 92 (13) had become the effective "residual clause" of the Canadian federal constitution. When the question was referred to the courts in test cases, the Judicial Committee of the Privy Council found several acts *ultra vires* of the Dominion Parliament.

The excerpts which follow, taken from the legal report of one of these cases, outline the arguments of the counsel for the Attorney-General of Canada (a team which included the future Prime Minister, L. S. St. Laurent) and the decision of the Board (as the Judicial Committee is called).

The Employment and Social Insurance Act was adopted by the Canadian Parliament in 1935 as a remedial measure for a serious unemployment problem which had spread throughout the whole of Canada as a result of the prolonged trade depression. The scheme of the Act is to set up a national employment service and to establish a national insurance fund against unemployment. The objection to the validity of the Act is that it is said to be legislation of the central Parliament in relation either to property and civil rights within each Province or to matters local and private within each Province as to which exclusive legislative jurisdiction is by s. 92, heads 13 and 16, assigned to the Provincial Legislatures. Canada supports the legislation as a valid exercise of the powers of Parliament for the following reasons: (a) Because the main provisions of the legislation are a valid exercise of the powers of the Parliament of Canada under heads 1 and 3 of s. 91 of the British North America Act, 1867, to raise money by a system of taxation and to appropriate the same for the public purposes touching the peace, order and good government of Canada indicated by the legislation. (b) Because unemployment has attained such proportions as to render it unquestionably a matter of national interest and importance and as to affect the body politic of the Dominion. (c) Because unemployment, through the growing mechanization of industry and other economic causes has ceased to be merely a local or Provincial problem, and has become one of national proportions, interest and importance. (d) Because as the Provinces have no power to control the migration of labour from one Province to another, and Provincial boundaries do not affect the movement of labour, legislation to deal effectively with the unemployment problem must be national in its scope. (e) Because the legislation is not in pith and substance legislation to regulate property and civil rights in the Province, but is an effort by the Dominion to provide a remedy for a social and economic condition of national concern relating to the peace, order and good government of Canada and its trade and commerce.

*   *   *   *   *

[The Board's ruling]

There can be no doubt that, prima facie, provisions as to insurance of this kind, especially where they affect the contract of employment, fall within the class of property and civil rights in the Province, and would be within the exclusive competence of the Provincial Legislature. It was sought, however, to justify the validity of Dominion legislation on grounds which their Lordships on consideration feel compelled to reject. . . . A strong appeal, however, was made on the ground of the special importance of unemployment insurance in Canada at the time of, and for some time previous to, the passing of the Act. On this point it becomes unnecessary to do more than to refer to the judgment of this Board in the reference on the three labour Acts, and to the judgment of the Chief Justice in the Natural Products Marketing Act which, on this matter, the Board have approved and adopted. It is sufficient to say that the present Act does not purport to deal with any special emergency. It founds itself in the preamble on general world-wide conditions referred to in the Treaty of Peace: it is an Act whose operation is intended to be permanent: and there is agreement between all the members of the Supreme Court that it could not be supported upon the suggested existence of any special emergency. Their Lordships find themselves unable to differ from this view.

> Richard A. Olmsted, Q.C., *Decisions of the Judicial Committee of the Privy Council relating to the British North America Act, 1867 and the Canadian Constitution 1867–1954* (Ottawa, 1954), Vol. III, pp. 208-9, 216-17.

THE VIEWS OF LATER COMMENTATORS

An Assessment of R. B. Bennett's Anti-Depression Measures

J. B. Brebner was a Canadian-born, Toronto- and Oxford-trained historian who retained a personal and scholarly interest in the land of his birth throughout his distinguished career as Gouverneur Morris Professor of History at Columbia University, New York. In his posthumously published *Canada: A Modern History* he traced the threatening trends toward political disintegration in Canada during the period under review.

Bennett was an able, vigorous New Brunswicker who had made a fortune as a lawyer and businessman, first in the West and later in central Canada. Material success, working upon his sincerity, humane concern, and self-certainty, had developed in him habits of dominance and assurance that commended him to bewildered Canadians in 1930 but that made him an unacceptably masterful and inconsiderate leader of a Cabinet. Perhaps he came to high office too late in life and with too little experience of the give and take that must characterize the federal executive in Canada. . . .

. . . He announced that he would end unemployment by retaliatory protectionism and other devices aimed principally to cut down purchases from the provocative United States by placing "Canada first and then the Empire," and by "blasting" a way into the markets of the world. . . .

One of the most interesting and in the long run significant aspects of his single term as prime minister was his discovery and use of the knowledge and ability of the civil service. Canadians in general had hitherto held the permanent administrative staff in distinctly low esteem, . . .

They overlooked the fact that a Civil Service Commission had been at work for some years instituting entrance by competitive examinations, classifying positions in terms of the accomplishments required, and arranging promotion by merit. . . .

* * * * *

Within Canada, Bennett's high protectionism had the obvious and predictable effect of sheltering central Canada and still further exposing the desperate margins. In 1934, N. M. Rogers startled not only the Nova Scotian Royal Commission to which he submitted the statement, but the rest of Canada as well, by his calculation that the tariff in effect subsidized each person in Ontario by $15.15 a year, and in Quebec by $11.03, but cost each person in the other seven provinces as much as $11.67 in Nova Scotia or $28.16 in Saskatchewan. Bennett succeeded, however, in using protectionism forcefully in the international area. In fact, Canada's reprisals for the stupid Smoot-Hawley tariff of the United States in 1930 and the still more stupid fiscal tariffs of 1932 were probably the most effective wakening shocks that the Americans received.

*   *   *   *   *

. . . Needless to say, he [Bennett] did not end unemployment, indeed by 1935 it was calculated that a tenth of the population was on relief. One after another, the provinces rejected the Conservatives locally and threw up strongly particularistic leaders who promised to remedy Ottawa's deficiencies by looking after individual Canadians instead of after large industry and the national bookkeeping position.

The Liberals under A. L. Macdonald won office in Nova Scotia in 1933 and under A. A. Dysart in New Brunswick in 1935. These Liberal premiers chanted "Maritime Rights" and other voices hinted at secession. In Quebec, the shaken Liberals . . . were undermined by the nationalists, the separatists, and all manner of demands for social legislation from within the party and without. After sundry maneuvers, the astute Maurice Duplessis capitalized the discontents with a new party, the *Union Nationale,* which was essentially separatist, conservative, autocratic, and extravagant, but earned popularity by fulminations and overt actions against Ottawa, against foreign financial domination, and against "Communism." After barely missing victory in November, 1935, Duplessis achieved it in August, 1936.

In Ontario, M. F. Hepburn carried the province for the Liberals in 1934 by a curious alliance between discontent, rural and urban, and the mining and financial interests of Toronto. He staged spectacular attacks against American and Quebec "power interests" and "foreign" industrial unionism, which he subsequently compromised, and kept in the limelight by vituperative campaigns against the Ottawa governments, Conservative or Liberal. In the West, the C.C.F. (Co-operative Commonwealth Federation) was strong enough outside Alberta to force open or tacit alliances of the older parties against it. Aberhart carried Alberta in 1935 by promises to pay all adults a "social dividend" of twenty-five dollars a month.

Canada was breaking up into rather demagogic principalities. Even within Bennett's Cabinet, H. H. Stevens, Minister of Trade and Commerce, became so disturbed by, and outspoken about, the social and economic abominations in commerce and industry, uncovered by the Royal Commission on Price

Spreads of 1934 that, after being forced to resign, he founded a political party of his own.

Tory radicalism.—Bennett's response to this situation was superficially shocking, but in keeping with his character. In a series of radio broadcasts during January, 1935, he announced an immense program of federal state intervention, relying considerably upon Ottawa's emergency powers for "peace, order, and good government," and on its treaty-making power in the form of accepting conventions of the International Labor Organization, so as to get round the obstacles set up by the Judicial Committee of the Privy Council.

Now Bennett and Herridge,* with the rather feverish aid of some able civil servants, prepared for Parliament, which dutifully passed them except for some amendments in the Senate, bills involving the federal government in the export marketing and interprovincial trade of natural products; agricultural debts and loans; minimum wages; maximum hours; prevention of child labor; unemployment insurance; antimonopoly; prevention of unfair and misleading business, commercial, and financial practices; relief; housing; public works; and so forth. Bennett's "Tory Radicalism" harmonized both with his nationalism and with his authoritarianism. A striking feature of some of the Bennett legislation was that certain breaches of it were made criminal, not civil, offenses.

. . . Few Canadians, however, were sophisticated in these matters and most of them did not know that outside North America such intervention or "planning" had historically been as congenial to the politico-economic Right as to the Left, with the liberals of the Middle holding it off as much as possible until political democracy destroyed their position.

It was in the midst of provincial revolts and of considerable confusion and muddled thinking, therefore, that King and the federal Liberals swept Bennett and the federal Conservatives out of power, indeed almost out of existence, in the autumn elections of 1935, in spite of promises of still further social and economic legislation from Bennett.

> J. Bartlet Brebner, *Canada: A Modern History* (Ann Arbor, 1960), pp. 456–7, 459–61.

In Praise of the Rowell-Sirois Commission

Excerpts from the Report of the Royal Commission on Dominion-Provincial Relations have appeared at a number of points in this book. Any short excerpt from its balanced recommendations would be misleading. The two extracts from commentators viewing the report from the 1960's indicate the range of interpretation.

---

* W. D. Herridge, brother-in-law of R. B. Bennett and sometime Canadian minister at Washington. While in the American capital he established close contacts with a number of the "Brain Trusters" responsible for the New Deal Legislation.

"The Most Important State Paper Produced in Canada"

J. B. Brebner's reference to the report follows his commentary on R. B. Bennett.

The Rowell-Sirois Commission.—Meanwhile, however, the ever more absurd state to which the federal constitution had been reduced by the Judicial Committee of the Privy Council* obviously threatened Canada with disintegration into nine principalities. To meet this threat, [Prime Minister] King in 1937 resorted to the Canadian agency of a Royal Commission on Dominion-Provincial Relations, . . . This able body, appropriately financed and calling on experts and conducting hearings all over the country, conducted a patient, thorough national inquest before reporting in 1940.

The Rowell-Sirois Report, with its appendices, was not only the most important state paper ever produced in Canada, but became at once a significant document in the general history of federalism. . . . Its recommendations proved to be more than the country could swallow, but they were the blueprint for political and economic, if not cultural, Canadian unity, and many subsequent developments have been in accordance with them, although sometimes effected in devious face-saving ways.

The report met separatism head-on by demonstrating the unevenness of wealth and prosperity across Canada and recommending that national revenues be raised and distributed in such a way as to ensure that no part be allowed to fall below a minimum level of well-being and security. This would involve federal responsibility for unemployment relief and insurance, and a new and flexible dispensation in the federal subsidies to the provincial governments so that they might maintain a uniform average level of social services.

Ibid., p. 462.

"Its Analysis Has Had Surprisingly Little Influence"

The views expressed by Professor Brebner reflect the opinion of the majority of the commentators on the Report and its significance. In a paper presented to a session of the Canadian Political Science Association in Montreal in 1961, Professor Donald Smiley presented a revisionist view in which the following passages appear.

On May 3, 1940, the Royal Commission on Dominion-Provincial Relations presented its report to the Prime Minister of Canada. This report, along with the specialized studies undertaken by direction of the commission, constitutes the most comprehensive investigation of a working federal system that has ever been made. In spite of the scope and quality of the commission's work,

---

* A reference to the decisions on Bennett's New Deal Legislation.

its analysis of federal-provincial relations has had surprisingly little influence on the directions that the theory and practice of Canadian federalism have taken since 1945. More specifically, the concept of provincial autonomy which is central to the commission's argument has been denied explicitly or implicitly by such influential writings on the Canadian federal system as the so-called Green Book proposals submitted by the federal government at the Dominion-Provincial Conference on Reconstruction in 1945, the Report of the Royal Commission on National Development in the Arts, Letters and Sciences, Mr. Maurice Lamontagne's book, *Le Fédéralisme canadien*, and the Report of the Quebec Royal Commission on Constitutional Problems, as well as by the actual developments in federal-provincial relations since the Second World War. . . .

The emphasis on provincial autonomy in the performance of a very wide range of public functions which pervaded the analysis of the Rowell-Sirois Commission has given rise to much less comment than the commission's relatively few but significant proposals for transferring particular provincial responsibilities to the federal authorities and for sharing functions previously the exclusive concern of the provinces between the two levels of government. Indeed, viewed against the constitutional impasse of the 1930's the report is a somewhat cautious document.

It is fundamental to the commission's analysis that the highly integrated nature of the Canadian economy makes it appropriate for the provinces to perform a very wide range of public functions without the direct involvement of the federal authorities.

It appears implicit in the commission's analysis that the desirability of provincial autonomy to safeguard regional particularisms is more pressing in relation to health, education, and welfare services than to the regulatory activities of government.

*   *   *   *   *

The commission had a precise idea of what it meant by provincial autonomy. A province has genuine independence only if it has the revenues at its disposal to carry out those functions for which it is responsible, free from federal control in respect to those functions; . . .

*   *   *   *   *

In summary, provincial autonomy is fundamental in the commission's concept of a viable Canadian federal system. Such autonomy was justified on three grounds—cultural, political, and administrative: (1) It is necessary for the preservation of provincial particularism; (2) It makes possible the effective accountability of provincial public authorities to provincial electorates, particularly in relation to the respective priorities that are placed on provincial programmes; (3) It makes possible the unified control over the administration of particular provincial functions necessary to the vigorous implementation of public policies relating to such functions.

To the commission, then, the major implications of the integration of the national economy lay in the desirability of giving the federal authorities exclusive access to the major field of direct taxation with the corresponding responsibility of effecting some redistribution of financial resources among the provinces rather than the alleged need for federal involvement in the range or standards of provincial functions.

> D. V. Smiley, "The Rowell-Sirois Report, Provincial Autonomy, and Post-War Canadian Federalism", *The Canadian Journal of Economics and Political Science*, XXVIII (February 1962), pp. 54–5, 56, 57–8.

Further Reading

The impact of the Great Depression on the individual and on attitudes to the existing social structure can most effectively be glimpsed through the verse and prose of those who experienced it. Anne Marriott, *The Wind Our Enemy* (Toronto, Ryerson Press, 1939), is a poem which evokes the complex of emotions experienced by the prairie-dwellers who witnessed the transformation of the world's bread-basket into a dust bowl. Among the novels that dwell on repercussions of the Depression, F. P. Grove, *The Master of the Mill* (Toronto, Macmillan, 1944), Morley Callaghan, *They Shall Inherit the Earth* (New York, Random House, 1935), and Irene Baird's less detached *Waste Heritage* (New York, Random House, 1939) deserve special mention. The files of the *Canadian Forum* for the decade should also be consulted for samples of the short stories and protest verse inspired by the conditions of the time.

The rapid rise of William Aberhart to political prominence in these years is traced in J. A. Irving, *The Social Credit Movement in Alberta* (Toronto, University of Toronto Press, 1959), the tenth volume in the series mentioned in the Further Reading section for Problem 16. Kenneth McNaught devotes three chapters to the Depression and the organization of the C.C.F. in *A Prophet in Politics: A Biography of J. S. Woodsworth* (Toronto, University of Toronto Press, 1959). Additional light is cast on the political appeal of R. B. Bennett's "New Deal" in an article by J. R. H. Wilbur, "H. H. Stevens and the Reconstruction Party", *Canadian Historical Review*, XLV (March 1964), pp. 1–28. That other members of the Liberal party were more receptive to the new current of political thinking than was Mackenzie King is demonstrated by Margaret Ormsby in "T. Dufferin Pattullo and the Little New Deal", in *ibid.* XLIII (December 1962), pp. 277–97.

Problem 18

Men and Machines — The Response of the Churches

With the exception of certain areas of education, church and state have been separated in Canada for over a century. Does this separation imply that the churches have no legitimate interest in secular affairs, or that they should at least remain silent on social problems? How have the churches defined their role? What in fact is the *proper* role of the churches in a modern industrial and urban society such as Canada? Are men's bodies as much the concern of the churches as men's souls?

The response of the Canadian churches to the problem-filled relationship of men and machines has varied between denominations, but it has shown over the past century a steady trend away from absolute faith in individualism, a rejection of the premise that the virtue of self-help can resolve the problems of industrial society, and toward a conception of Christian social responsibility as an alternative to the Marxist extreme of mechanistic collectivism. In brief, most churches have rejected two opposing assumptions of modern thought—first, that personal justification by faith will harmonize society, and second, that secular humanism can solve ethical problems.

The historical response, or responses, of the Canadian churches to industrialism has been precipitated by several crises in labour relations. The question of the churches' attitudes to capital and labour was first posed in an acute form by the Toronto printers' strike in 1872. Around the turn of the century, when prosperity and the tide of immigration heightened the industrial problem, the churches seemed to come together in the agitation for a Lord's Day Act that would ensure the factory worker of one day's rest in seven. The problem of leisure time inherent in a thirty-five hour week could not be foreseen in that age of sweat-shops and child labour. Although the pace of industrialism and secularism in Canadian society was intensified by the First World War, a major crisis did not recur until the Winnipeg general strike of 1919. Such separate strikes might temporarily crystallize the industrial problem for the churches, but the Great Depression produced such widespread and cataclysmic social and economic disorganization as to constitute an inescapable challenge to them. Their response to the Depression was confused by the fact that the churches themselves were victims of that Depression. A generation later the same issues of men, machines, and religion are being posed in a new form by automation in industry.

The Churches and the Printers' Strike

The first major crisis for industrial labour came with the Toronto Printers' Strike in 1872. Most church bodies did not deign to notice the strike because they considered it beyond the realm of their interests, but the few religious newspapers that did comment reveal a uniformly critical attitude.

A Presbyterian Opinion

The strike of the printers of Toronto, as the first movement in a grand campaign of Labour against capital, assumes national importance. We have before shown that the only true theory of the relation of the employer to employee rests on the same basis as that of buyer and seller, the commodity being "work" . . . When work-sellers talk of tyranny and oppression, as they are now doing, and are so prone to when the sale they have effected of their labour has not been as good as they wished, they not only display ignorance of the real facts of their case, but they recognize an idea and encourage its being held, which strikes at the very root of their personal independence and perpetuates their social demoralization as a class: that is, the old world notion of servility . . . The whole tendency of strikes is to harden class distinction, to justify class disabilities, and to create class hatreds . . .

No man ever rose above a lowly condition who thought more of his class than his individuality. In this new country, where every man who strives may advance in social power and rank, to teach men subordination to class movements, is to deprive them of those noble opportunities for personal advancement which are the peculiar glory and advantage of this continent.

The Witness (Halifax), 20 April 1872

An Anglican Viewpoint

The printers of the city have seen fit to usurp the control of the offices, an usurpation which needed and secured, by the force of its boldness, united and decided action on the part of those to whom alone that control legitimately belongs,—the Employers . . .

As to ourselves, the matter stands thus:—Our men had heretofore declared themselves satisfied with their labour and wages. But the insidious whimperings of a foreign-born League, circulated amongst them, their eyes were blinded under the excuse of opening them, so that to men *totally* unfit to judge of Canadian peculiarities of Labour, we have to give thanks for this ill-growth of antagonism between it and the Capital.

The Church Herald (Toronto), 28 March 1872

The Churches Recognize the Problem

Each decade brought increasing industrialization and urbanization to Canada until by the turn of the century the churches were awakened to the serious problems created by these related trends. Although the interdenominational Moral and Social Reform Council of Canada was formed in 1907, the churches usually reacted as separate entities to crises. The publication in 1907 of *Christianity and the Social Crisis* by the American clergyman, Walter Rauschenbusch, gave expression to the growing conviction that Christians are their brothers' keepers even in an industrial society and a free-enterprise economy. The following statements by Canadian churches stand in marked contrast to the sentiments expressed at the time of the printers' strike two generations earlier.

A Question to Be Faced

Has the hour struck when the Presbyterian Church should appoint an intermediary between itself and the "workingman"? The U.S. Presbyterian Church, North, took this step some years ago, and the wisdom of the appointment of Rev. Charles Stelzle has been amply vindicated. If Canada were one vast wheat field, the mission of the Church would be simple and direct; but with an army of loggers and navvies and miners in New Ontario, and an ever increasing multitude of operatives in the steel works, factories, smelters, and mines from Sydney on the Atlantic to the "black diamond" city of Nanaimo on the Pacific, the danger of divorce between the Church and the "workers" becomes more apparent, and the whole question more difficult and complex.

The Presbyterian, 8 February 1906

The Church and the Wage Earners

Is it a fact that the Church has lost its influence with the wage earning classes and that they are passing by on the other side? This is a question to which a sweeping and dogmatic answer cannot be given. There is too much reason to believe that in older countries in which men and women are crowded in great congested centres it is in a large measure true. In a comparatively young country like Canada in which the problem of the city has not yet assumed the acute form it **is** less true. But the same causes are at work and as wealth increases there is not only the danger of a widening chasm between the capitalist and the laborer, but also between the Church and the great army of toilers. And it is a danger against which those who are jealous for the honor of the Church of Christ and for the well being of the nation must be resolutely on guard.

* * * * *

. . . The Church with its wealth and culture and scholarship is in constant danger of regarding the organization as an end in itself rather than as a means for touching without distinction all sorts and conditions of men.

It is not enough to say that our church doors are open and that all are welcome. We cannot lay all the responsibility at the door of those who turn aside from our churches and say that their attitude is due to their crass materialism, their low ideals and lack of interest in higher things. In so far as there is any drift of the toiling classes from our church circles we must be ready to face squarely the question as to whether we are in any degree responsible.

The Presbyterian, 4 October 1906

We hold that the work of the Church is to set up the Kingdom of God among men, which we understand to be a social order founded on the principles of the Gospel—the Golden Rule, and the Sermon on the Mount—and made possible through the regeneration of men's lives.

We acknowledge with regret that the present social order is far from being an ideal expression of Christian brotherhood, and that the spirit of much of our commercial life is alien to that of the Gospel. We deplore the great evils which have their source in the commercial greed of our times, the money madness which leads men to oppress the unfortunate and to forget their obligations to the higher interests of society.

We deplore the lack of sympathy which too frequently exists between our more wealthy and less privileged individuals in society, leading to that most dangerous condition of indifference and sometimes contempt on the one hand and envy and distrust on the other. While we admit the right of both labour and capital to guard their interests by combination we condemn the disregard of the rights of the public and the individual which has been shown now by combinations of capital and now by combinations of labour.

While we admit that with the abounding and increasing wealth of our country, it is possible for the rich to grow richer without the poor becoming poorer, we deplore those existing economic conditions which tend to accentuate the inequality of opportunity open to the various classes of the community and to permit, through artificial and unfair conditions, the massing of the larger proportion of the wealth of the country in the hands of the few, with all the attendant economic and political dangers . . .

When the living wage is not made the first factor in determining the price of manufactured articles and the sweat shop scale of wages is so low that our maidens have set before them the awful choice between hunger and dishonour, and in the factory young children are stunted in mind and body by excessive labour, it is time for Christian citizenship to take up the Master's "whip of small cords" and drive these things from the holy places of our civilization, and for the Church to urge its members who in corporate bodies and otherwise, are served by labour, to keep themselves clear of guilt in these economic relations.

Journal of Proceedings, Seventh General Conference,
Methodist Church of Canada, 1906, pp. 274–6.

The Churches and the Winnipeg General Strike

The First World War stimulated industrialization, and the dislocations of the immediate postwar era resulted in widespread labour unrest that came to a head in the Winnipeg general strike during the late spring of 1919. Coming at a time when Communism had just overthrown the Tsarist regime in Russia and was threatening the status quo in several other European countries, the Winnipeg strike was considered by many to be the work of Bolsheviks intent on destroying free enterprise in North America, and so the strike contributed to the "Red Scare" that swept North America. The involvement of a few prominent Methodist and Anglican clergymen in the strike emphasized the gravity of the crisis as the churches were faced with taking a definite stand on the question of men and machines.

The General Assembly recognizes that the prevailing unrest is a sign of the vital effort of the nation to adjust itself to new and changing conditions. It also recognizes that this unrest is a belated protest against injustices that have been tolerated in our social system—the alienation of our natural resources, the tying up of land for the unearned increment in value, profiteering in the necessaries of life, the public indifference toward the conditions in which many of our people live and toward the wrongs they suffer, and they call earnestly for extensive reforms of the abuses complained of by Parliamentary action . . .

Industry, which includes both Capital and Labour, exists primarily for service. In order to serve, it must pay, but the object of its existence is service. All parties in industry have their obligations to meet, as well as their rights to secure, and the emphasis of the hour should be on the service, rather than on its reward.

The General Assembly would, therefore, remind both Capital and Labour that their first obligation is jointly to serve the people as a whole, and to give them the best service possible. Any attempt to lower the grade of the service rendered, or to take advantage of the public need, or in any other way to make gain their first consideration, forfeits the public confidence on which their standing in the community depends.

The General Assembly would remind the management of our industries of their obligation to promote in every way open to them the welfare and the interests of those who serve with them. The Assembly warmly commends movements now afoot in many of our industries towards the following ends:

Toward giving the workers a voice in determining the conditions under which their work is to be done, and a proper share in the control of industry;

Toward giving the workers an equitable share in the wealth jointly produced;

Toward co-operating with the State and with the workers themselves, in providing insurance against unemployment, accident and illness, and in providing pensions for old age and widowed mothers; . . .

The General Assembly affirms the sacredness of human personality, and would point out that such conditions of work must be secured as will afford to each worker the opportunity of the highest personal development.

In view of the tenseness of the present situation and of the perplexities that face men in every branch of industry, the General Assembly urges all parties to be conciliatory in spirit as they approach their problems, and suggests that the representatives of Capital and Labour confer carefully about all outstanding questions, in order that strife, with its attendant losses, may be averted at a time when the situation can be saved only by mutual good will and production to the full measure of our capacity.

The General Assembly sympathizes profoundly with the efforts of organized Labour to secure conditions for a more abundant life for the great mass of our people, and is anxious to co-operate with all interested bodies to that end. At the same time the Assembly would point out that organized Labour is now and must continue to be only a part of the world's workers and that the success of their cause depends on their winning the sympathy and confidence of the people, as a whole. The Assembly holds strongly that the following measures are necessary to this end:

Organized Capital and Labour should stand for each man rendering the fullest service of which he is capable.

Organized Capital and Labour should maintain the inviolability of agreements, both in spirit and in letter. Good faith is the foundation of all social stability, and when the representatives of Capital and Labour enter into agreements on the collective basis, for which both parties contend, such covenants should be observed.

The General Assembly affirms its conviction that the right of the workers to organize is fundamental in the present state of society, and that the right of the members of each craft to deal through their chosen representatives with the management of the industries in which they are working should be recognized at once by their employers and by the state.

In view of the fact that the rights of the entire community are imperilled by general sympathetic combinations, whether of Capital or workers, the General Assembly urges the Government at once to provide machinery for the adjustment of the differences and misunderstandings between employers and employed, and for the maintenance of the rights of all classes in the community.

*Acts and Proceedings of the Forty-fifth General Assembly of the
Presbyterian Church in Canada, 1918*, pp. 81–3.

What shall we say of [the sympathetic strike]? Nearly every newspaper of any authority condemns it. The Minister of Labour has condemned it, and the Hon. Sir Robert Borden has also condemned it in so far at least as it involves public servants such as post-office workers. In Winnipeg the firemen, the policemen and the post-office employees all went out on sympathetic strike. The Hon. Gideon Robertson, Minister of Labour, notified the post-office employees that they must report for duty or be dismissed, and as they refused to report they are all presumably no longer employees of the Government. This is certainly a very plain and simple way of dealing with the matter, but if it should precipitate a strike from the Atlantic to the Pacific amongst post-office employees, the case would not seem quite so simple. The Government itself is not so very sure of its position, and a nation-wide industrial conflict is the last thing anyone would desire.

* * * * *

It cannot be too clearly stated that these are not the days for the fighter, but for the peace-maker. Our people have been passing through most strenuous times, and they have borne nobly and uncomplainingly the burdens which have been laid upon them. They have sent their sons and brothers to the war, and they have done so without a murmur. They have borne the burden of bereavement, and they have had their dear ones come home lame, maimed, blind, deaf, and handicapped for all the future; and they have not rebelled. And they have faced the daily burden of increasing cost of living, seeing their scanty dollars every month buy a little less bread, and meat, and coal, and clothes; they have had the rent raised, and the taxes increased, until the dollar of four years ago is worth less than fifty cents; and they have borne it all. They have worn poorer clothes, eaten poorer food, spent less on simple luxuries, than ever in their lives before; and at the same time they have read the Government reports of huge fortunes made by corporations out of the very necessaries of life; and they have borne it all—because it was war.

The poor man in Canada is no better off to-day than he was a generation ago, and his standard of living is on a lower plane economically; and he becomes more acutely conscious of this, more resentful of it, and more determined to change the situation, as he sees all about him the evidences of increasing wealth in costly automobiles and luxurious living. It is within the power of the Government to insist that the poor man refrain from sympathetic strikes; but if it does so it were well that it exercise its power also upon the half-dozen or so of wealthy men who, by their refusal to agree to collective bargaining, have precipitated these strikes.

The Christian Guardian (Methodist Church), 4 June 1919, p. 5.

The Churches and the Depression

In the decade following the Winnipeg general strike, much of the socially conscious energy of the Protestant churches was merged through the 1925 union of the Methodists, Congregationalists, and Presbyterians. There is evidence that the minority of Presbyterians who rejected union also rejected the ideas of the "Social Gospel" and clung to nineteenth-century ideas of an individualistic laissez-faire society. Protestant social thought was also influenced by the Roman Catholic Church's traditional stress on corporate Christian benevolence and action. The testing time for men, machines, and churches alike came with the Great Depression. The religious response to massive unemployment and poverty tended to appear as support for or influence on secular reform movements rather than church-initiated programmes. The major exceptions to this were the co-operative schemes inspired by the Antigonish movement, and the back-to-the-land movement under Roman Catholic Church auspices in Quebec.

Christianizing the Social Order

Elements in Social Justice

38. As a fundamental motive in all her social effort, the Church, which is the Body of the living Christ, must proclaim the supreme worth of every

person as a child of God and a potential member of His Kingdom; she must, therefore, maintain that no man, with or without intent, shall be made to serve merely as an instrument of another man nor of any human institution; that employers shall not use their fellow men for the purpose of their private gain without regard for their human dignity, health and economic security, and should do their utmost to make possible for them the freedom and opportunity to live a worthy human life. Further, the Church must condemn business or financial methods, which, either in the interest of privilege or as impersonal forces, promote the accumulation of wealth in the hands of the few and rob the many of a decent livelihood.

39. A society approximating to the Kingdom of God on earth should ensure:

(a) That honest, capable and industrious persons shall have the opportunity as well as the responsibility of earning for themselves and their families a satisfactory livelihood, which should include humane living and working conditions, together with freedom and leisure for the awakening and development in them of whatsoever things are true, lovely and of good report.

(b) That the wage earner, the management and the provider of capital shall find equitable treatment. It is essential that wage earners and employers, while the present conditions of industry obtain, should bargain on equal terms through persons freely chosen by each group.

(c) That wage earners shall earn their wages by conscientious industry, that the management shall be efficient and exclude waste in production, and that the consumer shall find in the market price the minimum which will provide equitable treatment for all parties.

(d) That industry shall be so organized that the supply of the material needs of life will neither be interrupted nor exploited for sectional advantage.

(e) That the structure of the community shall be so ordered that no one shall be deprived of his chance to do the best he may with his gifts of mind and character, because of unjust outward circumstances.

(f) That the possession of money shall not be regarded as an end worthy in itself, nor its possessor be held in respect by the community by reason of his riches. The person of true wealth will be he who serves the community with what he has.

(g) That sometimes for co-operation within the nation or among the nations, renunciation of one's own desires shall be called for, and that exclusive privileges and economic advantage for one's self must yield to the larger common welfare, so that suspicions and animosities will be displaced by community of purpose.

The Christian Programme of Change

40. In the effort to achieve these aims alternative methods are open to us; but the Commission is agreed that two considerations must always be kept in

mind—the importance of stimulating individual initiative and the necessity for social co-ordination. Society will ever require the former, which, however, without the latter may result in wasted energy. The Commission does not find itself qualified to answer in detail the fourth question implied in the Council's remit, for the specific task of the Church in the process of reform is to be the light rather than the engineer of the City of God, to point direction and reveal goals rather than to elaborate programmes of successive changes. Yet it ventures to indicate the direction of some recent advances as suggesting possible extension. For example, the demand that all people have access to the means of full life as far as they are capable of it, involves an assured minimum provision against the fear of old age, unemployment, disability and accident, together with protection against compulsion to accept a wage which precludes the means of such a life. The idea of a public utility is also constantly being enriched. Almost every service now rendered as a public utility was originally an enterprise conducted for private gain. And it may be that extensions of this into fresh fields will bring the solution of many problems, provided security can be afforded from the dangers which attend political administration. Steps already taken in the curbing of the use of power and wealth for selfish ends point the direction of needed further progress.

One Spirit and Diverse Operations

Regarding the methods of future development we find in the Church three attitudes of mind. Many, recognizing the trend just referred to as operative in Canada and elsewhere, believe that it will lead, under the pressure of economic facts, to the gradual elimination from the social order of the evils here condemned; others are satisfied that this tendency will not of itself operate adequately unless there be explicit recognition from the start that every trace of competitive production for returns on private capital invested be eliminated. Yet others look to a great extension of voluntary co-operation under State auspices, but with the minimum of State compulsion. These three attitudes with many shades of difference are found widespread in the Church, and in the Commission itself there were representatives of each of these three opinions. We associate ourselves with the Anglican Bishops gathered from all parts of the world at Lambeth, in calling for a new spirit in Industry which will place co-operation for the general good above competition for private advantage. And we further associate ourselves with the demand of the recent Papal Encyclical that wealth, which has been derived from or enhanced by the operation of social growth, shall be distributed for the benefit of all rather than of the privileged few. We call attention to the embodiment of these ideas in recent acts of legislation and administration in Canada and elsewhere.

Report of the Commission on Christianizing the Social Order, *Record of Proceedings of the Sixth General Council of the United Church of Canada, 1934*, pp. 246–7.

The staggering fault of our modern social life confronting this year is unemployment. A recent statement is to the effect that at least 300,000 men at the time of writing are out of work. Of course, among them there are the criminal and the shiftless, but the great body are anxious to work not only for an income but for the work's sake, but are denied the opportunity. The serious aspect of unemployment is its demoralizing effect. The whole fibre of a man's being is soon weakened by an experience of this character. No one seems yet to have arrived at a solution, and a prominent weekly of the United States in an editorial draws attention to the possibility of considering methods of dealing with the situation as likely to result in more disastrous consequences than unemployment itself produces.

It is evident that there is at this time an open door into which the Church may enter. It should take advantage of the crisis to inculcate the Golden Rule, and it should exert itself to the utmost to see at least that the hungry are fed and the naked are clothed.

> Report of the Committee on Temperance and Moral Reform, *Acts and Proceedings of the Fifty-seventh General Assembly of the Presbyterian Church in Canada, 1930*, Appendices, p. 135.

THE VIEWS OF LATER COMMENTATORS

A Critical Voice from Winnipeg

Wesley College in Winnipeg was an active centre of "Social Gospel" thought. The late Principal Riddell comments critically on the involvement of certain Methodists in the general strike and on the strike's effects on his church.

During the strike eight men were arrested on the charge of seditious activity and revolutionary intent. Protracted and ineffective trials followed with no conclusive results. Among those arrested were J. S. Woodsworth, who had some time before figured prominently in the Methodist Church in Winnipeg but had recently resigned from the ministry, and William Ivens, who had lately been given "location" by the Manitoba Conference for his refusal to take the appointment assigned him. Both these men were former students of Wesley College. Through the agency of Mr. Ivens a labour church was formed. For a time it remained a vigorous centre of propaganda for the labour party. The Methodist people, as a whole, stood firmly loyal to the maintenance of law and order in the city. There were some, no doubt, among the Methodists who sympathized with the strikers. Some were loudly hostile to the movement. The Methodists suffered from the strike but the city suffered vastly more. Some observers declare that this agitation with others in the Methodist body had the effect of delaying for a time the consummation of Organic Union in the Negotiating Committee.

The Principal of Wesley College was asked in 1920, by the provincial premier, to be chairman of a committee to consider and report on the demand for the establishment of a minimum wage among women workers. Toward this he was decidedly favourable but not very successful. This request, however, indicated the attitude of the Provincial Government to the leadership of the Methodist Church.

J. H. Riddell, *Methodism in the Middle West* (Toronto, 1946), pp. 359–60.

Personal Evangelism or Social Gospel?

A Baptist historian discusses the impact of post-First World War problems on the churches, and the reaction of his own denomination.

. . . During the course of the First World War a new orientation of attitudes toward religious loyalties and Christian duties became very apparent. By the beginning of the 1920's it had become well established. The complex causes back of this condition cannot be analyzed but some of them may be indicated: the disillusioning effects of a world war; the spiritual unrest that followed the disappointed expectations of inevitable progress; a decline in moral standards; the increasing humanistic trend in religious thinking; the materialistic approach that invaded the field of education; the excessive emphasis on human comforts and the consequent depreciation of the more rugged qualities of self-reliance and thrift. The total effect of these changes on the churches was scarcely less than tragic. Congregations dwindled; a general apathy toward the discharge of religious duties set in; all over the Western world it became more difficult to interest people in church work or membership, and everywhere there was a suspicion of the older methods of carrying on religious work. The latter was particularly evident in the reaction against mass evangelism. The excessive emotionalism so frequently a part of the old-time mass evangelism was unacceptable to those who took pride in a more intellectual approach to religion which was often equally one-sided, and generally devoid of all emotion. The present growing emphasis on personal and visitation evangelism, and the return to a measure of mass evangelism are themselves a reaction against the sterility of the religious life of the two decades following the First World War.

One of the more constructive developments in this period has been the increased emphasis on the application of the Gospel to the solution of economic and social problems. Here, too, the Baptists have followed a trend which has included other denominations over a wide area. Among the Baptists this development came from two main sources: the contact of some of the younger ministers with exponents of the Social Gospel in the American theological schools, and the widely read writings of these same teachers, one of the most important of whom was Dr. Walter Rauschenbusch of Rochester Theological Seminary. These contacts served to sensitize the conscience and stimulate the enquiries of many of the younger religious leaders who were becoming alert to the evils of the economic and social order. Eager minds, well trained, and thoroughly consecrated to the task of advancing the Kingdom of God, were coming to feel there was something radically wrong with an order that would countenance gross inequalities of wealth—so many with "enough and to spare" and others underpaid and underprivileged. As this alertness became sharpened through contact with exponents of the Social Gospel, questions arose whether the strongly individualistic note in the preaching of the past had not missed the mark and left certain elements in society free to flourish at the expense of the weaker and those less able to protect themselves. The flagrant immorality that followed in the wake of the war, and the rising tide of intemperance, also served to direct a considerable body of thought with greater force to the need of a new social consciousness, and of a new sense of responsibility on the part of the churches as to their part in framing legislation that would help create a healthier moral environment. As time went on these views were expressed with greater frequency in both the pulpit and in the press, and soon appeared with new emphasis in the annual reports of the Board of Social Service.

G. E. Levy, *The Baptists of the Maritime Provinces, 1753–1946*
(Saint John, 1946), pp. 298–300.

Economic Dogmatists Trouble the United Church

George Pidgeon, first moderator of the United Church of Canada, had taken a prominent part in the social and evangelistic work of the Presbyterian Church before the Union of 1925. His biographer comments on Pidgeon's reaction to the Depression and contrasts it with the doctrinaire statements that often emanate from church committees.

The depression came as a particular shock to Canadians, who had not quite emerged from the Victorian era and who imagined that their social fabric was immune to sudden or unpredictable changes. Even the church union issue had been fought on a largely nineteenth-century battleground, with the evolutionary idealism of Tennyson and Browning running foul of the clan spirit of an earlier generation of immigrants. In the thirties, however, young theological professors began to enlist in the class struggle, and the old slogans of social reform were turned against the virtuous as well as the wicked rich. For the first time in Canadian history the church had to contend not merely with sin and indifference but with the denial of its primary axioms of faith and morality. Those who valued the evangelical tradition that had shaped the nation's character sought feverishly to repair its foundations.

*   *   *   *   *

. . . One of the weaknesses of United Church practice has been its tendency to give undue prominence to committee reports and to expressions of opinion by church courts. Committees of Evangelism and Social Service tend to be composed largely of people recruited for their special interest in a few causes, and resolutions are too often addressed to no one in particular. Reformers of the thirties would have been wiser if they had paid more attention to the education of the membership of the church, and less to zealous attempts to get resolutions passed. Their success in church courts affected the attitude of the business community to the United Church more than it did that of most United Churchmen to social issues. Thus it had a somewhat fraudulent aspect. Those who regretted the flood of resolutions included some . . . who were in sympathy with most of their aims, although others were far to the right.

Pidgeon undoubtedly dissented from the content of the resolutions, for like most reformers of the evangelical school, he was essentially a conservative in economics. There was nothing in this attitude inconsistent with his earlier enthusiasm for social reform. Conscious of a mission to seek and save the lost, evangelicals have always been eager to improve the lot of the dispossessed, and so have fought vigorously for the removal of economic abuses. On the other hand, their emphasis on the conversion of the individual has led them to distrust all forms of collectivism and, indeed, to be sceptical of all techniques of social reconstruction. Throughout his career Pidgeon maintained that the choice of an economic system is of little importance in comparison with the integrity of the men who run it, and despite his own generosity, and his constant readiness to help people in need, there can be little doubt that moral depravity distressed him more than material poverty. Holding such views, he had little in common with the radicals of the thirties, but there were other and more personal reasons for his opposition to them. . . .

. . . He feared that ideological controversy might weaken the new church irreparably. It endangered the growing together of denominational groups, for many Presbyterians looked upon political involvement as a Methodist specialty. It endangered the finances of the church, for wealthy men were threatening to withdraw support. Worst of all, it endangered the church's spiritual unity.

J. W. Grant, *George Pidgeon* (Toronto, 1962), pp. 118–19, 124–6

"The Day the Lord Hath Made" — Workers' Benefit or Workers' Bane?

The Lord's Day Act was passed in 1906 by the Canadian Parliament as a result of combined pressure from the interdenominational Lord's Day Alliance (established in 1895) and from organized labour. Its purpose was to assure workers of one day's rest in seven, but increased secularism and a reduced work-week have made the Act anachronistic and irksome to many Canadians, not least among the working class who feel its "puritanism" now unfairly restricts their enjoyment of leisure time. The Rev. A. M. C. Waterman, an Australian economic historian, suggests that the Lord's Day Act was even in its inception a piece of conservative religious legislation promoted by the churches rather than a statute for economic improvement.

The unions drew their membership from "Catholics and Protestants, Jews and Gentiles, and adherents of all creeds and even of no creed at all," and were not authorized by their constituencies to "give sanction to divine precepts." But they were perfectly willing to lend their weight to a movement whose aims—whilst profoundly divergent at a fundamental level—could be harnessed for the time to a specific objective of their own.

Two things are clear from this. First, the temporary league between the labour unions and the Lord's Day Alliance was entered upon because each party supposed it could use the power of the other for its own purposes. There was, to be sure, some tradition of alliance between Methodism and the working class movement, but already by 1906 this was largely a memory, and since that time it is safe to assume that the proportion of union members professing "no creed at all" has increased steadily.

Secondly, some members of the Lord's Day Alliance themselves were apparently under the impression that Bill No. 12 was, in essence, a piece of labour legislation. In view of the legal circumstances which gave rise to the bill, not to mention the distinctively "religious" tone given to its passage by Laurier and most others, this attitude is surprising. Still more surprising—in view of all subsequent judicial review—is the occasional revival in our own time of this discredited position.

It is probable, therefore, that temporary and local circumstances in pre-1914 Canada lent more efficacy to the attempts of Christians to influence public policy than might have been expected. Notwithstanding the Preamble to the Canadian Bill of Rights and the latest ruling of the Supreme Court of Canada on the force of its religious clauses, it seems almost certain that the degree of secularity has increased since 1906. It would appear that Christians as a class are unable to achieve more than a marginal impact upon public policy in any country as secular as Canada. . . .

A. M. C. Waterman, "The Lord's Day in a Secular Society", *Canadian Journal of Theology*, XI (2), April 1965, pp. 122-3.

The Modern Church — For the Masses or the Classes?

D. J. M. Heap, an Anglican priest who has worked for several years as an industrial labourer, criticizes the estrangement of the church from the workers and the effects of middle-class dominance over religion. The modern churches are painfully conscious of these problems and are trying by a variety of means to make religion a vital force in all aspects of modern society.

The worker not only lacks the chief form of social power in our country and in our Church, namely money, but he also lacks formal education. Until a century ago most workers could not read and write. The Church was then run by the educated, according as those with money paid the bill. Now the workers have all been to school—but the Church has leaped out of their reach again. We must now have fancy campaigns to raise money, with professional money-getters giving orders to clergy and elected officers alike; the slogan is "Where your treasure is, there will your heart be also," but a mere ten per cent of your treasure is supposed to make God think he has your whole heart. We must have glossy religious education programmes, either rocketting along on a university intellectual level or sharing in the gimmicks of radio, television, spectacular movies, and the Public Relations business. Pensions and building funds are so complicated that no worker can speak about them. The worker is not trained in public speaking or advertising. Even if he can school himself to speak and act in the meeting of the local congregation, he finds out sooner or later that the big decisions are made not there, but downtown. How like the factory.

As for the regular services of prayer, Bible reading, hymns, and teaching, the worker usually stays away. The teaching sets the tone, and that tone discourages him. Generally the Church in her teaching for several generations past has sided with the rich against the poor, with the employers against the workers.

One can, it is true, find statements made by Church leaders years ago upholding the dignity of work and the rights of organized labour. Nevertheless, I have not heard this judgment proclaimed in the weekly teaching of the Church. Still less have I seen it shown in the daily actions of Christian business-men or even Christian ministers.

. . . Where was the gospel? What did the Church say? There was hatred, bitterness, distrust, robbery, and death. Could we appeal to the Church for judgment, for real help? Not likely. The Church may give a handout to a man or his family, especially if he has been seen attending services, but the Church rarely risks the ill-will of the rich and powerful. Accordingly, the Church has nothing to say about our work, that part of our life which chiefly shapes our character and our spirit. The teaching services of our Church either drive the workers away or leave them cold.

* * * * *

For generations the working man has been shut out of full personal responsibility in his daily work, and the Church has consented. For generations the working man has been brought to baptism, marriage, and burial passive, expected only to be there and listen. For generations the working man has been effectively left out of the government of his Church. For generations the working man has watched the Church enjoy the favour and generosity of the owners of wealth and employers of labour, with little knowledge of the life of the working man, let alone care for it. How can he respond? How can he protest? How can he match his actions with his deepest sense of right and wrong? There is still the central act of the Church, depending solely (so he is taught) on one's will and mind and emotions. He can boycott it. Boycott, strike, withholding of one's presence and participation, is the characteristic means of working-class action. It seems that the workers are boycotting the worship services of the Church.

> D. J. M. Heap, "The Church and the Workers", *Canadian Journal of Theology*, X (2), April 1964, pp. 135–7.

Further Reading

Stewart Crysdale's *The Industrial Struggle and the Protestant Ethic in Canada* (Toronto, Ryerson Press, 1961)* traces the awakening of the social conscience in the Protestant churches as a result of the problems of industrialization. No comparable study of the reaction of the Roman Catholic Church has appeared. On the growth of the Social Gospel movement in Canada see Kenneth McNaught, *A Prophet in Politics* (Toronto, 1963)*, a biography of J. S. Woodsworth, *The New Christianity* (Toronto, 1920) by Salem Bland, the most articulate and influential spokesman for the movement; and *Towards the Christian Revolution* (Chicago, 1936) by R. B. Y. Scott and Gregory Vlastos. Pierre Berton's popular and controversial *The Comfortable Pew* (Toronto, McClelland & Stewart, 1965)* underlines the alienation of the people from the churches. The same theme is repeated in *Why the Sea is Boiling Hot* (Toronto, Ryerson Press, 1965)* by a group of Canadian journalists. Stewart Crysdale's *The Changing Church in Canada* (Toronto, Ryerson Press, 1965)* is a statistically documented study of the attitudes of United Church members toward current social and religious questions.

Problem 19

Middle Power Status — Illusion or Reality?

Since 1939 Canada has been playing a more active role in world affairs. Gone, apparently, is the preoccupation with "status" which marked the interwar period. During the 1950's, while Canadians were riding the crest of an economic boom at home, their nation achieved the high point of its prestige in international affairs. The confidence of the 1950's was succeeded by doubts and self-questioning in the 1960's.

Was there a significant change in the goals of Canadian foreign policy from the interwar to the postwar eras, or was there merely a shift in means reflecting shifts in the world power balance? Was the prominent Canadian role in the 1950's a result of a temporary dislocation of normal power relationships? Can a country the size and location of Canada initiate a foreign policy, or can it merely react to the policies of the superpowers? These are some of the questions that can be raised by the following readings.

Wartime Adumbrations of Postwar Policy

During the Second World War Canada assumed responsibilities which had no precedents in earlier struggles. From the fall of France to the German invasion of Russia, Canada was Britain's principal ally. Until some time after the entry of the United States, Canada remained the principal supplier of munitions to her allies. Men of other nationalities served under Canadian generals in Europe and under Canadian admirals in the North Atlantic. Canadian scientists participated in many of the "top secret" projects, including the development of the atom bomb.

Even while the war continued, Canadian leaders were already concerned about the role that Canada would play in the postwar world.

The Role of the Middle Power

In a speech delivered to the House of Commons on 9 July 1943, Prime Minister King outlined what the Montreal *Gazette* of the following morning described as "a new and wholly Canadian concept" for the organization of the postwar international institutions. He outlined the theory that a nation's representation on international bodies should reflect its ability to function effectively to further the objectives of that body. The acceptance of this doctrine (which would appear to reverse the prewar Canadian interest in status divorced from responsibility) would provide a special place for "middle powers" such as Canada.

In the view of the government effective representation on these bodies should be neither restricted to the largest states nor necessarily extended to all states. Representation should be determined on a functional basis which will admit to full membership those countries large or small which have the greatest contribution to make to the particular object in question. In the world there are over sixty sovereign states. If they all have nominally an equal vote in international decisions, no effective decisions are likely to be taken. Some compromise must be found between the theoretical equality of states, and the practical necessity of limiting representation on international bodies to a workable number. That compromise can be discovered, especially in economic matters, by the adoption of a functional principle of representation. That principle is likely in turn to find many new expressions in the gigantic task of liberation, restoration and reconstruction.

Canada, Parliament, *Debates of the House of Commons*, 1943 (Ottawa), p. 4558.

King Versus A Single Commonwealth Voice

While Canadian leaders favoured their country's playing a larger role in the postwar international scene, some Britons, concerned over their nation's diminished power base, looked, as did the imperial federationists of an earlier generation, to a more unified Commonwealth for compensation. On 24 January 1944, Lord Halifax, the British Ambassador to the United States, delivered a speech at Toronto, in which he said:

Today we begin to look beyond the war to the re-ordering of the world which must follow. We see three great powers, the United States, Russia and China, great in numbers, areas and natural resources. . . . If, in the future, Britain is to play her part without assuming burdens greater than she can support, she must have with her in peace the same strength that has sustained her in this war. Not Great Britain only, but the British Commonwealth and Empire must be the fourth power in that group upon which, under Providence, the peace of the world will henceforth depend.

J. W. Pickersgill, *The Mackenzie King Record*, Vol. 1, 1939–1944
(Toronto, 1960), pp. 636–7.

The following passage from the Hon. J. W. Pickersgill's published version of Mackenzie King's diaries provides an insight into the mind of the Canadian leader (who had been a prime architect of the decentralized Commonwealth) reacting to Halifax's proposal. His suspicion of "English Tories", his conviction of his own role of defender of the true interests of the Empire, and his appreciation of the immediate political implications are all noteworthy.

The next morning (January 25), when he "read something of what Lord Halifax had said at Toronto last night," Mackenzie King "was simply dumbfounded. It seemed such a complete bolt out of the blue, like a conspiracy on the part of Imperialists to win their own victory in the middle of the war. I could not but feel that Halifax's work was all part of a plan which had been worked out with Churchill to take advantage of the war to try and bring about this development of centralization, of makings of policies in London, etc. As Englishmen, of course, they seek to recover for Britain and the United Kingdom and the Empire the prestige which they are losing as a nation. In a moment, I saw that again it has fallen to my lot to have to make the most difficult of all the fights. This perpetual struggle to save the Empire despite all that Tories' policies will do—by fighting the Tories, save the British Empire from its dismemberment through their own policies. There is nothing truer than that, from the days of Lord North to the present, English Tories have learned nothing." He felt that Halifax's speech "marks the beginning of the real political campaign of this year. I should not complain about what Halifax has done, for he has handed me . . . an issue which ensures or should ensure the return of the Liberal party just as completely as Lord Byng, when he refused to grant a dissolution. I am perfectly sure that Canada will not tolerate any centralized Imperialism on foreign Policy." . . . He later told the Cabinet "I had never been more surprised. That it was what I had said many times would happen as soon as the war was over. I had not thought it would happen while it was on. I found all Members of Government thoroughly incensed. . . . I did not discuss the matter at length but said I would speak in Parliament on Monday. . . . There was mention that I would have to speak as Coldwell* had taken a very

---

* M. J. Coldwell, then leader of the C.C.F.

strong stand [in the press], and it would not do to let him steal our whole position."

Ibid., p. 637.

Canada and the Postwar Commonwealth

The Testimony of Nehru

It is highly unlikely that the centralized Commonwealth which Lord Halifax advocated could have survived the decolonization of the postwar era. Mackenzie King's self-evaluation of his role as preserver of the Commonwealth was confirmed in part later by Prime Minister Jawaharlal Nehru of India. Speaking at a banquet given in Delhi on 19 November 1958 in honour of the visiting Prime Minister of Canada, John Diefenbaker, Nehru referred to the encouragement King (as the grandson of a rebel, now first minister to the monarch) had given him during the freedom struggle.* He then expanded on the Canadian role in making a Commonwealth India could live in, singling out, with apparent disregard of his guest's political affiliations, two other Liberals for special commendation.

. . . And so a time came when we joined that family of nations of which Canada was one of the pre-eminent ones and in which indeed had played a very important part in that dynamic evolution which is characteristic of the Commonwealth. It was Canada really which led the way to independent nationhood within that family of nations.

So, when we attained independence, we gladly agreed to continue in that family, and while I do not wish naturally to differentiate, nevertheless I think I can say that we found it easiest of all to get on with the representatives of Canada, chiefly because they were receptive and they went out of their way to be friendly. . . . So, a little later another change came over the Commonwealth when we took a lead in another direction and became a Republic. That was a novel position which the Commonwealth had not faced till then.

Again, it may not be perhaps improper for me to say something that might be considered secret. It was the Canadian representative at the Prime Ministers' Conference in London [L. B. Pearson] who helped us greatly in finding a way out in this new position because we were anxious, in spite of being a Republic, to continue in that close relationship, and the Canadian Prime Minister of the

---

* King had communicated with Nehru in 1942 through the Chinese Government. Pickersgill, *op. cit.*, p. 408.

day [L. S. St. Laurent] also was anxious that we should continue, indeed others were too; but he did play perhaps a more important part in those talks than some others. Then again, whenever we have met, whether in the Prime Ministers' Conference or in the United Nations or elsewhere, because we have had many common dealings with each other, we have found this bond of friendship uniting us and understanding, even though we did not always agree.*

Suez, 1956

The Anglo-French invasion of Suez in October 1956 triggered crises in the Commonwealth and in the United Nations, two institutions through which Canadians hoped the world would resolve its differences by discussion and orderly procedures of negotiations and arbitration.

The Canadian role was critical and constructive. To facilitate the disengagement of the combatants, a United Nations Emergency Force was organized largely on Canadian initiative, equipped largely with Canadian material, and at first commanded by a Canadian.

It should be noted that the first suggestion by the Canadian delegate at the U.N. of the creation of such a force came in the early morning hours of 2 November, in an explanation of an abstention from voting. The vote on an American-sponsored resolution urging a cease-fire was called before the Canadians had an opportunity to speak. After the resolution was carried, L. B. Pearson pointed out:

This resolution does provide for a cease-fire, and I admit that that is of first importance and urgency. But, alongside a cease-fire and a withdrawal of troops, it does not provide for any steps to be taken by the United Nations for a peace settlement, without which a cease-fire will be only of temporary value at best. Surely, we should have used this opportunity to link a cease-fire to the absolute necessity of a political settlement in Palestine and for the Suez. . . .

*   *   *   *   *

I believe that there is another omission from this resolution to which attention has also already been directed. The armed forces of Israel and Egypt are to withdraw, or, if you like, to return to the armistice lines, where presumably, if this is done, they will once again face each other in fear and hatred. What then? What then, six months from now? Are we to go through all this again? . . .

---

* Text supplied by Information Service of India.

I therefore would have liked to see a provision in this resolution—and this has been mentioned by previous speakers—authorizing the Secretary-General to begin to make arrangements with member governments for a United Nations force large enough to keep these borders at peace while a political settlement is being worked out. I regret exceedingly that time has not been given to follow up this idea, which was mentioned also by the representative of the United Kingdom in his first speech . . . My own Government would be glad to recommend Canadian participation in such a United Nations force, a truly international peace and police force.

> Abridged from text quoted in J. Eayrs, *The Commonwealth and Suez: A Documentary Survey* (Toronto, 1964), pp. 319–20.

The Pearson Stand Criticized

Although L. B. Pearson was to receive the Nobel Peace Prize for his role in resolving the Suez crisis, his action and those of the government were criticized in Canada by those who interpreted the events not as a constructive measure but as an abandonment of kith and kin. Editorials in the Toronto *Globe and Mail* on 3 November (the day following the debate in the U.N.) and on 29 November reflect this attitude.

The Canadian Government added nothing to its prestige—or to Canada's—by its conduct at the week's emergency meeting of the United Nations General Assembly. External Affairs Minister Pearson did not actually cast Canada's vote against the Anglo-French effort to restore peace in the Middle East, but his abstention from voting had the same effect—assisting, in a passive way, the adoption of a United States resolution urging the British and French to withdraw.

After the vote had been called, with Canada and five other nations abstaining, Mr. Pearson got up and explained. The Canadian delegation, he said, found the U.S. sponsored resolution "inadequate"; it called for all the nations involved in the Middle East fighting to lay down their arms—but offered nothing beyond that, no means of ensuring the arms would remain laid down.

* * * * *

Mr. Pearson wants no more of this nonsense; hence his proposal for a Middle East police force that would maintain order while a permanent settlement was being worked out between Israel and her neighbours. But why a UN police force? No such body exists, or has any prospect of coming into existence. It would have been more practical to suggest a force drawn from the North Atlantic Treaty Organization—which at least has men and arms.

And why did the External Affairs Minister delay his criticism of the U.S. resolution until it had gone to a vote and been adopted; . . . Had he spoken before the resolution was voted upon, it could have been amended as he suggested . . .

It is not as if the idea of a Middle East police force hit Mr. Pearson suddenly, while the votes were being taken. He proposed it himself—had he forgotten?—in a House of Commons speech away back last February: saying then, as he said at the UN this week, that Canada would be willing to contribute to such a force. And this newspaper has been pressing the need of a Middle East force for the last five years. . . .

"Mr. Pearson Abstains", *Globe and Mail*, 3 November 1956, p. 5.

Almost four weeks later, when the matter was being debated in Parliament, the same newspaper's lead editorial observed:

Some of the extreme statements coming from some of the Opposition members in the Canadian Parliament—and the Government's angry reaction thereto—are giving the impression of a cleavage on foreign policy far greater than needs to exist. . . . Thus, the Government is stressing its deep attachment to the United Nations—all it has done was out of loyalty to the UN—and milking its proposal of a Middle East police force for all that proposal is worth.

For much more, in fact, than it is worth. The suggestion of a UN force was simply an expedient plucked out of thin air by a Government anxious to rescue itself from a position it should never have been in to start with. Ottawa has had no real confidence in the UN as an instrument of collective security; that is why, for almost ten years, the whole core of its stated foreign policy has been the North Atlantic Treaty Organization. By joining (indeed, it claims to have invented) NATO, the Canadian Government placed on record its lack of faith in the UN.

"Our Only Real Hope", *Globe and Mail*, 29 November 1956, p. 5.

NATO: Postwar Counterbalance to the United States?

References were made in the preceding editorials to Canada's stress on the North Atlantic Treaty Organization as the basis of its defence system. Other references appear in the commentaries which follow.* A feature of the formation of the alliance which is frequently commented upon was the initiative taken by Louis St.

---

* See below, pp. 336, 339, 340.

Laurent, a son of traditionally isolationist Quebec, who pressed for an agreement which involved maintaining Canadian military forces abroad. Prime Minister St. Laurent explained his position, stressing the common "North Atlantic" community, of which Canada was a part, in a speech to the House of Commons on 28 March 1949, from which the following extracts are taken. Later commentators, quoted below, note that the Canadian stress on the non-military aspects of NATO is almost unique. Was this stress a device to render the alliance more acceptable to Canadians by presenting it as a means of preserving and defending the homelands of their Western European heritage? Or was it a device to counter the cultural as well as economic and military attractions of the United States?

Well, the fear of subversive communism allied to Soviet might is in fact the mainspring of the development leading up to this North Atlantic security pact. Hon. members know what those developments were. On January 22, 1948, Mr. Bevin* declared that Soviet hostility to the European recovery program and Soviet obstructionism over the German settlement had convinced the United Kingdom government that the time had come to go ahead with plans for closer political and economic unity of willing western European states. Hastened in their negotiations by the communist seizure of power in Czechoslovakia in February and Soviet pressure for a treaty with Finland, the United Kingdom, France, and the Benelux countries signed the treaty of Brussels on March 17, 1948.

Under this treaty those signatory governments undertook that if any one of them should be the object of armed attack in Europe, the others would, in accordance with provisions in article 51 of the charter of the United Nations, afford the party so attacked all military and other aid and assistance in their power.

On the very day that this treaty was signed, hon. members will recall the impressive broadcast made by the President of the United States at noon, and will remember that the Prime Minister [then W. L. Mackenzie King] came into this house and declared, to the accompaniment of plaudits from all quarters in the house, that this treaty was a partial realization of the ideal of collective security by an arrangement under the charter of the United Nations, . . .

The President, in reporting to congress on the critical nature of the situation in Europe, had given this treaty his full support, and indicated that he was confident that the United States would extend to the free nations the help which the situation required.

* * * * *

* Ernest Bevin, British Foreign Secretary.

. . . The treaty, if signed, will bring together in alliance against war the free nations of the North Atlantic community which share a common heritage, a common civilization, a common belief in the purposes and principles of the charter of the United Nations and a common desire to live in peace with all peoples and all governments. . . .

This treaty is to be far more than an old-fashioned military alliance. It is based on the common belief of the north Atlantic nations in the values and virtues of our Christian civilization. It is based on our common determination to strengthen our free institutions and to promote conditions of stability and well-being. It is based on the belief that we have in our collective manpower, in our collective natural resources, in our collective industrial potential and industrial know-how, that which would make us a very formidable enemy for any possible aggressor to attack.

* * * * *

This is, of course, a serious step for this young nation, but I think it is a step that will implement the desire of all the Canadian people that civilized Christian nations should at some time abandon trial by might for the rule of law.

Canada, Parliament, *Debates* . . . , 1949, pp. 2063–4.

NORAD: Is the U.S. the Real Defender of Canada?

On 1 August 1957 the formation of the North American Air Defence Command (NORAD) was publicly announced, taking effect immediately. The command was established by executive agreement between the Canadian and American governments, with the air defence of the two countries placed under a single command structure in which the position of deputy commander-in-chief was reserved for a Canadian officer.

Although, as an executive agreement, its substance was not subject to Parliamentary approval, the question of NORAD was hotly debated in the Canadian Parliament.

The references to NATO made by Prime Minister John Diefenbaker in presenting the case for NORAD may be compared to the stress on NATO's compatibility with the purposes of the U.N., and to the Canadian stress on the non-military aspects of NATO. NORAD was a bilateral Canadian-American agreement.

Mr. Diefenbaker: As the house is aware, the machinery of defence cooperation between Canada and the United States had its origin in what is known as the Ogdensburg declaration of August, 1940, by the president of the United States and the then prime minister of Canada, Mr. Mackenzie King, foreshadowing the development of the closest defence collaboration between the United States and Canada. . . .

* * * * *

When Canada and the United States signed the North Atlantic treaty, the arrangements and procedures for defence collaboration were continued under the Canada-United States regional planning group as one of the regional groupings of NATO.

* * * * *

Collaboration in air defence was undertaken soon after the close of the last war, and a joint effort was made to develop a comprehensive air defence system for the common defence of North America. . . . In order to work out these intricate air defence problems of an operational and scientific nature, a joint Canadian-United States military study group consisting of service officers and scientists was set up.

One result of studies conducted by this group was a recommendation made to the chiefs of staff of both countries in December, 1956, for the establishment of a joint headquarters to provide for the operational control of the air defence of Canada and the United States. These recommendations of the joint study group were approved by the chiefs of staff of both countries and the United States Secretary of Defence approved these measures early in April.

This bilateral arrangement within the Canada-United States regional planning group of NATO is a further step in achieving the agreed NATO objectives for the Canada-United States regional planning group, . . .

* * * * *

This arrangement within the Canada-United States regional planning group was reported by both countries to the NATO council before it was made public.

It is realized that this comprehensive air defence system is a defence against the manned bomber, and it was recognized some time ago that steps should be taken to provide for defence against the further threat of the intercontinental ballistic missile. As early as July, 1956, negotiations were commenced for joint collaboration in the study of methods and procedures for dealing with defence against the ICBM. . . .

* * * * *

Mr. PEARSON: Interesting as his statement has been, Mr. Speaker, it certainly has not answered a great many of the questions in our minds concerning particularly the North American command, or NORAD, as it is called, and the implications of the action that has been taken by the government in regard to continental defence under that command. I refer to military implications and indeed political implications.

... Mr. Speaker, we must have all the available information and particularly the information with regard to the alteration, if there is any alteration, in the responsibility of the Canadian government for the actions of Canadian troops, and also the relationship of this command to NATO.

I notice that reference has been made to that relationship but not, if I may say so, in a form which gives me any clear indication that this command has any direct relationship to NATO whatever, or not in the sense that that relationship was established after debate and discussion in this house, as was done in so far as sending Canadian troops to Europe was concerned. The information we have received up to the present time has been inadequate, so far as I am concerned. After more complete information has been received I hope all the doubts we have will be removed, and that we on this side of the house will be able to support any move for continental defence in the interests of both countries and therefore in the interests of peace.

Canada, Parliament, *Debates* . . . , 1957–8, pp. 1059–61.

Is Neutralism a Solution?

By the end of 1950's the question was being raised whether Canada should abandon her alliances and serve the cause of peace as a neutral nation. A Canadian-born American citizen, James M. Minifie, presented this view in *Peacemaker or Powder-Monkey*, a book which became a best seller in Canada in 1960 and 1961. The following excerpts are from its concluding chapter.

This book is written in the belief that Canada can contribute more to the defence of democracy, the West, the North American continent and to its own defence as a neutral than as a member of a lop-sided alliance in NORAD, or of the straggling military consortium into which NATO has been debased. I believe that Canada can speak to the world in the language of freedom and peace to inspire mankind, much as the United States did before the cares of paramountcy, the need to placate dictators, the burden of arming and subsidizing half the world, and the objective and subjective handicaps of wealth muffled the accents of Jefferson, Lincoln and Wilson.

*   *   *   *   *

In the world today Canada, although not a major power, may play a part if it chooses as inspiring and decisive as that of the United States in earlier times. But not as the client of a power committed to the struggle for paramountcy. An impregnable neutralism must be its warranty of independence.

James M. Minifie, *Peacemaker or Powder-Monkey* (Toronto, 1960) pp. 172–3, 174.

THE VIEWS OF LATER COMMENTATORS

Conflicting Purposes Reflected in Canadian Views of NATO

The following excerpts are from an address prepared by Professor James Eayrs of the University of Toronto for presentation to Canadian and American air force staff officers in February 1961. He stresses the Canadian concern with the cultivation of associations beyond North America to counterbalance the preponderance of United States power.

Already a fairly substantial mythology has grown up around Canadian external policy; and one of the most widely accepted myths runs something like this: During the years between the two World Wars, Canadians and their governments were isolationist, distrustful of foreigners, more distrustful still of foreign commitments, jealous of sovereignty, hostile to the League of Nations, dead set against collective security; they thus contributed, in a small North American way, to the outbreak of conflict in 1939. But with the war—so runs the myth—everything changed. If Canada went into World War II as a myopic, withdrawn nation of the Americas, she is said to have emerged from the war as a nation of the world, conscious of the need for post-war order, ready to play her part in preserving peace through power. And the event cited as conclusive evidence of this noble metamorphosis is Canada's readiness, many months before the United States, to enter into a peacetime security alliance with the nations of Western Europe, and Canada's eagerness to become a founding member of the North Atlantic Treaty Organization.

The first part of this fantasy is fairly well matched by the facts. Where history is left far behind is in the second part, in the representation of the Second World War as a great watershed of Canadian diplomacy, dividing old out-dated attitudes from new progressive attitudes. For traditions do not that easily dissolve; the national mood is not that mercurial; the national memory not that short. There has in fact been no great revolution in Canadian foreign policy.... The Canadian concern with collective security in the North Atlantic area, manifest as early as 1947, so far from marking a revolution in our external affairs, is more properly explained as the result of the persistence of those Canadian attitudes shaping national policy during the "low dishonest decade" of pre-war years.

In his diary for April 9, 1948, the then American Secretary of Defense, James Forrestal, noted with evident perplexity the "curious fact ... that Canada is equally as strong as Britain for the formation of the alliance". The alliance in question was the proposed but as yet unnegotiated treaty between the United States and the five nations of Western Europe ... But no one closely familiar with the recent Canadian past would have remained perplexed for long by the fact that sentiment was stronger in Ottawa than in Washington for participation in a trans-Atlantic regional security arrangement. For such an arrangement offered at a stroke a ready-made solution for two of the most fundamental problems of Canadian external policy, preserving a measure of influence *vis-à-vis* the United Kingdom and the United States, and avoiding an agonizing choice between the policies of each.

The time-honoured solution to the first had been to play off one against the other. By 1945 this device would no longer work. Britain had ceased to be a Great Power; as a makeweight it was insufficient. But in association with the nations of Western Europe, the old balance might be restored in such a way as to save Canada from too close an association with the United States. Here was a main motive of Canadian interest in the project of the Atlantic Alliance; and, once the Alliance was formed, it may be seen at work in Canadian efforts to associate its Western European members in projects of continental defence, inviting Norwegians and Danes to take part in the operation of the northern radar systems (a proposal which, frowned upon by the Canadian military, came to nothing), or making NORAD, more obviously than it appeared to be, a NATO Command.

The solution to the second problem was the reverse of the first, for instead of playing off one against the other, it occasionally became essential for Canadian policy to bring the United Kingdom and the United States together. . . .

But while membership in the Atlantic Alliance admirably satisfied these traditional imperatives of Canadian foreign policy, it seemed to do so at the expense of another, no less deeply rooted, national tradition. This is the Canadian hostility to military approaches to international problems. . . . To the extent, therefore, that NATO was conceived as primarily a military instrument, applying the traditional military prescriptions to the ailments of post-war Europe, it was sure to be unattractive to the public. . . . On March 17, 1948, the Prime Minister declared (perhaps for the first but certainly not for the last time) that NATO must become more than a "mere military alliance". A year later Mr. Pearson, in his first speech in the House of Commons, developed the Canadian position in more detail:

> In the past, alliances and leagues have been formed to meet emergencies and have been dissolved as the emergencies vanished. It must not be so this time. Our Atlantic union must have a deeper meaning and deeper roots. It must create conditions for a kind of co-operation which goes beyond the immediate emergency. Threats to peace may bring our Atlantic Pact into existence. Its contribution to welfare and progress may determine how long it is to survive.

This view, writes a Canadian authority, "was disliked by the United Kingdom, regarded as unimportant by the American Secretary of State, and opposed as likely to interfere with the Marshall Plan". But the Canadian Government stuck with it; and was rewarded for its persistence by the inclusion in the Treaty of Article II, and by kindly references thereafter to Article II as "the Canadian article".

After admission as a founding member of NATO, Canada discovered an additional reason for stressing the need to extend NATO activities into non-military fields. This arose from what was sometimes and perhaps too optimistically described as "the Ottawa-New Delhi axis". 1949 had been a busy year for Canadian diplomatists. Not only had they set the seal on Canada's entry into the Atlantic Alliance, they had helped to make possible the retention of the Republic of India within a Commonwealth hitherto distinguished by the universality of the monarchical principle. A special relationship was henceforth to exist between the senior Member of the old "White Dominions" and the most important Member of what was shortly to become a predominantly Afro-Asian Commonwealth, a relationship no less valuable for the occasional exaggeration of its significance by Canadian statesmen and publicists. And here emerged a new dilemma. Canada had made NATO the cornerstone of its foreign policy. But NATO, in the eyes of its newly-found confidant in Asia, was a provocative instrument of Western imperialism. Was Canada, attracted to the Atlantic commitment by the prospect of being able to avoid having to choose between the United Kingdom and the United States, now to have to choose between NATO and New Delhi? . . . Only to the extent that NATO developed in such a way as to justify Jawaharlal Nehru's critique, clapping military blinders upon member governments, obscuring what the Indians believed to be the basic political and economic determinants of international conflict. And so the Canadian emphasis on the importance of NATO non-military activity received fresh impetus from this unexpected quarter.

> J. Eayrs, *Northern Approaches: Canada and the Search for Peace*
> (Toronto, 1961), pp. 57–61.

Concern with Achievement Rather than Credit Brings Success

Peyton Lyon had served with the Department of External Affairs before he reentered academic life as a political scientist at the University of Western Ontario. Although he wrote *The Policy Question* partly to influence the forthcoming election in 1963, his comments reflect the opinions of an informed observer proud of the achievements of the Canadian professional diplomatic corps. In an earlier passage in the book he referred to the neutralist arguments of James M. Minifie,* "Would we best promote the national interest—and

---

* See above, p. 336.

that of the world—by adopting the neutralist approach? The answer is a regretful but emphatic no."*

For most of the postwar period, Canada's economic and political health were the envy of the world. At the same time Canada came to be rated as one of the most effective and useful members of the international community. These two features of our reputation were related. Our strength appeared impressive very largely because most of the traditional powers were still exhausted by the ravages of war. . . . Dr. R. J. Sutherland, by taking a combination of gross national product and technological competence, calculates that Canada for a brief period after 1945 was "very probably, the fourth most powerful nation in the world."

Foreign observers believed that good management had contributed greatly to Canada's well-being. This belief, coupled with an awareness of our ability to extend much needed economic and military support, created a widespread disposition to heed Canadian views on international problems. . . .

Canadian ministers and diplomats were active in NATO and behind the scenes in Washington—much more so than the public realized. As promoters of military caution and diplomatic flexibility, they raised many points that ran counter to the thinking of important allies. The Canadians were particularly insistent that the West neglect no opportunity to negotiate sensible agreements with the Soviet Union, and they tried to ensure that the attitude of the West was so clearly defensive that it could not alarm outside countries. . . .

The degree to which Canadian diplomacy in the Pearson era was concerned with results rather than publicity has been noted by Max Freedman, the Canadian who represents the *Manchester Guardian* in Washington; according to him: "If there is such a thing as the Canadian tradition in diplomacy, it consists in not seeking national recognition for the ideas we have put into the common pool." As an example of this tradition, I recall a suggestion several members of the Department of External Affairs wished to have presented by the Canadian delegation in NATO; it was deleted from the telegram of instructions on the grounds that it was too good an idea for us to put forward as our own until we had tried to persuade the Americans that it was their idea.

Canada did not acquire influence because of her power; rather she achieved influence—and respect—very largely because we acted as if we were indifferent to prestige and power. In time, the policy-makers in other countries came to recognize the disinterested services of the Canadians and charged us with an increasing number of delicate assignments, such as the reappraisal of the NATO alliance, and membership on most of the United Nations peace-supervisory teams.

---

* Peyton V. Lyon, *The Policy Question: A Critical Appraisal of Canada's Role in World Affairs*. (Toronto, 1963), p. 58.

Without calling in question our basic commitment to the western alliance, our spokesmen in the United Nations earned for Canada the reputation of being a reasonable nation interested in the extension of areas of agreement and the lowering of international tension. We generally abstained from the exchange of insults that has characterized the Cold War and, by the quiet, persuasive pitch of our pronouncements, invited the representatives of all other powers to approach us in the expectation of a rational, constructive discussion of even the most inflammatory issues. Many nations wished to consult with us about proposed initiatives, and our support was prized. The Canadians acquired a reputation for having helpful ideas; this was probably owing less to the originality of our representatives than to their close contacts with a considerable variety of other delegations; it was also helped by the fact that we were sometimes asked, because of our good reputation, to take the lead in presenting joint resolutions. . . . Through their acceptability, tact, skill, and knowledge the Canadians came to perform a role in the United Nations similar to that of floor leader in the American Congress; the ill-coordinated nature of the representation in the General Assembly made this function particularly useful.

A high point in Canadian diplomacy occurred in 1956 when Lester Pearson achieved worldwide publicity, and later the Nobel Peace Prize, for his contribution to the containment of the Suez crisis. This crisis was especially painful for Canadians because it found our two closest associates, Britain and the United States, bitterly at odds. The entire Atlantic alliance was in peril, and the Russians appeared only too eager to fish in troubled waters. The proposal of an emergency force, which the Canadians introduced, was not particularly original. The significance of our role was rather the unique trust placed in us by the parties to the dispute—the British, Americans, French, Egyptians, Israelis, and also the Secretary General of the United Nations. The diplomatic credit which enabled us to serve at this crucial juncture had been accumulated through years of self-effacing, but active diplomacy.

Up until the Suez crisis, and its attendant publicity, Canadians had been unduly modest about what their country might achieve in world affairs. Our diplomats were not made to feel they were under great popular pressure to produce visible results. Moreover, according to one Gallup poll, most Canadians were displeased initially with the prominent role played by their representatives during the Suez crisis. . . .

* * * * *

Few Canadians now [1963] need to be told that their country has slipped in diplomatic effectiveness. . . . From an inflated belief in Canada's capacity to lead the nations along paths of sanity, we are swinging to the pessimistic conclusion that we shall have our hands more than full coping with domestic difficulties and the consequences of the new trading patterns other nations are establishing. In 1962 our docile acceptance of cuts in foreign aid and defence-spending indicated a disposition to abandon our international responsibilities.

This increasing defeatism is as little warranted as the earlier conceit; it is difficult to say which attitude is the more harmful to the role we should be playing in world affairs. . . . It would be helpful if we could learn that the limitations on our freedom of choice, which we find so frustrating, are also far from unique. . . .

*   *   *   *   *

Part of our difficulty is that Canada's closest associates are great or near-great powers; we aggravate our complexes when we judge ourselves by standards appropriate to them rather than to ourselves. . . . Nor do we notice as a rule that even the superpowers are chafing at the increasing restraints on their freedom. The Americans, for example, find it hard to understand why, even in areas where they are carrying the main burden of defence and economic development, they should often be obliged to heed the views of their allies. . . .

> Peyton V. Lyon, *The Policy Question: A Critical Appraisal of Canada's Role in World Affairs* (Toronto, 1963), pp. 86, 87, 88–90, 126, 127.

Further Reading

A book which is almost essential reading for anyone wishing to understand the processes, agents, and limitations of the formulation of Canadian foreign policy is James Eayrs, *The Art of the Possible: Government and Foreign Policy in Canada* (Toronto, University of Toronto Press, 1961). The biennial surveys of *Canada in World Affairs*, each by a different author, which are issued under the auspices of the Canadian Institute of International Affairs, are a useful introduction to the study of Canadian external relations. Livingstone T. Merchant, former American Ambassador to Canada, has edited *Neighbours Taken for Granted: Canada and the United States* (New York, Frederick A. Praeger, 1966), a collection of essays generally critical of Canadian pretensions to an independent role in world affairs. That Canadians still aspire to such a role is illustrated in Andrew Brewin, *Stand on Guard: The Search for a Canadian Defence Policy* (Toronto, McClelland & Stewart, 1965).

The book review pages of the *International Journal*, a quarterly published by the Canadian Institute of International Affairs, provide a guide to the growing stream of books on this general topic.

Problem 20

The Quiet Revolution — What Is Going On
in Quebec?

What do the French Canadians want? People across Canada are asking this question in voices that are angry, bewildered, or simply impatient. The *Front de Libération Québecois* has engaged in terroristic activities and urged the French Canadians to break "the shackles of colonialism". Marcel Chaput, holder of a McGill University Ph.D., has denounced the absurdity of French Canada's position and demanded independence in the name of dignity. Pierre-Elliot Trudeau has invited his fellow French Canadians to "throw down the totem poles and to violate the taboos", not in the name of nationalism (an ideology he abhors) but in the name of human reason and intelligence. Why this sudden great upheaval in Quebec?

Its basic cause has been the emergence in recent years of a new French-Canadian society that is entirely the product of the industrial forces, technological advances, and intellectual currents of the twentieth century. In structure and outlook, this new French Canada is essentially the same as the English-speaking societies of North America. It has its business class, its intellectuals, and its proletariat, and its aspirations are substantially those held by other North Americans "from Texas to Toronto".* Unlike, however, those societies whose structures and aspirations it shares, this new French Canada feels thwarted and frustrated. It considers that it is being denied its share of the good life.

Why do these French Canadians feel this way? Is it because the federal government has the powers and the revenues which the

---

* See the reading on p. 356.

government of Quebec requires to build a better society for them? If this is the case, Confederation is the principal villain, and the British North America Act would have to be substantially altered or even replaced to sweep away their grievances. Or is it because this new generation is living in a province whose way of life was shaped in an earlier age (the age studied in Problem 14) when the Church, the farm, and the classical college were the dominant institutions? If this is the case, what is taking place today is a French-Canadian family quarrel, a conflict between the generation of the college-bred technocrat and that of the village notable.

Today the Quiet Revolution is not yet a completed process. The provincial elections of 1966 have shown that the *Québecois* are not united in their will to change the face of their province. While some wish to move swiftly forward with their tradition-breaking reforms, others want to slow down the tempo of change, and yet a third segment of the population, that of the remote countryside, regards the Quiet Revolution with distrust and probably looks back wistfully to the days of Maurice Duplessis. However, one cannot help but wonder what would happen if the forces of change emerged victorious. Would French Canada then continue to exist as a distinct entity or would it eventually disappear as Jules-Paul Tardivel feared it would if it ever adopted the values of English-speaking North America?

Confederation and French Canada in 1917

The following is an excerpt from an article written by Lionel Groulx in the nationalist periodical *Action française* on the occasion of the fiftieth anniversary of Confederation. According to Groulx, great hopes had accompanied the birth of Confederation in 1867, but by 1917 it had become a regime of violated rights and broken promises.

Alas! What would the Fathers of Confederation say if they reappeared in our midst? Their descendants have taken less than fifty years to sabotage their great achievement. This work of destruction is now almost complete and our legacy to history will be one of the most striking examples of the dismal bankruptcies that often await federal unions. Verily, our politicians have spared nothing to make this proof conclusive. To continue the work begun outstanding men were required as leaders of our country. The successors of the Fathers should have reminded themselves of the fragility of these artificial constitutions drawn up in a few days. From history, Canada's public men could have learned of the congenital weakness of the political federation of this country. The central government lacked the power to rally the different entities for the pursuit of common goals and to enforce respect of mutual rights; as soon as possible it was necessary to mend this flaw. To offset the many separatist forces it was urgent that a Canadian spirit, a national soul, be rapidly created. This soul could not be the product of material progress, no matter how great, but only of common feelings and common ideals. . . .

* * * * *

Did Canadian statesmen have an understanding of this situation? . . . Instead of drawing the original populations closer together and through them to strengthen the national soul, our leaders thought it more practical to allow a horde of strangers to invade our home. . . . Our doors were opened to Americans and Englishmen preferably, the two classes of immigrants most likely to destroy Canadian patriotism: the first, who come from a land too close to Canada, change countries without changing their allegiance and become the most active agents of American penetration; the others remain under the spell of the mother country and can only endanger the progress of our autonomy by subordinating the interests of their land of adoption to those of their land of origin.

* * * * *

Meantime, the country's internal peace had been broken. . . . Barely five years after the two races had taken their oath of alliance, the stronger of the two had already begun to betray the weaker. In 1872, the school rights of the Catholics and Acadians in the Maritime provinces were attacked. From there the assault spread to the new territories of the West, to Manitoba and the Keewatin, then to Ontario, where the method used is the brutal one we know. Today, as we celebrate Confederation and as official speeches hypocritically speak of peace and national unity, all the French minorities are on the defensive and have to fight, not only for this right and that, but for the supreme right of existence.

. . . How can the government still invite us to respect the obligations we formerly contracted when it allows a regime of violated rights and broken promises to perpetuate itself against us? And for whom are we taken if it is believed that we will prolong much longer this alliance of dupes in which our race's only choice is between abdication and separation? Ah! how can a person love his country and not feel pain and anger when faced with the blunders of those little men who have ruined such a great hope?

L. Groulx, "Ce Cinquantenaire", *Action française* (July 1917), pp. 197–201 (translation).

The Doctrine of Provincial Rights

In many circles today, Maurice Duplessis is chiefly remembered for his corrupt government and his reactionary outlook in social and economic matters. He was, however, the first major political figure from French Canada to present a clear enunciation of the doctrine of provincial rights, and this was an extremely important first step in the political thinking of the Quiet Revolution.

Federalism alone can guarantee national harmony and can make Canada a great and strong nation by uniting, without merging them, the races and the regions of which she is composed.

It is one of the essential prerogatives of autonomous provinces to be able to raise, by means of direct taxation and in the way they deem best, the moneys necessary for the good functioning of public services and also for the application of the laws adopted by their parliaments; these prerogatives ought to be considered not only in terms of immediate needs but also to pursue a forward looking policy, since to govern is to foresee.

The federative system which necessitates, fundamentally, an attribution of public tasks, must also provide a correlative division of revenue sources. Of what benefit to the provinces would be the most extensive legislative and administrative powers if, on the other hand, they were prevented from collecting the revenues that the exercise of these powers demands?

A central government which would appropriate to itself the sources of taxation would, by this very fact, reduce the provinces to legislative impotence. Effectively, a province with no other revenues than federal subsidies would become a kind of inferior organism, under control of the authority which could measure out its means of subsistence. In other words, such a situation would amount to replacing the reins enabling one to drive with shackles that paralyze and enslave. It would amount to giving the key of one's house to another. This key is a fitting symbol of fiscal powers and indicates that one is master in one's home, as we desire and have a perfect right to be.

The Canadian constitution consecrates the exclusive right of the provinces to legislate respecting matters of very great importance, notably in regards to education, hospitals, asylums, institutions and charitable homes, public works within the province, administration of justice and all which touches property and civil rights. A progressive legislation in these domains necessarily entails considerable expense and clearly requires that the provinces have the right to raise the necessary moneys. Fiscal independence is all the more indispensable in the case of a province, such as the Province of Quebec, which is developing itself with giant strides; development which greatly enriches Canada but which exacts, on the part of the province, numerous and additional outlays in particular for new schools, new hospitals, for social legislation and for other provincial purposes.

Extract from a speech by Maurice Duplessis given at the Federal-Provincial conference of 1955. From *Proceedings of the Federal Provincial Conference 1955: Ottawa, October 3, 1955* (Ottawa, 1955), pp. 37–8.

Provincial Autonomy Is Not Enough

For the separatists, provincial autonomy is at best a half-measure. In the following passage Marcel Chaput, who became known nationally with his book *Pourquoi je suis séparatiste*, argues in favour of a fully sovereign state of Quebec.

THE TWO CHOICES FOR THE FRENCH-CANADIAN NATION

Remain a minority in a large country
Become a majority in a smaller country

REMAIN A MINORITY IN A LARGE COUNTRY

What we lack most

*   *   *   *   *

I begin with the postulate that the French Canadians form a nation like any other. And like all other nations, the French-Canadian nation has its good and bad points, a soul capable of love and reaction, aspirations to grandeur, a need for dignity and self-expression, the capacity for joy and tears, a feeling of solidarity. In short, the French Canadian needs a national identity, within the framework of concrete political structures and incarnated in universally accepted symbols.

*   *   *   *   *

The hour of decision

French Canada has arrived at its hour of decision. Its real problem is to decide now, once and for all, what it wants to be—an eternal minority, in eternal retreat in an immense country which doesn't belong to it, or a living and progressive majority, in a country which is smaller but all its own.

To those who choose to be a minority

The experience of ninety-four years of Confederation is enough to convince us that minority status in a two-nation country can lead only to mediocrity. To hope that by some sort of miracle the French-Canadian people should suddenly reform, demand with one voice that it be respected, become anxious to speak correctly, desire culture and great works, without the inspiration of an animating ideal—that is a dangerous case of delirium.

Let us suppose that the miracle should happen, and that our people should acquire the desired virtues of resistance—we would still remain a numerical minority, whose democratic responsibility would still and forever be to bow to the wishes, legitimate or not, just or not, generous or not, of a majority which is foreign to us in language and spirit.

The urgent need for orientation

Through the fault of its élite groups, the French Canadians are a people which doesn't know where it is going or what it wants. It is the victim of an immense confusion, torn between proposals that are as fantastic as they are contradictory.

Faced with this tangled mass of choices, it is absolutely necessary to choose one, once and for all; we must answer the one question we are allowed to ask—which of the choices, a bilingual Canada or an independent Quebec, will ensure the French-Canadian nation its greatest development? Personally, I have chosen independence.

> M. Chaput, *Why I Am a Separatist*, translated by Robert A. Taylor
> (Toronto, 1962), pp. 91–4.

A Strong Quebec Must Take Precedence over a Bicultural Canada

Ottawa has not remained oblivious to the separatist challenge and to French Canada's discontent with Confederation. In 1963 it formed a Royal Commission on Bilingualism and Biculturalism to examine the present state of Anglo-French relations in Canada and to report on what can be done to provide French Canadians with expanded opportunities for their language and culture outside Quebec. In the following passage René Lévesque, former Minister of Mines in the Lesage government, gives his views on this Royal Commission.

As defined by its terms of reference, the enquiry at best only promises to bring one possible benefit: a greater respect for, and a wider use of, French in the federal government departments and in the services controlled by the central government. This is not negligible, but it is obviously minor. However, there is also a risk of misplacing the proper emphasis, which could be very dangerous. We must not mislead others into believing, nor end up by convincing ourselves, that "biculturalism" is a basic goal or value.

It is infinitely more important to make Quebec progressive, free, and strong, than to devote the best of our energies to propagating the doubtful advantages of biculturalism. Moreover, if French culture is to spread, if the French language is to be respected, that will depend above all on the vigour, on the economic and political importance, of Quebec. These must become and must remain our first concern, by far our most decisive and constant preoccupation.

From an interview of René Lévesque by Jean-Marc Léger published in *Le Devoir* on 5 July 1963, translated by F. Scott and M. Oliver, eds., *Quebec States Her Case* (Toronto, 1964), pp. 144–5.

The Beginnings of Economic Nationalism

The traditional nationalism of French Canada was based on an agrarian philosophy that spurned participation in commerce, business, and industry. But the shift of population from country to city and from farm to factory which occurred in the early part of the present century resulted in new class structures and new socio-economic aspirations. French Canadians gradually became interested in the acquisition and exercise of economic power and this put them on a collision course with the English minority, which controlled the industries and natural resources of the province. The advent of this new type of nationalism is heralded in the following article by Edouard Montpetit, one of the pioneers of the science of economics in French Canada.

To each generation its role and its hardships. The task of our fathers was to repair the damages of defeat. To live and to grow, come what may, was their first concern. By increasing their numbers they were establishing the French fact. This was our first victory and it is perpetuated by our own existence and vitality. Later there were rights to be conquered and then defended. Our farmers successfully attended the school of politics. They studied the British constitution of which the victor had incautiously sung the virtues. Their clear and logical minds grasped its principles and then demanded their total application. . . . Today we exercise the rights they acquired and it is in this exercise that lies their safeguard. . . . But now the times have changed. Wealth, a new factor, has appeared. To the twin duties deeded to us by history we must add the one of keeping pace with the times by using our talents in new directions. We will never repeat often enough that for many people the national question is now an economic one. Not that wealth is the supreme good. . . . It is but a means, but such a powerful one that we cannot neglect using it. For us the economic conquest must be tomorrow's reality. It will give us equality if not superiority. It will even give us more than to others, for once we enjoy material sufficiency we will be naturally inclined to cultivate thought, to seek modes of expression, to diffuse the arts.

E. Montpetit, "Vers la supériorité", *Action française* (January 1917), pp. 1–2 (translation).

The Growth of Economic Nationalism

In Quebec as elsewhere in Canada the great Depression fostered the growth of new political formations. In 1934 a group of angry young Liberals broke with their party, which had held power at Quebec since 1897, and formed a new political grouping which they called the *Action libérale nationale*. It campaigned on a platform of extensive social, political, and economic reforms and returned twenty-six members to the Legislative Assembly in the elections of 1935. Shortly afterwards it merged with the provincial Conservatives led by Maurice Duplessis to form the *Union Nationale*. The following passage has been extracted from the programme of the *Action libérale nationale*.

IV. Economic reforms

1. The destruction by every possible means of the grip which the great financial institutions, the electricity trust, the paper industry have on the province and the municipalities.

2. To obtain lower electricity rates: the harnessing by the province, as the need may arise, of ungranted or unexploited water power resources; an immediate inquiry, by an independent commission specially appointed for that purpose and endowed with all necessary powers, to determine if it would be in the province's interest to acquire gradually at costs that would permit a substantial lowering in the present rates, the ownership of companies producing or distributing electricity in the province.

3. To fight the coal, gasoline and bread cartels by subjecting them to the competition of state-owned enterprises if necessary.

4. To fight the trust in the milk industry by grouping into a closed association all the province's milk producers.

5. A thorough investigation of the structures and methods of financing of the public utility companies and the reform of their finance.

6. The intensification and strict application of the Anti-Combines Law.

7. A policy of progressive rural electrification according to a determined plan and based on the one operating in Ontario.

> Programme of the *Action libérale nationale*
> *Le Devoir*, 28 July 1934 (translation).

An Indictment of French Canada's Present Economic Position

Raymond Barbeau is a prominent separatist and the author of books and articles on the subject of an independent Quebec. In the following passage he argues forcefully that economically, the French Canadians are a captive people.

Politicians assert that Quebec is in a period of full economic growth. They are right. But who are those who really profit from this expansion? Who are its prime organizers? Who are the owners of the great factories who reap the dividends and enrich themselves at the expense of the population? Who are those who seize our patrimony and use our natural resources to become fabulously rich? Who exploits our population, keeps it in misery and degradation, despises it as cheap labour, and forces it to remain unemployed? The responsible ones are the Anglo-American industrial magnates, who are assisted by the federal institutions and the policies of Ottawa over which French Canadians have no control at all.

* * * * *

Year after year foreign capitalists seize our industries and harm our businesses. All our economic possessions are absorbed by foreign finance, monopolies, and trusts. "No one will fail to notice," wrote M. Victor Barbeau in 1936, "that the concentration of capitals, their anonymity and irresponsibility, are for us as for other people a cause of social and moral dissolution." In his terrible account of our economic bankruptcy written in 1936, M. Barbeau asserted: ". . . as primitive peoples all over the world, who have been used as stepping stones by Anglo-Saxon megalomaniacs, we have been enslaved by merchants and industrialists. Those are our victors. We have followed them to wherever they have settled to make their money. We have become their lumberjacks, raftsmen, labourers and journeymen. We have built the canals for their boats and devastated our forests for their sawmills. . . . We are proletarians, fodder for their factories. We are a nation of petty clerks, petty workers, and petty rentiers; in brief, a nation of petty people."

R. Barbeau, *La libération économique du Québec* (Montreal, 1963), pp. 60–2.

Culture and Nationalism

French Canada's intellectual awakening is perhaps the most exciting aspect of the Quiet Revolution. The person who studies the ideas that have been expressed in Quebec during the past few years comes away convinced that what is taking place in the province today is essentially a revolution against old ways of French-Canadian life and thought. Dissatisfaction with these is very evident in the following passage written by the poet St. Denys Garneau, the gifted and tragic figure who died in 1943 at the age of thirty-one.

. . . Can culture be considered from the nationalist angle? It seems not. Culture is essentially human in its goal, it is essentially humanistic. Making French Canadians is perhaps a popular notion nowadays but it makes no sense. It is even opposed to sense and nature. One can take conscience of his person to perfect himself, not as self but as man. Every movement whose terminal goal is the self is sterile. . . .

*   *   *   *   *

Culture then means human improvement. It is something essentially humanistic. It proposes to make men, not French Canadians. There is no opposition here but only a distinction of priorities: to make men out of French Canadians and not French Canadians out of men. It is claimed that in making French Canadians one makes better men, but all methods which are not properly human in their goal can hardly avoid being restrictive and short-sighted. Thus all historical and nationalistic education. . . .

From the *Journal of St. Denys Garneau*
Benoit Lacroix, ed., *St. Denys Garneau* (Montreal, 1956), pp. 79–81 (translation).

The Inadequacies of the Policy of *Survivance*

In 1950 a small periodical called *Cité Libre* began to appear. Founded by Gérard Pelletier and Pierre-Elliot Trudeau, it soon established itself as an important journal of social and intellectual reform. The spirit of this new publication was well summed up in a single sentence of the first issue: "We are all here, we of a new generation whose turn it now is to express itself." The following passage by Pierre-Elliot Trudeau illustrated the general tone and outlook of *Cité Libre*.

For a long time adversity supplied us with a principle of action. Our entire policy consisted of saying no and we rightly called *chefs* those who were effective leaders of our resistance. Our people were then surrounded by very real dangers, principally ethnic and religious assimilation, and our national existence was defined as a negation of these hostile forces.

But to avoid evil is not enough; one must also do good. A Church that would never have emerged from the catacombs would have been an imposture; so in politics one can remain too long underground. If too many misfortunes compel this, the spirit is extinguished and what was heroic resistance becomes bestial obstinacy. Alas! Such is the case with certain nations that have struggled for too long and end up by believing that virtue is a negation.

I sometimes wonder if French Canada is not travelling along this blind alley. Some are elected to political office by defending the people against dangers that are either exaggerated or imaginary. Others manage their flocks by brandishing threats of eternal damnation. In brief, we seem far less interested in making friends than in denouncing enemies: Communists, English, Jews, imperialists, centralizers, demons, free-thinkers, and what else? We are told that this is forbidden and that not permitted. But does anyone ever speak of the sin of omission? Who accuses himself at one of his rare confessions of having sinned by not doing good?

"But we have preserved the language and the faith of our fathers. That is something positive."

That is a lie which illustrates very well how we have confused quantity and quality. Objective history will show that we began to lose everything the day our enemies became clever and pervasive and rendered our negations unjustifiable. Our language now has become so poor that we no longer realize how badly we speak it . . . our faith, so tenuous, has ceased to be apostolic. . . .

There are not many ways out of our quandary. We must stop trembling at the thought of external dangers, stop fortifying our traditions by sullying what is opposed to them, and consider by what positive actions we can uphold our beliefs.

We want to bear witness to the Christian and French fact in America. So be it. But let us sweep away all the rest. Let us submit to methodical doubt all the political notions of past generations; the strategy of *survivance* no longer serves the flourishing of the City. The time has come to borrow from the architect the style that is called functional, to scrap the thousand past prejudices that clutter up the present and to start building for the new man. Let us throw down the totem poles and violate the taboos, or better yet let us consider them as non-existent. Let us be coldly intelligent.

> P.-E. Trudeau, "Politique fonctionnel", *Cité Libre* (June 1950), (translation).

The Language of Defeat

In 1960 Jean-Paul Desbiens, Brother Jérome by his religious name, a teacher of the Marist Order, published anonymously a small book called *Les Insolences du Frère Untel*. It sold over 100,000 copies and became one of the province's all-time best sellers. The *Insolences* became chiefly known for its biting analysis of a type of French spoken in Quebec, which it described as *joual* (mispronunciation of *cheval*). But more broadly, the volume was an attack, made highly effective by a style that combined humour, anger, and sadness, on the general state of French-Canadian society.

Joual, this absence of language, is a symptom of our non-existence as French Canadians. No one can ever study language enough, for it is the home of all meanings. Our inability to assert ourselves, our refusal to accept the future, our obsession with the past, are all reflected in joual, our real language. Witness the abundance of negative turns of speech in our talk. Instead of saying that a woman is beautiful, we say she's not bad-looking; instead of saying that a pupil is intelligent, we say he's not stupid; instead of saying that we feel well, we say we're not too bad.

The day it appeared I read Laurendeau's comment to my class. My pupils realized that they spoke joual. One of them said, almost proudly, "We've founded a new language." They saw no need to change. "Everybody talks like us," they told me. Some said, "People would laugh at us if we talked differently from the others." One said—and it is a diabolical objection—"Why should we talk otherwise when everybody understands us?" It's not easy for a teacher, taken unaware, to answer this last proposition, which was made to me one afternoon.

Of course joual-speakers understand each other. But do you want to live your life among joual-speakers? As long as you want merely to chat about sports and the weather, as long as you talk only such crap, joual does very well. For primitives, a primitive language is good enough; animals get along with a few grunts. But if you want to attain to human speech, joual is not sufficient. You can make do with a board and some whitewash if you want to paint a barn, but finer tools are necessary for the Mona Lisa.

Now we approach the heart of the problem, which is a problem of civilization. Our pupils speak joual because they think joual, and they think joual because they live joual, like everybody around here. Living joual means rock'n roll, hot dogs, parties, running around in cars. All our civilization is joual . . .

Will you say I'm going back to the days of the Flood if I recall Bergson's words on the need for a supra-consciousness? We live joual because our souls are impoverished, and so we speak it . . . What can we do? The whole French-Canadian society is foundering. Our merchants show off their English company names, the billboards along our roads are all in English. We are a servile race; our loins were broken two hundred years ago, and it shows.

> *The Impertinences of Brother Anonymous* (Frère Untel), translated by
> Miriam Chapin (Montreal, 1966), pp. 28–30.

A Plea for Non-Denominational Schools

One of the more interesting aspects of the recent history of French-Canadian nationalism has been its transformation from an ideology with strong religious overtones into one that is essentially secular in character. In the late nineteenth century, for example, separate schools were considered one of the bulwarks of French-Canadian survival. Today, however, there is a growing demand in French Canada for the exclusion of religion from the classroom.

Confessional schools in Quebec are a screen behind which the clergy is concealed to impose a spiritual dictatorship (in the name of the supernatural) which has lasted long enough. Confessional schools in the second half of the twentieth century are more harmful than beneficial to the people of Quebec. For a long time the school was a place set aside to teach catechism and the road to heaven. Today it has become the road to life and a training place for the crafts and professions made necessary by the technological revolution. Surely the Church will find other ways of disseminating Christian precepts. She has even trained some of her bishops at the CBC!

The modern City is technological and secular and demands an education that has the same character. Today, Quebeckers are not free. They live behind the wheels of modern automobiles but under a medieval law. *When in our society a person can be born, married, have children or adopt them, avail himself of social services and of the law, provide his sons and daughters with schooling and employment, then die,* WITHOUT THE COMPULSORY INTERVENTION OF THE CHURCH, *freedom of conscience for believers as well as non-believers will be respected.*

Until then, because the presence of the Church is *compulsory* at every level of civil life, the citizen of Quebec is colonized much more deeply by the grip of Rome than by American dollars.

We demand a *Quebec that is secular* because that is the first step on the road to a *Quebec that is free.*

> Jacques Godbout, *Le Mouvement du 8 avril* (pamphlet no. 1 of the Mouvement laïque de langue française, Ottawa, 1966), pp. 6–7 (translation).

Two Commentaries on the Quiet Revolution

Because the Quiet Revolution is such a recent phenomenon, historians have not yet begun to study it intensively and it has been necessary to look elsewhere to find commentators on it. The first of the two readings that follow was written by Michael Oliver, a McGill University political scientist who is also director of research for the Royal Commission on Bilingualism and Biculturalism. This Royal Commission's Preliminary Report, published early in 1965, presents an excellent analysis of the Quiet Revolution. The second reading is an extract from it.

Why is it likely that the current wave of French-Canadian dissatisfaction with Confederation will persist longer and require more thoroughgoing accommodation than those of the past? After all, separatist movements are not a purely modern phenomenon. The spirit of Quebec independence can be traced far back into the nineteenth century.

The most general answer to this question is that today's demands are shaped by the social revolution in Quebec. This has to be elaborated, however, if it is to be a comprehensible reply. The social revolution is, roughly, the sum of industrialization, urbanization, expanded educational opportunity, and the impact of mass communications, especially television. It has led to a transformation in the image of the good life and the good society that most French Canadians hold. Instead of a vision of self-sufficing farm families linked together by parish institutions, asking only that the state protect them from outside influences, there has been substituted a basically urban model: one that resembles substantially that held by North Americans from Texas to Toronto. . . .

*   *   *   *   *

. . . It is because there has been indeed a social revolution that today's demands for a reconstructed Confederation are qualitatively different from those of past decades. Historical analogies have only very limited validity. It is just because French Canada now wants many of the things out of life that English Canada does that the cultures are on a collision course. If the good life means a comfortable city home, a car, an executive job, and a part in planning and executing big corporate projects, then Westmount and St. James Street have new significance. When these centres were known only in a mythical way, when they were unattainable and not all that desirable—then the fact that they were populated almost exclusively by English Canadians was only an occasional source of irritation. But when Westmount affluence becomes everyone's goal, when more and more people aspire to St. James Street jobs, when many are developing the skills and the outlook that make them confident that they can handle the command posts of a modern American community, then the fact that these are occupied largely by English Canadians has explosive potential.

*   *   *   *   *

But the forces released by Quebec's social revolution cannot achieve results fast enough to keep up with burgeoning demands. There must be, it is felt, some way to create heaven-on-earth overnight. Hostile forces must be at work hindering progress. There emerges, therefore, an analysis that is a *mélange* of fact and frustration: the relationship to English Canada is the barrier to Utopia; political independence will clear the way.

F. Scott and M. Oliver, eds., *Quebec States Her Case* (Toronto, 1964),
from the Introduction by M. Oliver, pp. 1–4.

. . . Why, suddenly, when apparently nothing has occurred to upset the traditional order of things, have more and more people decided that they can now 'no longer tolerate' the same 'shackles' which are nonetheless a century old? Could it be, as was suggested at a private meeting in Montreal, that 'among a people who had been walking somewhat bent over, two hundred thousand, five hundred thousand individuals had suddenly decided to pull themselves erect?' Or perhaps that 'Some good sturdy people trained to be docile, have stopped looking on obedience and poverty as a national vocation?' Through these quotations one catches a glimpse of the conflict between generations which is breaking out today in French Quebec. For it appeared to us that dissatisfaction was being most often expressed among representatives of the young, well-educated elite groups of technicians, engineers and executives. But they are not merely young; they belong more or less fully to the 'new world' of technology and management and are ready to take a leading part in it; they have the fullest confidence in themselves and plainly show their impatience in the face of the obstacles they meet.

* * * * *

The exasperation of the young elite groups . . . seemed to us to have been heightened by their beginning to sense their numerical importance and by their coming into collision with English-speaking people in positions of control. In comparison with the former mass of employees of the traditional type who for the most part were an army of workers with few special skills, the new elites stand out by their insistence on higher standards of culture and by their ambition to penetrate into the higher ranks of the economic hierarchy. But they did not express their demands particularly by denouncing competition between rivals in which they would be at a disadvantage, although indeed we were told repeatedly that having to do one's best in an unfamiliar language constitutes a real handicap. They appeared rather to base their arguments on the fact that the French Canadians form an overwhelming majority in Quebec. In other words they seemed to consider a status of economic inferiority to be incompatible with the fact of numerical majority.

* * * * *

In short, the French-speaking Canadians of Quebec who appeared before us belong—and they showed that they knew it—to a society which expresses itself freely in its own language, and which in various important fields is already master of its own activities, to which it gives the tone and pace it chooses. But at the same time most of those with whom we talked were of the opinion that this society had less than complete control of a number of crucial sectors in which it is active. This, then, seemed to us to be the root of the problem: a unique, functioning society does exist, but many of its members consider it to be deficient and want to make it more or less complete. Remove one of the terms of this two-part proposition and the problem disappears: either there would no longer be a society, and hence no longer any real basis for sustaining these demands; or else there would be nothing left to complete and the demands would disappear.

A Preliminary Report of the Royal Commission on Bilingualism and Biculturalism
(Ottawa, 1965), pp. 109–13.

Further Reading

The Quiet Revolution is a difficult subject to study because it is not yet a completed process and because its consequences for Quebec and the rest of Canada are not yet fully clear. Those interested in the point of view of some of the participants should familiarize themselves with three periodicals: *Cité Libre* which, in the 1950's, fought a long and lonely battle for intellectual freedom and social and political reforms; *Laurentie*, a right wing separatist publication; *Parti Pris*—first published in October 1963—which advocates making Quebec into a socialist republic, by the use of force if necessary. For the programs of the policy makers, one should consult the platforms of the provincial Liberal party in 1960 and 1962 and that of the Union Nationale in 1966.

Readers interested in analytical studies should refer to the three volumes of articles and essays given in the Further Reading section for Problem 14. To these should be added the following two books: E. C. Hughes, *French Canada in Transition* (Phoenix Books, University of Chicago Press, 1963)*, first published in 1943, is a case study of the effects of Anglo-American industrialization upon a French-Canadian small town; H. F. Quinn, *The Union Nationale: A Study in Quebec Nationalism* (Toronto, University of Toronto Press, 1963)*, is an analysis of the Union Nationale under Duplessis, which unfortunately tends to be superficial in places.

Finally there are three interesting journalistic accounts: P. Desbarats, *The State of Quebec: A Journalist's View of the Quiet Revolution* (Toronto, McClelland & Stewart, 1965)*; H. Bingham Myers, *The Quebec Revolution* (Montreal, Harvest House, 1964)*; T. S. Sloan, *Quebec—The Not-So-Quiet Revolution* (Toronto, Ryerson Press, 1965)*.

Problem 21

What Has Happened to Canada's Century?

Between 1911 and the late 1940's few Canadians concurred with Sir Wilfrid Laurier's confident assertion that the twentieth century would be Canada's century. Confidence returned in the 1950's, and Canadians were claiming proprietary rights to at least the last half of it.

Large-scale projects which captured the popular imagination as nation-building enterprises, and which also offered economic opportunities for the worker and the entrepreneur, were again being launched throughout the land. The prairies were freed from their dependence on the wheat crop with the discovery and development of vast oil and natural gas fields. The pipelines carrying these new products to markets in central Canada and the United States and to the Pacific Coast reproduced a modern counterpart of the railway-construction era, adding to and diversifying the east-west lines of communication, along with the Trans-Canada highway system and the micro-wave stations which multiplied the range of telecommunications.

Railway construction itself boomed again. New lines pushed into the north, to the iron ore of Quebec and Labrador, to nickel in northern Manitoba, and into the northern interior of B.C. The export demand, largely from a United States whose natural resources were now obviously being depleted, for Canadian products and services brought such modern communities as Elliot Lake, Ont., Thompson, Man., and Kitimat, B.C., into being in what earlier were wilderness sites.

During most of this decade the Canadian dollar brought a premium over the American. The United States government was placed in the unfamiliar role of petitioner, requesting the privilege of sharing in the construction (and consequent control) of the St.

Lawrence Seaway after the Canadian government in 1952 announced its intention of undertaking the long-discussed project as a Canadian venture.

By the 1960's the prevailing mood of optimism had been replaced by one of doubt. Government initiative passed from Ottawa to the provincial capitals. The identification of the Lesage administration in Quebec with the "Quiet Revolution" should not blind observers to the wider resurgence of provincial rightists in this decade.

Canadians were also becoming aware of the extent to which the boom had increased their dependence on American markets and capital. Was such economic dependence compatible with political independence? Continentalism, with its potential banes and blessings, again confronted Canadians.

The Optimism of the 1950's

The "prose poem" with which Bruce Hutchison in 1957 prefaced his description of Canada in mid-boom, in his appropriately titled *Canada: Tomorrow's Giant*, provides a suitable introduction to the optimistic era. Even in this period some concern is expressed over the nation's ability to withstand the attractions of continental integration.

Something strange, nameless, and profound moves in Canada today. It cannot be seen or labeled, but it can be heard and felt—a kind of whisper from far away, a rustle as of wind in prairie poplars, a distant river's voice, or the shuffle of footsteps in a midnight street. It is less a sound than a sense of motion.

Something moves as it has never moved before in this land, moves dumbly in the deepest runnels of a collective mind, yet by sure direction toward a known goal. Sometimes by thought, more often by intuition, the Canadian people make the final discovery. They are discovering themselves.

*   *   *   *   *

The sovereign question of Canadian life has always been whether anything lay here to be found, any separate and valid quality of our own, any indigenous substance to justify a nation.

That question has been answered in our time. It has been answered not by the nation's leaders and policies, but by the little, unknown people, of whom the great names, the great towns, the day's news, and all the known things are merely the shadow and reverberation.

The little people perceive for themselves a decisive event in the nation's history, unnoticed when it came to pass, undated, and still only half understood. In these last twenty years at most, probably in ten, they crossed the grand portage and watershed of their long march when no man saw the crossing. They crossed it blindly in the darkness; . . . and saw it behind them by a backward glance.

Until then the foreigner might predict and the Canadian admit to himself that a nation, or the semblance of a nation strung in shreds and clusters along four thousand miles of emptiness, could not permanently resist the magnetism of its mighty neighbor. Even today, in the full tide of material progress, the Canadian still asks himself whether his work is ultimately doomed by the neighbor's friendly economic penetration.

*　*　*　*　*

The Canadian whose father accepted Canada as a spiritual dependency of some external power is thinking of it now solely as a nation in its own right. Though the nation is diverse, confused, self-centered, a little dizzy and smug from success at the moment, it is essentially whole. . . . The Canadian knows, better than his father knew, that he belongs to it and no other.

Bruce Hutchison, *Canada: Tomorrow's Giant* (New York, 1957), pp. 3, 4, 5.

The Importance of Intangibles in Creating a National Spirit

Among the factors which encouraged the optimism of observers of the Canadian scene in the 1950's was the greater cultural and intellectual activity: the development of professional ballet companies, the Stratford Festival, the marked increase in scholarly activity in the humanities and social sciences in the newly flourishing universities. This upsurge was assisted, though not started, by sponsorship made possible by the federal government's acceptance of some of the major recommendations of the Royal Commission on National Development in the Arts, Letters, and Sciences which it established in 1949 under the chairmanship of Vincent Massey and which reported in 1951. Such recommendations as the creation of the Canada Council and the inauguration of federal grants for higher education (both established in 1957) could be interpreted as promoting federal encroachment on the provincial responsibilities. The commissioners therefore carefully stressed that a national purpose would be achieved by fostering the arts.

In the preamble to our Terms of Reference appears the following passage:

"That it is desirable that the Canadian people should know as much as possible about their country, its history and traditions; and about their national life and common achievements; that it is in the national interest to give encouragement to institutions which express national feeling, promote common understanding and add to the variety and richness of Canadian life, rural as well as urban."

There have been in the past many attempts to appraise our physical resources. Our study, however, is concerned with human assets, with what might be called in a broad sense spiritual resources, which are less tangible but whose importance needs no emphasis.

The . . . passage . . . suggests two basic assumptions which underlie our task. First, it clearly implies that there are important things in the life of a nation which cannot be weighed or measured. These intangible elements are not only essential in themselves; they may serve to inspire a nation's devotion and to prompt a people's action. When Mr. Churchill in 1940 called the British people to their supreme effort, he invoked the traditions of his country, . . . In the spiritual heritage of Great Britain was found the quickening force to meet the menacing facts of that perilous hour. Nothing could have been more "practical" than that appeal to thought and emotion. We have had examples of this truth in our own history. The vitality of life in French-speaking Canada and its effective coherence as a living community have come of a loyalty to unseen factors, above all of fidelity to an historic tradition. When the United Empire Loyalists came to British North America they were carried as communities through the years of danger and hardship by their faithful adherence to a common set of beliefs. Canada became a national entity because of certain habits of mind and convictions which its people shared and would not surrender. . . . It will flourish in the future in proportion as we believe in ourselves. It is the intangibles which give a nation not only its essential character but its vitality as well.

But tradition is always in the making and from this fact we draw a second assumption: the innumerable institutions, movements and individuals interested in the arts, letters and sciences throughout our country are now forming the national tradition of the future. Through all the complexities and diversities of race, religion, language and geography, the forces which have made Canada a nation and which alone can keep her one are being shaped. These are not to be found in the material sphere alone. Physical links are essential to the unifying process but true unity belongs to the realm of ideas. It is a matter for men's minds and hearts. Canadians realize this and are conscious of the importance of national tradition in the making.

Canada, Royal Commission on National Development in the Arts, Letters, and Sciences, 1949–1951, *Report* (Ottawa, 1951), pp. 3–5.

The Threat of Foreign Ownership

The postwar transformation and expansion of Canada's economy had been made possible by the massive influx of outside capital, especially from the United States. This infusion differed from the flow of British and other European capital into the United States in the nineteenth century. The typical investor was no longer an individual buying bonds, mortgages, or shares in a local company, a person whose estate would eventually be liquidated, putting the foreign-owned shares back on the market. The major investments now were made by large corporations, who established subsidiaries or bought up (and frequently revitalized) Canadian companies. There is much less opportunity to repatriate this type of foreign ownership. Successful corporations do not die, hence their estates are not liquidated every generation to satisfy succession duties and claims of heirs.

The threat of foreign ownership of Canadian industry was expressed forcibly in Walter Gordon's book, *Troubled Canada*. The author had been named chairman in 1955 of the Royal Commission on Canada's Economic Prospects, which had published its generally optimistic final report in 1957. In *Troubled Canada* he presented a table which represented the extent to which certain key Canadian industries were passing over to foreign control during the ten years 1948–1958. He then discussed the implications of this shift of ownership.

Non-Residential Control as a Percentage
of Selected Canadian Industries
1948, 1955, and 1958

	Control by United States residents			Control by all non-residents		
	1948	1955	1958	1948	1955	1958
Manufacturing	39	42	44	43	52	57
Petroleum and natural gas	*	73	69	*	79	75
Mining and smelting	37	55	51	40	57	60
Railways	3	2	2	3	2	2
Other utilities	24	6	4	24	7	5

* not available

. . . The influence of this foreign control is even greater than these few statistics suggest. To a considerable degree it is the larger companies that are foreign controlled and these companies tend to set the pace for, and in many cases dominate, the industries in which they operate.

*   *   *   *   *

There are thoughtful people both in Canada and elsewhere, including many professional economists, who see nothing harmful in the increasing control of Canadian industry by non-residents. They point out that Canada has gained enormously from the foreign capital that has been invested in our industries and resources, including that part of it that is invested in Canadian subsidiaries of foreign parent companies. Canada has benefited from access to research and technological developments in other countries that could not otherwise have been obtained. We have been provided with scientific, technical and managerial experience and know-how, the value of which it would be difficult to overestimate. In some cases, especially in the resource industries, Canadian subsidiaries have been provided with assured markets without which they could never have been justified or financed. . . .

But there are disadvantages also in having such a large proportion of our industry controlled by non-residents including United States parent companies. One of these is the obligation of such parent companies to see that the operations of their Canadian subsidiaries do not contravene United States laws, especially the anti-trust laws and the Trading with the Enemy Act. Moreover, it may not be good business for a United States parent company to encourage or even to permit its Canadian subsidiary to seek export markets in other countries, possibly in competition with itself.

*   *   *   *   *

The difficulties and irritations associated with absentee ownership are aggravated in our case because of the magnitude and the pervasiveness of foreign control of Canadian industries and resources. At times promotions are not filled from within the ranks of particular Canadian subsidiaries, or the technical and scientific personnel are not given sufficient opportunities to use their imagination and skills because the subsidiaries have access to the research work being done by the foreign parent company. . . .

It is not always appreciated, moreover, that there are subtle differences between the approach to business management in Canada and in the United States. . . .

There is another serious disadvantage in having such a large proportion of our industry controlled by non-residents. It inhibits the development and training of a large corps of experienced Canadian entrepreneurs, business managers, promoters and financiers. . . . [T]hese are the very people needed to spark new developments and expansion. . . .

*   *   *   *   *

Canadians may not have the same antipathy as have many American businessmen to the concept of public ownership, especially of certain public utilities, to the marketing of wheat by a government agency, or to a publicly owned broadcasting system. Our economic history has been different from that of the United States and we may be more influenced by developments in the United Kingdom, in France, and in other European countries. . . .

This brings us to a much more fundamental reason for Canadian fears about the increasing domination of our industries by Americans. This was clearly stated by the Royal Commission on Canada's Economic Prospects:

At the root of Canadian concern about foreign investments is undoubtedly a basic, traditional sense of insecurity vis-à-vis our friendly, albeit our much larger and more powerful neighbour, the United States. There is concern that as the position of American capital in the dynamic resource and manufacturing sectors becomes ever more dominant, our economy will inevitably become more and more integrated with that of the United States. Behind this is the fear that continuing integration might lead to economic domination by the United States and eventually to the loss of our political independence.

Those who share these fears . . . would like to see the trend towards an ever-increasing control of Canadian industry by foreigners reversed, gradually and over a period of time. They would like to see Canadian subsidiaries, the larger ones in particular, given a great deal more local autonomy. And this is not likely to happen as long as such subsidiaries continue to be wholly owned by their foreign parents.

* * * * *

[S]ome professional economists, including many government officials, . . . argue that a greater integration of the economies of Canada and the United States is desirable and in any case inevitable in the long run. . . .

Such views can be respected; but they may not be shared by others who firmly believe that Canada as a separate and independent nation will be able to do more for its own citizens—including those now unemployed—and more for the world at large than she could do as a dependency, even a semi-autonomous dependency of any other country. . . . Certainly many of our citizens are unhappy to see Canada as a nation losing a large measure of economic independence more or less by default. . . .

> Walter L. Gordon, *Troubled Canada: The Need for New Domestic Policies*
> (Toronto, 1961), pp. 84, 85, 88–9, 90–1, 97.

Canada Can Survive Economic Integration
If Canadians Want Her to Survive

Although *American Capital and Canadian Resources* was also published in 1961, the text was largely written during the academic year 1959–60 when the author, Professor Hugh Aitken, an economic historian at the University of California, Riverside, was visiting Queen's University. The optimism of the intellectual and cultural vitality of the 1950's is thus reflected in this commentary. The author's stress on cultural and intellectual vigour as a means of national survival reflects the views of the Massey Commission.* Also noteworthy are the references to Canadian efforts to counter American influence by fostering contacts outside this continent, and the suggestion that this "American influence" might really be a general twentieth-century technological society.

. . . The question is, then, whether resistance to continental integration would be likely to increase Canada's freedom of action in any significant degree.

It is essential in this connection to distinguish clearly between limitations on Canada's freedom of action that stem directly from the United States and those that arise merely because Canadians are living in the twentieth century. It may be possible to counteract the first type of restrictive influence, but the second is somewhat harder to deal with. Canada at present, like most other nations, finds itself caught up in a situation in which the range of alternative feasible courses of action is small. Economically and politically, present choices are limited by choices made earlier in time, by the choices of other sovereign states, and by the growing interdependence of human affairs in a world that daily grows smaller and more crowded. The impact of industrialism, mass literacy, scientific discovery, and the commercialization of culture is universal. No nation can hope to insulate itself from these pressures, and all nations find their freedom of action limited by the need to accommodate to them.

* * * * *

To Canada's formal sovereignty there is no threat. Any encroachment in this respect, direct or indirect, is certain to be resisted vigorously. . . .

* * * * *

. . . [W]e may expect Canada to place no serious obstacle in the way of closer economic integration with the United States, and to rely primarily on the United States for the strategic security of the continent, but at the same time to pursue consistently a policy of strengthening economic, political, and military ties with Europe. The proposed North Atlantic free trade area is merely an idealization of the general objective; if it does not prove feasible, other techniques for involving Canada in European affairs and Europe in Canadian affairs will be found. The strategy is one of exploiting to the full

---

* See above, pp. 361–2.

the economic benefits of proximity to the United States while neutralizing as far as possible the political and cultural consequences of economic integration by the maintenance of the European connection. Canada, in short, is attempting to bring in the Old World to redress the balance of the New. . . .

A strategy such as this may enable Canada to retain some freedom of action in the political and economic spheres. Whether it will serve to protect and foster a distinctively Canadian way of life is more doubtful. But here again a distinction must be made between pressures upon Canada that emanate specifically from the United States and those that have a more general origin. The major threat to the survival of distinctive cultural values in Canada is . . . twentieth-century industrialism, particularly the industrialization of communications. If Canada were less intimately involved in an economic sense with the United States, the pressures for uniformity in thought and action would still persist, though perhaps in more moderate form. Nations with cultural traditions far richer and more respected than Canada's are at present experiencing difficulties of much the same kind. They at least are in a position to fight a rear-guard action, defending a sense of cultural identity and difference that already exists. It is Canada's misfortune that she must attempt to develop a cultural tradition of her own at a time in the world's history when all the tendencies of technology and commercialization are working against her.

The forces which are tending to shape all societies of the western world into a common mould are not specifically American in origin. . . . It is natural . . . to argue that it is the cultural influence of the United States that is to be resisted. . . . Yet, is it not equally plausible to believe that what we see here is a common North American cultural pattern, a pattern on which both Americans and Canadians have embroidered a few distinctive variations but which nevertheless is the heritage and the creation of both? . . .

*   *   *   *   *

If Canadians lack faith in their ability to maintain a sense of identity in the face of economic integration with the United States, it can only be because they set a low estimate on the vitality and creativity of their own cultural life. It is not enough to point to differences between the two countries in population or other measures of size. Creativity—the ability to introduce cultural variations that survive and gain acceptance—is a matter of quality, not quantity. . . . Scotland was "teacher of the world" during most of the eighteenth century. German Austria, particularly Vienna, exercised a remarkable cultural influence on Germany and on Europe as a whole from the 1870's to the 1920's. And the tiny Swiss canton of Geneva from the time of Calvin produced a steady stream of thinkers of international reputation whose contribution to European science and literature was out of all proportion to the economic resources of the canton itself. Mere size cannot explain cultural vitality of this kind. . . .

Could Canada in the twentieth century come to exercise cultural leadership in North America as Scotland, Austria, and Geneva once did in Europe? . . . [T]he possibility is not to be dismissed offhand, and certainly not for any reasons connected with economic integration. Far more relevant are such considerations as the quality of Canada's educational system, the support and toleration granted to artists and creative thinkers, and the extent to which talent and originality are recognized and encouraged wherever they may be found. . . .

It may be that the future holds for Canada no better prospect than gradual absorption by the United States, a slow but cumulative process of integration that, beginning with the mundane affairs of trade and investment and the unfortunate imperatives of continental defense, finally leaves to Canada no more than the empty form of sovereignty. . . .

Yet it is possible that the outcome may be very different. Economic integration has brought tremendous benefits to Canada, and continues to do so. It is unlikely that the process will encounter serious resistance. What will be resisted will be any tendencies for the process to broaden beyond the economic sphere. . . . Only by unremitting scrutiny and criticism can Canadians take advantage of economic integration while at the same time maintaining their political independence and preserving their sense of cultural difference.

> Hugh G. J. Aitken, *American Capital and Canadian Resources*
> (Cambridge, 1961), pp. 184–5, 187, 189–95.

Can Canada Adjust to "Bilingualism and Biculturalism"?

The "Quiet Revolution", discussed in the preceding problem, caused some thoughtful and sober Canadians of both major language groups to question whether the national fabric could withstand the strains imposed by the more vigorous assertion of "the French Fact" and of English-speaking Canada's backlash to it. In their *Preliminary Report* the members of the Royal Commission on Bilingualism and Biculturalism, who had been appointed and had conducted hearings across the nation during 1963 and 1964, uttered the following warning:

What is at stake is the very fact of Canada: what kind of country will it be? Will it continue to exist? These questions are not matters for theoreticians only, they are posed by groups of human beings. And other groups by refusing to ask themselves the same questions actually increase the seriousness of the situation.

The chief protagonists, whether they are entirely conscious of it or not, are French-speaking Quebec and English-speaking Canada. And it seems to us to be no longer the traditional conflict between a majority and a minority. It is rather a conflict between two majorities: that which is a majority in all Canada, and that which is a majority in the entity of Quebec.

That is to say, French-speaking Quebec acted for a long time as though at least it had accepted the idea of being merely a privileged "ethnic minority". Today, the kind of opinion we met so often in the province regards Quebec practically as an autonomous society, and expects her to be recognized as such.

This attitude goes back to a fundamental expectation for French Canada, that is, to be an equal partner with English-speaking Canada. If this idea is found to be impossible, because such equality is not believed in or is not acceptable, we believe the sense of deception will bring decisive consequences. An important element in French-speaking Quebec is already tempted to go it alone.

* * * * *

From evidence so far accumulated, it appears to us that English-speaking Canadians as a whole must come to recognize the existence of a vigorous French-speaking society within Canada, and to find out more about the aspirations, frustrations and achievements of French-speaking Canadians, in Quebec and outside it. . . . They have to face the fact that, if Canada is to continue to exist, there must be a true partnership, and that the partnership must be worked out as between equals. . . . To some extent, they must be prepared to pay by way of new conditions for the future of Canada as one country, and to realize that their partner of tomorrow will be quite different from their partner of yesterday.

On the same evidence, it seems to us that French-speaking Canadians for their part must be ready to respond positively if there are to be truly significant developments toward a better partnership. It would be necessary for French-speaking Quebecers to restrain their present tendency to concentrate so intensely on their own affairs, and to look so largely inward. Problems affecting all Canada are their problems too. They would need to beware of the kind of thinking that puts "la nation" above all other considerations and values. They too, like the English-speaking, should forget the conquest and any psychological effects they think it left. They would have to avoid blaming English-speaking Canadians for shortcomings which are their own; and at times to remember that English-speaking Canadians have their feelings too. They, as well as the English-speaking, must remember that, if a partnership works, each party must give as well as get.

All ten of us are convinced that in the present situation there is a grave danger for the future of Canada and of all Canadians.

A Preliminary Report of the Royal Commission on Bilingualism and Biculturalism
(Ottawa, 1965), pp. 135, 138-9.

Alternative Definitions of Bilingualism and Biculturalism

Close to half the population of Alberta and Manitoba and more than half that of Saskatchewan are descended from other than French or British stock. This situation imparted a sense of unreality to the concept of "the two founding races" which seemed so self-evident in old Ontario and Quebec, an area lumped together as the exploiting "East" in the consciousness of many westerners. The following letter of Premier E. C. Manning of Alberta to Prime Minister L. B. Pearson, dated 28 May 1963, reflects this detachment.

My colleagues and I have given careful consideration to your letter of May 15th and to the Terms of Reference for the proposed Royal Commission on Bilingualism and Biculturalism.

In response to your request, we wish to advise that, while we are not opposed to such a study being undertaken, unless the Terms of Reference are clarified to make more explicit the objectives which it is hoped to achieve we have serious doubts as to its advisability and practical value.

To amplify, in the matter of biculturalism, if the objective is to encourage citizens of all racial and ethnic origins to make their maximum contribution to the development of one overall Canadian culture embracing the best of all, we feel this would meet with widespread endorsation and support.

If, on the other hand, the objective is to give some form of official recognition to a dual English and French culture, we suggest that this is unrealistic and impracticable and we doubt that it would meet with any widespread public acceptance.

In the matter of bilingualism, if the objective is to encourage Canadian citizens to become fluent in two or more languages, certainly on the part of most Canadians this would be welcomed.

If the purpose is to extend recognition of French as an official language in areas and spheres beyond those in which it was guaranteed official status at the time of Confederation, we feel that it would not meet with general public acceptance and the consequences, in our opinion, would impair rather than strengthen Canadian unity.

We offer these observations for your consideration in arriving at a final decision in the matter proposed in your communication.

Ibid., p. 170.

A Premature Obituary?

Pessimistic books about Canada date from the first Canadian settlements, although few of them matched the despair that Goldwin

Smith poured out in *Canada and the Canadian Question* (1891). Professor George Grant's *Lament for a Nation* is a very recent example of such pessimism. To the McMaster philosopher, the Canadian experiment was not merely failing: it had failed. All that remained was the problem of how to dispose of the remains.

As Canadians of all cultural traditions have been concerned with the problems of *la survivance* (and its equivalent in many other tongues), it seems appropriate that this collection of problems should end with excerpts from this interpretation by a despairing conservative of the total course of Canadian history.

The impossibility of conservatism in our era is the impossibility of Canada. As Canadians we attempted a ridiculous task in trying to build a conservative nation in the age of progress, on a continent we share with the most dynamic nation on earth. The current of modern history was against us.

A society only articulates itself as a nation through some common intention among its people. The constitutional arrangements of 1791, and the wider arrangements of the next century, were only possible because of a widespread determination not to become part of the great Republic. Among both the French and the British, this negative intention sprang from widely divergent traditions. What both peoples had in common was the fact they both recognized, that they could only be preserved outside the United States of America. The French were willing to co-operate with the English because they had no alternative but to go along with the endurable arrangements proposed by the ruling power. Both the French and the British had limited common ground in their sense of social order—belief that society required a high degree of law, and respect for a public conception of virtue. Both would grant the state much wider rights to control the individual than was recognized in the libertarian ideas of the American constitution. If their different conservatisms could have become a conscious bond, this nation might have preserved itself. An indigenous society might have continued to exist on the northern half of this continent.

*   *   *   *   *

. . . The inherited determination not to be Americans allowed these British people to come to a *modus vivendi* with the more defined desires of the French. English-speaking Canadians have been called a dull, stodgy, and indeed costive lot. . . . Yet our stodginess has made us a society of greater simplicity, formality, and perhaps even innocence than the people to the south. Whatever differences there were between the Anglicans and the Presbyterians, . . . both communities believed that the good life made strict demands on self-restraint. Nothing was more alien to them than the "emancipation of the passions" desired in American liberalism. . . . The early leaders of British North America identified lack of public and personal restraint with the democratic Republic. Their conservatism was essentially the social doctrine that public order and tradition, in contrast to freedom and experiment, were central to the good life. The British Crown was a symbol of a continuing loyalty to the state—less equivocal than was expected from republicans. In our early expansions, this conservative nationalism expressed itself in the use of public control in the political and economic spheres. Our opening of the West differed from that of the United States, in that the law of the central government was used more extensively, and less reliance was placed on the free settler. Until recently, Canadians have been much more willing than Americans to use governmental control over economic life to protect the public good against private freedom. . . . The early establishment of Ontario Hydro succeeded because of the efforts of an administrator, a politician, and a journalist, all of whom wrapped themselves in the Union Jack in their efforts to keep the development of electric power out of the hands of individual freedom.*

English-speaking Canadians had never broken with their origins in Western Europe. . . . That we never broke with Great Britain is often said to prove that we are not a nation but a colony. But the great politicians who believed in this connection—from Joseph Howe and Robert Baldwin to Sir John A. Macdonald and Sir Robert Borden, and indeed to John G. Diefenbaker himself—make a long list. They did not see it this way, but rather as a relation to the font of constitutional government in the British Crown. Many Canadians saw it as a means of preserving at every level of our life—religious, educational, political, social—certain forms of existence that distinguish us from the United States.

* * * * *

To turn to the more formidable tradition, the French Canadians are determined to remain a nation. During the nineteenth century, they accepted almost unanimously the leadership of their particular Catholicism—a religion with an ancient doctrine of virtue. After 1789, they maintained their connection with the roots of their civilization through their church and its city, which more than any other in the West held high a vision of the eternal. . . .

Nevertheless, indigenous cultures are dying everywhere in the modern world. French-Canadian nationalism is a last-ditch stand. The French on this continent will at least disappear from history with more than the smirks and whimpers of their English-speaking compatriots—with their flags flying and, indeed, with some guns blazing. The reality of their culture, and their desire not to be swamped, cannot save them from the inexorable facts in the continental case. Solutions vary to the problem of how an autonomous culture

* The three men were Sir Adam Beck, Sir Richard Whitney, and "Black Jack" Robinson. [Original footnote.]

can be maintained in Quebec. But all the answers face the same dilemma: Those who want to maintain separateness also want the advantages of the age of progress. These two ends are not compatible, for the pursuit of one negates the pursuit of the other. Nationalism can only be asserted successfully by an identification with technological advance; but technological advance entails the disappearance of those indigenous differences that give substance to nationalism.

* * * * *

All the preceding arguments point to the conclusion that Canada cannot survive as a sovereign nation. In the language of the new bureaucrats, our nation was not a viable entity. . . .

Canada has ceased to be a nation, but its formal political existence will not end quickly. Our social and economic blending into the empire will continue apace, but political union will probably be delayed. Some international catastrophe or great shift of power might speed up this process. Its slowness does not depend only on the fact that large numbers of Canadians do not want it, but also on sheer lethargy. . . . The dominant forces in the Republic do not need to incorporate us. A branch-plant satellite, which has shown in the past that it will not insist on any difficulties in foreign or defence policy, is a pleasant arrangement for one's northern frontier. . . . If the negotiations for union include Quebec, there will be strong elements in the United States that will dislike their admission. . . . [T]he formal end of Canada may be prefaced by a period during which the government of the United States has to resist the strong desire of English-speaking Canadians to be annexed.

George Grant, Lament for a Nation (Princeton, 1965), pp. 68–71, 75–6, 86–7.

Further Reading

Two books which are likely to survive as helpful statements of the temper of their times are Joseph Barber, *Good Fences Make Good Neighbours: Why the United States Provokes Canadians* (Toronto, McClelland & Stewart, 1958) and Gerald Clark, *Canada: The Uneasy Neighbor* (New York, D. McKay, 1965). The former was written by an American, and the latter by a Canadian who was revisiting his native land after a series of overseas assignments.

With the present rate of publication of scholarly works the bibliography of any book starts to become obsolete even before the book is published. Students, therefore, should familiarize themselves with such continuing bibliographical features as "Recent Publications Relating to Canada" appearing regularly in the *Canadian Historical Review*.

This book is printed in 11/12 and 9/11 Times Roman; problem numbers in 14 pt. Goudy bold, problem titles in 12 pt. Goudy light; main subheadings in 10 pt. Bodoni medium. Stock: 50 lb. Velvalur Opaque Litho (D/T).

2   3   4   5   6   7   8   9   10   Br   76   75   74   73   72   71   70   69   68